THE PHILIPPINES PAST AND PRESENT

THE MACMILLAN COMPANY
NEW YORK · BOSTON · CHICAGO · DALLAS
ATLANTA · SAN FRANCISCO

MACMILLAN & CO., Limited
LONDON · BOMBAY · CALCUTTA
MELBOURNE

THE MACMILLAN CO. OF CANADA, Ltd.
TORONTO

THE METAMORPHOSIS OF A BONTOC IGOROT.

Two photographs of a Pit-a-pit, a Bontoc Igorot boy. The second was taken nine years after the first.

THE PHILIPPINES
PAST AND PRESENT

BY

DEAN C. WORCESTER

SECRETARY OF THE INTERIOR OF THE PHILIPPINE ISLANDS
1901–1913 ; MEMBER OF THE PHILIPPINE
COMMISSION, 1900–1913

AUTHOR OF "THE PHILIPPINE ISLANDS
AND THEIR PEOPLE"

IN TWO VOLUMES—WITH 128 PLATES

VOLUME II

New York
THE MACMILLAN COMPANY
1914

Norwood Press
J. S. Cushing Co. — Berwick & Smith Co.
Norwood, Mass., U.S.A.

CONTENTS

VOL. II

APPENDIX

LIST OF ILLUSTRATIONS

VOL. II

THE PHILIPPINES PAST AND PRESENT

CHAPTER XIX

EDUCATION

No work accomplished since the American occupation is of more fundamental and far-reaching importance than that of the Bureau of Education. In order to appreciate it one must gain some familiarity with the conditions which prevailed in Spanish times.

The first evidence of the Spanish governmental attitude toward education in the Philippines is found in a royal edict of March 21, 1634,[1] in which Felipe IV orders all archbishops and bishops to take steps for the education of the Filipinos in the Spanish language and in Christian doctrine.

That this decree was more honoured in the breach than in the observance is evident from another royal decree of June 20, 1686,[2] in which the king reminds civil and religious authorities that the non-observance of the decree of 1634 will be charged against them.

Neither of these documents provided for financing the scheme of education ordained, but a decree of December 22, 1792,[3] did make financial provision for the establishment of Spanish schools for natives. The salaries of teachers were to be paid from the royal treasury, and deficits were to be made up from the communal properties and treasuries.

Although this was the first practical attempt to introduce general native education, there are evidences that individual opportunities were offered to, and embraced by, Filipinos. It is probable, too, that in certain

[1] Blair and Robertson, Vol. 45, p. 184.
[2] *Ibid.*, Vol. 45, p. 186.   [3] *Ibid.*, Vol. 45, p. 222.

localities the most generous of the Spaniards opened private schools.

The College of San José was founded in 1601, the University of Santo Tomás in 1619. Neither made provision for educating natives. They were established for the children of Spaniards only, although both later admitted Filipinos. But in the rules for the short-lived college of San Felipe (1641–1645),[1] Corcuera lays down the following: "The college servants shall be of influential Pampango families, and they shall be taught to read and write in the Spanish language, and shall be given clerkships if they show aptitude therefor." We learn that when the charity school of San Juan de Letran passed under the control of the Dominicans in 1640, native boys were admitted, on payment of fees, to share the advantages offered charitably to Spanish orphans.[2]

Primary education for Filipinos secured no real foothold until 1863.[3] In that year, by royal decree, a school system originally planned for Cuba was extended to the Philippines. It made provision for the beginnings of primary instruction in all municipalities of the islands. A summary[4] called forth by a circular of March 1, 1866, gives information with regard to the progress actually made. This summary fixes the number of towns at nine hundred, the number of children attending school at one hundred thirty-five thousand boys and twelve thousand two hundred sixty girls, and the number of schools at sixteen hundred seventy-four, but it gives the number of buildings actually in use for schools as only six hundred forty-one. Instruction in Spanish was not always, or even generally, given.

In 1863 provision was also made for the establishment of a normal school at Manila. In 1893,[5] forty years later,

---

[1] Blair and Robertson, Vol. 45, p. 175.
[2] Ibid., Vol. 45, pp. 213–265.
[3] Census of the Philippines, Vol. III, pp. 578–590.
[4] Ibid., Vol. III, p. 591.   [5] Ibid., Vol. III, pp. 579–580.

the actual appropriation for the Normal School was $5525. Fourteen years after the American occupation, the appropriation for the Normal School was $56,476.42, in addition to $224,500 spent for new buildings and furniture.[1]

In 1892 there were two thousand one hundred seventy-three schools. The attendance of these schools was small and irregular. In 1896, at the outbreak of the insurrection, the Spanish had in operation a public school system which could call upon the Normal School for teachers and also upon such graduates of private schools as cared to undertake the work. Naturally the latter were few. Between 1863 and 1893, the Normal School had enrolled two thousand and one students.

This may be contrasted with the number of schools which, under the present régime, prepare the pupils for teaching, as well as for other occupations. Including the students of the Philippine Normal School, the Philippine School of Arts and Trades, the Provincial High and Intermediate Schools, nearly thirty-seven thousand pupils are now following studies which fit them more or less to undertake the work of giving instruction to others.

In addition to the Normal School, the Spanish established a Nautical School in 1820, a School of Commercial Accounting and of the French and English Languages in 1839, and an Academy of Drawing and Painting. Their final system of public instruction was not badly planned, but it was never actually put into full operation.

From the beginning of the insurrection against Spain in 1896 until the beginning of the insurrection against the United States in 1899, most of the public schools were closed. The schoolhouses were used for barracks, prisons, or hospitals. No attempt was made to keep them in repair, and what scanty equipment they had once possessed was for the most part destroyed or stolen.

Between 1899 and 1901, many of these buildings were

[1] Report of Director of Education, 1911–1912.

repaired in towns which were occupied by American soldiers, and the beginnings of a public school system were made by our victorious army. Wherever our flag was raised a public school was soon established, soldiers often serving as teachers, and the moral effect of this upon the Filipinos was very great.

The city of Manila was naturally the first place to receive attention. Three weeks after our army entered it on August 13, 1898, seven schools were opened under the supervision of Father W. D. McKinnon, chaplain of the first California Regiment. In June, 1899, Lieutenant George P. Anderson was detailed as city superintendent of schools for Manila, and during the following school year he had an average of forty-five hundred pupils enrolled in the primary schools. Captain Albert Todd was detailed to act as superintendent of schools for the islands, but on May 5, 1900, in anticipation of the transfer of the islands from military to civil government, he gave way to Dr. Fred W. Atkinson, who had been chosen by the Philippine Commission as superintendent of public instruction. This title was changed later to that of director of education.

On January 21, 1901, the commission passed Act 74, the basis of the present school law. It provided for the appointment of one thousand American teachers to begin the work of establishing a school system carried on in English. Appointments were made as rapidly as possible. By the end of the year, seven hundred sixty-five American teachers were at work.

When provision was made for the appointment of this large number of Americans, it was with the idea that they should act as teachers of English in schools over which there should be Filipino principals, but there was, at that time, no body of Filipino teachers properly prepared to carry on school work, and by force of circumstances, this plan was soon altered.

Ten school divisions were established, covering the

archipelago. Each was presided over by a division superintendent of schools. The teachers were theoretically subject to his control, but the divisions were so large that it was impossible for him to exercise control very effectively. It is perhaps well that many of the teachers were left free to employ their own ingenuity in meeting local conditions.

The school system finally established represents a composite of the recommendations of hundreds of teachers scattered throughout the archipelago, and these recommendations were based on hard-earned experience.

One of the first duties of teachers was to begin the training of Filipino assistants. This took form in the organization of so-called *aspirante* classes, into which the best of the Filipino youth who were old enough to teach, and who had already received some education, were gathered. These *aspirante* classes were often held side by side with classes in the primary schools first established by American teachers, and by the beginning of the year 1902 some of the brightest pupils were able to assist in primary school work. These classes made possible the establishment of organized primary schools under the control of American teachers with Filipino teachers in the lower grades. Their graduates formed the nuclei of the first secondary schools, which were established in 1903.

The difficulties which teachers had to overcome at the outset were numerous. In some of the older and richer towns there were stone or brick schoolhouses more or less fit for occupation. In such cases a small number of old wooden benches and a few square feet of blackboard were usually available. Sometimes there were books provided by the army: Baldwin's readers in English or in rudely translated vernacular; Frye's geographies translated into Spanish; and possibly Spanish editions of the history of the United States. This stock was greatly improved during the latter half of 1902, and teachers were furnished books and supplies as rapidly as transportation facilities permitted.

In 1901 the number of school divisions was increased to eighteen, and in 1902 to thirty-six, making the school divisions identical with the thirty-six then existing political subdivisions of the islands. The organization of the public school system gradually crystallized and assumed something of the form which it has to-day. Barrio [1] schools were opened, and the work of American teachers who were detailed to supervise them was thus greatly increased.

The school system took permanent shape in 1903 and 1904. As it now stands it is controlled by the director of education, who is responsible for its conduct. Serving with him, and subject to his control, are an assistant director and a second assistant director. The directors have immediate charge of the general office, which has the following divisions: records, accounting, buildings, property, academic, industrial and publications. Each has a chief who is directly responsible for its work.

The islands are now divided into thirty-four school divisions, corresponding, except in two cases, to provinces. Each has its superintendent of schools.

The divisions are subdivided into districts, over each of which there is a supervising teacher who is responsible for the conduct of its work. Certain of the intermediate schools are under supervising teachers, while others are directly under division superintendents.

The school system to-day extends to the remotest barrios. It is organized and equipped for effective work, and ready to carry out promptly and effectively the policies determined upon by the central office.

In each province there is a central provincial school offering intermediate and secondary courses. Only twelve of them now give a full four-year course. Others offer three years, two years or one year of secondary work.

[1] Barrios are small outlying villages.

There is also a manual training department attached to the provincial school, or a trade school. So much for the provincial school system.

At Manila we have the Philippine Normal School, with an attendance of six hundred sixty-nine, and the Philippine School of Arts and Trades, with an attendance of six hundred forty-one. Also, there are the School of Commerce and the School for the Deaf and Blind, both supported directly from insular funds. The School of Household Industries has recently been established for the training of adult women in embroidery, lacemaking and similar arts, so that they may return to their provinces to establish little centres for the production of articles of this nature. This is most important work. The Filipinos are endowed with great patience, and with extraordinary delicacy of touch and manual dexterity. If productive household industries based on these valuable characteristics are generalized, the prosperity of the common people will be very greatly increased.

Of the school system in general it can be said that Filipino teachers have been gradually employed for the lower grades, and Americans have thus been freed to take charge of the higher instruction. Primary instruction is now in the hands of Filipinos, and intermediate instruction is rapidly being turned over to them. In July, 1913, there were about eighty-five hundred Filipino teachers, with an estimated total enrolment of five hundred thirty thousand pupils. The total enrolment in primary schools was approximately four hundred ninety thousand, in intermediate schools thirty thousand nine hundred, and in secondary schools six thousand. When we compare these figures with the hundred and seventy-seven thousand reported by the Spanish government in 1897, and when we consider the fact that attendance at that time was extremely irregular, it is evident that noteworthy progress has been made. Mere figures, however, come far short of telling the whole story. There has been very great improvement in the quality of the instruction given. In the old days children "studied out loud," and the resulting uproar was audible at quite a distance.

On their arrival in these islands, Americans found that the educated Filipinos as a rule held honest manual labor in contempt, while many of those who had managed to secure professional educations did not practise their professions, but preferred to live a life of ease. There were doctors who made no pretence of treating the sick, and lawyers who had studied simply for the standing which the title would give them. The Bureau of Education has brought about a profound change in public sentiment; a change of basic importance to the country. It was apparent at the outset that any educational system adhering closely to academic studies would simply serve to perpetuate this condition of affairs. Fortunately, those in charge of the situation were untrammelled by tradition, and were free to build up a system that would meet actual existing needs. The objection to manual labor offered much difficulty, but it has been largely overcome. There was, furthermore, a feeling against industrial work on the part of the people in many regions, based on the idea that teachers meant to supplement their salaries by the sale of the industrial products of the schools. This prejudice, which seemed formidable at first, disappeared when the bureau took up in earnest the introduction of industrial education and vocational training.

Just as the academic organization grew out of local conditions, so did industrial education accommodate itself to existing circumstances. In the Spanish *colegios*, girls had been taught to do exquisite embroidery and to make pillow lace. In various parts of the islands, hat weaving was carried on by families or groups of families. The making of *petates*,[1] of rough but durable market baskets and of sugar bags constituted widespread local

[1] Sleeping mats.

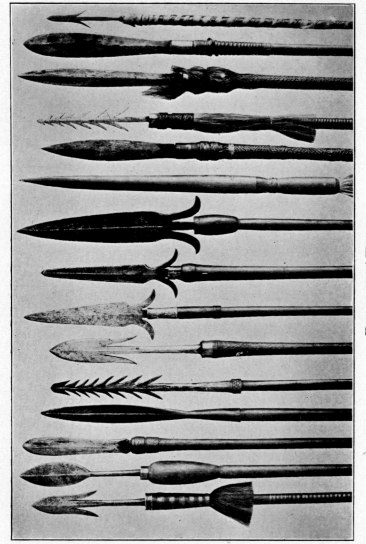

HEAD-HUNTERS' WEAPONS.

industries. American teachers were quick to see how these vagrant arts could be organized and commercialized. An intense rivalry sprang. up between supervising teachers, and as a result the arts of pillow lace-making, embroidery, Irish crochet, hat weaving, basketry and macramé work have been introduced and standardized throughout the primary and intermediate schools. The excellence of the output is truly astonishing.

Courses in housekeeping and household arts also received early attention. The social and economic conditions in the Philippines are such that the so-called "domestic science" course of American schools is quite inadequate to meet the needs of Filipina girls. Specialized instruction in hygiene, in the care of the sick, in household sanitation and in the feeding and care of infants is included in this course of housekeeping and household arts, which was taken by fifteen thousand two hundred twenty-seven girls during 1912–1913.

School gardening was introduced at an early date. This course now includes the school garden, in which each pupil has his own individual three and a fourth by thirteen foot plot, and home gardens which are not less than four times the size of the school plot. By this arrangement eighty per cent of the garden work is carried on at the homes of the pupils or on vacant lots under the direct supervision of teachers.

In the beginning much of the school agricultural work was not very practical. Teachers who themselves knew nothing about agriculture were wedded to the small "individual plot" idea, which I regret to say still continues to prevail in some of the schools. On a bit of ground about three feet by six the pupil might plant one tomato plant, one *camote* vine, one grain of rice, two or three eggplants and a flowering plant or two. This gave him helpful open-air exercise, but taught him nothing about agriculture. Weeks after the school year had opened I once visited a number of school gardens in Mindoro and found that several of them consisted of rectangular plots marked off on solid sod with shells picked up on the beach ! On my return I told the director of education that three active hens would have done far more toward preparing soil for cultivating than had all the children in these towns.

These conditions have changed rapidly since the adoption, three years ago, of a definite policy of agricultural education consisting of standard school and home gardens and farm schools for Filipinos; and large communal tracts of land cultivated at the Settlement Farm Schools for non-Christians.

Lieutenant-Governor Frederick Lewis of Bukidnon was as deeply disgusted with the former play agriculture as was I. Exercising, I fear, rather arbitrary authority over the local Filipino teachers, but with my connivance, he persuaded them to turn their active, strong schoolboys loose on large tracts of the beautiful prairie land found near almost every school in the sub-province, and raise crops. As a result of this experiment, first carried out at Tankulan, each boy took home a bushel or two of unhulled rice. Parents were enthusiastic, and so were the boys. From this small beginning came the so-called farm-settlement schools, of which there are thirty-eight among the non-Christian tribes. On large, well-fenced, carefully cultivated tracts of ground the schoolboys grow *camotes*, upland rice, corn, bananas, cowpeas, beans, pineapples, egg plants, arrowroot, and in some cases, cacao and coffee. Instead of learning what individual plants will do when grown quite by themselves under abnormal conditions, they learn to produce real crops. They become interested in the introduction of American sweet potatoes in place of the less nutritious *camotes*, in the selection of seed corn, in the generalization of the better varieties of bananas, and in other practical matters. Incidentally they largely furnish the school food supply.

It is of course true that in many of the Filipino towns

sufficiently extensive tracts of land cannot be had near the schools to make such a system possible, but, wherever it can be done, school children should be taught how to raise crops on a commercial scale, instead of spending their time on small individual plots of ground. Even the latter procedure has good results. It teaches them not to be ashamed to work. It also makes possible the introduction of home gardens, and through this means brings the practical production of vegetables into the home life of the people, with the result that unused yards and vacant lots are put under cultivation.

The system of establishing home gardens is one which meets with my unqualified approval. In 1911–1912 there were no less than twenty-two thousand nine hundred fifty-eight of these. It is said to be true that a large percentage of them soon pass into family care, and thus not only help to educate parents, but become a permanent additional source of food supply.

The schools have proved a useful medium through which to bring about the introduction of new and valuable plants. There are many school nurseries in which grow thousands of seedlings, and these are distributed at opportune times.

Woodworking is one of the industrial branches which received first attention. As previously stated, every one of the thirty-eight provinces has either a trade school with first-class equipment, or a manual training department attached to the provincial school. Eighteen schools have already been established as regularly equipped trade schools. The Philippine Normal School and the Philippine School of Commerce offer special advantages to those studying for the profession of teaching, or for a business career.

Previous to 1909, industrial instruction was only partially organized. Experience had shown, by that time, that it was expedient to introduce a degree of specialization into the courses of study at an early stage of the child's development. Special intermediate courses were therefore organized to meet this need. After finishing the four-year primary course, the child may choose between a course in teaching, a course in farming, a trade course, a course in housekeeping and household arts and a general intermediate course. Relatively few children are at present able to take up secondary courses, and it is therefore necessary to provide in the lower grades for instruction which will prepare them for some vocation. So important has become this line of instruction that it has been found necessary to maintain, in the general office, an industrial information department, under a division chief, which employs a botanist, a designer, four native craftsmen and a force of travelling supervisors who inspect trade schools, machinery, school gardens, building sites and the general industrial work done throughout the public school system. This system of industrial instruction receives the fullest support from the Filipino people.

The following quotation from the twelfth annual report of the director of education serves to give some idea of the extent to which industrial instruction has been developed in the Philippines : —

"As is at once evident, with requirements so definitely fixed for industrial work in the schools, the great majority of the pupils who are enrolled must be engaged in some branch of this work. An examination of the figures included among the statistical tables of this report will show that of the total enrolment of 235,740 boys and 138,842 girls during the month of February, 1912 (an average month), 216,290 boys and 125,203 girls — 91 per cent of the entire monthly enrolment — were doing some form of industrial work. More specifically, it will be found that 21,420 boys were taking manual training and trade work; 96,167 boys were engaged in school gardening and farming; 15,463 girls were also engaged in garden work; and 68,194 girls were taking up various lines which go under the general caption of minor industries. . . . Further in this connection it will be found that in the subject of lace-making alone 16,439 girls were receiving instruction; in embroidery, 12,339; and in cooking 4768. There were 22,965 boys and

7709 girls making hats in the industrial classes, 40,264 pupils making mats, and 104,424 studying the art of basketry.

". . . 1309 pupils were enrolled in the regular trade school classes; 924 in regular trade courses in other schools; and 7360 in the shops operated in connection with provincial and other intermediate schools. In 401 school shops having an enrolment of 19,949 boys, articles to the value of ₱142,189.74 were fabricated and from this product, sales to the amount of ₱131,418.13 were made during the school year 1911–12. In addition to the above, 10,356 pupils were doing work in 236 primary woodworking shops conducted in connection with municipal primary schools in all parts of the Islands. The figures for trade and manual training are taken from the March report."

This most important result is due in very large measure to the determination of the Honourable Newton W. Gilbert, while secretary of public instruction, to give a practical turn to the activities of the Bureau of Education. I must confess that at first I was profoundly dissatisfied with the work which this bureau was doing, for the reason that, in my opinion, it tended to produce a horde of graduates fitted to be clerks, in which event they would naturally desire to feed at the public crib, or be likely to become *abogadillos*,[1] who would be constantly stirring up trouble in their own towns, in order to make business for themselves.

Much of the industrial work originally provided for was at the outset carried out in a haphazard and half-hearted way. Under Mr. Gilbert's administration it has been hammered into shape, and we now see in prospect, and in actual realization, practical results of vital importance to the country.

Personally, I feel especially indebted to Mr. Gilbert for his attitude relative to school work among the non-Christian tribes. The children of the hill people are naturally hard-working. In some places they were being actually taught idleness in the schools, and in most the

[1] Literally, "little lawyers." This designation is commonly applied to pettifoggers.

education given them was of little practical value. I found Igorot children in Lepanto studying geography. I asked a boy what the world was, and was told that it was a little yellow thing about the size of his hand! This was a fairly accurate description of a map, the significance of which had utterly failed to penetrate his understanding. Filipino teachers who were not considered fit for appointments in the lowlands were being foisted off on to the unfortunate hill people, as they were willing to accept very small salaries in lieu of none at all. Prior to Mr. Gilbert's assumption of office, my frequent complaints had produced no practical result. He was kind enough to say to me at the outset that he would give very serious consideration to my opinions in the matter of educational work among the people of the non-Christian tribes. To-day industrial work has taken its proper place in schools established for them, and considerable numbers of them are being fitted for lives of usefulness, although it is still true that school facilities among them are, as a rule, grossly inadequate. In Ifugao, for instance, with at least a hundred and twenty-five thousand inhabitants, there are but two schools. In Kalinga, with some seventy-six thousand inhabitants, the first school has just been opened. However, this condition will doubtless be remedied in time.

The former tendency of Filipinos to prepare themselves for trades or professions and then not follow them has been largely overcome. Most of the students graduating from the Philippine Normal School take up the profession of teaching, and practically all of the graduates of the Philippine School of Arts and Trades are following the lines of work which they have studied. And now I come to what I deem to be one of the most important accomplishments of the Bureau of Education.

Before the American occupation of the Philippines the Filipinos had not learned to play. There were no athletics worthy of the name. Athletic sports had their begin-

nings in the games played between soldiers. Gradually
Filipinos became interested enough to attend contests of
this nature. Later, through the influence of American
teachers, they began to take part in them. As soon as
athletic sports reached a point where competition between towns and provinces was possible, they aroused
the greatest enthusiasm among the people. To-day,
the athletic policy of the Bureau of Education is heartily
approved by all classes. At first, highly specialized
sports were introduced, but the necessity for developing some form of group athletics in which a large percentage of the pupils would take part was soon made manifest.
For the past few years this programme has been pushed.
Eighty per cent of the pupils now participate in some form
of athletics, and the number steadily increases.

The results are justifying the hope of the original pro-
moters of this athletic programme. The physical development of the participants has been wonderful. The spirit
of fair play and sportsmanship, hitherto lacking, has
sprung into being in every section of the islands. Baseball not only strengthens the muscles of the players, it
sharpens their wits. Furthermore it empties the cock-
pits to such an extent that their beneficiaries have attempted to secure legislation restricting the time during
which it may be played. It has done more toward abolishing cockfighting than have the laws of the commission
and the efforts of the Moral Progress League [1] combined.
It is indeed a startling sight to see two opposing teams
of youthful savages in Bukidnon or Bontoc "playing the
game" with obvious full knowledge of its refinements,
while their ordinarily silent and reserved parents "root"
with unbridled enthusiasm!

Annual meets between athletic teams from various
groups of provinces, and a general interscholastic meet
held each year at the Philippine Carnival, offer advan-

---

[1] An organization which long vigorously combated the cock-pits,
but failed to bring about their abolition.

tages of travel to boys who have seldom if ever left their homes, and promote a general understanding between the various Filipino peoples. In the "Far Eastern Olympiad" held at Manila in 1913, in which China, Japan and the Philippines participated, the victorious teams representing the Philippines were largely composed of schoolboys.

When the American school system was organized, it was found that adequate accommodations for school children were almost entirely lacking. In some of the towns there were long, low stone or brick buildings, small and poorly lighted. They were usually located in the larger centres of population, and had no grounds that could be used for play or garden purposes. In most of the *barrios*, there were no schoolhouses at all.

The American teachers at once set to work to put the old buildings into decent condition. Some private houses were rented, and others were donated, for school purposes. In a number of cases the teachers attempted, as best they could, to construct buildings for the thousands of pupils who wished to avail themselves of school privileges. At that time the whole burden of such construction fell upon the municipalities. The insular government had given them no aid. Many mistakes were made during these early days, and many of the buildings then erected have long since fallen into ruin. The experience gained has demonstrated the folly of spending large sums of money on anything but strong, permanent construction. It will be necessary, for a long time, to depend to some extent upon temporary buildings ; and when these can be erected at low cost they are good provisional expedients, but destructive storms and the ravages of wood-eating insects quickly reduce them to ruins.

The demand upon local funds for the maintenance of schools was so pressing, and these funds were so limited, that it was found impossible to erect modern buildings without insular aid. When the necessity for help was

The Three Leading Men in the Funeral Procession of an Ifugao who has lost his Head to the Enemy.

brought to the attention of the insular authorities, the commission responded by enacting a bill which appropriated $175,000 from the congressional relief fund for the construction of school buildings. Two years later $150,000 were appropriated and, in August, 1907, an additional $175,000 were voted for this purpose. A total of $500,000 was thus made available by the Commission before the Philippine assembly came into existence. This amount was augmented by provincial and municipal funds and voluntary contributions, and the erection of twenty-two buildings for provincial high schools, twenty-six for trade and manual training schools, and fifty-seven for intermediate schools other than provincial was thus made possible.

The first act of the Philippine Assembly was to vote for an appropriation of $500,000, available in four equal annual instalments, to aid municipalities in constructing school buildings. The bill was duly approved by the commission and became a law. Under its terms, municipalities received $2 for every dollar furnished locally, the maximum insular allotment for one project being $2500. This bill was later supplemented by an act which appropriated an additional $500,000 under similar conditions. Three subsequent acts have been passed, each appropriating the sum of $175,000 for the aid of municipalities in constructing school buildings under such conditions as the secretary of public instruction may see fit to prescribe. The funds made available by the three appropriations last mentioned are being used chiefly for the erection of large central school buildings at provincial capitals.

The sums appropriated by the Philippine Legislature since the assembly was established have made possible the construction of five hundred twenty-nine school buildings, of which two hundred seventy-three are finished and three hundred nineteen are being built.

There have been additional appropriations for the construction of a Philippine Normal School already completed at a cost of $225,000, a girls' dormitory now building to cost $147,000 and a building for the Philippine School of Arts and Trades to cost approximately $250,000.

The bureau has required that school sites for central schools shall have a minimum of one hectare[1] of land, and the barrio schools a minimum of one-half hectare, for playgrounds and gardens. There have been secured to date three hundred eighty-nine school sites of ten thousand or more square metres, and six hundred forty-three sites of at least five thousand square metres. These represent the results obtained during the past three years.

The Bureau has formulated a very definite construction policy. Its programme may be outlined briefly as follows : —

1. The preparation of a set of standard plans for permanent buildings which provide for a unit system of construction whereby additions may be made without injury to the original structure, and which shall be within the limited means available.

2. The selection of suitable school sites.

3. A decent and creditable standard in temporary buildings.

4. The proper care and maintenance of schoolhouses and grounds.

5. The equipment of every school with the necessary furniture and appliances of simple but substantial character.

From the beginning, other branches of the government have clearly seen that no agency is so effective as the Bureau of Education in the dissemination of knowledge among the people. It has therefore been called upon frequently to spread information, either through classroom instruction or through the system of civico-educational lectures established by an act of the Philippine Legislature. The Bureau of Health has frequently requested it to instruct the people in the means to be used for the prevention of diseases, particularly cholera, smallpox and dysentery, and has always met with a ready response. Great good has doubtless been accomplished

[1] A hectare is equivalent to two and a half acres.

in this way, but with regret I must call attention to the fact that in connection with a matter of fundamental importance the Bureau of Education has signally failed to practice what it preached, or at all events what it was requested to preach. The Philippines are constantly menaced by epidemic diseases, such as cholera and bacillary dysentery, while amœbic dysentery occurs in every municipality in the islands and is a very serious factor in the annual death-rate, hook-worm disease is common, and typhoid fever is gradually increasing in frequency. The question of the proper disposition of human feces is therefore one of fundamental importance. It seems incredible, but is nevertheless true, that in connection with a large majority of the modern school buildings which have been erected there are no sanitary facilities of any sort whatsoever. The condition of the ground in the rear of many of these buildings can better be imagined than described. This state of affairs not only sets an evil example to the children, but exposes them to actual danger of infection with the above-mentioned diseases. In many of the special provincial government towns where a great effort has been made to have the people clean up, I have found school grounds and the private premises of school teachers, including, I regret to say, those of American school teachers, to be in a more unsanitary state than were any others in town; and finally, in despair of securing improvement in any other way, I have fallen back on the courts and caused teachers responsible for such conditions to be brought before justices of the peace and fined.

The Teachers' Camp at Baguio was long maintained in a shockingly unsanitary condition; and as a result many persons who went there seeking health and recreation became infected with intestinal diseases, and were incapacitated for work during more or less prolonged periods. In dealing with this situation I finally resorted to radical measures, but got results.

Such a state of affairs is wholly incomprehensible to

me. School-teachers should be the first to set the people practical examples in sane living, which means sanitary living, and should improve the great practical opportunity afforded by the public schools to bring home to their pupils certain homely but much-needed lessons in ordinary decency.

In another important particular the Bureau of Education has, in my opinion, fallen short of performing its manifest duty. Not only does beri-beri kill some five thousand Filipinos outright, annually, and cripple ten times as many, but it is believed to be a determining factor in the deaths of large numbers of infants through its untoward influence upon their mothers. As previously stated, the fact that it is due to a diet made up too largely of polished rice has been demonstrated beyond a reasonable doubt. Persons who eat unpolished rice do not contract it. *Tiqui-tiqui*, the substance removed from rice in the process of polishing, has proved to be a very effective remedy for it. The use of polished rice should therefore be discouraged, yet at the Philippine Normal School, where the brightest and best youths of the land receive their final education before going out to teach their fellows, polished rice is furnished the students; and the director of health, and I myself, have sought in vain to have the unpolished article substituted for it.

The secretary of public instruction has stated, with obvious truth, that it is only when polished rice forms a very large element in the diet that there is actual danger of its causing beri-beri, and so far as I am aware no case of beri-beri has occurred at this school; but the practical result of the present practice will be that the graduates, while instructing their pupils in the dangers of the use of polished rice, will themselves continue to use it. There exists at the present time a foolish prejudice against unpolished rice, which, although far more nutritious and actually more palatable than the polished article, does not look so attractive and is commonly considered "poor man's food." So long as the instructors in the public schools continue to teach by precept that its use is dangerous, and by example that it is safe, the undiscriminating and ignorant Filipino public, which does not draw fine distinctions, will be encouraged to continue to eat it, will eat it in excess, and will pay the penalty. The Bureau of Education has coöperated with the Bureau of Lands in instructing the people as to the right to acquire homesteads and free patents. It has also given the Bureau of Public Works assistance in promoting the campaign for good roads. Its system of civico-educational lectures has met with fair results. Thousands of people have secured information relative to the rights and duties of citizens, the prevention of human and animal diseases, and the growing of corn, coconuts and other useful crops. A corn-raising contest in 1912 was participated in by more than thirty thousand boys, and thousands of people attended the demonstrations which formed a part of the campaign. This is a most important matter. Corn is a far better food than rice.

At first the only books available for use in the schools were those prepared for American children. These were soon found to be unsuited to the needs of Filipino children, and teachers were set to work to prepare more suitable text-books. Book companies in the United States quickly interested themselves, and as a result there is now in general use a comprehensive series of text-books particularly adapted to the needs of Filipinos.

In the secondary grades American text-books are quite generally used, although a few special texts dealing with literature, rhetoric, economic conditions and colonial history have been prepared in the islands.

In order to keep the teacher in the field well informed, the Bureau of Education has issued a large number of bulletins and circulars on matters of current interest. These bulletins have covered instruction in domestic science, drawing, manners and right conduct, school buildings and grounds, embroidery and athletics, and have conveyed information as to the general and special courses of study followed in such schools as the School of Arts and Trades, the School of Commerce and the Normal School. They have received much commendation from educators in the United States and the Orient.

When public schools were first opened children crowded into them by thousands. With them came many adults who believed that they could learn English in a period of a few weeks, or in a few months at the most. No doubt they entered the schools in many cases with the idea of thus conciliating the victorious American nation. It was not long until they realized that there was no royal road to learning. Then came a slump in attendance. Largely through the influence of the American teacher and his Filipino assistants, the attendance was again built up. This time the people clearly understood that education is not a matter of a few months or weeks. It is greatly to their credit that they have now settled down to a realization of what public education is, and are giving the public school system most loyal support.

The industrial programme has been accepted with enthusiasm, and without doubt there are in the islands to-day thousands of people who believe that it is a Filipino product.

There is an interest in athletic sports that can hardly be equalled in any other country. The crowds of enthusiastic spectators that attend every meet of importance testify to the hold that such sports have taken upon the people, whose attitude toward all forms of education is such that it needs only adequate revenue to develop an effective school system along the broadest lines.

Manhood suffrage does not exist in the Philippines. The qualifications for an elector are as follows: he must be a male citizen at least twenty-three years of age, with a legal residence of six months previous to election in the municipality where his vote is cast, and must belong to at least one of the three following classes : —

1. Those who, previous to August 13, 1898, held the office of municipal captain, *gobernadorcillo*, *alcalde*, lieutenant, *cabeza de barangay*, or member of any *ayuntamiento*.

2. Those who hold real property to the value of $250 or annually pay $15 or more of established taxes.

3. Those who speak, read or write English or Spanish.

With a population of approximately eight million people, there were, in 1912, two hundred forty-eight thousand qualified voters. Of these a large number had obtained the franchise because they belonged to class 1 or class 2. Death yearly claims its quota from both these classes, but the public schools more than make up the decrease by their yearly contribution. Any boy who finishes the primary course possesses the literary qualifications of an elector, and will become one on attaining legal age.

In 1912 there were graduated from the primary schools 11,200 pupils, of whom approximately 7466 were males; from the intermediate schools 3062 pupils, of whom 2295 were males; and from the secondary schools 221 pupils, of whom 175 were males. In that year alone the schools therefore contributed 9936 to the contingent of persons qualified by literary attainments to vote. Of these 175 are perhaps capable of intelligently holding municipal and provincial offices, and to this number may probably be added half of the 2295 intermediate male graduates, making an increase of 1362 in the possible leaders of the people.

The public schools, however, do not limit their contributions to that part of the electoral body having literary qualifications only. Vocational training, it is true, is limited in the primary grades to cottage industries; but no pupil is graduated from the primary schools with only literary qualifications. In some form or other, he has had a vocational start. His own energy must determine the use he makes of it.

The intermediate schools add vocational training to

increased academic training. All their graduates have
done three years' work in the general course, leading to a
literary course in the high schools, the course in farming,
the course in teaching, the business course, the course
in housekeeping and household arts or the trade course.

Of the graduates of secondary schools a small part have
highly specialized vocational training; but the great
majority have followed the literary course and have
undoubtedly done this with the idea of entering political
life. Rome was not built in a day, and in spite of her-
culean American efforts, it will be a long time before
Filipinos cease to regard a certain kind of literary culture
as the proper basis for statesmanship. It has been said
of them that they have "the fatal gift of oratory"! The
future leaders of the Filipino people, dependent or independent, must be the output of the public schools.
The danger is that the number of would-be leaders will
be disproportionately great in comparison with that of
the useful but relatively inconspicuous rank and file.

There are in the Philippine Islands fully twelve hundred
thousand children of school age. The present available
resources are sufficient to educate less than one-half of
that number.

The claim has been made that a due proportion of the
very limited revenues of the insular government has not
been expended for educational purposes. It is not justified by the facts. It is certainly important to keep the
Filipinos alive, and if this is not done, they can hardly be
educated. The expenditure to date [1] from insular funds
for health work, including cost of necessary new buildings,
has been approximately $9,630,000; that for educational
purposes, also including buildings, approximately
$21,376,000.

As a simple matter of fact, the Bureau of Education
has been treated not only with liberality but in one regard with very great leniency. Taking advantage of

---

[1] End of fiscal year 1913.

THE SACRED TREE OF THE IFUGAOS.

This great tree at Quiangan is considered sacred by the Ifugaos of that region.
They believe that when it dies they too will perish.

the friendly attitude of the legislative body and of the people toward education, one of its earlier directors incurred expense with utter disregard for appropriations. He repeatedly made deficits of $150,000 to $250,000 and then in effect calmly asked us what we were going to do about it. After stating that I, for one, would never vote to make good another deficit incurred by him while he was allowed to remain in the service, and at a time when I was threatening to hold the director of forestry personally responsible for a deficit of $5000 resulting in his bureau from unforeseen expenditures by forest officers in remote places, and therefore more or less excusable, I learned that the usual shortage in the Bureau of Education had again occurred and was being covered by the quiet transfer of a sum approximating $200,000.

The present director of education believes that the total number of children who would enter the public schools without compulsion, if adequate facilities were provided, is approximately eight hundred thousand. Until revenues materially increase not many more than five hundred thousand of these can be educated, if due regard is had for other imperative necessities of the government and the people. If the people of the United States, or any political body composed of them, really desire to help the Filipinos toward the practical realization of their ideal of an independent, self-sustaining government, let them stop talking about the advisability of now conferring upon the present generation of adults additional rights and privileges, and provide the hard cash necessary to make intelligent, well-trained citizens out of the three hundred thousand children who are now annually left without educational advantages which they earnestly desire, and greatly need.

Under the Spanish régime private education as distinguished from that provided for by the government attained considerable importance. At the time of the American occupation, Santo Tomás, the oldest university under the American flag, had colleges of medicine and surgery, theology, law, engineering and philosophy. There were also numerous private so-called "colleges" for boys and girls and very numerous smaller private institutions. At first the establishment of public schools had no apparent effect on those conducted privately other than to induce them to introduce the study of English, but as years went by, the organization, modern methods and industrial development of the public schools forced the private institutions into activity. The law provides that the secretary of public instruction may give approval and recognition to such private schools as meet certain requirements, and in 1910 a division superintendent of schools was detailed to assist him in carrying out this provision. His report for the period ending September 1, 1912, is a very interesting document. It compares the Philippine private schools with those of South America, very much to the disadvantage of the former. It notes particularly the lack of manual training in boys' schools and the lack of standardization in the manual training of girls' schools; and speaks of the allegiance of the Filipino institution to the classical programme of mediæval institutions of learning. It is a notable fact, however, that English is gaining. Thirty-four private schools are giving their entire primary and intermediate courses in that language; nine are giving primary, intermediate and high school courses in it, and two are so giving all courses, including the college course.

These private institutions are employing public and normal school graduates as teachers to a constantly increasing extent. They are bringing their courses of study into conformity and competition with those of the public schools; are introducing athletics; using standard patterns and materials in their industrial work, and rapidly improving their buildings and equipment. During the year 1911–1912 improvements to the value of $100,000 were made in four of the Manila private schools:

the Jesuits are planning a new college to cost $1,000,000; the Dominicans an expenditure of $500,000 on a new university, and the *Liceo de Manila* looks forward to becoming the most modern and best equipped school in the islands.

Twenty-five private schools have already received government recognition and approval.

No account of education would be complete without mention of the University of the Philippines. Higher education is the great conscious goal of Filipino desire; and to meet the growing need for it, an act passed June 18, 1908, established this institution. Subsequent amendments authorized, when practicable, colleges of liberal arts, law, social and political science, medicine and surgery, pharmacy, dentistry, veterinary science, engineering, mines, agriculture and fine arts. At present there are in actual operation the colleges of liberal arts, veterinary science, engineering, medicine and surgery, law, agriculture and the school of fine arts. Instruction in pharmacy is given in the College of Liberal Arts, and instruction in forestry is given in the College of Agriculture. By special acts of the Philippine legislature, several scholarships have been provided, but for the most part the university is open only to those who can afford to live in Manila during their period of attendance.

The opening of some of these colleges has served sharply to call attention to one of the present weaknesses of the Filipino people. It is but a few years since agriculture was well-nigh prostrated as a result of the decimation of cattle and horses throughout the islands by contagious diseases. The need for well-trained veterinarians was, and is, imperative. Filipinos properly qualified to undertake veterinary work would be certain of profitable employment. A good veterinary course was offered in 1909. At the same time the School of Fine Arts was opened. No one took the veterinary course the first year. Admissions to the School of Fine Arts were closed when they reached seven hundred fourteen.   At the end of the school year 1912–1913 the students in the Veterinary College numbered twenty-seven as compared with six hundred ninety-four in the School of Fine Arts. The grand total enrolment of this latter institution since its organization is thirty-two hundred twenty-nine, while that of the Veterinary College during the same period is forty-seven.   It is necessary to restrict attendance at the School of Fine Arts.   Until there is a livelier and more general interest in saving carabaos than in painting them, the country will not attain to a high degree of material prosperity through the efforts of its own people.

I take genuine pleasure and pride in briefly describing the work of the Philippine Training School for Nurses. I have always believed that young Filipina women would make excellent trained nurses, and I earnestly endeavoured to have a certain number of them included among the first government students sent to the United States for education soon after the establishment of civil government.   In this effort I rather ignominiously failed. The prejudices of the Filipino people were then radically opposed to such a course, and my colleagues of the commission were not convinced that it would lead to useful practical results.

To the Bureau of Education must be given credit for inaugurating the movement which has resulted in the firm establishment of the profession of nursing in the Philippine Islands as an honourable avocation for women. At an early date it employed an American trained nurse to give instruction, and inaugurated a preparatory course at its Normal School dormitory.   The work at the outset could not be made of a very practical nature, but after a number of bright and well-trained young women had become interested in it arrangements were perfected for giving them actual training at the government institution then known as the Civil Hospital.   Here strong racial prejudices of the Filipinos were gradually overcome, and the student nurses soon showed themselves to be unexpectedly practical, faithful and efficient.

Later when the great Philippine General Hospital was established it became possible for the Bureau of Health to open a school under the immediate control of the chief nurse, and to take over all the work of training nurses. Students at this school are supported at government expense while in training. Its opportunities and advantages are open to young men, as well as to young women, and may be extended to a number not exceeding one hundred six of each sex at a given time.

The training of young women began sooner, and thus far has resulted more satisfactorily, than has that of young men, although many of the latter are now making good progress.

The work is popular, and as there are more candidates than places only the more promising are admitted. They have shown that they possessed common-sense by avoiding the traps set for them by Filipino politicians and newspaper reporters. Their tact and self-respect have brought them safely through many embarrassing, and a few cruelly trying, situations forced upon them by the unkindness or brutality of those whom they have sought to serve. Their gentleness and kindness have endeared them to their patients, and it is now a common thing for Americans to request the services of Filipina nurses. Their faithfulness and efficiency have won the confidence of patients and physicians alike. Their courage has enabled them to triumph over the prejudices of their own people, and to perform many hard, disagreeable tasks, and meet some very real dangers, without faltering. The gratefulness which they have shown for the opportunity to help their people, no less than for the interest taken in them by Americans, has won them many friends. The training of Filipina nurses has passed far beyond the experimental stage; it is a great success.

Instruction in the Philippine Nurses' Training School is now largely given by members of the university faculty and the graduates of this school must certainly be numbered among the most highly educated women of the Philippines. More of them are sadly needed, not only in government institutions, but in private hospitals, and especially in the provincial towns, where a few of them are already engaging in district nursing with unqualified success. The country might well get on for the present with fewer lawyers, and fewer artists, if the number of nurses could be increased.

Equally praiseworthy is the work of the students and graduates of the College of Medicine and Surgery, which is housed in a commodious and adequate building. Their theoretical instruction is of a very high character, and they have almost unrivalled facilities for practical clinical work in the Philippine General Hospital. Entrance requirements are high and the course of study is severe. A number of the best students do post-graduate work in the hospital, where they are employed as internes and assistants. As a result, the college is turning out graduates admirably qualified for the great work which awaits them among their own people.

The other colleges of the university are, for the most part, doing their work efficiently and well, and as a rule their students are showing appreciation of the opportunities afforded them, and are utilizing them to good advantage.

Important educational work is being carried on by various bureaus of the government. The Bureau of Lands has an excellent school for surveyors. The Bureau of Printing is in itself a great industrial school, and ninety-five per cent of its work is now done by Filipinos trained within its walls, while many others who have had practical instruction there have found profitable private employment.

An excellent school is conducted in Bilibid Prison with

convicts as teachers. A very large proportion of the prisoners receive practical instruction in manual training and are fitted to earn honest livings when their sentences expire. Furthermore, they readily secure employment, as the men discharged from this institution have in many cases earned well-deserved reputations for honesty and industry.

All the women confined at Bilibid are taught to make pillow lace.

At the Bontoc Prison, the non-Christian tribe convicts of the islands are taught useful industries, and so satisfactory are the results that I have formed the habit of calling the institution my "university."

At the Iwahig agricultural penal colony convicts are taught modern agricultural methods under a system such that they gradually become owners of houses, land and agricultural implements and may in the end have their families with them so that they are well settled for life when their sentences expire, if they take advantage of the opportunities given them.

The educational policy which the United States has adopted in dealing with the Filipinos is without a parallel in history. I am glad to have assisted in its inauguration, and I am proud of its results, which will make themselves felt more and more as the years go by. Even now English is far more widely spoken in the Philippine Islands than Spanish ever was, and this is a boon the magnitude of which cannot be appreciated by those who have not had brought home to them by experience the disadvantages incident to the existence of very numerous dialects among the inhabitants of one country.

When it is remembered that in the present instance each of these dialects is very poor in literature, and that its use is limited to a million or two of human beings at the most, the enormous value of instruction in English will be realized, to some extent at least.

CHAPTER XX

THE EXPLORATION OF NON-CHRISTIAN TERRITORY

AT the time of their discovery the Philippine Islands were inhabited by a very large number of distinct tribes the civilization of which was directly comparable with that of the Negritos, the Igorots and the Moros as they exist to-day. Do not understand me to imply that the Negritos, the Igorots and the Moros have attained to the same stage of civilization.

The Negritos belong to a distinct race. They are woolly-headed, nearly black, and of almost dwarfish stature. They seem to be incapable of any considerable progress and cannot be civilized. Intellectually they stand close to the bottom of the human series, being about on a par with the South African bushmen and the Australian blacks.

The Igorots are of Malayan origin. They are undoubtedly the descendants of the earlier, if not the earliest, of the Malay invaders of the Philippines, and up to the time of the American occupation had retained their primitive characteristics.

The Moros, or Mohammedan Malays of the southern Philippines, exemplify what may be considered the highest stage of civilization to which Malays have ever attained unaided. They are the descendants of the latest Malay invaders and were, at the time of the discovery of the islands, rapidly prosecuting an effective campaign for their mohammedanization.

At the outset the Spaniards made extraordinary progress in subduing, with comparatively little bloodshed, many of these different peoples, but the Moros at first successfully resisted them, were not brought under anything approaching control until the day of steam gun-boats and modern firearms, and were still causing serious trouble when Spanish sovereignty ended.

As time elapsed the political and military establishments of Spain in the Philippines seem to have lost much of their virility. At all events the campaign for the control and advancement of even the non-Mohammedan wild peoples was never pushed to a successful termination, and there to-day remains a very extensive territory, amounting to about one-half of the total land area, which is populated by non-Christian peoples so far as it is populated at all. Such peoples make up approximately an eighth of the entire population.

When civil government was established I was put in general executive control of matters pertaining to the non-Christian tribes. Incidentally, a word about that rather unsatisfactory term "non-Christian." It has been found excessively difficult to find a single word which would satisfactorily designate the peoples, other than the civilized and Christianized peoples commonly known as Filipinos, which inhabit the Philippines. They cannot be called pagan because some of them are Mohammedan, while others seem to have no form of religious worship. They cannot be called wild, for some of them are quite as gentle, and as highly civilized, as are their Christian neighbours. The one characteristic which they have in common is their refusal to accept the Christian faith, and their adherence to their ancient religious beliefs, or their lack of such beliefs as the case may be. I am therefore forced to employ the term "non-Christian" in designating them, although I fully recognize its awkwardness.

While serving with the First Philippine Commission I was charged with the duty of writing up the non-Christian tribes for its report, and tried to exhaust all available sources of information. The result of my investigations was most unsatisfactory to me. I could neither find out how many wild tribes there were, nor could I learn with any degree of accuracy the territory which the known tribes occupied, much less obtain accurate information relative to their physical characteristics, their customs or their beliefs.

The most satisfactory source of information was the work of Blumentritt, an Austrian ethnological writer; but Blumentritt had never set foot in the Philippines, and I suspected at the outset what later proved to be the case, that his statements were very inaccurate. He recognized more than eighty tribes of which thirty-six were said by him to be found in northern Luzón.

As it was obviously impossible to draft adequate legislation for the control and civilization of numerous savage or barbarous peoples without reliable data on which to base it, and as such data were not available, I had to get them for myself, and undertook a series of explorations, carried out during the dry seasons so far as possible, in order to gather my information on the ground.

I first visited Benguet in July and August, 1900.

On my second northern trip I traversed the province of Benguet from south to north, arrived at Cervantes in Lepanto, and was about to leave for the territory of the Bontoc head-hunters when I received a telegraphic summons to return to Manila for the inauguration of Governor Taft on July 4, 1901.

The following year such time as could be spared from my duties at Manila was necessarily devoted to the search for a suitable island for the site of a proposed leper colony; but in 1903 I was able to make a somewhat extended exploring trip, traversing the country of the Tingians in Abra, passing through the mountains which separate that province from Lepanto, visiting the numerous settlements of the Lepanto Igorots and continuing my journey to Cayan, Bagnin, Sagada and Bontoc; and thence through various settlements of the Bontoc Igorots to Banaue in the territory of the Ifugaos.

ENTRANCE TO THE QUIANGAN SCHOOL-HOUSE.

The Ifugao boys on either side of the stairway helped build this remarkable structure.   Most of their companions in the work were older, but all were of school age.

The latter portion of the trip was not unattended with excitement. A few weeks before a fairly strong constabulary detachment, armed with carbines, had been driven to the top of a conical hill in the Ifugao country and besieged there until a runner made his way out at night and brought assistance. We felt that there was some uncertainty as to the reception which would be accorded us. The Bontoc Igorots who accompanied us did not feel that there was any uncertainty whatever as to what awaited them, but were more than anxious to go along with us, as they were spoiling for a fight with their ancient enemies.

We had to use them for carriers to transport our baggage, and each carrier insisted on having an armed companion to lug his lance and shield. As a precautionary measure we took with us twenty-five Bontoc Igorot constabulary soldiers armed with carbines, while each of the five American members of the party carried a heavy six-shooter. We also had with us a dog which was supposed to be especially clever at seasonably discovering ambushes and giving warning.

We were able to use horses more or less as far as the top of the Polis range, but the trail down its eastern slopes was impracticable for horses and dangerous for pedestrians.

We shivered for a night on a chilly mountain crest, and the next day continued our journey to Banaue. When still several miles from the town, we were met by an old Ifugao chief with two companions. They marched boldly up to us and inquired whether we were planning to visit Banaue. On receiving an affirmative reply, the chief asked if our visit was friendly or hostile. I assured him that we were friends who had come to get acquainted with the Ifugaos. He said he was glad to hear this, but that after all it did not really matter. If we wished to be friends, they were willing to be friendly; but if we wanted to fight, they would be glad to give

us a chance.   As he and his companions were facing a
column of eighty-seven armed men I rather admired his
courage.

He next presented me with what I now know to be an
Ifugao gift of friendship, to wit, a white rooster and six
eggs, after which he took from one of his companions a
bottle filled with *bubud*,[1] and having first taken a drink
to show me that it was not poisoned, handed it to me.
I did my duty, and we were friends.

We then proceeded on our way to Banaue, being obliged
to plunge down through the rice terraces to the bottom of
a deep cañon and then climb two almost perpendicular
earthen walls before reaching the house of the chief.

I was completely exhausted when I began this climb,
and did not feel comfortable clinging like a tree frog to
the face of a clay bank with nothing to support me except
rather shallow holes which could be better negotiated by
Ifugaos, possessed of prehensile toes, than by men wearing
shoes.   Seeing my predicament, an Ifugao climbed down
from above, pulled my coat-tails up over my head and
hung on to them, while another came up behind me,
put his hands on my heels and carefully placed my toes
in the holes prepared for their reception.   Thus aided, I
finally reached the top.

The Ifugaos did not invite us to enter their houses,
but allowed us to camp under them.   I was assigned
quarters under the house of the chief.   It was tastefully
ornamented, at the height of the floor, with a very striking
frieze of alternating human skulls and carabao skulls.

One of my reasons for coming to Banaue at this time
was that I had heard that the people of seven other
towns had recently formed a confederation and attacked
it, losing about a hundred and fifty heads before they were
driven off.   I therefore thought that there might be a
favourable opportunity to learn something of head-hunting,
and to secure some photographs illustrating customs

---

[1] A fermented alcoholic beverage made from rice.

which I hoped would become rare in the near future, as indeed they did.

Trouble promptly arose between our Bontoc friends and the Ifugaos. The Bontocs wanted to purchase food. Some baskets of *camotes* were brought and thrown down before them and they were told that they were welcome to *camotes*, which were suitable food for Bontoc Igorots and pigs, but that if they wanted rice they would have to come out and get it. As twenty-five of them were armed with carbines and all the rest had lances, shields and head-axes, they were more than anxious to go, but this we could hardly permit! So we put them in a stockade under guard, and subsisted them ourselves, a thing which necessarily rendered our stay brief, as provisions soon ran low.

The Ifugaos of Banaue showed themselves most friendly, but warned us that a large hostile party was waiting to attack us at Kababuyan, a short distance down the trail. My mission to the Ifugao country was to establish kindly relations with the people rather than kill them, so I did my best to get on good terms with the inhabitants of the more friendly settlements.

The day before we left, people came in haste from a neighbouring village to advise us that one of their men had lost his head to the Ifugaos of Cambúlo, and begged us to join them in a punitive expedition, assuring us that there were numerous pigs and chickens at Cambúlo and that our combined forces would have no difficulty in whipping the people of that place, after which we could have a most enjoyable time plundering the town, while they would secure a goodly toll of heads which might be advantageously employed in further ornamenting their Banaue homes. They were greatly disgusted when we declined to join them, and said they would do the job anyhow, as no doubt they did.

First, however, they insisted that we come with them to see that the story they had told us was true. We soon overtook a procession carrying a very much beheaded man who was being borne out for burial on his shield, and were readily granted permission to attend his funeral. It was an interesting and weird affair. After it was over we hastened back to Banaue, in constant fear of breaking our necks by falling down the high, nearly perpendicular, walls of the rice terraces, on the tops of which we had to walk. Most of us discarded our shoes, in order to minimize the danger of a fall. One member of the party, who insisted on wearing his, glissaded down a steep wall and had to be pulled out of the mud and water at the bottom. Fortunately he was not injured.

Having succeeded beyond our expectations in establishing friendly relations with the Ifugaos of Banaue we took our departure, requesting them to tell their neighbours about us and promising to visit them again. I returned to Bontoc and made my way to Baguio in Benguet through the Agno River valley, stopping at numerous settlements of the Benguet Igorots on the way.

It was not possible for me to make further explorations in the territory of the Luzón wild people until 1905. In this year I set out, accompanied by Mr. Samuel E. Kane, an American who spoke Ilocano exceptionally well, and Colonel Blas Villamor, a former Insurgent officer, who was more familiar with the territory which I desired to visit than any one else of whom I could learn. He had established friendly relations with some of its inhabitants during the insurrection.

We visited several of the wilder settlements of the Tingians in Abra, then made a hard climb over Mount Pico de Loro and descended its eastern slopes to the Tingian village of Balbalasan in the Saltan River valley. Its people, while not really head-hunters, were often obliged to defend themselves against their Kalinga neighbours, and were consequently well armed.

After a brief rest we continued our journey down the Saltan River, visiting settlements on the high hills in its immediate vicinity.

At Salecsec we had an extended conference with an old chief named Atumpa, a very acute man of wide experience and sound judgment, who exercised great influence in the territory through which we had just passed.

Atumpa, satisfied as to our good intentions, consented to accompany us into the Kalinga country. A Kalinga chief named Saking, whom Villamor had known during the insurrection, met us here, and told us of a war trail into his territory which would greatly shorten our proposed journey, and make it possible for us to reach in one day the first of the previously unknown Kalinga settlements of the Mabaca River valley.

Saking, observing that the people in the Saltan valley had cleaned off their old trails, and in some cases had built new ones for our convenience, went ahead of us to his own country in order to try to persuade his people to do some trail work, leaving us to follow him.

Our route lay over the top of a high peak called "Dead Man's Mountain" because a good many people who tried to climb it never came down, the true explanation of their failure to appear being no doubt that they perished from exposure during violent storms.

While ascending this mountain I suffered an attack of partial paralysis of the legs, due, as I now have reason to believe, to heart strain, but was able to continue the journey after a brief rest and the use of stimulants.

A considerable part of our trip down the steep northern slopes of this mountain was made by utilizing a stream bed in lieu of a trail, and was in consequence very uncomfortable and somewhat dangerous, as the chance for broken bones was good. Fortunately, however, no one was badly hurt.

At the first Kalinga village we found about a hundred and twenty fighting men armed with shields and head-axes, but Saking and his brother Bakidan at once came forward to greet us and we did not suspect mischief.

I had brought with me from Manila a great bag of

newly coined pennies. They looked like gold, and we distributed them among the warriors, who were greatly delighted and promptly proceeded to place them in the ends of the huge ear plugs which the men of this tribe are so fond of wearing. Every one seemed friendly enough at the outset, but soon a rather disturbing incident occurred.

There were eight chiefs present. I noticed that they suddenly withdrew a short distance and squatted all together in a circle as if by word of command. After a brief but very animated discussion they rose simultaneously, and six of them started down the trail at a run, while Bakidan and Saking came to us and somewhat anxiously suggested that it was time to be moving on.

Our way lay through enormous *runo* grass which closed in over our heads, so that we were marching in a rather low tunnel through the vegetation. Bakidan went ahead of us, Saking brought up the rear, and both were evidently on the alert. Bakidan suggested that we keep our revolvers handy, which we did.

A short march brought us to Saking's place. Here a still larger body of fighting men awaited us, and there were no women in evidence except Saking's wife, who, at the direction of her husband, came forward, and under his instructions sought to shake hands with us. This was a new ceremony to the Kalingas, and she gave us her left hand.

Standing in a conspicuous place in front of Saking's house were two baskets filled with flowers which were wet with blood. We surmised, rightly, as it later proved, that these baskets had contained human heads just before our arrival, and that we had interrupted a head-cañao.[1]

---

[1] *Cañao* is the word commonly used by the northern Luzón wild men in designating a feast or ceremony. In Ahayao it is also used as an adjective to designate a place which may not be approached, being then equivalent to "taboo."

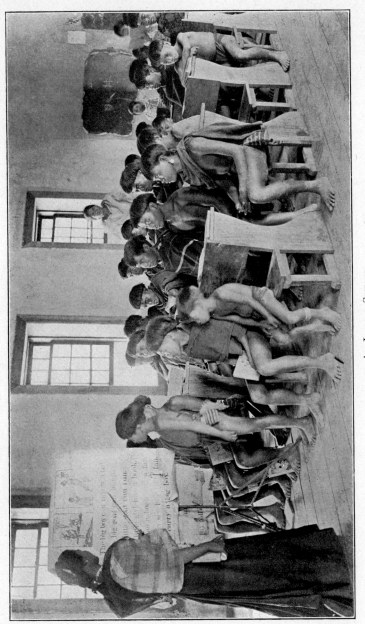

AN IFUGAO SCHOOL.

A *Filipina* woman is teaching *Ifugao* boys to read *English*.

One did not need to be an expert in the moods of wild men to see that the people of this place were feeling ugly, and after shaking hands with Saking's wife we promptly marched on.

It was fortunate for us that we did so. We later learned that the conference of the eight chiefs which aroused our suspicion had been held to discuss our fate. Six of them were in favor of killing us immediately, arguing that we were the first white men to penetrate their country; that they might have to carry our baggage, which would be a lot of trouble; and that if they allowed us to pass through others might follow us, whereas if they killed us they would have no further trouble with strangers. Saking was severely criticized for having told us the whereabouts of the war trail over which we had come, and was appointed a committee of one on extermination, with power to act. In fact, he was directed to take his people and kill us, but he declined to obey instructions, and the other chiefs had run down the trail ahead of us in order to gather a sufficient force to wipe our party out. Saking's people were somewhat loath to act under the orders of any one else, and our sojourn among them was so brief that they did not have time definitely to make up their minds to attack us.

We now rapidly completed our journey to Bakidan's place, where we were to spend the night. Here again a crowd of armed fighting men awaited us. It was momentarily augmented by the arrival of recruits from the villages through which we had just passed.

Still unsuspicious of mischief, we turned our revolvers over to one of our Ilocano companions, a man named Lucio, who had served as Aguinaldo's mail-carrier during the latter days of the insurrection. We then walked into the middle of the crowd and sat down on pieces of our own luggage.

Bakidan immediately brought me a small wicker basket of very dirty looking bananas. I was nauseated as a

result of severe exertion in climbing Dead Man's Mountain, and the bananas did not look appetizing, so I thanked
him and put the basket on my lap. Instantly I felt
strong tension rising in the crowd. We had brought along
chief Atumpa and several friendly Kalingas from the
Saltan River valley. They seized their head-axes and
stepped in behind us, facing out. Bakidan instantly withdrew into his own house, and from a point where hardly
any one except myself could see him made emphatic
gestures, indicating that I was to eat. Little suspecting
the significance of the act, but desirous of placating his
outraged feelings if he felt that his hospitality had not
been appreciated, I hastily peeled a banana and took a
bite. To my amazement, there was an instant and obvious relaxation of tension in the crowd. The Kalinga
warriors loosened their grip on their head-axes and began
to walk about and talk. My own old men also assumed
an air of indifference.

Much puzzled, I made up my mind to look into this
matter further, and later learned that when people from
one Kalinga settlement visit those of another if the latter
wish to be friendly it is customary for them to offer the
visitors salt if they have it, bananas if salt is lacking, and
water in the event that neither salt nor bananas are
available. If the visitors wish to accept the friendship
thus proffered, they promptly eat or drink, as the case
may be; otherwise it is understood that they have come
looking for trouble.

Bakidan had ceremonially proffered the friendship of
himself and his people, and in my ignorance I had practically declared war on the whole outfit! When I learned
these facts I asked Bakidan why they did not kill us at
once. He said they were afraid. I expressed my surprise that they should be afraid of three unarmed men, and
he explained that it was very bad etiquette in the Kalinga
country for a person with a head-axe to go behind another,
and that we had amazed every one when we walked into

the midst of that gathering of armed men and sat down with our backs to half of them. They instantly concluded that we had, concealed about our persons, some new and strange device with which we could annihilate a crowd, hence they were afraid !

Here, as at Saking's place, we had interrupted a head-*cañao*. The head had been smuggled out of sight just before our arrival. The *cañao* was now renewed and continued all night, although the head was not again put in evidence. It is needless to say that we attended. We witnessed one of the weirdest sights I have ever seen.

The following day was spent in distributing presents to the Kalinga head-men, in taking photographs, and in getting a little much needed rest. As evening drew near Bakidan suggested that it was about time we formally made friends with each other. We were beginning to feel rather far away from home, and wanted all the friends we could get, so promptly acceded to his suggestion and repaired to his house at eight o'clock, the hour he had indicated.

The ceremony proved very simple. His wife fried some boiled rice in fat — dog fat as we afterward learned, but fortunately we did not know this at the moment! We all squatted on the floor, Bakidan facing us, and the dish of fried rice was placed between us. He squeezed a mass of it into a ball and gave it to me. I ate it, and then rendered him a similar service. He ate in turn, and we were friends ! The same procedure was followed with each of my companions.

In the midst of the ceremony there came a very unexpected interruption. A Kalinga woman was standing near me holding a torch. She had been silent and had seemed timid. I chanced to stretch out my right hand palm up. To my surprise she uttered an exclamation which was almost a shriek, seized my wrist and began to point excitedly to the lines in my palm. The other Kalingas gathered about, evidently greatly interested.

Several of them showed the lines in the palms of their own hands, and an animated conversation ensued. I asked what it all meant, and was informed that I was going to become a man of great influence! I had already modestly introduced myself as the ruler of all non-Christians, so found this reply unsatisfactory, but could get no other.

It was fortunate indeed for us that we made friends with Bakidan. On the following day we continued our journey down the valley. Our baggage was carried by women, children and a few old and more or less decrepit warriors who obviously felt deeply insulted at being required to render such a menial service, and were decidedly resentful toward Bakidan for having ordered them to do it.

Before we started Bakidan warned us that the Kalingas were queer people, and in consequence it would be well for us very quietly to go around certain of their settlements. Others we would visit. Their inhabitants would be sure to invite us to stay and enjoy their hospitality. He would second every such invitation. We were to pay no attention to his words, but were to note whether or not he sat down. If he did, we might accept the invitation. Otherwise we must plead an urgent engagement farther down the valley and move on.

Things came out exactly as he had foretold. In several villages we heard noises decidedly suggestive of head *cañaos*, and discreetly circled these places. We declined all invitations seconded by Bakidan when he did not seat himself, and rested comfortably for a time in several villages where he did.

Toward noon we walked straight into an ambush laid for us in the *runo* grass, discovering it only when Bakidan began to deliver a forceful oration in which he set forth the fact that he had a right to stroll down his own valley with a party of friends without being annoyed by having his fellow tribesmen hide beside the trail and prepare to throw lances.

Bakidan, who was himself a famous warrior, told these

men that they might kill us if they saw fit to do so, but must kill him first. Apparently rather ashamed of themselves, they came out on to the trail and slunk off to their town. Bakidan, greatly disgusted, suggested that we follow them and lunch in their village just to show that we were not afraid of them, and we did this.

After lunch I photographed a number of our late opponents, and we then continued our journey, escorted by a Kalinga chief named Bogauit from Took-Took. This man had previously descended to the Cagayan valley, where he had seen white people, and hearing of our advent in the Kalinga country, and fearing that we might have trouble in getting carriers for our baggage, had come with his fighting men to help us out.

The people of his village received us in a most friendly spirit, and after attending a bit of a *cañao* organized in our honour, and doing our best to entertain the crowd with a few simple experiments in physics, and some sleight-of-hand tricks, we retired, as we supposed, for a peaceful night's rest.

No such good fortune awaited us. We were aroused in the middle of the night by a fearful din only to find our hut surrounded by a great circle of armed men. The people who had attempted to ambush us earlier in the day had repented of their action in letting us pass through unharmed, had gathered a strong force of fighting men, had surrounded our house and were now vociferously demanding to be allowed to take our heads.

Old Bakidan was apparently fighting a duel with their chief in the midst of the circle. The two men were dancing around each other with cat-like steps, occasionally coming to close quarters and clashing shields, then leaping apart, swinging their head-axes and obviously watching for an opportunity to strike home. Had either of them gained any decided advantage of position he would doubtless have used his head-axe, and this would have started a fight which could have had but one ending.

Owing to a mistake made when the ammunition for our trip was purchased, we had just twenty-two revolver cartridges amongst us, and in the darkness they would have been worth about as much as so many firecrackers. The roof of the house was dry as tinder; a blazing brand thrown on it would promptly have forced us into the open. We should have been met by a flight of head-axes and lances, and this book would not have been written!

The majority of the crowd were determined to take our heads. The Took-Took people, greatly outnumbered, were evidently on the fence, and Bakidan was our only advocate. He still insisted that any one who wished to kill us must kill him first. His reputation stood him in good stead, and no one tackled the job. The uproar continued until nearly morning. *Bási*, a strong native liquor, was constantly passed. Indeed, every one but Bakidan had been drunk when we were first awakened. Finally food was handed around, and when the excited warriors stopped yelling in order to eat it the liquor had a chance to work, and most of them went to sleep.

We might probably have then effected our escape for the time being, but it was utterly impossible for us to get out of the country without the assistance of the Kalingas, and we decided to see the thing out right there.

In the morning the crowd was uglier than ever. As we crossed the little plaza they suddenly closed in on us with the obvious intention of doing for us, and we thought the end had come. At this critical moment a diversion was created in our favour by the wholly unexpected arrival of a letter brought in by a Kalinga runner. It had followed us all the way from Abra, and contained information about two pieces of baggage which were missing when we started. Its arrival greatly alarmed the hostiles, who interrogated me as to whether soldiers were coming. They had heard of soldiers, but had never seen them. I assured them that the arrival or non-arrival of soldiers

The Sub-provincial Building at Quiangan.

All the work of preparing materials for this building and of erecting it was done by Ifugao school-boys under the direction of a foreman. It was not quite completed when this photograph was taken.

would depend on the way they treated us, and to our utter amazement, they presently faded away.

The Took-Took people again showed themselves friendly when their unwelcome visitors had departed, and made us bamboo rafts on which we descended the river.

Our voyage was a decidedly adventurous one. Our rafts were repeatedly smashed by the swift current. As we approached each Kalinga village we were met by a reception committee carrying a bunch of bananas, followed at a short interval by a crowd of fighting men fully armed, and were thus given an opportunity to decide whether there should be peace or war. Needless to say, we voted for peace every time. I ate bananas until it was difficult to find room for more !

We spent the night at the *rancheria* of a friendly, white-haired old chief who had been to Tuguegarao, the capital of Cagayan, and knew a few words of Spanish. The next day we reached the settlement of Chief Doget, who had a wonderful house of red *narra*, a wood which closely resembles mahogany. It was furnished with beds, chairs and tables obtained from the Spaniards. Here we were able to rest in peace.

After sleeping the clock twice around, we continued our journey, and at dusk reached the Filipino town of Tuao, glad enough to get back to civilization and feeling that the kindly Providence which watches over fools, drunken men and children had had its eye on us. Without escort, and armed only with six-shooters rendered almost useless by lack of ammunition, we had completed the first trip ever made through the Kalinga country, and had done it without firing a shot and without losing a man.

This trip marked for me the beginning of friendly relations with the Kalingas. They have never since been interrupted, and now, when I ride a fast American horse rapidly over the splendid trails which cross their country from south to north and from west to east, or meet at Lubuagan the fighting men who were once so anxious to take my head but now make a long journey yearly in order to see me, I realize, as perhaps no one else does, how very materially conditions in Kalinga have changed.

It had been our intention, after spending a brief period in recuperation at Tuao, to proceed to Malaueg and continue our journey through the absolutely unknown country of the Apayaos, but we found it impossible to secure guides. The leading men of Malaueg, who came to Tuao to meet us, assured us that there were no trails known to them, which was untrue, and added that they would not under any circumstances consider trying to enter the territory of the fierce Apayao head-hunters.

We accordingly proceeded to Tuguegarao, the capital of Cagayan, intending to descend the Cagayan River to Aparri, go overland to Abulúg or Pamplona and there get guides and carriers.

At Tuguegarao, however, we found assembled the presidentes of all the Cagayan towns. Those from Abulúg and Pamplona positively assured me that there were no trails thence into the Apayao country, and that guides and carriers would be absolutely unobtainable. I insisted that I would visit their towns and ask them to accompany me, whereupon they actually wrung their hands and wept, complaining that the people of Apayao used bows and poisoned arrows.

In disgust I told them that I would abandon the trip for that year, but the following year would go to Laoág in North Ilocos, cross the "Cordillera Central" and come out through the Apayao country, taking with me Ilocano guides and carriers, as the Ilocanos were real men.

I then proceeded up the river to Ilagan and went overland through Nueva Vizcaya, ultimately crossing Ifugao from east to west and thoroughly exploring the territory from which I had been excluded on my previous trip; proceeding thence to Bontoc and Cervantes over a route new to me, and finally returning through Benguet and Pangasinán to the railroad, where I took train for Manila.

The following year I carried out my promise, taking
with me Colonel Villamor, who had rendered very valuable and satisfactory assistance on my previous trip.   I
also had three white companions, Dr. Paul C. Freer,
superintendent of government laboratories, Major Samuel
Crawford and Lieutenant L. D. Atkins.   These officers
commanded a detachment of twenty-five Ilocano constabulary soldiers which I reluctantly took along,
warned by my experience of the previous year and convinced by the arguments of my Ilocano carriers, who
declined to accompany me unless I took an armed
escort.

Prior to my departure from Manila I had received an
urgent telegram from the governor of North Ilocos informing me that one Abaya, a wild Tingian from Apayao,
had been sentenced to a term of imprisonment in Bilibid,
the insular penitentiary, and urging me to arrange if
possible to have him detained at Laoag until my arrival there, which I did.

On reaching Laoag, I was amazed to find a large delegation of fully armed Apayao men waiting for me at the
river bank.   They followed me to the house where my
quarters were to be, and sat down on the stairway, with
the obvious intention of seeing that I did not leave without their knowledge.

On asking the meaning of this occurrence, I was told
that they were friends of Abaya and wished to talk with
me.   When given an opportunity to do so, they told me
a singular tale, which admirably illustrates the relations
prevailing in that region between the wild men and their
Filipino neighbours.

Abaya was one of a few men in Apayao who dared to
descend to the lowlands.   He came down occasionally,
bringing tobacco and wax to barter for cloth, steel, salt
and other necessaries not obtainable in Apayao.   Being
unable to speak Ilocano well, he obtained a Filipino agent
known as his "commissioner," who transacted his busi-

ness for him, withholding for himself a liberal percentage of the proceeds.

On the occasion of his last visit to the lowlands, the "commissioner" had told Abaya that he had a Negrito slave who was planning to escape, and had directed him to take his head-axe and kill the Negrito, promising him half of a large pig in payment for this service.

Abaya, nothing loth, hastened to execute the order, hunting up the Negrito and aiming a terrific blow at him. Fortunately the Negrito saw it coming and jumped so that he received it on his shoulder instead of his neck. It inflicted a horrible wound, but he nevertheless ran away so fast that Abaya was unable to catch him and finish the job. He returned and regretfully reported his lack of success to his "commissioner." To his amazement he was arrested, taken to Laoag and held for trial. Both he and his friends were convinced that the reason for this was his failure to kill the Negrito, and the friends assured me in the most positive terms that Abaya had done his very best and that it was through no fault of his that the Negrito had escaped! They demanded his immediate release.

Meanwhile I had been informed by the governor of the province that Abaya's people had threatened to come and wipe out the village where his "commissioner" lived, and also to kill all of the Negritos in that vicinity in revenge for the arrest and imprisonment of their chief.

It struck me that the "commissioner" was the man who ought to be in jail, but I did not care to allow the Apayao people to think that they could make such threats with impunity, so asked them whether it was true that they were planning to wipe out the village in question. They said yes. I then told them that they must not do it. They expressed a willingness to obey any instructions that I might give to them. I asked whether their promise to let the village alone was dependent upon Abaya's being set at liberty, and they answered no. We then took up the question of killing the Negritos. They were greatly amazed that I should object to this, urging that they had always fought the Negritos, and that the latter were bad people who constantly made trouble with their poisoned arrows; theretofore it had been considered commendable to kill as many as possible. However, they said that they would let the Negritos alone if I insisted upon it, irrespective of whether or not Abaya was released. Having duly impressed them with the fact that the matter of the release of Abaya must stand on its own merits, and could not be made to depend on their subsequent good or bad conduct, and having interviewed the Filipino judge who sentenced Abaya and learned that he had been puzzled to know what to do and was heartily in favour of having him pardoned, I telegraphed to the acting governor-general requesting that this be done, and continued my journey, leaving word that Abaya should follow me if set at liberty.

He was promptly pardoned. His people insisted that he join them and take to the mountains, but he told his friends that since I had secured his release he would do what I had asked. He overtook me before I had finished my second day's march, and stayed with me until I gave him leave to go his way !

Our climb over the cordillera was by no means a pleasure trip. We were forced to use beds of streams and Tingian warpaths in lieu of trails. At one time our way lay over wet limestone rocks which were slippery as ice. Here our hobnailed shoes were a positive source of danger. The feet of our carriers were badly torn, and we ourselves suffered from occasional falls on the sharp rocks. We secured the help of some additional Tingians whom we met journeying to the coast, paying them liberally enough so that they were willing to abandon their proposed trip and accompany us.

We sent all of our Tingian companions ahead to give notice of our friendly intentions before reaching the first village in Apayao, but its inhabitants nevertheless ran away. Thoroughly exhausted, we decided to spend a night there. In the course of the afternoon our men were able to bring in some of their fellow tribesmen who lived in the vicinity, and we made friends with them.

From this point a half day's march brought us to the head-waters of the Abulúg River at a point where it was navigable for bamboo rafts. We delayed at a little village until we could construct rafts enough to float our large party, and then started downstream, knowing that we should meet plenty of people, for the Tingians of Apayao are fond of placing their villages on river banks.

Our trip was a wild and adventurous one. Fortunately I had purchased some twenty dollars' worth of beads and with these I made at least twenty-five hundred presents! The friendship of the women at the first town which we met was thus secured, and thereafter the "grapevine telegraph" worked ahead of us and we found waiting delegations of women and girls on the river bank at almost every village. So long as they were about, it was reasonably certain that the men would not make any hostile demonstration.

The trip proved a great success in every way. Many of the numerous settlements which we visited were at war with each other. One had just been attacked, and a number of its people had lost their heads, literally. We were constantly warned that the residents of the next town down the river were "bad people" and that "five hundred" of them were waiting in the river bed to attack us, but only once were we in any real danger of being molested, and even then diplomacy prevailed.

We were careful to respect local customs. One town was reported to be *cañao*, which is equivalent to "taboo," because of the death of the wife of the headman, and we religiously kept away from it. Another was *cañao* because of a virulent epidemic of smallpox, and we were more than willing to keep away from that one!

We bumped down rapids and shot over several low falls. Again and again our rafts were torn to pieces and we were precipitated into the rushing stream. At one time a constabulary soldier was under water for some ten minutes, and we thought him dead when he was first fished out, but finally succeeded in resuscitating him.

We had been told that the trip would take eight days and had made our plans accordingly. It took fifteen. Food ran short. Shoes and clothing gave out. Some of our soldiers were dressed in clouts before we reached civilization, and crawfishes on which our men could pounce along the edges of the river were out of luck!

I shall long remember the shout of delight which our Filipino companions set up when we finally passed through the last mountain gap and came out into the open country, but as a matter of fact the most disagreeable part of our journey lay before us. Up to that time our progress had been rapid and exciting. Now the current of the river grew sluggish, and we were largely dependent on it, as our rafts were too heavy to paddle and the stream was in many places so deep that we could not pole them.

We found ourselves in the country of very wild Negritos. Our Tingian friends had informed us that these people would certainly sneak up and shoot arrows into our camps at night, but nothing of the sort occurred. On the contrary, through the liberal use of scarlet cotton cloth, we were able to establish very friendly relations with the Negritos encountered, some of whom gave us in exchange deer meat enough for a feast, which was highly appreciated by all concerned.

On arrival at Abulúg we were received with great surprise by the people, who had heard that we had been attacked and killed. There I developed malaria and contracted bronchitis.

We made our way up the Cagayan River to Ilagan and thence proceeded overland to the Kalinga villages in the vicinity of Sili. At the latter place we had an amusing experience. Knowing that we were going to Mayoyao, some Ifugaos from that town had joined our party for protection. A delegation of Sili Kalingas waited on us during the lunch hour and politely asked to be allowed to take the heads of these Ifugaos, saying that they needed some fresh heads, and that it would save a lot of trouble if they could have these, so providentially brought to them by their respective owners. I explained to them that we really needed the Ifugaos, and they politely waived their claim to them in our favour !

I had been assured that I could ride a horse to Mayoyao in two and a half days. The trip took five days. Much of the way horses were worse than useless. Before we reached our destination my bronchitis had developed into pneumonia and I was very ill. My white companions on the Apayao trip had long since left me, but at Ilagan I had been joined by Señor Claraval, who was later elected governor of Isabela, and by an American school-teacher. Colonel Villamor had stayed with me. Now all my companions turned back and I continued my journey accompanied only by Ifugaos and by a young lieutenant of constabulary named Gallman, who had then just come to the Ifugao country but was later destined to play a most remarkable part in bringing its warlike people under control and starting them on the road toward civilization.

Our route from Mayoyao to Banaue of necessity followed the Ifugao war trails, which invariably run along the crests of mountains so as to command a view in both directions. The country through which we passed was frightfully broken, and I could hardly stand.

Wherever it was humanly possible to do so, the Ifugaos carried me in a blanket slung under a pole. They took me up almost perpendicular ascents in this way, but in some cases the ascents were *quite* perpendicular and the descents the same, so that I had to try to climb, constantly falling as the result of weakness and exhaustion,

IFUGAO CONSTABULARY SOLDIERS.

These men are brave, efficient, and loyal. They shoot with extraordinary accuracy. The Filipino officer at the left, Lieutenant Maximo Meimban, has long rendered efficient service in Ifugao.

in spite of the efforts of the Ifugaos to keep me on my feet. We reached Dukligan at dusk and there we spent the night.

In the morning I found myself unable to rise, so took a stiff dose of whiskey. As this failed to produce the desired result, I took a second and finally a third. Under the potent influence of the stimulant I managed to get up. The willing Ifugaos carried me clear to the rice terraces near Banaue, making a joke of the hard work involved. There were always a dozen men on the pole, and whenever one set of carriers grew weary there was a scramble, closely approaching a fight, to determine who should be allowed next to take their places.

These jolly people constantly gave a peculiar shout which was ridiculously like an American college cheer. Ill as I was, I almost enjoyed the trip, and conceived a great liking for the splendidly developed men who were seeing me through in such gallant style. Had it not been for their kindness, I should certainly have left my bones somewhere between Mayoyao and Banaue.

They were determined to lug me through the rice terraces, but as it took at least four men to carry me, and the weight of the five of us was sufficient to cause the tops of the high terrace walls to crumble so that I had several narrow escapes from falling down them, I climbed out of my extemporized hammock, took one more big drink of raw whiskey and on the strength of it managed to stagger along to the river, where I was amazed to find a horse awaiting me. Nothing ever looked better to me than did that somewhat decrepit animal!

I was absolutely unfit to travel, but having rested at Banaue for half a day, and realizing that it was imperatively necessary that I should get to a doctor at once, I made what was then record time to Banaue, Bontoc, Cervantes and Baguio, and on arrival at the latter place proceeded to go to bed and be comfortably ill.

Tramping over the northern Luzón mountains with

my lungs partly solidified left my pumping machinery in such shape that I have never since been able to make a hard trip on foot, but that is no longer necessary. Splendid horse trails now make travel through this region a pleasure.

When we crossed Apayao only one other white man had achieved the feat. This was a good missionary priest who in 1741 traversed the country between Abulúg and one of the North Ilocos towns.

Lieutenant Gilmore's [1] Filipino captors took him and his companions across a corner of Apayao, and instead of murdering them in the forest, as they had been ordered to do, turned them loose. They made their way across a portion of the territory traversed by us, and had reached the Abulúg River and were attempting to build rafts when overtaken by a rescue party of American soldiers. All hands then descended the river to the town of Abulúg, and proceeded overland to Aparri.

Colonel Hood, who was commanding the United States forces there, declined to let them enter the town until they had been provided with decent clothing, thinking that the sight of American soldiers clad in clouts might be too much of a shock to the inhabitants !

In 1907 I was able to land at various points along the then absolutely unknown Pacific coast of northeastern Luzón, but failed to get into touch with the Negritos, who constitute its sole inhabitants, until near Palanan, the northernmost settlement of Filipinos on the east coast.

With this trip my exploration work in northern Luzón ended, although I have ever since made extended annual trips through the non-Christian territory of the island.

During the years covered by this hasty narrative, I also made trips to the territory of the wild men in Mindoro, Palawan, and Mindanao, as opportunity offered. In Spanish days I had lived among the Moros and had

[1] Lieutenant Gilmore, U.S.N., was captured at Baler in the summer of 1899, and held a prisoner for many months.

visited the mountains of Negros and Panay and seen
something of the wild men living there, so that I finally
gained a fairly comprehensive knowledge of the non-
Christian tribes of the Philippines, having seen representatives of nearly all of them,[1] and lived for longer or
shorter periods among all except some of the more unimportant peoples in the interior of Mindanao.

As a result of these personal investigations I was able
to reduce to twenty-seven the eighty-two non-Christian
tribes said by Blumentritt to inhabit the Philippines;
to determine with reasonable accuracy the territory occupied by each, and not only to become familiar with
the manners and customs of the people of each important
tribe, but to establish relations of personal friendship
with many chiefs and headmen which have proved invaluable to me in my subsequent work for the betterment
of the non-Christian peoples which has so irritated certain Filipino politicians who have wished to continue to
oppress and exploit them, or, like Judge Blount, have
sought to minimize their importance.

The latter individual seems to regard my past efforts to
portray actual conditions among the wild men as a personal grievance, and has devoted an entire chapter to the
shortcomings of "Non-Christian Worcester." In it he
says of me that I impressed him as "an overbearing bully
of the beggar-on-horseback type"; that I am "the P. T.
Barnum of the 'non-Christian tribe' industry"; that
"in the early nineties he [Non-Christian Worcester]
had made a trip to the Philippines, confining himself
then mostly to creeping things and quadrupeds — liz-
ards, alligators, pythons, unusual wild beasts, and
other forms of animal life of the kind much coveted
as specimens by museums and universities," and goes

[1] The only tribes of which I have not seen representatives inhabit
the region of the gulf of Davao in Mindanao. It is doubtful whether
they are really tribally distinct from the Bagobos, Bilanes and other
tribes living near the coast.

on to tell how it was that "the reptile-finder ultimately became a statesman." The Honourable Judge summarizes his views concerning me by stating that he "considers Professor Worcester the direst calamity that has befallen the Filipinos since the American occupation, neither war, pestilence, famine, reconcentration nor tariff-wrought poverty excepted." He describes the experience on which he bases these statements as follows: "During all my stay in the Philippines I never did have any official relations of any sort with the Professor, and only met him, casually, once, in 1901."

This latter statement is correct to the best of my recollection. "A man is known by the company he keeps." I feel that I have been fortunate in my friends and singularly blessed in my enemies! If I do not in turn attack the Philippine career of Judge Blount, it is not for lack of abundant ammunition, but for the reason that I believe that the American public will be more interested in the truth or falsity of the allegations concerning more important matters which we respectively make than in our opinions of each other.

The Judge seems to have overlooked the fact that invective is not argument. I leave to him the use of needlessly abusive and insulting language. He has also apparently overlooked the further fact that disregard of the truth is apt, sooner or later, to bring its own peculiar reward. Later I call attention to certain of his misstatements concerning the wild peoples of the Philippines, and correct them.

CHAPTER XXI

The Government of the Non-Christian Tribes

When I visited Benguet in July and August of 1900, I found conditions there such that the early establishment of civil government seemed practicable and desirable. The people had taken no part in the insurrection and nowhere in the province was there any resistance to American authority. An act providing for the government of the province and its settlements was accordingly passed on November 23, 1900, Benguet being thus the first province to pass from the control of the military.

In drafting this act I was fortunate in having the co-operation of Mr. Otto Scheerer, a German citizen who had lived for a number of years among the Benguet Igorots, understood them fully and was most kindly disposed toward them.

The Benguet law, in considerably amplified form, was applied to Nueva Vizcaya when that province was organized on January 28, 1902, and on April 7, 1902, a carefully considered act entitled "An Act providing for the Establishment of Local Civil Governments in the Townships and Settlements of Nueva Vizcaya" was passed by the commission.

On May 28, 1902, the province of Lepanto-Bontoc was established. It had three sub-provinces, Amburayan, Lepanto and Bontoc. The two Nueva Vizcaya acts above mentioned were made applicable to it, and to its towns, respectively.

On June 23, 1902, an act was passed organizing the province of Palawan (Paragua) and extending to it, and to its towns, the more essential provisions of the two Nueva Vizcaya acts.

559

On the same day Mindoro was incorporated with the province of Marinduque under the regular Provincial Government Act, which was then being made applicable to all provinces populated chiefly by Filipinos. As might have been anticipated, it did not prove feasible properly to administer the affairs of Mindoro under this act, and on November 10, 1902, a province of Mindoro, including the main island and numerous neighbouring small islands, was established under a law embodying the essential provisions of the Nueva Vizcaya Act. Certain provisions of the Nueva Vizcaya township and settlement act were made applicable to its municipalities, while on December 4, 1902, other provisions of the same act were made applicable to the settlements of the wild Mangyans, who occupy the whole interior of this great island so far as it is occupied at all.

The desirability of uniform legislation for the government of the non-Christian tribes, except those of the Moro Province, soon became evident, and after much experience in the practical working of the several acts above mentioned under the conditions presented in the five provinces, Benguet, Nueva Vizcaya, Lepanto-Bontoc, Palawan and Mindoro, I drafted the so-called "Special Provincial Government Act," and "The Township Government Act." The former was made applicable to the five provinces above mentioned, and the latter to all settlements of non-Christian tribes throughout the Philippines except those of the Moro Province.

On August 20, 1907, an act was passed carving the province of Agusan out of territory which had previously belonged to Surigao and Misamis, and organizing it under the Special Provincial Government Act.

Finally, on August 18, 1908, the Mountain Province was established in northern Luzón.

At the same time that the Ifugao territory was separated from Nueva Vizcaya there was added to the latter province the Ilongot territory previously divided between Isabela, Tayabas, Nueva Ecija and Pangasinán.

Before considering the details of the work accomplished in the several special government provinces and sub-provinces, I will state the general principles which have been found useful in bringing the non-Christian peoples under control and in establishing friendly relations with them, and will explain how these principles have been applied in actual practice.

I have always considered the opening up of adequate lines of communication an indispensable prerequisite to the control and development of any country, and this is especially true of the territory of the wild man. No matter how unruly he may be, he is apt to become good when one can call on him at 2.30 a.m., since that is the hour when devils, *anitos* and *asuáng* are abroad, and he therefore wants to stay peaceably in his own house! Again and again we have built a trail to an ugly, fighting, head-hunting settlement whose people have at first thrown spears at our road labourers, but later, when they found that the trail was really going to arrive, have ended by building one out to meet it. Constabulary garrisons which we have expected to be forced to establish have often proved unnecessary when communication was opened up.

We have had scanty funds for public works in these regions. At the outset I had to get along with four or five thousand dollars a year in the territory now included in the Mountain Province and the task which confronted me seemed utterly hopeless. Nevertheless, I made a beginning and did the best I could. Now the Mountain Province has annual receipts of about $85,000, of which some $65,000 are expended for public works and permanent improvements. This is made possible by the fact that the salaries and wages of the provincial officers, and certain contingent expenses as well, are met by direct appropriation of insular funds.

Another principle to which I have steadfastly adhered is never to impose taxes on a wild man until he can be made to realize that direct good to him will result from their collection. One of several reasons why the Spaniards never could dominate the hill people of Luzón was that they insisted at the very outset upon exacting "tribute" from them. The hill people regarded the money thus contributed as a present to the man who collected it, and rebelled against making presents to people who did not treat them well and whom they did not like.

The most important tax in the special government provinces is the so-called "public improvement tax."

The law imposing it does not become operative on the non-Christians of any given territory without the prior approval of the secretary of the interior.

It provides for the collection from every able-bodied adult male between the ages of 18 and 55 of an annual contribution of two pesos.[1] The taxpayer is allowed to render ten days of service upon public works in lieu of cash payment if he prefers, and most non-Christians do prefer to settle the obligation in this way. All money derived from this source is expended on public works, going to pay for supervision, dynamite, powder, caps, fuse, steel, road tools and the like, as it is seldom necessary to hire labourers.

We paid for all labour on the first trails constructed, and it was only when the people themselves learned to comprehend the usefulness to them of improved means of communication that I made the public improvement tax applicable to them.

Except under very special circumstances, I did not allow the construction of a trail with a grade higher than six per cent. There are two reasons for this rule. First, the torrential rain-storms of the tropics rapidly destroy high-grade trails in spite of all efforts to provide adequate drainage; second, if trails are constructed on low grades, every shovelful of earth which is thrown is just so much accomplished toward the eventual opening up of cart

[1] Equivalent to one dollar.

BONTOC IGOROT HEAD-HUNTERS.

These men were expecting to be attacked at the time this photograph was taken.

roads, carriage roads or automobile roads, the whole subsequent question involved being one of widening and surfacing.

In constructing a trail we first carefully stake what seems the best possible line between the two points to be connected; then build on this line a path which is cut into the hill [1] four feet, the dirt being thrown outward. No special effort is made to give the bank a proper slope; the Almighty does this in the course of the first rainy season, when the earth sloughs off on to the trail in those places where it stands too steeply. It is then promptly thrown off the road-bed while still loose, and much hard pick and shovel work and many "pop shots" are thus saved. Only the most necessary drainage is provided before the first rainy season, for the reason that experience has shown that what seem dry beds of streams and look as if they would be converted into raging torrents during the rainy season sometimes then hardly carry water enough to wash one's face in; while, on the other hand, destructive torrents come charging down the crests of hogbacks in places where one would least expect them, and cut out the trail completely where they strike it. With the first rain the maintenance gangs get to work, noting where drainage is especially needed and providing it, throwing off loose earth and stones when slides occur, and widening the trail or cutting off sharp corners when not otherwise engaged.

American and Filipino road foremen were at first used for trail construction, but the Igorots, Ifugaos and Kalingas, all of whom are very intelligent people, soon learned to serve as foremen. I had Ifugaos who ran about clad in clouts only, but were nevertheless quite capable of carrying a road or trail across the face of a precipice, doing all of the powder work.

The wild men soon learn to take great pride in their trails, and usually keep them in an excellent state of re-

[1] Nearly all our trails are on steep mountain sides.

pair. It is a remarkable fact that on the thousand miles of road and trail which have been constructed since the American occupation in the Mountain Province and Nueva Vizcaya no one has as yet been murdered. In the wildest regions there has been an understanding from the outset that people travelling over government roads were to be let alone!

The establishment of government, and of a decent state of public order, have gone hand in hand with the opening up of lines of communication. Wherever practicable it is highly desirable to police the wild man's country with wild men, and this has proved far easier than was anticipated. The Bontoc Igorots make good, and the Ifugaos most excellent, constabulary soldiers. They are faithful, efficient, absolutely loyal and implicitly obedient. The Ifugaos are born riflemen, and their carbine practice is little short of marvellous when one considers their very limited experience. Natural fighters as they are, the people of these two tribes make the best of soldiers. They are absolutely fearless, and fight much as do the Ghurkas of India. Benguet Igorots and Kalingas are now being enlisted as constabulary soldiers, and from the very outset the people of many of the non-Christian tribes of the islands have been used as policemen in their own territory.

The annual inspection trip which the secretary of the interior is required by law to make to every province organized under the special provincial government act has become very important in the control and advancement of the non-Christian tribes.

It is now customary to hold *fiestas*, or as they are locally designated, *cañaos*, at central points, to which are invited great numbers of the wild people from the neighbouring country. At the outset these gatherings served to bring together men who had hardly seen each other except over the tops of their shields when lances were flying. They were all friendly with me, but they were by no means friendly with each other, and trouble threatened on vari-

ous occasions.   Within the space of thirty seconds I have
seen a couple of thousand men draw their war knives
and snatch up their lances, and have feared that a record
killing was about to occur, but in the end the excited
warriors always quieted down.

We took advantage of these great gatherings to bring
about the settlement of old difficulties between hostile
towns and they have thus proved an important factor in
the establishment of peace and order throughout the
wild man's territory.   Furthermore, they afford excellent
opportunity to discuss past events and future plans under
the most favourable conditions.   I well remember the occasion on which the Ifugao headman of Quiangan requested that the public improvement tax be imposed upon
them and their fellow tribesmen.   There was at that time
but one decent trail in this sub-province.   It had been
built by paid labour.   Some of the headmen who had
gone to Bontoc with me had seen excellent trails there
and had asked why Ifugao could not have some just as
good.   I had replied that the Bontoc Igorots were more
civilized then the Ifugaos and had come so to appreciate
the benefit of trails that they were willing to build them
without being paid for their labour.   Vehement exception
was taken to my contention that the Bontoc Igorots were
further advanced than the Ifugaos.   The latter insisted
that they were much better men than the Igorots, and
could and would build better trails.   I explained to them
in detail the practical working of the public improvement
tax, and asked if they would be willing to have this contribution imposed on them.   They insisted that they wanted
it, and I finally gave it to them, although I doubted their
ability to bring their people into line.   On the following day
there was a precisely similar occurrence at Banaue.   I soon
found that I had underrated the influence of the headmen.
That year twenty thousand Ifugaos worked out their road
tax.   The following year twenty-four thousand men rendered the prescribed ten days' service; and the number

has steadily increased year by year ever since, with the result that the sub-province is crisscrossed with trails, many of which are already wide enough for considerable distances to permit the passage of automobiles if they could be brought there, while the main line of communication with Bontoc on the one hand and the capital of Nueva Vizcaya on the other is open for cart travel from the western to the eastern boundary of the sub-province.

At many of the *cañaos* we have athletic contests, which the wild men, with their splendid physical development, greatly enjoy. It is much better for two hostile towns to settle their differences by a tug-of-war, or a wrestling match, than by fighting over them, and they are now often quite willing to adopt these more pacific means provided the audience is sufficiently large and enthusiastic, for the average wild man has a very human love of playing to the gallery. He takes to the athletic contests of the American like a duck to the water, and soon learns to excel in them. No sooner is a *cañao* over than those who have taken part in it begin to look forward to the next one, and the small expense involved is repaid a thousand fold in the good feeling produced.

In the course of a year the people of each of the non-Christian tribes do many things for us simply because we want them to, and it seems only fair that we should give them at least one opportunity during the same period to have a good time in their own way.

The personal equation is of vital importance in dealing with wild men. They know nothing of laws or policies, but they understand individuals uncommonly well.

The men in immediate control of them must be absolutely fearless, must make good every promise or threat, must never punish except in case of deliberate wrong-doing committed in spite of warning duly given, and must, when punishment is thus made necessary, inflict it sternly but not in anger. The wild man thus dealt with is likely to call quits when he has had enough, and if he promises to behave must be treated like a man of his word, which he usually is.

As a result of such just, firm and kindly treatment governors and lieutenant-governors soon find themselves endowed by their people with powers far in excess of those conferred on them by law. They are *ex officio* justices of the peace, but are just as apt to be asked to settle a head-hunting feud between towns, which has caused a dozen bloody murders, as a quarrel growing out of the joint ownership of a pig. They are the law and the prophets, and no appeals are taken from any just decisions which they may make, nor is their authority questioned. On the contrary, their people usually object when sent to the courts, as is of course often necessary.

These officers are always on the watch for opportunities to get the people of hostile towns to swap head-axes, or dance together, and so become friends.

When one town has been in the very act of raiding another the timely appearance of an unarmed *Apo* [1] has sufficed to shame the culprits into laying down their arms and going home without them.

No one who has not seen for himself can appreciate the courage, tact and patience of the handful of Americans who have not only brought under control the wildest tribes of the Philippines, but have established the most friendly relations with them.

Having now outlined in a general way the principles which have been followed in the work for the non-Christian tribes of the special government provinces, I will set forth some of the more important results which have been obtained.

In Benguet, which under the Spanish régime was organized as a *comandancia*,[2] there dwell a kindly, in-

---

[1] An untranslatable term of respect and affection given by the fighting men of northern Luzón to rulers whom they like.

[2] A designation applied to a political division of less importance than a province, governed by a military officer.

dustrious, self-respecting, silent tribe of agriculturists known as the Benguet Igorots. Governmental control was established over them by the Spaniards. They have never indulged in head-hunting nor caused any serious disturbance of public order, but have persistently refused to give up their ancient religious beliefs, and for this reason were not allowed by the Spaniards to obtain education, so that, with rare individual exceptions, they were completely illiterate. When I first visited their country I found the men clad in clouts, supplemented in the case of the more wealthy by cotton blankets. The women usually wore both skirts and upper garments, and bound towels around their heads for turbans.

The Benguet Igorots were formerly compelled to trade for the necessaries of life in the lowlands of the neighbouring province of Union, where they were shamelessly exploited by the Filipinos. They had been obliged by the Spaniards to pay taxes for which they received no adequate return. They had furthermore been roughly treated by the Insurgents during the war, and were extremely fearful and timid. Men ran away at my approach. Women overtaken unexpectedly on the trail leaped down the steep mountain sides, squatting where they first struck the ground and covering their faces with their hands.

It proved a simple matter to establish friendly and helpful relations with these simple and gentle people. Fortunately for them Mr. Otto Scheerer, who had lived among them for years, helped organize their settlements. Some of them were still so wild that they ran away at his approach, sitting up on the high mountain sides and watching him from a distance, but declining to come down. Patience, perseverance and kindness soon overcame their fears, and local governments were established in the several settlements.

Travel through Benguet was then dangerous and difficult because of the condition of the trails, which were mere footpaths. None of the streams were bridged. Work was promptly begun upon a trail system, and now one can ride a large horse rapidly to every settlement of importance.

At first the people had nothing to sell, and no money with which to buy what they needed. From time to time they packed coffee and Irish potatoes down to the lowlands and traded them for salt, cloth and steel, which they needed, and for *vino*, which was poison to them.

We have protected them in their property rights and encouraged them to increase their agricultural holdings. As they were too ignorant to understand and exercise their right to obtain free patent to small tracts of land which they had long occupied and cultivated, I sent out a special survey party to help them make out their applications in due form.

The gradual development of Baguio, first as a health resort and later as the summer capital, afforded them an ever increasing market for their products; while trail construction, the opening of the Benguet Road and the erection of buildings at Baguio made it possible for every one desiring it to secure remunerative employment. In the old Spanish days they had been forced to build trails without compensation, and to feed themselves while doing it. When they realized that the new régime had come to stay, their gratitude knew no bounds.

For a time they could not be persuaded to try the white man's medicines, but ultimately the wife of the most important chief in the province, who was dying of dysentery, was persuaded to let Dr. J. B. Thomas, a very competent American government physician, treat her case. She recovered, and the news spread far and wide. After that Igorots came in constantly increasing numbers to the hospital which had meanwhile been established, and to-day their sick and injured are often carried to it from a distance of fifty miles or more.

Schools were soon established in several important

settlements. The boys proved apt pupils. At the outset parents would not allow their girls to attend. Gradually the prejudice against sending them to school was overcome, and at three different places girls are now given instruction in English and in practical industrial work.

The children learn English readily and the old folks pick it up from them. Mrs. Alice M. Kelly, who started the first Igorot school, taught her boys respectfully to salute her in the morning, and shortly thereafter American travellers over the Benguet trails were addressed by Igorots with the cheerful greeting, "Good morning, Mrs. Kelly." Their feelings were doubtless identical with those of the traveller in Japan to whom a beginning student of book English said, "Good morning, Sir, or Madam, as the case may be!"

The Benguet Igorots have responded quickly to the opportunities afforded them, and several serious dangers which have threatened their progress have been met and overcome.

The Filipino peoples will never become victims of alcoholism. They drink in moderation, but seldom become intoxicated. The non-Christian peoples, on the contrary, never lose an opportunity to get boiling drunk. All of them make fermented alcoholic drinks of their own. Fortunately most of these beverages are comparatively mild and harmless; but if a hill man can get hold of bad vino or worse whiskey he will get so drunk that he thinks he has to hang on to the grass in order to lie on the ground.

The Filipinos had long taken advantage of this weakness of the Benguet-Lepanto Igorots to debauch them with *vino* and cheat them while they were intoxicated. I regret to say that since the American occupation some white men who wanted them as labourers have used liquor as a bait. Because of these conditions, and of more or less similar ones throughout the rest of the wild man's territory, I drafted and secured the passage of an act mak-

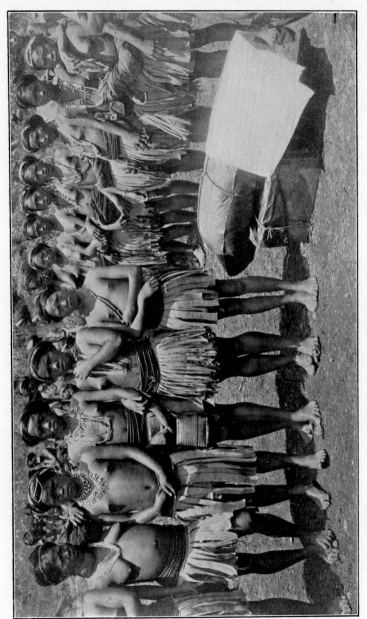

Bontoc Igorot Women in Banana-leaf Costume.

ing it a criminal offence to sell or give white man's liquor to a wild man, or for such a man to drink such liquor or have it in his possession.   This law has been very successfully enforced.   Although Benguet-Lepanto Igorots have sometimes succeeded in purchasing liquor at Baguio or Cervantes, their use of strong alcoholic stimulants has steadily decreased, and throughout much of the wild man's territory strong drink is absolutely unobtainable.

The Benguet Igorots have an abiding love for gambling, and some of them learned new tricks, which did them no good, through contact with Filipinos when working on the Benguet Road.   Strict enforcement of the law against gambling has, however, prevented any considerable spread of this evil.

One of the most interesting results thus far obtained is the arousing of a strong commercial instinct among them.   It was literally true at the outset that one could not buy from them an egg, a chicken or a basket of *camotes*, much less a pig or a cow.   Now special market buildings have been erected for them at Baguio, and they are thronged on Sundays.   The Igorots have money and spend it wisely.   They also have farm products to sell, know what they are worth, and insist on getting full value for them.   Among other things there may be mentioned sleek cattle, the best fat hogs grown in the Philippines, chickens, eggs, cabbages, Irish potatoes, peas, beans, tomatoes, squashes, camotes and strawberries.

There have been some interesting episodes in connection with the work for the Benguet Igorots.   At one time it became necessary for the provincial governor, Wm. F. Pack, to undergo a severe and dangerous surgical operation.   Word spread through Benguet that the doctors were going to cut him to pieces.   Palasi, an old Igorot chief of Atok, gathered his cohorts and came in hot haste to Baguio to stop it.   He was assured by Governor Pack himself that the cutting was to be done with his consent, but still entertained some doubts about the matter and asked to be allowed to be present. His request was granted. There was then no operating room in Baguio, so one was extemporized in the governor's house. He walked out to the operating table, and Palasi, who was standing by, once more asked him if he was to be cut up with his own consent, offering to stop the performance even then if the governor so wished !

On March 30, 1913, I sat at a luncheon given at Trinidad, Benguet, in honour of former Lieutenant-Governor E. A. Eckman, who had just been promoted to the governorship of the Mountain Province. At the long tables were seated a representative gathering of decently clad Benguet Igorot head-men, the hosts of the occasion. They understood the use of knives, forks and spoons. At the close of the luncheon they presented Governor Eckman with a beautiful silver cup. The presentation speech was made by an Igorot named Juan Cariño, who had been shot and badly wounded by American soldiers from whom he foolishly endeavoured to escape in 1900 !

Fortunately old Juan was not killed. Like every other Igorot in Benguet he is to-day a good friend of the Americans. The people of his tribe are now sober, industrious, cheerful, contented and prosperous. As time passes they keep cleaner, wear more and better clothes and build better houses. In this case, at least, a primitive people has come in close contact with the white man and has profited by it.

Lepanto, like Benguet, was a *comandancia* in the Spanish days. Its Igorot inhabitants are fellow-tribesmen of their Benguet neighbours, and like them are, and have long been, peaceful agriculturists, raising *camotes*, rice, coffee and cattle. They also mine gold and copper. In the extreme southeastern and the extreme northern parts of Lepanto the people are wilder and less law-abiding than those of Benguet, and some of them are prone to indulge in cattle stealing.

This subprovince has one Ilocano town, Cervantes,

which was made the capital of the province of Lepanto-Bontoc. At the outset communication with the coast was maintained over a very bad horse-trail crossing the coast range at Tilad Pass. It zigzagged up one slope of the mountains and down the other on a grade such as to make travel over it very difficult. Furthermore, after reaching the lowlands on the west side of the range, it crossed a river some fourteen times. During the rainy season there were weeks at a time during which this stream could not be forded. In the early days of the American occupation a good wagon road was built from the coast to the point where the trail began, and the trail itself was put in the best possible condition. It was subsequently well maintained, but after the establishment of a Filipino provincial government in South Ilocos the wagon road was allowed to fall into such a state of neglect that travel over it, even for persons on horseback, became impossible during wet weather. Mr. Kane, the supervisor of the Mountain Province, was nearly drowned in mud when trying to ride over it, being thrown from his horse into soft ooze so deep that his hands did not reach bottom, and had it not been for a timely rescue by Filipinos who chanced to be passing, he would certainly have lost his life.

Although forty or fifty thousand pesos' worth of supplies were annually sent into the mountain country by the people of South Ilocos over this trail, that province refused to spend a peso in keeping the connecting road up. The constantly growing trade of the mountain country made it, in my opinion, necessary that it should have a good outlet to the coast, and a route for a road was surveyed from Cervantes directly west over the Malaya range, traversing the subprovince of Amburayan from east to west and coming out at the municipality of Tagudin. In order to prevent the occurrence of a state of affairs such as had rendered the Tilad Pass trail practically useless during much of the rainy season, this Ilocano town was annexed to Lepanto-Bontoc, thus giving the province a route to the coast within the limits of its own territory.

The people of Tagudin were at first inclined to protest against annexation to the country of the non-Christians, but soon discovered that the change was greatly to their advantage. Their town had long been threatened with destruction by the encroachment of the Amburayan River, and they had appealed in vain to South Ilocos for help. The Mountain Province gave them assistance in the construction of a protecting wall which held the river within bounds and adequately safeguarded the town. Their business rapidly increased when Tagudin became the western terminus of an important trade route. They soon began to take an active interest in improving local conditions, and their municipality was gradually changed from a dirty, down-at-the-heel place to a neat, clean, sanitary town in which its people could take justifiable pride. An old feud which had long separated the leading men into two parties so bitterly hostile to each other that the mere fact of advocacy of a given measure by one of them was sufficient to cause determined opposition to it by the other, died out, and Tagudin is to-day quite a model place in comparison with the general run of Filipino towns.

The opening up of transportation lines has placed the people of Lepanto within much easier reach of a market for their rice, coffee and cattle. The successful combating of cattle disease by the Bureau of Agriculture has been a great boon to them, as has the suppression of the liquor traffic. Schools have been established in a number of their settlements. Last, but by no means least, their lives are no longer endangered by the head-hunting Bontoc Igorots. They are now a peaceful, prosperous people, and are progressing steadily in civilization.

In Spanish days there was a *comandancia* known as Amburayan wedged in between the provinces of La Union and Ilocos Sur. After the American occupation this territory was at first organized as a part of Ilocos Sur, but it soon became necessary to make of it a separate subprovince and add it to Lepanto-Bontoc, to the end that its people might be adequately protected. In contact on two sides with Christian Filipinos, they were shamefully maltreated and oppressed, and they appealed to me for help.

Filipinos were graciously permitting them to cut firewood and lumber in the public forests, and taking the lion's share of the products in return for their consent! They were debauching the Igorots with *vino*. I remember particularly the case of one unfortunate individual who owned five carabaos, two of which got to fighting. As usually happens with these animals, the one that was whipped ran away, and the victor blindly pursued it. Both charged over a precipice and broke their legs. The owner killed them, dressed them, and divided the meat among his family and friends. He was arrested, given a mock trial for killing carabaos without a license, and fined three carabaos — all he had left — which of course went to his persecutors!

Instances of this sort of thing could be indefinitely multiplied.

Amburayan was freed from the *vino* traffic soon after it became a subprovince of Lepanto-Bontoc. This alone was a great boon to its Igorot inhabitants, who little by little were helped to assert their rights as they gained greater confidence in their American lieutenant-governor and learned to go to him freely with their troubles. They had so long been helpless and hopeless that it was some time before they could be convinced that a new day had dawned for them.

And now let us betake ourselves to the country of the real wild man, and consider briefly past and present conditions in the subprovince of Ifugao.

The people of the tribe known as Ifugaos are a remarkable lot. Their country is almost entirely made up of exceptionally steep mountain sides with hardly a naturally level piece of ground in it. On almost precipitous slopes they have built wonderful series of irrigated rice terraces held in position by stone retaining walls which have been laid without mortar or cementing material of any kind, and are so skilfully constructed that they withstand even the terrific rains which sometimes occur during typhoons. Accurate rainfall statistics for Ifugao are not obtainable, but, as we have seen, in the neighbouring subprovince of Benguet, there is of record a period of twenty-four hours during which forty-nine and nine tenths inches of rain fell ! Under such conditions as this, exceptionally good work is necessary to prevent structures of any sort built on mountain sides from sliding into the valleys below.

Up to the time of the American occupation the Ifugaos had always been inveterate head-hunters. Unlike the Bontoc Igorots, who depend on large numbers of fighting men for protection, they live in small villages usually placed in inaccessible spots which can be reached only by ascending the almost perpendicular rice-terrace walls.

Not only were the people of this tribe then constantly fighting among themselves, but they from time to time raided the Bontoc country or that of the Kalingas, and they persistently victimized the people of Nueva Vizcaya, making travel so unsafe on the main road between Nueva Vizcaya and Isabela that the Spaniards found it necessary to maintain several garrisons along it, and forbade private persons to pass over it without a military escort. Even so, parties of travellers were cut down from time to time, the savages making their attacks at the noon hour when Spanish soldiers had a way of going to sleep beside the road.

I have already narrated my earliest experiences in this subprovince, which occurred in 1903, and have called attention to the fact that when I returned in 1905 I was able to traverse it from east to west without the slightest danger. This condition of affairs was due to the efforts of Governor Louis G. Knight, supplemented by those of Captain L. E. Case of the Philippine constabulary, who had established his headquarters at Banaue and had exercised a strong influence over his unruly constituents. Perhaps I ought to change my statement and say that order was established by Captain Case, assisted by Governor Knight. Captain Case was very fortunate in his dealings with the Ifugaos. He was a kindly man, who won their friendship at the outset. He resorted to stern measures only when such measures were so imperatively necessary that the Ifugaos themselves fully recognized the justice of employing them.

On my trip through the Ifugao country in 1906 I was accompanied from Mayoyao to Banaue by Lieutenant Jeff D. Gallman, who had come to the former place to meet me. This young man had been especially selected by Colonel Rivers, of the Philippine constabulary, to be trained for work among the Ifugaos. Never was a selection more fortunate. When Captain Case injured himself by over-exertion in climbing a steep, terraced mountain side in the hot sun, and had to return to the United States for recuperation, Gallman took up his work and devoted himself most effectively to the task of bringing the Ifugaos under control, protecting them, and improving their conditions. He was a dead shot with revolver and carbine; was absolutely fearless; was of a kindly, cheerful disposition, and soon not only won their respect but gained their love.

As the years went by, the Ifugaos came to regard him as but little less than a god. He had extraordinary success in training them for service as constabulary soldiers. On the occasion of the first general rifle competition between all the constabulary organizations in northern Luzón ten Ifugao soldiers were sent to the lowlands to participate. Gallman, who had trained them, was travelling with me at the time, so they were taken down by a comparatively inexperienced officer who, instead of selecting the best ten men from among the ninety possible candidates, took ten from the twenty who happened to be stationed at Mayoyao.

The hot climate of the lowlands troubled them. The Filipino constabulary soldiers made fun of them because they wore no trousers, and bedevilled them in various ways. The best shot among them lost his nerve in consequence. Nevertheless, when the competition was over they ranked Nos. 1, 2, 3, 4, 5, 6, 7, 8, 9, and 10, respectively, an Ilocano soldier from the lowlands being tied with the last man for tenth place!

Ifugao soldiers are submissive to discipline, obey orders implicitly, and are loyal and brave to a fault. When on duty they attend strictly to business. No prisoner ever yet escaped from one of them. This is more than can be said of the Bontoc Igorots. It is of record that on one occasion when a prisoner guarded by a raw recruit of the latter tribe made a break for liberty, the recruit followed him, firing as he ran. After missing the fleeing man five times, he threw his carbine at him, lance-fashion, and speared him with the bayonet! So long as an Ifugao has a cartridge in his magazine he does not indulge in bayonet practice.

The same general policy was pursued in Ifugao which had been found so effective elsewhere. Lines of communication were opened up; after a short time criminals were for the most part apprehended and turned in by the head-men themselves; whenever possible, hostile towns were left to sulk until they had learned from the experience of their neighbours that there was nothing to be afraid of or to complain about, and voluntarily came into the fold; head-hunting was suppressed with a heavy hand, but only after due warning as to what the fate of transgressors would be. It is now some six years since a head has been taken in this region. Travel not only in Nueva Vizcaya but in Ifugao itself is at present absolutely safe, and general conditions as to law and order

A BONTOC IGOROT TUG-OF-WAR.

The government now encourages field sports among the wild people as an outlet for energies which were formerly expended in head-hunting. The Bontoc Igorots, the Ifugaos, and the Kalingos take the keenest interest in contests like that here shown.

are better than those which prevail in many American communities. The people have been assisted in the construction of irrigation ditches, and little by little are being persuaded to come down from their steep and over-populated mountain sides to the neighbouring fertile, level vacant plains. They are loyal and friendly to a marked degree, and I experience no greater pleasure than that which I derive from travelling through their country.

Credit for this happy result is chiefly due to the efforts of Jeff D. Gallman, who speedily rose to be a captain in the constabulary and at an early date was made lieutenant-governor of Ifugao. He has done a monumental work for civilization in the Philippines.

The Kalinga country was at the outset administered as a part of Bontoc. This made that subprovince so large that one lieutenant-governor could not hope satisfactorily to cover it, especially as there were no good lines of communication. Although a constabulary garrison was early stationed at the town of Lubuagan, comparatively little progress was made in bringing the Kalingas under effective control until their territory was made a separate subprovince of the Mountain province and Lieutenant-Governor Walter F. Hale, of Amburayan, was transferred to it as its lieutenant-governor.

Lieutenant-Governor Hale has now been in the special government service longer than any other man who remains in it, and has an admirable record for quiet efficiency. Like Gallman, he is a man with chilled-steel nerve, and he needed it in the early days in Kalinga where the people, who had been allowed to run wild too long, did not take as kindly to the establishment of governmental control as had the Bontoc Igorots and the Ifugaos. The Kalingas are a fine lot of head-hunting savages, physically magnificently developed, mentally acute, but naturally very wild. Hale soon made friends with many of the local chiefs, and thereafter when he received invitations from outlying *rancherias* to come over and have his head taken would quietly accept to the extent of setting out accompanied by a few soldiers, or none at all, and talking the matter over with the people who had made the threat! In the end they always decided that he was too good a man to kill.

Here, as in Ifugao, we felt our way, avoiding trouble with hostile settlements as long as it was possible to do so. And here, as in Bontoc and Ifugao, head-hunting was abolished and law and order were established practically without killing. In a few instances settlements which absolutely refused to come into the fold, and persisted in raiding and killing in the territory of people who had already become friendly, were given severe lessons, which they invariably took in good part.

One of the pleasant things about dealing with people like the Kalingas and the Ifugaos is their manliness when they fight. They let one know, so plainly that there can be no mistake about it, whether they are friendly or hostile, and even if thoroughly whipped they bear no ill will provided they know that they deserve a whipping, but come calmly walking into camp to tell you that they have had enough and are going to be good. And they keep their promises.

In Kalinga, as elsewhere throughout the Mountain Province outside of Apayao, an admirable trail system has now been opened up and travel is not only safe but comfortable. The people are most friendly and loyal, and while head-hunting has not completely disappeared, cases of it are extremely rare and occur only in the most remote parts of the subprovince.

Apayao has proved a hard nut to crack. As previously stated, I made a trip across this subprovince from west to east in 1906, without encountering any hostility whatsoever. Unfortunately, the officer who commanded my escort saw fit to go blundering back there with a constabulary command a few weeks later. He managed to get into a fight and was whipped and chased out of the country. A so-called punitive expedition was then sent in, which came near meeting a similar fate, but finally withdrew in fairly good order after having inflicted slight damage on the town of Guennéd, the people of which made the original attack.

Apayao was at first organized as a subprovince of Cagayan, and Colonel Blas Villamor, who had accompanied me on my two longest exploration trips through northern Luzón, was appointed its lieutenant-governor. The attitude of the provincial officials of Cagayan toward the difficult task which confronted them in Apayao was most unsatisfactory. Indeed, the governor of that province informed me that in his opinion the best way to settle the Apayao problem was to kill all of the inhabitants. As Colonel Villamor reported that there were some fifty-three thousand of them[1] this procedure would have presented practical, as well as moral, difficulties ! I myself was of the opinion that the Apayao people, who proved to be wild Tingians, were altogether too good to kill.

Colonel Villamor was a native of Abra, where approximately half the population is made up of Tingians who have attained to a high degree of civilization. He was already quite familiar with the dialect spoken by these people, and speedily learned the language of their wild brethren in Apayao, many of whom understood Ilocano, which was his native tongue.

At the outset he made excellent progress in bringing . his people under control. The task was undoubtedly more difficult than that in any other subprovince of the Mountain Province, both because the Spaniards had failed to penetrate into this region, leaving the people untouched by civilization up to the time of the American occupation, and for the further reason that their head-hunting is connected with religious beliefs. They think that when a man dies his prospect for a good time in the

---

[1] This statement proved to be untrue. They number about twenty-five thousand.

future world is bad unless the members of his family take a head within six months, and this idea has a tendency to keep society in a somewhat disturbed condition.

For reasons which I have never been able fully to fathom, Villamor's progress in establishing governmental control grew steadily slower as time went by, and ultimately came to a standstill. During my absence from the islands it was deemed best to accept his resignation, for reasons not immediately connected with his administration of the affairs of his subprovince. Before surrendering his post he caused word to be spread among the Tingians that the kindly policy which had thus far been pursued in dealing with them was to be superseded by one of severity, greatly alarming them, and seriously retarding work which he had quite auspiciously begun. There was absolutely no justification for his statements, as no one thought for a moment of dealing with the Apayao Tingians in a fashion differing at all from that invariably followed in our relations with non-Christians in the special government provinces.

Mr. Norman G. Connor was appointed to succeed Señor Villamor. Mr. Connor had been acting governor of Nueva Vizcaya and had rendered very satisfactory service. He has made material progress in establishing control over the people of Apayao, where the work of trail construction has now begun. At the outset communication was maintained by boats on the Abulúg River and its branches, near which most of the wild Tingian villages are situated, but it is a dangerous stream to navigate, especially when in flood, and lines of land communication must therefore be opened up.

We found the subprovince of Bontoc peopled by a tribe of wild, warlike, head-hunting Igorots over whom the Spaniards had never been able to establish effective control. At the time of the American occupation their numerous settlements were constantly at war with each other, and with the Kalingas and the Ifugaos as well.

The Bontoc Igorots build large towns and depend on the numbers of their hardy fighting men for protection. Each town formerly kept a profit and loss account of heads with every town of its enemies. Physically these people are splendid men, and we soon found that they were usually both brave and fair in their fighting, formally making and breaking peace, and serving due notice on their enemies before attacking.

If a small town felt itself aggrieved by a big one, it would send a messenger to say, "You have more fighting men than we have, but they are no good! Pick fifteen of the best from your thousand and send them to a certain place at a certain time to meet fifteen real fighting men selected from among our five hundred." At the appointed time the thirty warriors would meet in deadly combat, while their fellow-townsmen looked on.

The Bontoc Igorots are naturally truthful and honest, and they soon became most friendly, gladly bringing many of their troubles to their lieutenant-governor for settlement. Fortunately, head-accounts between different towns can be adjusted by proper payments made by those who hold the highest scores. We took advantage of this fact to establish peace between the towns, and when once established it was, as a rule, religiously kept.

Trail construction was promptly inaugurated and has been steadily pushed. Most of the towns have thus been made readily accessible.

When friendly relations had been established, and we were in a position to back orders with force if necessary, settlement after settlement was warned that head-hunting must cease and was further informed as to what would happen if the mandate was disobeyed. Certain dare-devils promptly broke over, partly, I fancy, to see what would happen, and partly, no doubt, because they found the influence of tribal customs too strong to resist. We made our warnings come true. One settlement required three bitter lessons. For others a single mild one

sufficed. The majority of the towns were content to get
their experience vicariously. We were amazed at our
own success in stopping this horrible practice. At the
outset we burned towns if their people engaged in head-
hunting.[1] The Igorots recognized the justice of this
action because the whole town was invariably cognizant
of, and party to, every head-hunting raid made by any
of its people. Later, when head-hunting became comparatively rare, we began to deal with the individuals concerned. They were arrested, brought before the courts,
and tried like any other criminals. To-day head-hunting
in Bontoc is almost unknown. When it does occur the
people themselves usually capture and turn over the culprits.

The respect of the Bontoc Igorots for the law is extraordinary. In 1910 a Constabulary soldier shot the
presidente of Tinglayan without just cause. The people
of the place rushed to arms, meaning to kill the soldier.
Chief Agpad, assisted by the son of the murdered man,
took station before the door of the house in which the
assailant had sought refuge, and the two stood off their fellow-townsmen, saying that the government had promised
to kill evil-doers and that this man must be turned over
to the government to be killed ! When I passed through
their town a few weeks later, with Governor-General
Forbes, they begged to have him killed promptly.

In the early days I myself had a rather stormy clash
with some of the Bontoc Igorots. During Aguinaldo's
long flight he had passed through half a dozen of their
towns, as had the American soldiers who pursued him.
The Igorots did not like this, so tore out the trail to
Ifugao, between Bontoc and Samoqui, and built high-
walled rice paddies where it had been, with the result
that persons making the journey had to use the river bed
for several miles. This was all very well if the river was
low, but was no joke if it chanced to be in flood.

[1] Not so serious a matter as it may seem, when houses are made
of grass and can be speedily rebuilt.

I ordered that the trail be rebuilt, the Igorots to be
paid for their work, and for the resulting damage to
their rice fields, and this was done.

The lieutenant-governor was a weak man, and the
Igorots, after getting their money, tore the trail out again
and rebuilt their stone terrace walls across the place
where it had been, just to see what he would do about it.
He did nothing. I found things in this condition when I
arrived, and was obliged to come down the river bed at
dusk, with the result that my horse and I took several
impromptu baths.

The Samoqui warriors came dancing out to meet me,
playing their *gansas* [1] and making a grand hullabaloo.
Summoning my sternest expression, I refused to shake
hands with them, telling them to go home and to report
at Bontoc at nine the following morning.

The fighting men of the town of Bontoc met me on the
other side of the river, and I served them the same way.
The official under whose nose they had destroyed the
trail was greatly alarmed, and assured me that if I
ordered it rebuilt, as I told him I would do, there would
be a fight, and the Igorots would cut the heads off all the
Americans in town, including the ladies. He added,
"Think how the ladies would look without any heads!"
While this was a disquieting reflection, I remained ob-
durate.

At the appointed hour the Samoqui and Bontoc men
appeared, armed with head-axes and lances. I asked them
if they would rebuild that trail, and they said no! I told
them that if they did not I would cut their main irri-
gating ditch and put a constabulary guard on it to see
that it was not repaired until they changed their minds.
This might have meant the loss of their rice crop. They
knew me quite as well as they did their lieutenant-governor, and promptly rebuilt the trail for nothing, as I
told them they must.

[1] Bronze timbrels.

When the Mountain Province was established, the town of Bontoc was made the capital, as Cervantes, which had been the capital of Lepanto Bontoc, was hot, had proved unhealthful, and was not centrally situated. Bontoc has a cool, delightful climate, is near the geographic center of the province, and from it radiates a road and trail system of constantly increasing importance. Things have moved rapidly there since the status of the place was changed.

To-day the town has modern public buildings of brick and stone. The brick have been made, burned and laid by Igorots. Much of the stone has been cut and laid by Igorots. The mortar used has been mixed by Igorots with lime burned by Igorots. Some of the carpenter work has been done by Igorots. There is a modern hospital to which the Igorots flock. There are schools in which Igorot boys and girls learn the English language, and become adept in the practice of useful industries.

Perhaps the most unique of the Bontoc institutions is the provincial jail. Years ago I discovered to my horror that a two-year sentence to Bilibid, the insular penitentiary, was a death sentence for a hill-man! Not all who were sent there died, but the average term of life of men from the hills was two years only, while those who served out their sentences and returned to their mountain homes had invariably become adepts in crime as the result of prolonged contact with vicious Filipinos. I promptly drafted an act providing for the establishment at Bontoc of a penitentiary where all prisoners from the highlands should be confined, and the commission passed it. The prison has been made a real educational institution. Most of its inmates have been guilty of crimes of violence, committed in accordance with tribal customs, and are not vicious at heart. The jail building is perfectly sanitary. Its occupants are required to keep their persons clean and their quarters both clean and in perfect order. They live amid healthful surroundings and receive abundant and

BONTOC IGOROT BOYS LEARNING TO MAKE FURNITURE.

Their teacher, Mr. Hora, has staked hundreds of miles of trail in the Mountain Province, and supervised the construction of the wonderful stone school-house built by the Ifugao boys of Quiangan.

nourishing food. They are taught useful trades and are
compelled to work hard, which they do not in the least
mind, as industry is the rule in the mountain country.
They usually leave the jail better men than when they
entered it, and thereafter, instead of being a menace to
law and order, assist in their enforcement and maintenance.

We do odd things with some of these prisoners. Last
year we paroled a man from Ifugao who had a score of
heads to his credit. Learning that his people believed
him to be dead and were greatly troubled, we told him to
go home, show himself to them, tell them how he was
treated in jail, and come back. He did it !

Proof of the kindliness of the relations which have
existed with the Bontoc Igorots is found in the fact that
no member of this tribe has ever yet turned his hand
against an American. On the contrary, there are not a
few Americans who owe their lives to Igorots. Agpad, of
Tinglayan, has twice dived into rivers swollen by typhoons
and rescued Americans who had sunk for the last time
beneath the rushing, muddy waters, while their fellow-
countrymen stood by paralyzed with fear.

Last year there occurred an event of profound significance. In the past, American officials have often worked
hard for days to get representatives of two hostile towns
to dance together, for this would make friends of them.
On the occasion in question there had gathered at Bontoc
to meet me representatives from every settlement in the
subprovince. Each town had brought its *gansas* and its
dancers. On the second day of my visit the people of
one of the towns started a dance on the plaza. They
were promptly joined by representatives from another
town which had long been hostile to them. People from
yet other towns followed suit, until finally the plaza
swarmed with a great crowd of dancers in which every
settlement in the subprovince was represented. Even
at that late day I should not have dared to attempt to

bring about such a thing. It happened of itself, and to the initiated told an eloquent tale of the results of our years of patient work !

The first time I climbed Polis Mountain, on my way from the Bontoc country to the land of the Ifugaos, four Igorots went ahead of me, armed with head-axes and lances, carrying their shields in position. At each turn in the steep, worn-out trail, they drew back their lances ready to throw. I had eighty-six armed men with me, and knew that I might need them. To-day I travel through the length and breadth of the Mountain Province unescorted and unarmed. Furthermore, I usually take my wife with me.

Prior to 1903, if an Ifugao showed himself on the north side of the Polis range he lost his head. Now people of this tribe stroll into the town of Bontoc almost daily. They travel north through the Bontoc Igorot country to Lubuagan, in Kalinga, and west to Cervantes, in Lepanto, or even to Tagudin on the coast, crossing three subprovinces on the latter trip. They also go south to Baguio.

All freight was formerly packed in from the coast on men's backs a distance of eighty odd miles over steep, narrow, stony trails which were really foot-paths. Now it comes in carts over a good road which has a maximum grade of six per cent.

The people of the settlement had to get their water from the river. Now it is piped into town.

There was not a shop in the place, and every one had to go to the coast to make the smallest purchases. There are at present half a dozen good stores, beside the provincial exchange, a store where the government sells the Igorots what they want at reasonable prices, thus preventing shopkeepers from overcharging them.

Commodious quarters for visiting Igorots and Ifugaos have been provided, and there is a fine market where they may display and sell their products. This market is a busy place.

The population is rapidly increasing, now that head-hunting has practically ceased. The area of cultivated lands steadily grows larger, for the men are freed from the necessity of being constantly under arms, and we are helping them to get more irrigation water, so that they can extend their rice fields.

There are a thousand or so Bontoc Igorots in Benguet to-day, contracting for railroad excavation work. Times have changed.

When Nueva Vizcaya was first organized, its non-Christian inhabitants greatly outnumbered its Filipino population, as there were at least one hundred fifteen thousand Ifugaos in addition to several thousand Ilongots and a few Benguet Igorots, locally known as Isinayes, who had strayed over the boundary line. With the transfer of the Ifugao territory to the Mountain Province, the Filipinos were left in the decided majority. Later all of the Ilongot territory which had previously belonged to the provinces of Isabela, Tayabas, Nueva Ecija and Pangasinán was added to Nueva Vizcaya, in order that the members of this wild and primitive tribe might be brought under one provincial administration.

The Ilongots are a strictly forest-inhabiting people. Many of them have a considerable admixture of Negrito blood and live a semi-nomadic life. Their settlements, which are small and more or less transient, are usually situated in remote and inaccessible places surrounded by the densest jungle. It is at present impracticable to open up horse trails through their country, for the number of inhabitants is so small, in comparison with the area occupied, that such trails could not be built with Ilongot labour, nor indeed could they be maintained even if built. One main trail· is, however, being constructed, and it is planned to build foot trails from this to the more important of the settlements which it does not reach.

A special assistant to the Provincial Governor of Nueva Vizcaya for work among the Ilongots has been appointed and assigned to duty at Baler, on the Pacific coast of Luzón, from which place he can more conveniently reach the Ilongots east of the coast range. These people were very wild at the outset, and it proved difficult to establish friendly relations with them, but this has now been successfully accomplished, and their fear of the white man is largely a thing of the past.

There is a school for Ilongot children at Campoté. They prove to be bright, capable pupils.

At the same place there has been established a government exchange, where the Ilongots can sell such articles of their own manufacture as they wish to market, and can purchase what they need at moderate cost.

They still fight more or less with each other, but depredations by them upon Filipinos have ceased.

CHAPTER XXII

THE GOVERNMENT OF THE NON-CHRISTIAN TRIBES
(*Continued*)

THE province of Mindoro includes numerous small islands, all peopled by Tagálogs, and the main island of Mindoro, which has a narrow broken fringe of Tagálog settlements along its coast. Its whole interior is populated, so far as it is inhabited at all, by the Mangyans, a primitive semi-nomadic tribe which is of Malayan origin but has considerable Negrito blood. No one knows even approximately how many of them there are, for although the island has been crossed in several different places, much of it is still quite unexplored. In most of the interior regions thus far visited the population is very sparse, but one quite thickly settled district has been found. It is believed that the Mangyans number something like 15,000.

The Filipino settlements were so disorderly, filthy, and unhealthy that the energies of the first governor, Captain R. G. Offley, and those of his successor, Captain Louis G. Van Schaick, were to a large extent expended in efforts for the betterment of the Tagálogs. It is a pleasure to record the fact that these efforts met with a very large degree of success.

The condition of most of the Tagálog towns is now good. Mangarin is the chief exception to this statement. Its surroundings are such as to make it impossible successfully to combat malaria, from which every one of its inhabitants suffers. We are still endeavouring to persuade its unfortunate people to move to a healthy site!

Governor Offley did some work for the Mangyans. They have advanced but slightly beyond the Negritos in civilization. Many of them live under shelters not worthy of the name of huts, and in the vicinity of Mt. Halcon even the women are clad only in clouts. Houses are placed singly in the dense forests, or at the most are gathered in very small groups. It proved a most difficult undertaking to persuade any considerable number of Mangyans to gather together and construct decent dwellings. It had been their custom to abandon their forest homes whenever a death occurred, leaving behind all their belongings, and perhaps even changing their names on the theory that their old names were unlucky and new ones might prove advantageous.

With admirable patience Governor Offley organized a little village called Lalauigan on the south coast of Mindoro. Lalauigan has prospered. It is very clean; the houses of its Mangyan residents are quite presentable. The neighbouring fields are planted with corn and rice. It has a school, and the children prove to be apt pupils.

Another Mangyan village, organized near the west coast, was short-lived. The Tagálog Filipinos look with great disfavour on the gathering of the Mangyans into settlements where they can be protected, as this renders it difficult to hold them in a state of peonage. Whenever Governor Offley got a little group together, they did their best to scatter it. In this instance they passed the word that smallpox had broken out in a neighbouring Tagálog village. All Mangyans are deathly afraid of this disease, and this particular set built a great fire, jumped through the flames to purify themselves from contagion, took to the hills, and have not been seen since!

While in hearty sympathy with the admirable work which was being done among the Tagálogs, I was dissatisfied with the failure to push explorations in the interior more actively and to get more closely in touch with the wild inhabitants. When the Tagálog settlements had at last been put in really good condition, I gave Governor Van Schaick, who had succeeded Governor Offley, positive instructions that more attention must be paid to the Mangyans. He then began active explorations, and pushed them with considerable success up to the time when he was compelled to tender his resignation by the terms of the Army Appropriation Bill for 1913, which necessitated his return to his regiment. Prior to his departure he succeeded in establishing a new Mangyan village which has continued to prosper up to the present time. His successor, Governor R. E. Walters, was kept from actively pushing exploration work during the past "dry" season, by unprecedented rains.

Road and trail construction began several years ago and is going forward as rapidly as limited funds will permit.

The great trouble with the Tagálogs of Mindoro is that nature has been too kind to them. They have only to plough a bit of ground at the beginning of the rainy season, scatter a little rice on it, and harvest the crop when ripe, to be able to live idly the rest of the year, and too many of them adopt this course. However, some good towns, like Pinamalayan, are waking up as the result of immigration from Marinduque.

Two great services have been rendered to the more orderly of the inhabitants of Mindoro, which was, in Spanish days, a rendezvous for evil-doers from Luzón. Indeed, it was the most disorderly province north of Mindanao. An excellent state of public order has been established, and there has not been an armed *ladrone* [1] in the province for years. It was famous for its "bad climate." We have shown that its climate is good, making its towns really healthful by merely cleaning them up.

The establishment of a great modern sugar estate on the southwest coast has doubled the daily wage, and given

[1] The words *ladrones* and *tulisanes* are used indiscriminately in the Philippines to designate armed robbers and brigands.

profitable employment to all who wanted to work, and the people are beginning to bestir themselves. The public schools, of which every town has one, are materially assisting the awakening now in progress.

Palawan, like Mindoro, is made up of one large island, which bears the name of the province, and a number of smaller ones. Indeed, it includes more small islands than does any other province, with the possible exception of Moro.

The bulk of its Christian population are found on the smaller islands, several of which are very thickly settled.

The non-Christian inhabitants are divided between three tribes, — the Moros, Tagbanuas and Bataks. The latter are Negritos of very pure blood. Their number is quite limited. They extend across the island from the east coast to the west in the region north of Bahia Honda.

Until within a short time there have been Moro settlements scattered along both east and west coasts of the southern third of the main island. The Moro population of Palawan is largely composed of renegades who have been driven out of Joló, Tawi Tawi, Cagayan de Joló, British North Borneo and Banguey by their own people because of infractions of the laws of their tribe. When the province was organized, they were not cultivating a hectare of land amongst them. They lived in part by fishing, but chiefly on what they stole, or on the products of the labour of the hill people in the interior, many of whom they enslaved or held in a state of peonage, taking their rice and other agricultural products with or without giving compensation, as seemed to them good.

The hill people, who occupy the higher mountains in the interior of southern Palawan, and who in the central and northern portions of the island extend down to the very coast, are known as Paluanes in the south and as Tagbanuas elsewhere. Tagbanuas are also found on

A Conference with Ifugao Chiefs.

From left to right the Americans are: Governor William F. Pack of the Mountain Province, the author, and Lieutenant-governor Jeff D. Gallman of Ifugao.

Dumarán and Linapácan, and quite generally throughout the Calamianes Islands, especially on Culion and Busuanga. I have failed to discover any real tribal differences between the Paluanes and the Tagbanuas and believe that they should be classed as one people, although the Paluanes are more inclined to stand up for their rights than are the Tagbanuas, and by using blow guns and poisoned arrows have succeeded in keeping the Moros out of the interior highlands. They were, however, long forced to trade with the Moros in order to obtain cloth, steel, salt and other things not produced in their own country, and so were at their mercy.

The Tagbanuas are a rather timid and docile people, giving evidence of a considerable amount of Negrito blood. They are at times quite industrious, and raise considerable quantities of rice and *camotes*, but live, in part, on fish, game and forest products.

Communication in this province was very difficult. The main island of Palawan, which is some two hundred fifty miles in length and very narrow, extends in a northeasterly and southwesterly direction, and as a result both of its coasts are swept by each monsoon so that there are only about two months of the year when travel by sea in small boats is comfortable and safe. At the outset there was not a mile of trail on the island. This latter condition is being rapidly remedied.

The first governor appointed for the newly established province of Palawan was Lieutenant E. Y. Miller, U. S. A., a man of splendid physique, tireless energy, and indomitable courage.

Governor Miller set to work very actively to better the condition of the Filipinos and to establish friendly and helpful relations with the non-Christians.

The bulk of the Christians are unusually poor and ignorant and many of them were held in a miserable state of peonage by a few *caciques*. Vigorous efforts extending through a long term of years have weakened the grip of the *caciques*, but have by no means broken it.

At an early date the new governor won the admiration of the Moros, who like courage, by a series of very brave acts. A number of constabulary soldiers who were coasting along the west shore of Palawan in a sail-boat went ashore, leaving their rifles on board guarded by two or three of their comrades. They also left several Moros on the boat, and the latter, watching their opportunity, killed the guards and got away with the rifles, taking them to Dato Tumay, their chief, who armed his people with them.

Governor Miller, with Captain Louden, of the constabulary company concerned, promptly attacked Tumay's place and drove him into the hills. Tumay took refuge in a Tagbanua village, never dreaming that he would be pursued into the mountain fastnesses. Miller and his companions succeeded in getting into the place before Tumay knew they were in the vicinity, and there followed a fight to the death at close quarters. Two soldiers, standing one to the right and one to the left of Governor Miller, were shot dead, but he was not scratched.

On a number of other occasions he displayed a bravery approaching recklessness. Hearing that a fleet of some fifty Moro boats had put to sea on a piratical expedition, he embarked in a twenty-foot launch accompanied only by a captain of constabulary, and the two of them ran down and disarmed the pirates and sent them home. They nearly sank their tiny launch with the dead weight of the weapons which they took on board. The thing seems preposterous, and only Miller's extraordinary moral influence over these unruly people made it humanly possible.

When I visited Palawan on my regular inspection trip in the year 1909, I found Mrs. Miller much worried about her husband, who was absent from the capital, having gone to arrest some Moro murderers at Lara. As usual, he had taken with him only a constabulary captain and three or four soldiers, and Mrs. Miller feared that he might be killed.

I hastened down the coast of the island at the full speed of my steamer, keeping a close watch for his boat, and finally located it at Bonabóna, where he had succeeded in arresting several of the criminals. On his way down he had stopped at Lara and had learned that a brother of the local chief, Dato Pula, was responsible for the murder, having ordered it and paid the assassins who committed it, one of whom was lurking in the vicinity, while others had gone to Bonabóna. Governor Miller called upon Dato Pula to deliver both his brother and the murderer, who was then at Lara, and stated that he would be back on a certain day to receive them. As he insisted on returning at the appointed time and attempting to arrest these men, I took him on my steamer, together with his American companion and one constabulary soldier. The other soldiers remained on his boat to guard the prisoners he had already taken.

We returned to Lara, but were unable to land in front of the town as a heavy surf was thundering on the beach. A mile to the north we found a sheltered spot where we could safely disembark and our little party, consisting of Governor Miller armed with a six-shooter, a constabulary captain armed with a Winchester shotgun and a six-shooter, a constabulary soldier armed with a carbine, ex-Insurgent Colonel Pablo Tecson armed with my double-barrelled shotgun, Governor Pack of the Mountain Province, my brother George S. Worcester, and my stenographer, all of whom were without weapons, and myself carrying an automatic Winchester rifle, marched on the town. Governor Miller sent the soldier ahead to warn the Moros that they must meet us unarmed. A small reception committee did so.

On the very outskirts of Lara we waded a creek nearly

up to our necks in water, then marched up the street and entered Pula's house. Just as we did so I saw twenty or thirty fully armed Moros come in on the run and hastily conceal themselves in one of the numerous neighbouring houses. I further promptly discovered that two rooms partitioned off in the corners of the great living room of Pula's house were crowded full of men armed to the teeth, and that a second-story room, immediately under the roof and over our heads, was similarly occupied. I asked Governor Pack quietly to ascertain how many of the houses in the village were occupied by fully equipped fighting men, and he soon informed me that every one of them was packed. We estimated that there were several hundred warriors in town, which meant that Pula had raked the coast of the island north and south for miles and brought in every male Moro big enough to wield a weapon.

We seated ourselves on a table, back to back and facing out, with our own weapons very handy, and had a talk with Pula which lasted until late in the afternoon. Standing within striking distance of us most of the day, were two stalwart Moros, each of whom had a kriss dagger firmly gripped in his right hand and concealed between his folded arms. When one remembers that the average Moro fighter does not seem to know when he is dead, but keeps on doing damage after he ought to be busily occupied in passing to the other world, it will be seen that our situation left much to be desired.

Under the pretext of sending for a phonograph with which to entertain the crowd while our negotiations continued, I communicated with the captain of our steamer, advising him of the facts. He got out ammunition for his two one-pounder rapid-fire guns and took up a position immediately in front of the town. We did not ask him for reënforcements, believing that any attempt on his part to send them would precipitate an attack on us.

Never did I pass a more peculiar, or a more unpleasant,

day. Miller steadfastly insisted that Pula's brother and the hired assassin be given up. Pula produced two thoroughly cowed Tagbanuas whom he had induced by threats to declare that they had committed the murders, and most emphatically declined to turn over either his brother or the true murderer. Our discussions were punctuated by tunes played on the phonograph which created great excitement among the Moros, some of whom got up and danced to the music !

Finally, late in the afternoon, Pula gave in, turned the murderer over to us, and promised to turn over his brother, but said that the latter must first be allowed to go home to get some clothes, and that he would then send him on board our ship.

We improved this our first opportunity to beat a retreat without losing face. Our Moro "friends" bid us good-by on the beach, then armed themselves and followed us at a short distance as we marched back to the landing place where our launch was pounding in the surf, awaiting our return. Three strong fighting parties came out of the dense vegetation which bordered the beach immediately after we had passed the places where they were concealed. They had obviously been waiting there to cut off our retreat if trouble started, and could most certainly have done it. In fact, they could have shot us down from the brush without showing themselves.

It required all the self-control which I could muster to keep my back toward the strong and constantly growing group of armed men who followed us, and to look unconcerned, yet I knew, as did every other member of the party, that our seeing the light of another day probably depended on our ability to do both things. The slightest evidence of alarm would have precipitated a fight which could have had but one outcome for us.

When opposite the launch, we turned and faced the Moros and then the several members of the party went aboard, one at a time. Never did a widening strip of water look better to me than did that which finally began to separate us from the shore.

To our great amazement Dato Pula kept his word and sent his brother on board !

No man ever laboured more diligently for the good of alien peoples than did Governor Miller. He evolved a wise plan for improving the condition of the Tagbanuas living in the vicinity of Puerto Princesa, many of whom, as is so often the case with the uncivilized peoples of the Philippines, were reduced to a state of peonage by their Filipino neighbours. A large reservation was set aside for their exclusive use, and they were persuaded to retire to it. At the cost of infinite labour and pains Governor Miller built there a fine set of school buildings, and the Bureau of Education started a school which gives instruction in English, arithmetic and manual training to Tagbanua boys and girls.

Governor Miller's keen interest in this project led him to stop to inspect the progress of the work when returning from a long trip around the island. In the face of a coming storm he ascended the Aborlan River to the school site, where he remained until after dark, oblivious of the fact that a tremendous downpour of rain in the neighbouring mountains had produced a sudden flood in the river. Returning to his launch, he jumped on board and cast off before the engine was started. The current swept the launch away like a straw, carried it in close to the bank, and an overhanging branch, which ordinarily would have been high above the water, struck the governor a stunning blow on the head, knocking him overboard. He never came to the surface, and twenty-four hours elapsed before his body was recovered.

Mr. John H. Evans, then serving as lieutenant-governor of Bontoc, in the Mountain Province, was appointed in his place, and I took him around the Palawan group of islands to introduce him to his unruly subjects. On arrival at Puerto Princesa we were told that the occupants of a fleet of Moro boats were already raiding and killing along the southern coast of the island, and we accordingly took on board Captain Moynihan of the Philippine Scouts, with thirty of his soldiers. The report proved unfounded, but nevertheless the soldiers came in very handily.

I landed at Culasián Bay on the west coast, meaning to ascend a river to the settlement of Dato Tumay, the man whose people had on a former occasion fought Governor Miller with captured constabulary rifles and been soundly whipped. Finding no one on the beach, we walked up the river bank for a short distance to a group of half a dozen tightly closed houses which looked as if they might belong to fishermen. Here we were met by a splendidly dressed glad-hand delegation, who greeted us rather too effusively. My suspicion was further aroused by the fact that only three of them carried weapons, in sight at least. The weapons of a Moro chief are just as much a part of his full dress as are the garments he wears. I had a few moments' friendly conversation with these people, during which I noticed that several of them displayed a marked inclination to get behind me. This I did not like, so took up a position with my back to the river. Presently I suggested that we had come to call on Dato Tumay. The following conversation ensued : —

"You cannot go to see him."

"Why not? Are the trails in bad condition?"

"There are no trails."

"Are you not Dato Tumay's people?"

"Yes."

"How did you come down if there are no trails?"

"We came down the river."

"Very well, we will go up the river."

"You cannot do that."

"Why not?"

"There are no boats to carry you."

"How did you come down?"

"In those boats. [Pointing out two tiny dugouts barely able to carry two men each.] You and one of your friends can go up in them if you like. Two of our men will paddle you."

This proposition did not seem attractive to me, so I suggested that I would take a little walk up the river. I had been positively assured that there was no other boat in the vicinity, but at the very first turn discovered a suspicious looking trail running up into the bushes and following it found a fully rigged war-canoe over which freshly cut brush had been hastily thrown. I suggested to the Moros that this looked very much like a boat. They replied that it leaked. I asked them to put it into the water, stating that I liked to see boats leak. Not a Moro stirred. We had brought twenty-five soldiers ashore with us, as Tumay's reputation was by no means of the best, and I now called to some of them to come and put the boat into the river. In passing back of the group of Moros, one of these men stubbed his toe on the shaft of a lance which was hidden in the grass, and fell on his nose. He raised the lance as he recovered his feet, then stooped and picked up a second one, trailed them behind him until he reached a position in front of me and dropped them on the ground. Both had the sheaths removed from their long steel heads. Another soldier kicked around in the grass a bit and produced a serpent kriss which had been drawn from its scabbard. Still another fished up a *baróng*.[1]

I asked the ranking Moro present what was the meaning of these weapons, concealed at our very feet. He said that they were afraid that we would steal them and had therefore hidden them. I asked him whether any white man had ever stolen anything from them, and also why they had hidden them there, where we were likely to cut our feet on them, instead of in the forest which was not fifty yards away. Obviously there was no satisfactory

---

[1] A fighting knife of deadly effectiveness.

FINISHED TRAIL BUILT BY IFUGAOS.

Approximately a thousand miles of such trail have been built in the Mountain Province and Nueva Vizcaya under American rule.

answer to these questions and he had no time to attempt any, for one of the soldiers stooped down and pulled out of the grass from beside his very hand a forty-five caliber single-action revolver, cocked and with all six cylinders loaded. Fearing to be taken at a disadvantage, I said to the soldiers, "Make these men sit down, and search the place for arms."

The soldiers repeatedly ordered the Moros to sit down and the order was translated to them in their own language by my interpreter. Not a man obeyed. On the contrary, one of them turned his back and started off at a quick pace, disregarding repeated orders to halt. Theoretically he should have been shot.

Practically, I had ordered the soldiers not to fire under any circumstances unless some Moro drew a weapon. Mr. Olney Bondurant, assistant to the provincial governor for work among the Moros, had been taking a hasty look back of the houses and was returning to tell me that they were full of armed men. The Moro above mentioned, just before meeting Bondurant, reached into a bush and drew out two of the cruel fighting knives known as *baróngs*. They were in their flat sheaths, and lay one on top of the other. Snatching the upper one from its scabbard, he struck a wicked blow at Bondurant as the latter passed him on the trail. Bondurant, who was quick as a cat, dodged the blow, then whirled and shot his assailant. Instantly armed men with drawn weapons began to boil out of the houses on the side farthest from us, and those soldiers who were in a position to see them promptly opened fire. Other Moros also began to pop up at the edge of the forest, and we had a bit of a scrimmage, lively enough while it lasted. I took no part in it, but with three soldiers helping me compelled eleven men of the group with whom we had been talking to sit down, and kept them sitting until the unpleasantness was over, as I wanted to talk with them. I then told the head man to stand up.

He was very reluctant to do this, obviously expecting to be shot, but no such fate was in store for him. On the contrary, I gave him a lecture, told him where certain wounded and certain dead Moros were to be found, and instructed him and his people first to care for the wounded ; second, to bury the dead ; third, to go to Tumay's place and tell him that although I had come to make a friendly call on him, my party had been attacked by his people, but that the only men who had been hurt were those who had endeavoured to use their weapons on us. I further-more directed him to tell Tumay that he must come across the island to the place where Mr. Bondurant lived, and explain this extraordinary occurrence. We then took our departure, marching down the beach a mile to our launch, and expecting every moment to be fired on from the dense forest close at hand.

We learned from a wounded Moro that our party had been mistaken at a distance for that of Governor Miller. On his last trip around the island he had been threatened by Tumay, who surrounded him with a strong body of armed men and talked to him in a very insulting manner. Miller, who had but a single companion, knew himself to be at Tumay's mercy, and believing that he was in grave danger of being killed and that only a bluff could save him, slapped Tumay's face vigorously and then gave him a strong piece of his mind. Tumay, overawed at such temerity, allowed him to depart in safety. Before leaving, Governor Miller exercised his lawful authority to order Tumay to take his people and move to the east coast of the island.[1] Tumay begged that his people be

---

[1] A governor of a province may, with the approval of the Secretary of the Interior, require members of a non-Christian tribe to take up their residence on land reserved for such purpose if he deems such a course to be in the interest of public order. The object of this provision is to make it possible to compel lawless persons to live in reasonably accessible places. In only three instances has it been necessary to exercise this authority. Tumay and his people were outlaws and were living in a nipa swamp where it would have been almost impossible to attack them successfully.

allowed to harvest some rice which he said they had planted, and Governor Miller, not knowing whether or not the statement was true, and not being in a position to investigate it, allowed him two weeks to be spent in this way.

I was about Governor Miller's size. When I landed Tumay's people mistook me for him, and thought that he was returning with soldiers to punish them for having disobeyed him, or to enforce his order that they move to a more accessible place. Hence the plan for the attack, which was rather clever. While the reception committee entertained us, the men concealed in the woods were to open on us. As we turned to deal with them the ones hidden in the houses were to attack us from the rear, and the reception committee were then to join in. When they found themselves mistaken as to the make-up of the party, which was larger than they had expected, there was delay and confusion, and the attack fizzled.

A few days later Tumay actually started across the island in obedience to my instructions, but on the way he met two recalcitrant Moro chiefs who encouraged him to stand out, saying that they and their people would help him fight the Americans, and he turned back. I accordingly asked that a hundred scouts be sent after him, and this was done, fifty of them marching over the mountains to cut off his retreat and fifty coming on a coast-guard boat which was intended to serve as a base of operations and afford a place to which injured men might be brought for treatment. Strict instructions had been given that there was to be no firing, except in self-defence, when women or children were liable to be hit. These orders were strictly adhered to, and Tumay was twice allowed to escape when he could have been shot down if it had not been for the danger of killing Moro women and children. Ultimately, after the non-combatants had surrendered, his armed band was overtaken early in the morning, and fired from ambush into the approaching scouts. The return fire killed or wounded most of them, but Tumay got away. It was stated by some of his followers that he was badly wounded, but this proved to be untrue. A little later he voluntarily surrendered, as he had been deserted by his people and was reduced to dire straits.

The misconduct of Tumay and his men gave me a reason for moving the Moros from the west coast of Palawan, where they were living in mangrove or nipa swamps. It was hard to approach their settlements under any circumstances, and very dangerous to do so if they were disposed to be hostile. The west coast of Palawan was a no-man's land, difficult of access on account of weather conditions and numberless uncharted reefs. It had long been a safe haven for evil-doers who fled from other portions of the Moro country to escape the vengeance of their fellows, and there was no possibility of compelling them to abandon their evil practices unless they were transferred to more accessible regions.

Governor Evans, with my approval, now issued the necessary instructions to them, and they were all moved to the other side of the island, together with their household goods and chattels of every description. Once there they were assisted in procuring building materials, and were fed until such time as they were able to take care of themselves. Only the old, the infirm, and women and children who could not support themselves by working were given food gratis. Trail construction was inaugurated, and all able-bodied persons were given an opportunity to engage in this or in other honest labor for a good wage payable either in money or in rice.

At the end of a year I visited these Moros at their new homes near Bonabóna, going ashore without a weapon of any sort, and finding them more friendly than could reasonably have been anticipated. I sent for old Tumay and had a very frank talk with him about past differences, in the course of which I asked him if he had had enough. He assured me that he had, and I then suggested that we forget the troubles which were behind us and try to get on better in future. He promised to do his part, and has faithfully kept his word.

In August, 1912, I again visited the Moros of this region and to my great surprise was greeted as if I were a member of their royal family. They carried me ashore through the surf in a chair covered with a fine piece of purple brocade. Two men equipped respectively with a five-foot blue and a five-foot yellow umbrella, struggled with each other to see who should protect my delicate complexion from the sun. Wonder of wonders, the wives of the ranking chiefs were present in a dancing pavilion which had been erected for our benefit, this being the first time that these women had ever shown themselves in public. I learned that Hadji Mohammed [1] had explained to them that the women of other nations were getting progressive, and had argued that they ought to follow suit. The poor things were dreadfully frightened, and sat with their backs toward us, covering their faces with gayly colored cloths if we so much as glanced toward them, but they were there, anyhow!

At noon the Moros sat down with us to a fine luncheon of their own providing. This is the first time in my eighteen years of residence in the Philippines that I have known a Moro to sit at meat with a white man, or for that matter with any person not a Mohammedan.

After the meal several chiefs insisted on my visiting them individually, and I found that entertainment had been provided at each of their houses. Old Dato Tumay, with only one woman to help him, had built the best house in town, and was cultivating with his own hands the largest piece of land farmed by any Moro in Palawan. He was greatly pleased when I complimented him on the good example he was setting. Later I referred to it in my annual report, and the assistant to the governor for work among the Moros read to him what I had said. The old

---

[1] One of the most influential of the Palawan Moro chiefs.

man was delighted. He immediately called the local chiefs together and delivered a long lecture on the advisability of settling down and tilling the soil. The principal request that the Moros made, on the occasion of this visit, was that they be furnished agricultural implements and seeds.

Tumay was very ill with dysentery. From the ship I sent him medicine and a case of milk. He recovered in due time.

Moros are uncertain people to deal with, but I believe that we are now on the right road so far as concerns those inhabiting Palawan, and that with a continuance of the present policy there will be no further serious trouble with them.

The Tagbanua reservation and the school established in connection with it have proved a great success. A large number of Tagbanuas have settled on the reserve and are farming industriously, while their boys and girls are making rapid progress in school, where they obtain practical instruction that will make them better and more useful men and women.

In Southern Palawan the wild people of the highlands, who have never yet allowed any one to enter their country, are being persuaded to come down to the coast by the establishment of little government trading posts where they can sell their few products at good prices, and can purchase what they need at a reasonable figure.

All in all, things are moving forward steadily in Palawan, although many of the Filipino settlements are still filthy and unsanitary. Encouraged by the results obtained in Mindoro, I have inaugurated an active campaign to compel these people to clean up, and anticipate success. One thing which renders it difficult to deal with some of the Filipinos of this province is that in its more remote districts they are showing a marked tendency to scatter out into the forests where they make *caiñgins*, or forest clearings, and live in tiny huts. Little by little they are gravitating back to the barbarism from which they originally emerged, and under existing laws they are free to do this if they like. I regret that this tendency is by no means confined to the province of Palawan. The Spaniards dealt with it in no gentle manner, but we are powerless to do more than argue against it.

The cost of the work in Palawan in valuable human lives has been dear. No one can at the outset fill the place of a man like Governor Miller, who had become invaluable not only as a result of his personal characteristics, but because of his years of experience and of the regard in which he was held by his people. Unfortunately his life is not the only one which has been sacrificed for the good of the inhabitants of this province. Mr. W. B. Dawson, who organized the work of the Tagbanua Industrial School and was in a fair way to make a success of it, died of malignant malarial fever contracted at his post of duty. Mr. William M. Wooden, who succeeded him, in his anxiety to return more quickly to his post after a brief absence, leaped overboard from a launch and was drowned while trying to swim ashore. Mr. Olney Bondurant, assistant to the provincial governor, who did admirable work among the Moros and the Tagbanuas in Southern Palawan, and though suffering from dangerous illness never gave up, but rendered service in the field on the very day of his death, also fell a victim to pernicious malaria.

If the results obtained by these splendid men, who amid lonely surroundings and in the face of manifold discouragements, bravely and effectively carried on their country's work, are to be *permanent* results, then I hold that the price has not been too dear, but if they are to be destroyed by the premature withdrawal of American control these sacrifices are pathetic indeed.

All of the territory in Northern Mindanao east of Dapitan and north of the eighth parallel of latitude was at the outset divided between the provinces of Surigao and

Misamis. It is generally conceded that these provinces had been worse governed under American rule by their Filipino officials than have any others, and it was to be anticipated that, under such circumstances, their very numerous non-Christian inhabitants would prove to have been very badly mistreated. Sinister rumours reached me from time to time as to what was occurring, but I had no competent persons whom I could send to make investigations on the ground, and intended to defer action until I could go myself.

Matters were finally brought to a crisis by reports from Catholic priests, school-teachers and other reliable persons setting forth a condition of affairs which seemed to demand immediate remedial action. The commission had previously made a liberal sum available for work among the Bukidnon people of Misamis, and I had endeavoured to bring about the prosecution of this work by the Filipino provincial officials, but my efforts had been fruitless. Not one *centavo* of the funds appropriated had ever been expended. No Filipino provincial official had so much as visited the main Bukidnon country, the borders of which were distant less than three hours' ride from the provincial capital.

The Bukidnon people are industrious. They raise a large part of the coffee, hemp and cacao exported from Cagayan, the capital and the principal port of Misamis. They were being robbed when they sold their produce. A common procedure was to instruct them that they must sell to certain individuals at absurdly low prices, and if they did not promptly obey, to bring charges of sedition against them and throw them into jail. As a matter of fact, they hardly knew the meaning of the word sedition.

Depredations upon them were by no means confined to the town of Cagayan de Misamis. Filipinos from the coast invaded their territory, debauching them with *vino* and purchasing their property when they were

A DIFFICULT BIT OF ROCK WORK ON THE MOUNTAIN TRAIL IN BENGUET.
This trail has since been widened. It formerly required nerve to ride a horse around the corner where the Igorot is standing.

drunk; getting them into crooked gambling games and cheating them, or swaggering around armed with revolvers and so terrorizing them that they surrendered their belongings. It was common for a Filipino to go into the Bukidnon country with nothing but the clothes on his back, and soon to return with three or four carabaos heavily laden with hemp, coffee, cacao, or gutta percha.

Although the provincial governor had appointed, in some instances, men whom he had never seen as presidentes of settlements, the settlements were in reality without government, and their discouraged and disgusted people were betaking themselves to the mountains whence they had been brought years before by Jesuit missionary priests. The wilder members of the Bukidnon tribe, and the Manobos in the southern part of the province, who had never abandoned their mountain homes, were preying upon their neighbours, and committing crimes of violence undisturbed.

In the Agusan River valley conditions were nearly as bad. The people along the main stream were for the most part broken-spirited Manobos. Their settlements had been parcelled out among the members of the municipal council of Butuan to be plundered. The activities of these "Christian" gentlemen had been such that a number of Manobo villages were already completely abandoned, while the people of others were gradually betaking themselves to secure hiding-places in the trackless forests which stretch east and west from the banks of the Agusan.

Both in the Bukidnon and in the Manobo country the trade in bad *vino* was being actively pushed. The principal business on the Agusan River at that time was shipping it up-stream. Opium was being imported in considerable quantities from Cebu. The use of this drug was already established among the people of Butuan, and was gradually spreading up the river. The wilder Manobos, who lived some distance back from the stream, and the Mandayas along its upper waters, were killing and plundering without let or hindrance.

These statements, coming as they did from absolutely reliable witnesses, convinced me that I had allowed work for non-Christians in other parts of the archipelago to interfere unduly with investigations which I should have made in this region. As the legislation under which we were working for the betterment of the wild people had now taken final form, all that was necessary in order to begin active operations looking to the correction of these untoward conditions was to cut off a province from Surigao and Misamis and organize it under the Special Provincial Government Act. In view of the relative unimportance of the Filipino population in Misamis and Surigao, and of the lamentable conditions which had arisen there under Filipino provincial officials elected in accordance with the provisions of the Provincial Government Act, I suggested that both provinces be reorganized under the Special Provincial Government Act. This would have had the effect of making their officials appointive. American governors who would have protected the non-Christian inhabitants could have been put in office. Unfortunately, the first session of the Philippine Legislature was about to be held, the assemblymen having already been elected. Every member of the commission present, American and Filipino, agreed with me that the course which I suggested would be in the interest of the inhabitants of these two provinces, but they all shied off when it came to taking the needed action because of the political hullabaloo which would most certainly have resulted. I was forced to accept the best compromise I could get, and a law was passed providing for the establishment of the province of Agusan with two sub-provinces to be known respectively as Butuan and Bukidnon. Butuan took in the whole Agusan River valley as far south as the eighth parallel of latitude, and east and west to the crests of the two watersheds. It also included some territory on the west coast of the northern peninsula of Mindanao. Bukidnon included all of the territory inhabited by the people of the same name, and that of some wild Manobos in central Mindanao.

Armed with the law creating the new province, I proceeded to investigate conditions on the ground, and actually to establish the provincial government. At the town of Butuan, situated about five miles up the Agusan River, and accessible to good-sized steamers, I was met by Frederick Johnson, a captain in the Philippine constabulary who had had wide experience in dealing with the non-Christian tribes of the Moro Province and had been very successful in this work. At my request he had been appointed governor of the Province of Agusan, of which the town of Butuan was the capital.

We hired a launch, driven by a one-cylinder engine, from a man named Wantz, and in it proceeded up the river, taking the owner along to run the boat. It was paid for by the day, and I was warned before I started that Wantz had his own ways of lengthening journeys. I soon discovered that this was true. Before starting I had indicated the settlement which must be reached before dark, but the engine soon began to wheeze and thump dolefully. It happened that I knew something about gasoline engines, and this one sounded to me as if it were running with the spark advanced too far, but I could not discover the adjusting mechanism, so exercised diplomacy, involving Wantz in a discussion of the intricacies of modern gasoline engines, and stating that I had an automobile with a very convenient attachment for advancing and retarding the spark. He promptly and proudly showed me the device on his engine for the same purpose. It was hidden away where I could not have found it. After he had instructed me in its operation I quietly retarded the spark, and the engine began to work in a most cheering manner. In order to punish Wantz, I insisted that we keep on until we reached our prescribed destination, in spite of the time we had lost.

We had a prophet of evil on board who predicted that Wantz would certainly have the engine thoroughly stacked by the next morning, and he did. We had planned to start at daylight, but, when we climbed down to the boat in the gray dawn, found him puttering over its machinery. He said that the cylinder was "froze up." As the temperature did not seem to warrant such a result, I got him to explain to me what was wrong, and after watching him put on and take off the cylinder-head several times, discovered that he had an ingenious contrivance so arranged that by giving a single push he could put the make-and-break spark connection out of commission from the inside of the cylinder. I myself adjusted it properly, compelled him to put on the cylinder-head without touching his disarranging mechanism, and we went on our way. For some time I watched him closely, and while I continued to do so, the engine ran beautifully, but ultimately I had to go ashore to inspect a rotting Manobo settlement, and while I was gone he queered it again in such a manner that I could not find the cause of the mischief. We had speedy revenge, however, for while we were negotiating a swift rapid the engine died, with the result that the launch nearly turned turtle and narrowly escaped being wrecked. This frightened Wantz, and after a few mysterious manipulations on his part the engine began to "put, put, put" again most cheerfully, and we ascended the rapid without difficulty.

On the evening of the third day we reached a Filipino settlement called Talacógon, seventy miles up the river. Wantz began to complain that he was sick, and as Talacógon would have been a very comfortable place to lie over, I opined that his ailment would become acute before morning. At four o'clock I sneaked down to the river bank by a back street to see what was going on. He was whistling cheerfully. I beat a careful retreat, then came ostentatiously down the main road to the pier. Sepulchral groans were now issuing from the launch, and Wantz was not visible. I found him writhing on its bottom in assumed agony. By this time I had become convinced that a native *banca* with a few good oarsmen would be better than a launch with such an engineer, so told him I was sorry he was ill, gave him permission to return to Butuan, and offered to pay what I owed him on the spot. When he found that it was not my intention to pay for the time consumed by the return trip his symptoms became less alarming, and he expressed hope of ultimate recovery. Interrogated as to the probable date when he would be prepared to continue the journey, he put it three days ahead. I told him that I could not wait so long. Gradually he reduced to half a day the time which the reëstablishment of his health would require, but I told him that I could not wait, and that his recovery must be immediate if he was to continue with us. This was too much of a jolt to his pride, and when we were ready to embark he was still too ill to start ! We accordingly loaded our belongings into two *bancas* each some sixty feet long, lay down on our backs in their little cabins, and continued on our way upstream.

The trip up the Agusan River is a most wonderful one. Nothing could surpass the magnificence of the tropical vegetation along its banks. The sportsman finds himself constantly diverted. Great fruit pigeons and huge hornbills frequently fly over one's boat, or perch in trees where they can be shot from the river. Monkeys abound. Huge crocodiles may occasionally be observed sleeping on the banks. Wild hogs are plentiful, but usually keep out of sight. The trees are hung with a marvellous drapery of vines, orchids and ferns, and, as the stream is so broad and deep as to render its navigation easy, one can lean back and enjoy to the full the beauties of nature displayed in prodigal abundance on every side.

We found the human inhabitants of this wonderful

region a highly unsatisfactory lot. The Manobo families were living either singly, scattered along the river, or grouped in little villages composed of a dozen or two rotting huts and surrounded by the accumulated filth of years. As was to be anticipated under the circumstances, most of the people were full of malaria, and many suffered from repulsive skin diseases. They had little cultivated ground. The growing and cleaning of hemp was their only resource, and they had become so accustomed to having the products of their labour taken from them by the people of Butuan that they had almost given up working. They listened with dull, uncomprehending hopelessness to our story of better days to come, and it soon became evident that nothing but practical experience would convince these helpless people that times were going to change.

The Filipinos of Talacógon were an especially lazy, vicious lot, who did no work themselves, but sponged or stole a living from their non-Christian neighbours. Forest trees were springing up on the plaza of this town. Its streets were deep in mud, and its sanitary condition beggared description. I was really afraid to stay overnight. I ordered the people to clean up, and they laughed at me. I ultimately made them clean up, but they successfully resisted my efforts to do so longer than the people of any other town ever did, and several years passed before I was at all satisfied with results.

Our progress up the river was unimpeded until we reached what is shown on the maps of Mindanao as a series of extensive lakes, but is in reality a huge and trackless swamp. Some years before a very severe earthquake had caused the subsidence of a vast forested area along the banks of this portion of the Agusan River, with the result that the old river-bed was completely broken up, and the river below this point reversed its flow for some time until the depressed region had been filled up by the water which entered it from all sides. There were no well-established channels through this submerged forest, and navigation in it was dangerous unless one had experienced guides.

In order that such guides might be always available, the Spaniards had compelled a number of them to live on the outskirts of the swamp at a place called Clavijo. The ground on which their houses stood was under water most of the year. They were a miserable, sickly lot. Most of them were suffering acutely from malaria, and all were very anxious to abandon the ill-fated site of their village, — a thing which, it is needless to say, they were promptly permitted by us to do. Having secured the services of several of them, we continued our journey toward Bunauan, but found the stream which we ascended after extricating ourselves from the swamp so choked with rubbish that it was frequently necessary either to clear channels or to haul our heavy boats over masses of dead tree trunks, branches, bamboo, etc. From Bunauan we returned to Butuan and sailed for Cagayan de Misamis.

While passing along one of the main streets of the latter town on my way to the provincial building, I discovered Bukidnon people buying *vino* by the demijohn. The law prohibiting the sale of alcoholic liquors to members of non-Christian tribes was then in effect throughout the archipelago. One of the first questions which I put to the Filipino governor was whether he had taken the necessary measures to see that this law was enforced. He replied in the affirmative. I asked him what he had done. He said that he had sent letters to the several Bukidnon settlements telling the people that they must not buy *vino*. I asked him if he had warned the dealers in his own town that they must not sell to the Bukidnons, and he replied, "It has not occurred to me to do that!"

Having explained to the governor the terms of the law establishing the province of Agusan, and the reason for its adoption, I proceeded across the bay to a *barrio* which then was, and still is, the point of departure for the interior, planning to start at daylight the following morning. I had with me my private secretary Mr. Zinn, and Mr. Frederick Lewis, who had just accepted appointment as lieutenant-governor of the sub-province.

Lewis had taken a number of Zamboanga Moros to the St. Louis Exposition and had also assumed charge of the Lake Lanao Moros there when their manager misbehaved and it became necessary to dispense with his services. He had looked after his people so carefully and so well that some of the hardened old sinners from Lake Lanao actually wept when they parted company with him on the beach after their return from the United States! He was a tireless rider, and the country which he was to govern was a horseman's country *par excellence*.

Our transportation for the trip was in charge of a Filipino lieutenant of constabulary, named Manuel Fortich, and I was not greatly pleased with this arrangement, as we had a hard journey ahead of us which might be rendered difficult or even dangerous by lack of efficiency on the part of the man who looked after our saddle animals and our carriers. I soon learned, however, that no better man could have been selected for this task.

We marched at daylight, as is my custom when travelling overland in the provinces. At midnight a mounted Filipino messenger, sent by the *caciques* of Cagayan, had started ahead of us to frighten the people of the towns which we proposed to visit so that they would take to the hills. In this he was partially successful. When we reached the small settlement of Tancuran late in the afternoon, after a hard day's work, the only inhabitants left were a few old cripples who had been too sick or too feeble to run away. However, many of those who had fled were hiding in the underbrush near by. Lieutenant Fortich, who had already made himself invaluable to us, soon rounded up quite a number of them, and they were in turn despatched for their friends.

This little village was in a deplorable state of abandon-

A FLYING FERRY IN OPERATION.

ment. Only a few of its houses were habitable. It had been well laid out by some good Jesuit missionary priest, but its streets and plaza were choked with a jungle of tropical vegetation through which ran trails resembling deer paths! There was absolutely nothing growing in the vicinity which could furnish food for a human being.

Lieutenant Fortich ultimately got together quite an audience for me. We squatted around a cheerful campfire and discussed the past and the future until late at night. I was delighted to find that my auditors took a keen interest in my statements. They soon gained courage to tell me freely of the abuses which they had suffered, and while obviously not optimistic over my promises of better things, were evidently willing to be shown.

Just before we turned in Lieutenant Fortich asked me at what time I would like to start in the morning. I said "five o'clock." He replied, "Very well." While his remarks were gratifyingly in accord with the biblical injunction to "let your conversation be yea, yea; nay, nay," I feared that he did not fully comprehend the difficulties involved in an early start, so decided to take a hand myself when the time came. I accordingly arose at three-thirty A.M., and nearly fainted when I found that the horses were already munching their grain and, wonder of wonders, that the carriers were eating their breakfast. The usual thing is to be informed, when you are about an hour on your way, that the carriers have had no breakfast, and to be forced to sit down and wait while they cook and eat their morning meal. I went back to bed, convinced that I had discovered a new kind of Filipino constabulary officer. I got up again at four o'clock, dressed, and went to the table at four-thirty, finding a piping hot meal ready. When at five o'clock I descended the stairs of the house where I had spent the night, my horse was saddled and waiting at the gate. All I had to do was to climb aboard. Meanwhile I had not heard an order given, or a word spoken in a tone above that of ordinary conversa-

tion. Throughout the trip Lieutenant Fortich continued
to display quiet efficiency. I jotted his name down in
my mental notebook as that of a man to be used later.
He is to-day the lieutenant-governor of Bukidnon, and
a most faithful, competent and efficient public officer.

During my first day's ride I had had a decidedly startling experience. On leaving the sea beach one climbs
rather abruptly for some nine hundred feet and then comes
out on a wonderful plain. After riding over this beautiful
stretch of level country for some time I could not longer
resist the temptation to attempt to take a panoramic
series of views showing it, so dismounted, set up my
camera and made three exposures, rotating the instrument so as to get a panoramic effect. I worked with my
back toward my companions, and became so absorbed in
my task that I failed to notice that they were moving on.
When I finally turned around I discovered to my utter
amazement that I was alone, save for the carrier who
packed my camera and plates. In every direction an
apparently unbroken plain stretched for miles, and
there was not another human being in sight. My companions had disappeared from off the face of the earth.
I actually began to fear that I had taken leave of my
senses. Nothing which has ever befallen me has given
me such a curious sensation. However, one tangible
thing remained; to wit, a well-marked trail through the
grass. I followed it, and before I had gone three hundred
yards came to the brink of a precipitous cañon down
the wall of which my companions were zigzagging. From
the point where I had taken my photographs it was absolutely impossible to detect the existence of this narrow
crack in the earth. We soon learned, to our sorrow, that
this first cañon was only one of many.

At its bottom was a raging torrent which we forded
with difficulty. My fool horse got frightened and turned
down-stream where the current was swiftest, and I narrowly escaped taking an impromptu trip down rapids

which would have hammered me into insensibility against the rocks.

Until we reached Malaybalay the conditions encountered in the several villages through which we passed were similar to those which we had found at Tanculan : houses abandoned for the most part, and always in a lamentable state of neglect; sanitary conditions very bad; streets and plazas overgrown; an abundance of coffee bushes in some of the villages, but no visible source of food supply anywhere, except for a few scraggly banana plants.

At the outset we had found all the villages deserted, but in each case had managed to get some of the people back and hold a friendly interview with them. The "grapevine telegraph" got to working, and soon they began to await our arrival. At Malaybalay they gave us quite an ovation. This town was comparatively clean; the grass on the plaza was neatly cut. All in all, conditions were so encouraging that I decided that it should be the capital of the subprovince.

The following day we continued our journey to Linabo, where I heard of a Filipino engaged, as usual, in terrorizing the inhabitants and taking their products from them. I twice sent him courteous requests to come to see me, and then had him unceremoniously brought into my presence. He was carrying an ugly looking, heavy-calibre six-shooter. I demanded the document which justified his possession of this weapon, and as he could produce nothing more satisfactory than a note from the governor of Misamis authorizing him to use it in that province, I took his gun away from him. He assumed a threatening attitude and warned me that he was a friend of the provincial governor, but I told him that he was not a friend of mine, and started him on his way to the coast.

This occurrence was known throughout Bukidnon within three days, and as the man in question was influential the fact that his claws had been at least temporarily trimmed greatly encouraged the people.

From Linabo we returned by a different route, visiting the old settlement of Sumilao, the site of the original Jesuit mission in Bukidnon, and spending a day in endeavouring to reach a constantly disappearing village named Nanca. We had gathered from the written report of a lieutenant of the United States army that Nanca was distant from Sumilao about two hours' ride. We reached it after dark, having travelled steadily throughout the day except for some thirty minutes taken for lunch, and having, I firmly believe, broken the world's record for the number of cañons encountered in the course of a fourteen-hour ride.

Nanca proved to be a very interesting Bukidnon village, as its people retained their picturesque tribal dress and most of their primitive customs. I became much interested in finding out about its organization, and the part that each family took in its affairs, and asked the persons present what each man did. I finally came to a particularly fine-looking white-haired individual, and when I inquired about him my informant replied: "Oh, he does not do anything. He is a philosopher!" Then the crowd shouted with laughter. We decided that the Bukidnons were not without a sense of humor.

A hard half day's ride brought us back to Cagayan de Misamis, and I sailed at once for Manila, leaving Lieutenant-Governor Lewis to face his difficult task alone. As I had anticipated, trouble promptly began. The wealthiest people of Cagayan had always lived off the unfortunate Bukidnons, and had no intention of relaxing their grip. I have deeply regretted that I did not myself visit the remaining villages in the valley of the Cagayan River and explain to their inhabitants the change in their fortunes. Agents of the Cagayan *caciques* had been busy there while I was occupied on the other side of the subprovince, and shortly after my arrival at Manila a telegram was received from the provincial

governor, saying that the Bukidnons were asking for a
brown governor, instead of a white one, and were reported
to be preparing ropes and poison with which to commit
suicide.

Now these simple people of the hills had no intention
of committing suicide, nor did they want "a brown governor." Their petitions were prepared by Cagayan *caciques* and they were forced to sign them.

In the part of the subprovince which I had visited the
conspirators against the new government made little
headway. Nevertheless their vicious activities continued, and later, on several occasions, they succeeded in
frightening the people of one or another of the then
rapidly growing towns so badly that they took to the
hills, and Mr. Lewis had to hunt them up and persuade
them to come back again, which he always succeeded in
doing.

When I returned to inspect Bukidnon a year later, I
found that a marvellous change had already been brought
about. Model villages had taken the place of the ram-
shackle affairs which I had found on my first visit. The
houses were grouped around spacious plazas on which
the grass had been so carefully cut that they had already
begun to look like lawns. Streets were kept so clean
that one could literally pick up a dropped pin without
the slightest difficulty. Where the streets reached the
open prairie, bars were provided to keep stray animals
out of town. Every yard was neatly fenced. All domestic animals were properly confined if not out at pas-
ture. Every village was perfectly drained, the slope of
the land being such that all drainage promptly ran off
onto the prairie. Yards were immaculately clean and
were planted with useful food-producing crops. Little
cultivated fields were already beginning to appear near
the outskirts of the towns. This latter change greatly
delighted me. These poor, ignorant people had always
believed that the prairie soil was worthless for agricultural

purposes, and that in order to grow crops it was necessary for them to go to the distant mountains, clear forest land and plant it. Furthermore, they had been quite unable to break the prairie sod and bring the underlying soil under cultivation with such simple agricultural implements as they possessed.

At the request of Lieutenant-Governor Lewis, I had furnished two disk plows with the necessary animals to pull them, in order that the land might be plowed the first time for those who were willing to cultivate it. Thereafter they were left to care for it themselves. This plan had aroused great enthusiasm. As I approached Sumilao I saw a crowd of men busily engaged in some task, and when I drew near was amazed and delighted to find that, although the disk plow intended for use at that place had arrived before the animals which were to pull it, fifteen men had harnessed themselves to it and were vigorously breaking the sod. I decided on the spot that the Bukidnon people had a future, and have never changed my mind. The progress which they have since made is almost unbelievable.

Efforts to destroy the government which we had established in Bukidnon, and to reëstablish the system of peonage under which its peaceful, industrious inhabitants had so long groaned, were persistently continued. During my third annual inspection trip, I found that there was a plan on foot to trump up criminal charges against Lieutenant-Governor Lewis and Señor Manuel Fortich, whose services I had meanwhile secured as an assistant to Mr. Lewis upon his severing his connection with the constabulary. The efforts of the mischief-makers had become so persistent and so vicious that I decided to declare war on them. Accordingly, I ran over to Cagayan and summoned the provincial officers and several other prominent citizens, with whom I went straight to the point, telling them that I had not anticipated that they would readily adapt themselves to the changed conditions which resulted from the separation of Bukidnon as a distinct subprovince, and had patiently waited three years for them to accept the inevitable, but that I had grown weary of their constant efforts to nullify the work which we were doing, and that I was aware of the plan to destroy the usefulness of Lewis and Fortich; adding that they must let the Bukidnon officials alone, and that in the event of future failure to do so I would temporarily transfer my office to Cagayan de Misamis and devote my time and attention to making things interesting for certain of them. I named no names, and it was not necessary to do so. The individuals referred to knew whom I meant.

Conditions now rapidly improved for a time, but in November I was called to Washington to be investigated by the Committee on Insular Affairs with reference to my administration of public and friar lands, and the enemies of the Bukidnon government promptly became active. Governor Lewis was arrested and tried on two criminal charges, while his assistant, Señor Fortich, was charged with murder, no less. If the charges of *estafa* and falsification of public documents brought against Lewis failed, it was proposed to prosecute him for adultery, the minimum penalty for which in the Philippine Islands is imprisonment for two years, four months and one day.

Fortunately, it took but a short time to show that the cases against those two young men were spite cases pure and simple, and they collapsed miserably. Other charges were promptly brought.

There had been a sad mix up, resulting from an ill-defined boundary line between Bukidnon and the Moro Province, for which I myself was directly responsible, as the papers concerning it were on my desk awaiting action when I was called home, and in the rush of a hurried departure I had overlooked them. Lewis and Fortich had been unjustly blamed for the result. I now took a hand in the game myself, and the whole matter was satisfactorily cleared up. Lewis was promoted to the governorship of the province of Agusan, and Fortich was made lieutenant-governor of Bukidnon, a position which he has filled ever since with great credit to himself and advantage to the Bukidnon people.

The progress which has been made in Bukidnon is really wonderful. At the outset there was not a decent trail in the subprovince. Now one can go nineteen miles inland to the Mañgima River cañon in an automobile, and it will be soon possible so to continue the journey ten miles further to Maluco. Excellent low-grade horse trails, many miles of which are already wide enough to serve as automobile roads as soon as the line to the coast is completed, connect the principal settlements of Bukidnon proper, which also have telephonic communication, the people having gladly undertaken to cut and erect the necessary poles and build and maintain the lines, if furnished instruments, wire, insulators and tools. They have kept their bargain, and there are constant demands for an extension of the system, under similar conditions, to the more remote mountain villages.

There was not a bridge or a culvert in the subprovince. Pack animals were constantly being swept away by the rushing currents of the larger rivers, or perishing miserably in mud when attempting to cross soft-bottomed creeks. Now one may ride from the sea-coast to Malay-balay without wetting the feet of one's horse, and in so doing one will cross more than a hundred substantial bridges and culverts built by the Bukidnons themselves. As a rule, even the largest bridges have cost the government no more than the price of their iron bolts and braces. The people have voluntarily and cheerfully done the work, in order to get the benefits which would result. In some cases heavy hardwood timbers have been dragged for fifteen miles or more by teams of hundreds of men. All bridges are roofed, and they afford fine camping places

A WILD TINGIAN OF APAYAO.

The Tingians of Apayao have proved to be the most difficult of the hill-tribes of Northern Luzon to bring under effective governmental control. With them head-hunting is connected with religious beliefs and observances.

for travellers and their pack animals. Incidentally the load which pack animals can comfortably carry has been more than doubled.

Old villages have increased greatly in size, and numerous new ones have been established. All have spacious plazas and streets which are beautifully kept. The mountains are almost depopulated. The hardy old fighters who used to frequent them have become peaceful agriculturists. Houses are neat and clean. Yards are fenced, planted with useful crops, and well cultivated. Each house has its own sanitary arrangements. No domestic animals are allowed to run at large in towns.

Rich, cultivated fields surround the villages and each year stretch farther and farther out over the neighbouring prairies. Coffee production is increasing by leaps and bounds, and blight is disappearing from the plantations as the result of intensive cultivation. The people are well fed and prosperous. Their condition steadily improves. They have been taught the value of their products, and encouraged to insist on receiving it.

Practically every village has its schoolhouse and its schoolmaster's house, voluntarily built free of charge by the inhabitants. Children are sent to school by their parents and learn rapidly. On my second visit I found the boys trying to play baseball, using joints of bamboo for bats, and big, thick-skinned oranges for balls. I sent to each of the more important towns a complete baseball outfit, and now the boys certainly know, and can play, the game.

These results have been accomplished practically without bloodshed or rough treatment of any sort. Only in the rarest instances, and in dealing with the very worst of the hill men, who were professional murderers, has a shot been fired.

When the subprovince was invaded by bands of savages from the mountains of Butuan and from the neighbouring Moro Province, the people requested firearms so that they might protect themselves. Some twenty-five old carbines were furnished them, and they organized an effective force which pursued the evil-doers and policed them up very effectively.

Marámag, one of the most recently established villages, is in the very heart of Mindanao. Two years ago a good many of its leading citizens were living in tree-houses. During August, 1912, I found them cutting the grass on their plaza with a lawn-mower!

Another thing which has made me rub my eyes and wonder if I were awake was the discovery that the people of this subprovince were clothing themselves and their children in garments purchased from Montgomery, Ward & Co., of Chicago, Illinois, U. S. A.! The explanation is simple. The Cagayan shopkeepers persist in cheating them at every opportunity, and the house of Montgomery, Ward & Co. does not. Although Chicago is far away, the mail service is nevertheless good!

Death has just summoned Leoncio, one of the most remarkable men who has yet arisen among the Bukidnon people. We found him an absolutely illiterate heathen. With no other instruction than that given him by lieutenant-governors Lewis and Fortich, he learned to lay out and build roads and trails on any desired grade, to construct bridges which will be standing twenty years hence, and to erect public buildings which would be a credit to any man compelled to use such materials as those available in Bukidnon.

At the time of his death he was just finishing a bridge three hundred feet long across the rushing Culaman River. This structure has a galvanized iron roof, contributed by the enthusiastic residents of Sumilao.

The healthful rivalry between towns is one of the delightful things about Bukidnon. Each desires to have better buildings, better streets, better bridges, better roads and better schools than its neighbours.

I experience no keener pleasure than that which I enjoy

on my annual trips through Bukidnon. There is always something new to see. The people are most grateful for the help which has been given them. Their friendliness and their loyalty cannot fail to touch the hearts of all who know them. They are now well housed, and well fed. Their children are being given in liberal measure the education which had previously been denied to them. The Bukidnons are to-day a prosperous, progressive people, happy and contented. I have an abiding faith in their future if they are given a chance.

When they meet their old Filipino oppressors on trips to the coast, the latter grit their teeth and remark under their breath: "Oh, very well. This is your inning now, but ours will come! The Americans are going soon, and then we will square our little account with you. You will pay dearly for your 'insubordination'!" Having set the feet of these people on the road which leads onward and upward, shall we leave them to their fate?

Conditions in Butuan have improved far more slowly than in Bukidnon. The climate is less favourable. Bukidnon is a highland country with a white man's climate. The Agusan River valley is usually hot, and always damp. The town of Butuan was considered the worst misgoverned municipality in the Philippines on the date of its separation from Surigao, and it was certainly one of the filthiest. I have sunk to my knees in the mud of its streets. It is to-day a beautifully kept and sanitary place, and is certainly not misgoverned.

As I have already said, the Manobo inhabitants of the wretched villages along the banks of the main Agusan River were a sickly, filthy, broken-spirited lot, besotted with *vino* and in danger of becoming victims of the opium habit. It is almost a physical impossibility completely to suppress the opium traffic because of the ease with which the drug is smuggled, but the *vino* traffic has been suppressed. The chief business on the Agusan River was formerly the transportation of *vino* up-stream. It is now the transportation down-stream of Manila hemp raised by the people of the valley.

The villages have been greatly improved and rendered reasonably sanitary. The best of them compare not unfavourably with some of the Bukidnon towns. The people improve, but radical improvement will not be in evidence until the next generation comes on.

Transportation facilities have been greatly increased by freeing several of the more important branches of the Agusan River from snags, and so opening them for launch navigation. Two good canals have been cut through the swamps, and communication by launch has thus been opened with the upper Agusan valley.

There is an industrial school for Manobo boys, and a number of the villages have primary schools.

Doubtless the most important single factor in improving the condition of the Manobos has been the establishment of a series of government shops at which they can sell their products for a fair price, and buy what they need so cheaply that it almost seems to them as if they were receiving presents.

Governor Frederick Johnston, who is largely responsible for these improved conditions, laboured ceaselessly to bring them about. At the outset he had no launch transportation and lived for weeks at a time in native canoes or *bancas*. He was fearless and tireless. When the time came for him to take long overdue leave I had no competent person to put in his place, and in deference to my wishes he continued at his post for nearly two years. At the end of that time it was found that one of his legs, which had been injured on an early exploring expedition, had become cancerous, and that immediate amputation was necessary. This made it impossible for him to continue his work, and crippled him for life. He had borne his trouble uncomplainingly, and I had not even known of its existence. Although a man of mature years, he bravely entered upon the study of medicine, hoping to prepare himself for a useful life, but the operation had come too late. Cancer reappeared, and for a year he was dying by inches. In a way I am responsible for it. Do you think he laid it up against me? You shall judge for yourselves.

He used to write a copy-book hand. Just before leaving Manila I received from him an almost illegible letter in which he economized words as if composing a cablegram. It brought the tears to my eyes. He said : —

"I thank you for your slavery book just received. If strength is left me to read it, I shall read it though I do nothing else in this life.

"I have had letter in preparation to you since last June but I haven't strength to sit at the machine. I expect now to die before New Year.

"I have offered surgeons to take all chances, but they decline to operate, stating that they would consider operation deliberate murder.

"This is first letter I write since last September. If I do not get strength to finish typewritten letter I have given instructions it be sent when I am dead. I cannot write with pen ; I have tried it.

"If you hear no more, please remember I never forgot you. Sorry you leave the Secretariat — so sorry I can't tell you.

"I am ready to die. I know that I have lived unselfishly for what I thought was right and good, and death is nothing. If this should be the last, then accept from the man that was always your man and will be your man until he dies, a last Good-by."

A few days later he went to his reward.

The loyalty of such a man is a precious possession.

The lot of the non-Christian tribes inhabiting the regularly organized provinces is not a happy one. The township government act is applicable to their settlements, and the provincial officers have the same powers and duties with reference to them as have the corresponding officers in the special government provinces. In both cases these powers are exercised subject to the approval of the secretary of the interior, but in providing for the government of non-Christians in Christian provinces, we overlooked one very essential detail. Neither the secretary of the interior nor any one else has authority to compel the governors or provincial boards of these provinces to act. They have discovered that efforts to improve the condition of the ignorant and primitive peoples intrusted to their charge can be very effectively nullified if they merely sit still and do nothing, and almost with one accord they have adopted this policy. Exception should be made in favour of North Ilocos, South Ilocos, Pangasinán, Ambos Camarines, Iloilo and Zambales. No other provinces have made any real effort to help their non-Christian population, and the funds set aside by law to be expended for this end simply go on accumulating in their respective treasuries, as I have managed to convince them that efforts to divert such funds to purposes not authorized by law will not prosper. The law should be so amended as to provide that if provincial boards fail to act, the secretary of the interior may do so.

The organization of the Moro Province was provided for by an act passed on June 1, 1903. It is the largest single province in the Philippine Islands, including within its limits more than half of the great island of Mindanao with various small islands adjacent thereto, and Basilan, Joló, Siassi, Tawi Tawi, Sibutu, Cagayan de Joló and the very numerous other small islands stretching between Mindanao and North Borneo. It is divided into five districts, each with a district governor. The province has a governor, a secretary, a treasurer, an attorney, an engineer and a superintendent of schools.

The four officials first named constitute a legislative council the acts of which are subject to the approval of the Philippine Commission.

The province is allowed to expend the moneys accruing from the customs dues paid at Joló and Zamboanga, which are ports of entry, but is not fully self-supporting. The insular government pays for the Philippine constabulary serving there. Until within a very short time the provincial officials have been almost exclusively officers of the army of the United States. In my opinion this arrangement has been a bad one, not because of the character of the men who have done the work, many of whom were of exceptional ability and were admirably fitted for the performance of the duties which fell to their lot, but because no one of them has retained a given office long enough to carry a policy through to its logical conclusion and get the results which might thus have been obtained. Indeed, the lack of a fixed policy, combined with some unnecessary and unjustifiable killing, explain, in my opinion, the fact that the results accomplished have come far short of what might have been expected when one considers the splendid body of men from which the provincial officials have been drawn.

Noteworthy public improvements have been made in places like Zamboanga and Joló, but the country of the hill people, which ought to have been crisscrossed with trails long ere this, is still not opened up. Tribes like the Mandayas would, if given the opportunity, advance as rapidly as have the Bukidnons, but such opportunity has not been given to them to any considerable extent.

Having heard much of the Mandaya villages near Mati, I improved the opportunity to visit them in August, 1912, only to find to my amazement that the local constabulary officer, who ought to have been in the closest possible touch with these people, did not even know the way to their settlements. At another place where some 1400 hill people had been compelled to come down from their native mountains and settle in a village which could have been made a model of cleanliness, and should have been surrounded by rich cultivated fields, not half enough ground had been cleared to furnish food for the inhabitants, even under the most favourable circumstances. The houses were falling down; the streets were deep in mud; the garden patches were overgrown with weeds;

more than half of the people had taken to the hills again in a search for food, and small blame to them! I found here as fine appearing a young constabulary officer as one could hope to meet, eating his heart out because he had nothing to do! Neither he nor any of his soldiers spoke the local dialect. He was supposed to be running a store, among other things, for the benefit of the hill people. I asked to see it, and it took him half an hour to find the key! In sixty minutes I could have set him work enough to keep him busy for three months. All that he needed was some one to direct him, but there was no one to do it. With the best intentions in the world he was using his soldiers to chase a lot of poor hill people back into a village where they ought never to have been asked to live. In other words, the Moro Province, having brought these people down and ordered them to settle on a site selected for them, had signally failed to back its own game. I myself would not think of trying to compel members of a wild tribe to live in any given place, unless it were necessary to do so in the interest of public order. Life in villages can, and should, be made so attractive to them that they will be glad to adopt it.

The Moros, with their fanatical religious beliefs and prejudices, present a very grave problem. Conditions have undoubtedly greatly improved in Davao, Cotabato and Zamboanga. I am not sufficiently familiar with affairs in the Lanao district to express an intelligent opinion concerning them. So far as concerns Joló, it is my opinion that things have come to a bad pass there; that life and property are not as safe to-day as they were during the early days of the American occupation, and that we have progressed backward for some time. However, Joló pirates have at least been pretty effectively kept off the sea, and that in itself is a very important result.

It is idle to suppose that the Moros can be subdued and made into decent citizens by throwing kisses at them. It

TINGIAN GIRLS THRESHING RICE.

was certain from the start that they would transgress. In my opinion, if we are to cure them of their evil tendencies, we must first warn them that they will be punished if they misbehave, and then make the warning come true. This has been done, but to another very important part of the programme which I deem essential to success, comparatively little attention seems to have been given. When people who have been punished for misbehavior have had enough they should be afforded a chance to quit, and indeed should be encouraged and helped to do so. No grudge should be borne for past misdeeds after the account has once been settled. Occasions have not been lacking in the Moro Province on which men have been treated with severity when they should have been treated with kindness.

In the Moro, native racial characteristics have been profoundly modified by religious beliefs. Men endowed with such magnificent courage as the Moro warriors often display certainly have their redeeming qualities. The same old policy that has won with the Ifugaos, Bontoc Igorots and Kalingas, and is winning with the wild Tingians and Ilongots, has been tried in dealing with the renegade Moros of Palawan with a considerable degree of success. It is my firm belief that it will work with the Moros of Mindanao, Basilan, Joló and Tawi Tawi, but substantial and permanent progress cannot now be anticipated for many years. The Moros must be given more than a square deal, or results will not differ essentially from those which have attended the efforts of Japan to subdue the hill people of Northern Formosa, or those of the Dutch to subdue the Achinese.

Recently nearly all of the army officers holding positions in the Moro Province have been replaced by civilians. This is a move in the right direction; not, I repeat, because the men thus displaced are incapable of achieving success if given the opportunity, but because continuity of policy is absolutely essential to success and is impracticable if the men charged with carrying out that policy are to be constantly changed. The next governor of the Moro Province should be a civilian and should be selected with the greatest care. He should be able, energetic, fearless, tireless and young. He should be kept in office for twenty years if he will stay so long. The task which awaits him is real man's work.

CHAPTER XXIII

Corrigenda

I trust that the foregoing incomplete outline of what has been accomplished toward bettering the condition of the non-Christian tribes of the Philippines has at least sufficed to convey some idea of the nature of the task which has confronted us and of the spirit in which it has been approached. Before considering further the difficulties which have been successfully met and the problems which still remain unsettled, I will correct some of the numerous misstatements which have been made relative to the unimportance of the non-Christian tribes, the nature of the work done for them, and the motives of some of those who have engaged in it.

I once heard it said that the trouble with Blount's book was that it contained five thousand lies, that the correction of each would require, on the average, two pages of printed matter, and that no one would read the resulting series of volumes!

I have not counted the misstatements of this author. They are sufficiently numerous to make it impracticable to answer them all in detail. It is hard to know just what to do in such a case, as one must run the risk of giving undue importance to them by noticing them, or of creating the impression that they cannot be answered by ignoring them.

Under all the circumstances it has seemed to me well to reply somewhat fully to his more important allegations relative to non-Christian tribe matters, for the reason, among others, that many of his statements embody the more important claims of the Filipino politicians relative thereto; and to add that it would be equally easy to

637

riddle his contentions relative to most other matters which he discusses.   He says: —

"Professor Worcester of the Philippine Commission has for the last twelve years been the grand official digger-up of non-Christian tribes.   He takes as much delight at the discovery of a new non-Christian tribe in some remote, newly penetrated mountain fastness, as the butterfly catcher with the proverbial blue goggles does in the capture of a new kind of butterfly." [1]

I have never had the good fortune to discover even one new tribe, the net result of my explorations and studies having been to reduce the number of such tribes claimed to inhabit the Philippines from eighty-two to twenty-seven, and to throw serious doubt on the validity of several of those which I still provisionally recognize.   Blount adds: —

"Professor Worcester's greatest value to President Taft, and also the thing out of which has grown, most unfortunately, what seems to be a very cordial mutual hatred between him and the Filipinos, is his activities in the matter of discovering, getting acquainted with, classifying, tabulating, enumerating, and otherwise preparing for salvation, the various non-Christian tribes." [2]

It is quite true that the Filipino politicians have bitterly resented my making known the facts relative to the existence of numerous uncivilized peoples in the islands, but to the charge that I hate the Filipinos I must enter an emphatic denial.

Fifteen years ago I expressed my opinion of them in the following words: —

"The civilized native is self-respecting and self-restrained to a remarkable degree.   He is patient under misfortune, and forbearing under provocation.   While it is stretching the truth to say that he never reveals anger, he certainly succeeds much better in controlling himself than does the average European. When he does give way to passion, however, he is as likely as not to become for the moment a maniac, and to do some one a fatal injury.

[1] Blount, p. 543.   [2] *Ibid.*, p. 573.

"He is a kind father and a dutiful son. His aged relatives are never left in want, but are brought to his home, and are welcome to share the best that it affords to the end of their days.

"Among his fellows, he is genial and sociable. He loves to sing, dance, and make merry He is a born musician, and considering the sort of instruments at his disposal, and especially the limited advantages which he has for perfecting himself in their use, his performances on them are often very remarkable.

"He is naturally fearless, and admires nothing so much as bravery in others. Under good officers he makes an excellent soldier, and he is ready to fight to the death for his honour or his home.

*   *   *   *   *   *   *

"With all their amiable qualities it is not to be denied that at present the civilized natives are utterly unfit for self-government. Their universal lack of education is in itself a difficulty that cannot be speedily overcome, and there is much truth in the statement of a priest who said of them that 'in many things they are big children who must be treated like little ones.'

"Not having the gift of prophecy, I cannot say how far or how fast they might advance, under more favourable circumstances than those which have thus far surrounded them. They are naturally law-abiding and peace-loving, and would, I believe, appreciate and profit by just treatment.

"In the four months which separate May 1, 1898, from the day when the manuscript for this volume leaves my hands, important events have crowded on each other's heels as never before in the history of the Archipelago. Whatever may be the immediate outcome, it is safe to say that, having learned something of his power, the civilized native will now be likely to take a hand in shaping his own future. I trust that opportunities which he has never enjoyed may be given to him. If not, may he win them for himself." [1]

This opinion, which I trust will not be considered unkindly, has not been modified in its essentials as a result of many additional years of life in the Philippines. I have unexpectedly had a hand in giving to the Filipinos opportunities which they had never before enjoyed.

[1] "The Philippine Islands and Their People," by Dean C. Worcester, p. 480.

I drafted the act under which the municipalities of these islands to-day govern themselves; the act creating the College of Medicine and Surgery where young Filipino men and women may receive the best of theoretical and practical instruction; the act creating in the Bureau of Lands a school of surveying as a result of which the present dearth of Filipino surveyors will soon end; the provision of law creating and providing for the Philippine Training School for Nurses, which is preparing hundreds of young Filipino men and women to practise a useful and noble profession. I drafted the legislation which created a forest school, where many bright Filipino lads are now being trained for the government service. I drafted the provision of law which gives to all Filipinos the right to make personal use of timber from the government forests without paying a cent therefor, and the act which makes it possible for municipalities to have communal forests, reserved for the special and exclusive benefit of their citizens.

I fought for eight years to get the money for the Philippine General Hospital, where nearly ninety thousand patients, the vast majority of whom are Filipinos, are treated annually either in beds or at the several clinics; I have approved, and indeed compelled, the appointment of a staff for that institution largely made up of Filipinos, and I have steadily supported the Filipino members of that staff when insulted or unjustly accused, as I regret to say they sometimes have been, as a result of race prejudice with which I have no sympathy.

I am the official ultimately responsible for the establishment and maintenance of a health system which indisputably saves the lives of hundreds of thousands of Filipinos every year, and has practically rid their country of smallpox, plague and cholera.

All of the employees of the Weather Bureau, which comes under my executive control, are Filipinos.

I could name a score of other important measures, hav-

TYPICAL MANOBOS.

ing for their sole object the betterment of the condition of the Filipinos, and extension to them of increased opportunity to demonstrate their capacity, which I have originated. I have never knowingly opposed a measure which would produce this result.

I frankly admit that I have declined to approve the appointment of a Filipino to any position under my control simply because he was a Filipino. I have insisted that appointees have higher and better reasons to claim consideration, among which may be mentioned decent character and ability to do the work of the positions to be filled. No living man entertains more genuinely kindly feelings toward the peoples of these islands, Christian and non-Christian, than do I. An allegation that I hate the Filipinos comes with especially bad taste from a man who himself never ceased to criticise them, and to denounce them as utterly incompetent and worthless throughout his Philippine career, but who finally experienced an eleventh-hour conversion on the eve of a presidential election which was likely to bring into power another political party.

Blount has worked out a theory, peculiarly his own, to the effect that the non-Christian peoples have been set aside as a field for purely Protestant missionary activities, and that I am a party to this scheme. In this connection he says : —

"It seems that the Catholic and Protestant ecclesiastical authorities in the Islands get along harmoniously, a kind of *modus vivendi* having been arranged between them, by which the Protestants are not to do any proselyting among the seven millions of Catholic Christians. So this field of endeavour is the one Professor Worcester has been industriously preparing during the last twelve years. [1]

"Obviously, every time Professor Worcester digs up a new non-Christian tribe he increases the prospective harvest of the Protestants, thus corralling more missionary votes at home for permanent retention of the Philippines.[2]

[1] Blount, p. 580.   [2] Blount, p. 581.

"But neither Bishop Brent nor any one else can persuade him [1] that it is wise to abandon the principle that Church and State should be separate, in order that our government may go into the missionary business. Since it has become apparent that the Philippines will not pay, the Administration has relied solely on missionary sentiments. . . .

"The foregoing reflections are not intended to raise an issue as to the wisdom of foreign missions. They are simply intended to illustrate how it is possible and natural for President Taft to consider Professor Worcester 'the most vauable man we have on the Philippine Commission.' The Professor's menagerie is a vote-getter." [2]

The first passage quoted has the merit of being ingenious, and embodies a half truth. Bishop Brent deems it inadvisable to try to proselytize Catholic Christians, and outside of Manila his co-workers confine their efforts to the conversion of persons other than Filipinos. They conduct missions for non-Christians at Sagada and Bontoc in Bontoc, at Baguio in Benguet, and at Zamboanga in the Moro Province.

In Manila they conduct a mission for Filipinos in connection with a hospital which does most valuable work, but they mean to leave Catholic Filipinos alone.

The Catholics recognize no corresponding limitations. They conduct missions for the Benguet-Lepanto Igorots at Baguio, Itogon, Kabayan, Cervantes and elsewhere; for the Bontoc Igorots at Bauco and Bontoc and for the Ifugaos at Quiangan.

The other Protestant denominations having missions in the Philippines work chiefly among the Catholics.

I have absolutely no connection with any such enterprises except that I have helped to make them possible in the wild man's territory by the establishment of law and order there, and have sometimes made both Catholic and Protestant missionaries my agents for administering simple remedies to sick persons who might otherwise have perished miserably.

[1] Blount.   [2] *Ibid.*, pp. 581–582.

To this extent, and to this extent only, has our government gone into the missionary business.

I am proud to count Bishop Brent and Archbishop Harty among my personal friends. I am in complete sympathy with the purposes which actuate both of them in prosecuting Christian missions. I have sometimes disapproved, personally, of methods employed by their subordinates in this work, and have felt free to tell them so!

Blount complains bitterly over the exhibition of members of non-Christian tribes at the Louisiana Purchase Exposition. For a wonder he admits that Tagálog and Visayan Filipinos were also exhibited. He fails to record the fact that a commission of highly educated and cultured Filipino men and women were sent to the exposition and travelled quite widely in the United States, so that they were seen, and heard of, by great numbers of people who never visited St. Louis at all. Of the exhibition of wild men, he says : —

"I think no deeper wound was ever inflicted upon the pride of the real Filipino people than that caused by this exhibition, the knowledge of which seems to have spread throughout the islands." [1]

And he rather ingeniously gives it to be understood that I was responsible for this exhibition, although he carefully avoids stating that this was the case.

I am quite as strongly opposed to the exhibition of members of the Philippine non-Christian tribes as is Blount himself, but for very different reasons hereinafter set forth. As such peoples constitute an eighth of the population of the Islands, I also object to the attempt of certain Filipino politicians to conceal the fact of their existence, and to the efforts of certain misguided Americans to minimize the importance of the problems which their existence presents. Let us look the facts in the face. The Moros are as "real" as the Tagálogs.

[1] Blount, p. 576.

The average Filipino does not object in the least to the exhibition of wild people. On the contrary, he is just as much interested in them as is the average American, and goes to see them whenever the opportunity offers. It is only the Filipino politician who pretends to see any actual immodesty in scanty costumes worn with the innocence with which Adam and Eve were endowed before the fall. The truth is that the politician himself does not really object to this semi-nudity, to which he is already sufficiently accustomed among his own people in his own native town, but he plays it up for political effect.

The pedigree of the average Filipino politician very frequently runs back to white or Chinese ancestors on the father's side. In his heart of hearts he resents his Malay blood, and he particularly objects to anything which reminds him of the truth as to the stage of civilization which had been attained by his Malay ancestors a few centuries ago.

If he be a member of the Philippine Assembly, he further and bitterly resents his lack of authority to legislate for the Moros and other non-Christian tribes, and is ever ready to support his frequently reiterated demand for such authority by arguing the unimportance of these peoples, and that of the problems which their existence presents. Up to the time when the assembly was established and was denied the power to legislate for the non-Christians, my occasional illustrated lectures on the wild peoples, given at Manila, were very liberally attended by Filipinos, not a few of whom I am glad to say still continue to patronize them when occasion offers.

My own attitude toward the exhibition of non-Christians, and my reasons therefor, are set forth in the following official correspondence, with which I will dismiss this phase of the subject : —

(Telegram.)

"PACK[1] BONTOC, MANILA, Dec. 4, 1909.

"Schneiderwind is back with his Igorots some of whom have as much as two thousand pesos due them. Am trying to arrange to have this money put in postal savings bank to protect them from themselves. Schneiderwind is after another party of wild people to take to Europe. Has asked about Ifugaos and Apayaos. Have told him strongly opposed to taking these people to other countries for exhibition purposes and will place all possible obstacles in his way if he attempts to do so. If after this warning he enters Mountain province to secure people for exhibition purposes give him no assistance but use every legitimate means to prevent his getting them. Give proper and seasonable instructions to your subordinates.

"WORCESTER."

On April 22, 1910, in returning to the Governor-General a petition dealing with the exhibition of wild people I placed upon it this indorsement : —

"Respectfully returned to the Honourable, the Governor-General.

"The undersigned is strongly opposed to the sending of members of wild tribes to the United States or to other civilized countries for exhibition purposes. Apart from all other considerations experience shows that the men and women thus taken away from their natural surroundings are apt to be pretty thoroughly spoiled and to be trouble makers after their return.

"The undersigned has recently informed Mr. R. Schneiderwind that he would, if necessary, do everything in his power to prevent the latter gentleman from taking another set of Igorots away from the Philippines for exhibition purposes. This, too, in spite of the fact that Mr. Schneiderwind has apparently been very considerate in his treatment of the Igorots whom he has taken to the United States for exhibition purposes.

"The undersigned would assume the same attitude toward any other person endeavouring to obtain Igorots for exhibition purposes."

The advocates of the "united people" theory for these islands are forced to insist on the unimportance of the non-Christian tribes and it is needless to say that Blount

---

[1] William F. Pack, governor of the Mountain Province.

does this. His contentions on the subject are rather concisely stated in the following passage : —

"You see our Census of 1903 gave the population of the Philippines at about 7,600,000 of which 7,000,000 are put down as civilized Christians; and of the remaining 600,000 about half are the savage, or semi-civilized, crudely Mohammedan Moros, in Mindanao, and the adjacent islets down near Borneo. The other 300,000 or so uncivilized people scattered throughout the rest of the archipelago, the 'non-Christian tribes,' which dwell in the mountain fastnesses, remote from 'the madding crowd,' cut little more figure, if any, in the general political equation, than the American Indian does with us to-day."[1]

If there were ten million American Indians who were in undisputed occupation of half the territory of the United States, this statement might in a way approximate the truth. Blount's ten-year-old population figures are a trifle out of date, but before demonstrating this I wish to show certain peculiarities in his method of manipulating them. He says : —

"That the existence of these wild tribes — the dog-eating Igorrotes and other savages you saw exhibited at the St. Louis Exposition of 1903-4 — constitutes infinitely less reason for withholding independence from the Filipinos than the American Indian constituted in 1776 for withholding independence from us, will be sufficiently apparent from a glance at the following table, taken from the American Census of the Islands of 1903 (vol. ii., p. 123) : —

ISLAND	CIVILIZED	WILD	TOTAL
Luzón	3,575,001	223,506	3,798,507
Panay	728,713	14,933	743,646
Cebu	592,247		592,247
Bohol	243,148		243,148
Negros	439,559	21,217	460,776
Leyte	357,641		357,641
Samar	222,002	688	222,690
Mindanao	246,694	252,940	499,634

"I think the above table makes clear the enormity of the injustice I am now trying to crucify. Without stopping to use

[1] Blount, p. 577.

your pencil, you can see that Mindanao, the island where the 'intractable Moros' Governor Forbes speaks of live, contains about a half million people. Half of these are civilized Christians, and the other half are the wild, crudely Mohammedan Moro tribes. Above Mindanao on the above list, you behold what practically is the Philippine archipelago (except Mindanao), viz. Luzón and the six main Visayan Islands. If you will turn back to pages 225 *et seq.*, especially to page 228, where the student of world politics was furnished with all he needs or will ever care to know about the geography of the Philippine Islands you will there find all the rocks sticking out of the water and all the little daubs you see on the map eliminated from the equation as wholly unessential to a clear understanding of the problem of governing the Islands. That process of elimination left us Luzón and the six main Visayan Islands above as constituting, for all practical governmental purposes all the Philippine archipelago except the Moro country Mindanao (*i.e.* parts of it), and its adjacent islets. Luzón and the Visayan Islands contain nearly 7,000,000 of people, and of these the wild tribes, as you can see by a glance at the above table constitute less than 300,000, sprinkled in the pockets of their various mountain regions. Nearly all these 300,000 are quite tame, peaceable and tractable, except, as Governor Forbes suggests, they 'might possibly mistake the object of a visit.'" [1]

This is all very well unless you take the Judge at his word and turn to the page of the census report referred to, but if you do this a rude shock awaits you, for instead of the table above quoted the following is the table which you will find : —

TABLE 1. — TOTAL POPULATION, CLASSIFIED AS CIVILIZED AND WILD, BY PROVINCES AND COMANDANCIAS.

PROVINCE OR COMANDANCIA	TOTAL POPULATION	CIVILIZED	WILD
Philippine Islands	7,635,426	6,987,686	647,740
Abra	51,860	37,823	14,037
Albay	240,326	239,434	892
Ambos Camarines	239,405	233,472	5,933
Antique	134,166	131,245	2,921
Basilan	30,179	1,331	28,848

[1] Blount, pp. 567-568.

TABLE 1. — *Continued*

PROVINCE OR COMANDANCIA	TOTAL POPULATION	CIVILIZED	WILD
Bataán	46,787	45,166	1,621
Batangas	257,715	257,715	——
Benguet	22,745	917	21,828
Bohol	269,223	269,223	——
Bulacán	223,742	223,327	415
Cagayán	156,239	142,825	13,414
Cápiz	230,721	225,092	5,629
Cavite	134,779	134,779	——
Cebú	653,727	653,727	——
Cottabato	125,875	2,313	123,562
Dapitan	23,577	17,154	6,423
Dávao	65,496	20,224	45,272
Ilocos Norte	178,995	176,785	2,210
Ilocos Sur	187,411	173,800	13,611
Iloílo	410,315	403,932	6,383
Isabela	76,431	68,793	7,638
Joló	51,389	1,270	50,119
La Laguna	148,606	148,606	——
La Uníon	137,839	127,789	10,050
Lepanto-Bontoc	72,750	2,467	70,283
Leyte	388,922	388,922	——
Manila City	219,928	219,928	——
Marinduque [1]	51,674	51,674	——
Masbate	43,675	43,675	——
Mindoro	39,582	32,318	7,264
Misamis	175,683	135,473	40,210
Negros Occidental	308,272	303,660	4,612
Negros Oriental	201,494	184,889	16,605
Nueva Ecija	134,147	132,999	1,148
Nueva Vizcaya	62,541	16,026	46,515
Pampanga	223,754	222,656	1,098
Pangasinán	397,902	394,516	3,386
Paragua	29,351	27,493	1,858
Paragua Sur	6,345	1,359	4,986
Rizal	150,923	148,502	2,421
Romblón	52,848	52,848	——
Sámar	266,237	265,549	688
Siassi	24,562	2 97	24,265
Sorsogón	120,495	120,454	41
Surigao	115,112	99,298	15,814
Tarlac	135,107	133,513	1,594
Tawi Tawi	14,638	93	14,545
Tayabas [2]	153,065	150,262	2,803
Zambales	104,549	101,381	3,168
Zamboanga	44,322	20,692	23,630

[1] Sub-province of Tayabas.   [2] Exclusive of sub-province of Marinduque.

From this it will be apparent to the reader that the Judge takes some rather unusual liberties even with such information as was available nine years before he finished his book. I have quoted the actual table in full, as it is useful for reference.

In the middle of the page referred to by Blount there begins another table showing "Total Population, Classified as Civilized and Wild, by Islands." This table occupies four and one-half solid pages, and therefore does not closely resemble the one foisted on the public by him.

It includes 323 islands, from which the Judge has selected eight which happened to suit his purpose, giving it to be clearly understood that the islands which he has not included are "rocks sticking out of the water" and "little daubs you see on the map" "eliminated from the equation as wholly unessential to a clear understanding of the problem of governing the Islands."

Among the "rocks" and "little daubs" thus eliminated are Mindoro with an area of thirty-eight hundred fifty-one square miles, and Palawan with an area of four thousand twenty-seven square miles. Of the islands included, Leyte has twenty-seven hundred twenty-two square miles; Cebu, seventeen hundred sixty-two square miles; and Bohol, fourteen hundred eleven square miles. Incidentally, neither Leyte, Cebu nor Bohol have any non-Christian inhabitants at all, while all of Mindoro and Palawan, with the exception of narrow broken strips along the coast are populated by wild people, hence it is convenient for him to ignore them.

In spite of his suggestion that it is not necessary to use the pencil in connection with his table, I ventured to do so, in connection with his statement that "Luzón and the Visayan Islands contain nearly 7,000,000 of people." On his own showing they contain 6,158,311.

And now for the real facts. At the time the census enumeration was made Apayao had been crossed by a white man only once and that more than a hundred years ago. Extensive portions of Ifugao and Bontoc, and the greater part of Kalinga, were unexplored, as were the interior of Mindoro and most of the interior of Palawan, to say nothing of immense regions in Mindanao. As a matter of fact, we do not to-day know with any accuracy the number of Mangyans in Mindoro, nor the number of Tagbanuas in Palawan, but it has been conclusively demonstrated that the latter were greatly underestimated by the census enumerators. There will be found in the appendix [1] a table giving in detail the present accepted estimate of the non-Christian population of the islands, which numbers at least a million seventy thousand.

It is reasonably certain that the necessary corrections in the figures for several provinces for which the present estimates are admittedly too low will raise the total slightly.

Blount has made a further statement relative to the non-Christian population of Luzón which is indeed extraordinary. He says : —

"Of the 7,600,000 people of the Philippines almost exactly one-half, *i.e.* 3,800,000, live on Luzon, and these are practically all civilized." [2]

The table on the opposite page, giving the census estimate of the non-Christian population of Luzón and the present accepted estimate, shows how erroneous is this statement.

It will be seen that the census estimate of non-Christian inhabitants in the province of Luzón was 224,106 and the present accepted estimate is 440,926.

In explanation of his extraordinary statement that practically all of the people of Luzón are civilized Blount has inserted the following foot-note : —

[1] Page 999.   [2] Blount, pp. 231–232.

An Old Bukidnon Chief.

He is wearing the head-dress of scarlet and gold which may be donned only by those who have killed many enemies.

"**223,506** is the total of the uncivilized tribes still extant in Luzon, Philippine Census, vol. ii., p. 125, but they live in the mountains, and you might live in the Philippines a long lifetime without ever seeing a sample of them, unless you happen to be an energetic ethnologist fond of mountain climbing." [1]

PROVINCE OR SUBPROVINCE	CENSUS ESTIMATE	PRESENT ACCEPTED ESTIMATE
Abra	14,037	14,037
Albay	892	892
Amburayan	—	10,191
Ambos Camarines	5,933	5,933
Apayao	—	23,000
Bataan	1,621	1,621
Batangas	000	000
Benguet	21,828	28,449
Bontoc	—	62,000
Bulacan	415	415
Cagayan	13,414	15,000
Cavite	000	000
Ilocos Norte	2,210	2,210
Ilocos Sur	13,611	13,611
Ifugao	—	125,000
Isabela	7,638	(?)
Kalinga	—	76,000
La Laguna	000	(?)
La Union	10,050	000
Lepanto	—	31,194
Lepanto Bontoc	70,283	000
Nueva Ecija	1,148	862
Nueva Vizcaya	46,515	6,000
Pampanga	1,098	1,098
Pangasinán	3,386	3,386
Rizal	2,421	2,421
Sorsogon	41	41
Tarlac	1,594	1,594
Tayabas	2,803	2,803
Zambales	3,168	3,168
Total	224,106	440,926

Also you might live in the Philippines a long lifetime and never see anything but wild people. The question of

[1] Blount, p. 232.

where they live is not intimately connected with that of
their number, which is the point under discussion.

Blount devotes considerable space to alleged newspaper
accounts of "a speech" said by him to have been delivered
by me in the Y. M. C. A. auditorium at Manila. I
delivered two illustrated lectures there, entitled respectively "The Non-Christian Tribes of the Philippines,"
and "What has been done for the Non-Christian Tribes
under American Rule."

In the course of the latter discourse I made the point
that Filipinos who claim that conquest confers no right of
sovereignty are hoist with their own petard, for the simple
but sufficient reason that the Negritos were the aborigines
of the Philippines and were later conquered and driven out
of the lowland country into inaccessible, forested mountain
regions by the Malay invaders who were the ancestors
of the present Filipino claimants not only to the territory
thus conquered, but to territory which was held up to the
time of the American occupation by wild tribes whom they
now propose to conquer and rule if given the opportunity !

My shaft struck home and called forth a howl of rage
from the politicians, which was the louder because I
further expressed with entire frankness my firm belief
that the Filipinos were unfit to govern the non-Christian
tribes, whether or not they were fit to govern themselves.

In the course of further reference to the above-mentioned
lecture, Blount says : —

"Another of the Manila papers gives an account of the speech,
from which it appears that the burly Professor succeeded in
amusing himself at least, if not his audience, by suggestions
as to the superior fighting qualities of the Moros over the
Filipinos, which suggestions were on the idea that the Moros
would lick the Filipinos if we should leave the country. (The
Moros number 300,000, the Filipinos nearly 7,000,000.) The
Professor's remarks in this regard, according to the paper, were
a distinct reflection upon the courage of the Filipinos generally
as a people." [1]

[1] Blount, pp. 583–584.

Here, as is so often the case, he finds newspaper statements more suited to his purpose than cold facts. I yield to no one in my admiration for the courage of Filipinos, and have expressed it on a score of occasions. In my first book on the Philippines I made the following reference to it : —

"I once saw a man in Culion who was seamed and gashed with horrible scars from head to foot. How any one could possibly survive such injuries as he had received I do not know. It seemed that his wife and children had been butchered by four Moros while he was absent. He returned just as the murderers were taking to their boat. Snatching a machete, he plunged into the water after them, clambered into their prau, and killed them all. When one remembers the sort of weapons that Moros carry, the thing seems incredible, but a whole village full of people vouched for the truth of the story." [1]

This was not the only tribute which I paid to the courage of the Filipinos [2] and I have never made a statement intended to reflect on it in the slightest degree. It is true that their fighting ability is on the average far below that of the Moros, and I may add that the same thing holds for Americans on the average.

It is really funny to see how Blount sometimes tells the truth in spite of himself. He takes me to task for amusing myself "by suggestions as to the superior fighting qualities of the Moros over the Filipinos," and here is what he says on the same subject : —

"Again, because the Filipinos have no moral right to control the Moros, and could not if they would, the latter being fierce fighters and bitterly opposed to the thought of possible ultimate domination by the Filipinos, the most uncompromising advocate of the consent-of-the-governed principle has not a leg to stand on with regard to Mohammedan Mindanao." [3]

"Consistency, thy name is not Blount !"

[1] The Philippine Islands and Their People, by Dean C. Worcester, p. 481.

[2] See p. 639.

[3] Blount, p. 230.

The Moros are religious fanatics. I have known one when bayoneted to seize the barrel of the gun and push the bayonet through himself in order to bring the man at the other end within striking distance, cut him down, unclasp the bayonet and, leaving it in the wound to prevent hemorrhage, go on fighting. I have known two Moros armed with bamboo lances to attack a column of two thousand soldiers armed with rifles. It is an historic fact that Moro *juramentados* [1] once attempted to rush the walls of Joló and kept up the fruitless effort until they blocked with their dead bodies the rifle slits, so that it became necessary for the Spanish soldiers to take positions on top of the walls in order to fire. I have known a Moro, shot repeatedly through the body and with both legs broken, to take his kriss in his teeth and pull himself forward with his hands in the hope of getting near enough to strike one more blow for the Prophet.

The Filipinos are afraid of the Moros and they have the best of reasons to be. The relative numerical insignificance of this little Mohammedan tribe of desperate fighters has little to do with the question under consideration. Their number has for centuries borne substantially the same proportion to the total population of the Philippines which it now bears, yet no one can deny that it is but a short time since they harried the archipelago from south to north and from east to west. The shores of Northern Luzón and the neighbouring islands are to-day dotted with the forts which were built for defence against them. The town of Polillo, on the northernmost island off the east coast of Luzón, is still surrounded by a high wall built to protect its inhabitants from the Moros. The churches at Cuyo, Agutaya, Culion, Linapacan and Taytay stand inside of strong stone fortresses in which the people took refuge when the Moros descended on their towns. Back of Bacuit a cave high up in a cliff was kept provisioned that it might serve a similar purpose. Not only were the

[1] Men who have taken a solemn oath to die killing Christians.

Filipinos unable to protect themselves against these bloodthirsty pirates of the south, but the Spaniards were for nearly two and a half centuries unable to afford them adequate protection. When I was in Tawi Tawi in 1891 the Moros of that island were still actively engaged in taking Filipino slaves and selling them in Borneo.

With all of our resources we have not as yet been able to establish a decent state of public order in the little island of Jolo. No serious minded person, familiar with the facts, with whom I have ever talked, believes for a moment that the Filipinos could establish an effective government over the Moros, or could keep them at home. They are wonderful boatmen and when once at sea in the little crafts of their own building are liable to strike the coast of the Philippine Islands at any point. When it is remembered that this coast is longer than that of the continental United States, the impossibility of adequately protecting the whole of it becomes immediately manifest. It would be always possible, under Filipino rule, for the Moros to strike defenceless towns, and where they struck the only resource of the inhabitants, whether Filipinos, Europeans or Americans, would be in speedy flight. It should be borne in mind that one Mohammedan who is earnestly desirous of being killed while fighting Christians can chase a good many unarmed citizens into the tall timber, brave though they may be!

I venture here once more to express the deliberate opinion that if American control were withdrawn from these islands and some other civilized nation did not interfere to restore a decent state of public order, the Moros would resume the conquest of the Philippines which they were so actively and effectively pushing when the Spaniards compelled them to abandon it, and would slowly but none the less surely carry it through to a successful termination.

The inaccuracy of Blount's statements regarding matters

covered by absolutely conclusive documentary evidence is well typified by the following : —

"The Philippine Assembly, representing the whole Filipino people, and desiring to express the unanimous feeling of those people with regard to the Worcester speech, unanimously passed, soon after the speech was delivered, a set of resolutions whereof the following is a translation." [1]

The resolution which he quotes was never passed by the Assembly which on February 3, 1911, four months after my Y. M. C. A. lecture,[2] and while I was absent in the United States, passed another and quite different one criticizing language "ascribed" to me, without ever making any effort to ascertain from me what was really said. I might quote the two in parallel columns, but I grow weary of showing the details of Blount's false or mistaken statements, and refer those interested to the official records which he perhaps did not take the precaution to consult.

I gave the Assembly and every one else interested in the matter a chance to attack me by incorporating in my annual report for 1910 every important statement made at the lecture in question and by adding various new ones for good measure, but there was no response ! It is a time-honoured procedure, but one of somewhat doubtful real value, to build up a man of straw in order to have the pleasure of tearing it to pieces. I must decline to assume responsibility for statements which I did not make.

Blount says he thinks that Nueva Vizcaya is my

"'brag' province, in the matter of non-Christian anthropological specimens, both regarding their number and their variety." [3]

With regret I must call attention to the fact that he thinks wrong. In Nueva Vizcaya as originally constituted there were representatives of three non-Christian tribes, to wit, the Ifugaos, numbering approximately

[1] Blount, p. 584.   [2] Delivered October 10, 1910.   [3] Blount, p. 577.

TYPICAL STREET IN A FILIPINO TOWN.

Contrast the neglect here shown, with the care given the village streets in Bukidnon, yet the Filipinos desire to govern the Bukidnons.

A TYPICAL BUKIDNON VILLAGE STREET.

a hundred and fifteen thousand; the Ilongots numbering perhaps five thousand; and the Isinayes, who were numerically unimportant.

Years before Blount wrote his book the number of wild tribes was reduced to two and that of their individuals to approximately seven thousand by changes in the provincial boundary. As we have seen, there are slightly more than one million non-Christian inhabitants in the archipelago. These facts are of interest chiefly for the reason that they show how grossly unreliable are his statements.

Finally he seeks to convey the impression that the hill people are a rather harmless and lamb-like lot. He says:—

". . . while I was there,[1] though we knew those people were up in the hills, and that there were a good many of them the civilized people all told us that the hill tribes never bothered them. And on their advice I have ridden in safety, unarmed, at night, accompanied only by the court stenographer, over the main high-road running through the central plateau that constitutes the bulk of Nueva Vizcaya province, said plateau being surrounded by a great amphitheatre of hills, the habitat of the Worcester pets."[2]

Had Blount taken this ride before the time when the American government established control over the Silipan Ifugaos there might have been a different story to tell needing some one else to tell it, for the Ifugaos were not by any means the gentle and harmless people that one would infer them to have been from reading the above-quoted statement.

At Payauan, a strongly held point within the plateau referred to, they annihilated a Spanish garrison. At Aua, further back in the hills, they did the same thing. The Spaniards never established control over the Ifugao country, into extensive portions of which they never even temporarily penetrated. On the main trail which connected the town of Bagabag, in Nueva Vizcaya with the nearest town in the province of Isabela,

[1] In Nueva Vizcaya.   [2] Blount, p. 577.

over which Blount rode, the Spaniards found it necessary to maintain two garrisons. There were also garrisons at the terminal towns on this trail and it was
prohibited to travel it without military escort. Even
so, parties were repeatedly cut up by the Silipan Ifugaos,
and the very soldiers who constituted their guard were
again and again caught sleeping and butchered.

It is only very recently that the murderous raids of wild
men on the Filipinos of Isabela have been finally checked.

Many a time have the Filipinos of Bagabag, in Nueva
Vizcaya, thanked me for making their lives and property
safe by quieting the Ifugaos. Ilongots killed Filipinos
in the outskirts of Bayombong, the capital of Nueva
Vizcaya, long after Blount left the province, and during
a period shortly preceding his arrival conditions were very
bad throughout the Cagayan valley.

On August 29, 1899, the Insurgent governor of Nueva
Vizcaya reported [1] that he had only a few rifles, that the
"Igorrotes" were preparing to attack the towns, and that
he had been forced to kill and wound a number of them.
On September 6, General Tirona in Cagayan asked that
General Tinio be ordered to give him some of his rifles
to protect the people, as the "Igorrotes" were cutting off
heads and the towns were in danger. Tirona said that he
had nine hundred rifles; Tinio thought that he himself
had some two thousand and could spare two hundred as the
conditions along the coast were not as serious as the conditions inland with the savages preparing to attack.[2]

In July, 1899, the governor of Benguet asked that orders
should be given prohibiting "Igorrotes" from leaving
their own towns as they were growing restless and would
probably soon become dangerous. The Benguet people
are the most pacific of all the hill men.

In October, 1899, the Ilocanos of Lepanto petitioned
Aguinaldo to send them arms with which to defend themselves against the people of the hills, who objected to

[1] P. I. R., 150. 4.   [2] *Ibid.*

being forced into paying what the governor of Benguet Province called "voluntary contributions" for the support of the war. When an attempt was made to collect, they abandoned their towns and took refuge in the hills. Next to the Benguet Igorots, those of Lepanto have the best reputation for quiet and orderliness.

From Simeon Villa's diary, heretofore referred to, we learn that Aguinaldo's armed escort was attacked again and again by Ifugaos, Kalingas and Bontoc Igorots when he passed through their country.

The people of these three tribes, and the Ilongots, and the wild Tingians of Apayao, were fierce, war-like, unsubdued head-hunting savages at the time of the American occupation.

Friendly as is our present relationship with the former head-hunters of Luzón, and excellent as is now the condition of public order in their territory, we still often have the fact brought home to us that the blood-lust of these sturdy and brave fighters is only dormant. A steady hand must be held on them for many a year to come.

The problems which the primitive peoples of the Philippines present are neither few nor simple. We shall not get far by ignoring them or misrepresenting them. Let us look them squarely in the face.

CHAPTER XXIV

Non-Christian Tribe Problems

AND now let us try to gain a clear appreciation of some of the problems actually presented by the existence of the non-Christian peoples of the Philippines.

They belong to twenty-seven tribes at the most. Probably this number will ultimately be somewhat further reduced. The number of dialects spoken is greatly in excess of the number of tribes, as the people of a single tribe sometimes speak three or four well-marked dialects.

The tribes are divided between two wholly distinct races, to wit, Negritos and Malays.

The Negritos are of very low mentality and are incapable of any considerable degree of civilization. Many of them are kept in a state of abject peonage, and not a few are held in actual slavery, by their Christian Filipino neighbours. In revenge for the abuses which they suffer they are prone to commit criminal acts, and the problem which they present resolves itself into protecting them from their neighbours and their neighbours from them. The latter thing would be easy enough if the former were practicable, but unfortunately their neighbours cannot be persuaded to let them alone, and never do it except under compulsion.

The people of all the Malay non-Christian tribes, with the exception of certain Negrito *mestizos*, are undoubtedly capable of attaining to a fairly high degree of civilization. Physically and, in my opinion, mentally the people of several of the hill tribes are decidedly superior to their lowland Filipino neighbours, who have degenerated to some extent as a result of less favourable climatic conditions and other causes.

In social development these Malay tribes vary from the semi-nomadic Mangyans of Mindoro to the highly civilized Tingians of Abra, who are in many ways superior to the Ilocanos with whom they live in close contact. Some of these tribes, like the Benguet-Lepanto Igorots and the Tingians, are peaceful agriculturists; others, like the wild Tingians of Apayao, the Kalingas, the Bontoc Igorots, the Ifugaos, the Ilongots, the Manobos and the Mandayas, are, or recently have been, fierce fighters prone to indulge in such customs as the taking of human heads for war trophies, or even the making of human sacrifices to appease their heathen divinities.

The Moros, who are numerically stronger than are the people of any other one tribe, stand in a class by themselves on account of their strong adherence to the Mohammedan faith and their inclination to propagate it by the sword. Who would hold them in check if the Americans were to go? Certainly not the Filipinos. They have never been able to do it in the past, and they cannot do it now.

All the non-Christian tribes have two things in common, their unwillingness to accept the Christian faith and their hatred of the several Filipino peoples who profess it. Their animosity is readily understood when it is remembered that their ancestors and they themselves have suffered grievous wrongs at the hands of the Filipinos. In spite of all protestations to the contrary, the Filipinos are absolutely without sympathy for the non-Christian peoples, and have never voluntarily done anything for them, but on the contrary have shamelessly exploited them whenever opportunity has offered. They have never of themselves originated one single important measure for the benefit of their non-Christian neighbours, and their attitude toward the measures which have been originated by Americans has always been one of active or passive opposition. Their real belief as to what should be done with the wild people is that they should be used if they can be made useful, but should be exterminated if they become troublesome. Governor Pablo Guzman, of Cagayan, actually said to me that the best thing to do with the wild people of Apayao, then supposed to number fifty-three thousand, might be to kill them all.

Americans have adopted a firm but kindly policy in dealing with the non-Christian tribes and have met with extraordinary success in winning their good-will and weaning them from the worst of their evil customs. Even with those of the Moros who live outside of the island of Joló considerable progress has been made. Head-hunting has been abolished among the Ifugaos, Igorots and Kalingas with an ease which was wholly unanticipated.

In all work for the wild people the attitude of governors and lieutenant-governors has proved to be a matter of fundamental importance. The problem in each province or subprovince has been a one-man problem. He who would succeed in handling wild men must be absolutely fearless, for if he is not, they are quick to discover the fact and to take advantage of it. He must protect his people from injustice and oppression, or they will lose faith in him. He must have a genuinely friendly feeling toward them, and must bear them no ill will even when they misbehave. They will not object to severe punishment when they know that it is deserved, but after being punished feel that the slate has been wiped clean, and that they are making a fresh start. They believe in letting by-gones be by-gones, and their officials should meet them half way in this.

The following occurrence illustrates my point. Before all the settlements of Ifugao had been brought under control, Lieutenant-Governor Gallman had a headman acting as a policeman, who rendered invaluable service and was allowed to carry a gun. No one dreamed that he would ever be molested. When on a trip to Lingay he became overheated, and stopped to bathe in a stream, leaving his gun on the bank. Some young men improved the opportunity thus afforded to attack him. One of them threw a lance into him, and then they all started to run away. Such was his reputation and influence that he succeeded in compelling them to return and pull the lance out, but he was fatally hurt and soon died.

After his death they took his head and his gun, and immediately thereafter the Lingay people sent to Gallman a challenge to come and fight them. He promptly accepted their invitation, taking a few Ifugao soldiers with him. He found the country deserted. Women, children, pigs and chickens had been sent into the forested mountains. Roofs and board sides of houses had been removed so that there remained only the bare frameworks which could not readily be burned.

For some time Gallman encountered no opposition. He at last grew careless and walked into an ambush. He was met with a volley of stones and a volley of lances. Fortunately for him the stones arrived first and one of them, striking him in the face, knocked him senseless. Another injured his right hand and knocked his revolver from his grasp. The lances passed over him as he fell. He slid for some distance down the almost precipitous mountain side, and his soldiers thought him dead. When he recovered consciousness, he heard them talking close to him. They agreed that they must do two things: first, prevent his head from being taken; and, second, punish his assailants. Before he could call to them they charged the latter and scattered them right and left. Gallman staggered to his feet, hunted around until he found his revolver, and rejoined his men. It was known that their opponents had had ten guns before killing the policeman and taking his. There followed a marked unpleasantness, at the end of which Gallman had the eleven guns, and most of those who had been using them had been gathered to their fathers. He then returned to his station at Banaue.

Three days later the headmen of Lingay came walking in, shook hands and announced that they had had enough. Gallman asked them why they had been so foolish. They replied that as they already had ten guns, when they got one more the young men became overconfident, thought that they could whip the constabulary, get their guns also and dominate all that part of Ifugao. The old men said that they had warned the young fellows that their plan would result in disaster, but as they were not to be dissuaded, and as they were their young men, had finally joined in. They said, however, that they were glad things had come out as they had, for the young men would now behave themselves, and it is worthy of note that they have done so ever since.

Six weeks later, when I visited Banaue, the one survivor of the eleven gunmen came in and danced with the other Ifugaos on the plaza, apparently as happy as any of them.

How many Filipinos are there who have the courage, the kindliness, the knowledge of primitive human nature and the sympathy with it which would enable them to treat the really wild barbarians as Gallman and Hale have treated them? Thus far I have found one, and one only.

In a previous chapter[1] I have told the story of a Kalinga with whom I had just made friends according to the formula of his tribe who put his life in deadly peril twice within the space of twenty-four hours in order to save mine when it was gravely endangered by his fellow-tribesmen. Is such real friendship possible between Filipinos and non-Christians? Not at present. A lot of ancient history must first be lived down.

In the Philippines it has invariably been true that the wild man has in the past been more or less completely despoiled of the fruits of his labour by his so-called "Christian" neighbours whenever compelled to do business with them in order to obtain some of the necessaries of life.

[1] Page 542.

A TYPICAL IMPROVED BUKIDNON HOUSE.

A TYPICAL NEGLECTED FILIPINO HOUSE.

In the Bukidnon villages all the people now take pride in keeping their houses in good repair. Houses like the one here shown are frequently seen in neighboring Filipino towns.

He is accustomed to receive a mere pittance for his products, and to pay enormous prices when he makes purchases. The opening of the so-called "government exchanges," which are stores where the products of the surrounding country are purchased and where the things required by the hill people are sold at a small margin of profit, has proved very useful in the establishment of friendly and helpful relations with them. In some places they have been persuaded to grow new and more profitable crops. Some of the Benguet Igorots, for instance, now raise strawberries for sale at Baguio, although a few years ago they had never seen them.

If in control, would the Filipinos reverse the policy they have heretofore always followed in commercial dealings with the wild men? Most assuredly not.

The Igorots, Ifugaos and Kalingas are adepts in the use of irrigation water, and know how to terrace the steepest mountain sides so as to employ it advantageously wherever it is available. The giving of help in running main irrigation ditches through rock has been especially appreciated by them. The money which we expend for this purpose goes for the establishment of proper grade lines, the providing of necessary supervision and the purchase of explosives and tools for rock work. The people concerned are more than glad to contribute all necessary labour free of charge.

Would the Filipinos continue to make funds available for such improvements in the wild man's country? A thousand times no! Before any one disputes me, let him show one instance where they have done any such thing in any one of the very numerous provinces where the expenditure of funds for non-Christians is under their control.

In dealing with tribes which have been accustomed to live by families, or small groups of families, and to select very inaccessible places for their homes, it is of course necessary to persuade them to live in larger groups and in reasonably accessible places before much progress can be made toward improving their condition. This is usually not a very difficult task if one goes about it in the right way.

In Bukidnon, for instance, where we are still bringing people down from the tree-tops, in which they and some of their ancestors have lived for centuries, and settling them in well-ordered and beautifully kept villages, when new arrivals come in to inspect the towns and interrogate me as to the conditions under which they may take up residence there, I often have conversations like this: —

"What about this life in town?"

"Look around and see for yourself. Talk with the people and hear what they have to say about it. They will tell you whether they like it or not, and why."

"But what do I have to do if I wish to live in town?"

"A piece of ground will be assigned to you and on it you must build a decent house like those you see. This house is for you and your family, not for me. I come here only once or twice a year and at the most stay over one night, so I do not need your house. The lieutenant-governor does not need it. When he comes he stays at the *presidencia*. He will not let any one take it away from you."

"Very well. What else?"

"You will have to build a good, tight fence around the lot given you and keep your domestic animals inside it. You must also clean it up thoroughly, removing all vegetation and filling all the low places so that water cannot stand in them. Then you must keep it clean."

"What is the use of that?"

"The *búsaos*[1] who cause sickness do no like clean places and stay away from them."

"I never heard of that."

"Ask the people who have tried keeping their yards clean, and they will tell you that it is true."

[1] Evil spirits.

"Well, what else?"

"As long as you have to keep your yard clean you might as well plant something useful in it, so that you will get a good return for your labour."

"That is a good idea. Is there anything more?"

"Yes. You must take up a piece of the beautiful prairie land near town, build a fence around it to keep out the wild hogs and deer, and plant it with rice, *camotes* or something else that will give your family plenty of food and if possible leave a surplus to sell, so that you can buy better clothes with the money you make."

"But I cannot break this thick prairie sod."

"The ground will be ploughed for you the first time. After that you must look after it yourself."

"Is that all?"

"No. There is one additional very important thing. I am getting old and fat,[1] and I can no longer scramble around over these hills as I used to do. I want to come and see you every year, and find out how you are getting on. You will have to help build good trails for my big horse, working ten days every year, or paying two pesos, so that some one else can be hired to work in your place. Everything else that I have told you must be done, if you come to town, is for your benefit, not for mine, and even the trails are only partly for my benefit. You will find it easy and safe to travel over them, and when you want to go to market, your carabao will be able to pack three or four times as much as he can now carry over bad paths."

"Will I gain any other advantages by living in town?"

"Yes, two very important ones. You and your family will be safe from attack, and you will have a chance to send your children to school."

"Must I come and live in town if I do not want to?"

"By no means. If you prefer to live up a tree in the mountains, no one will interfere with you so long as you

---

[1] This is only too true!

behave yourself. There are plenty of mountains and plenty of trees."

As a result of the simple arguments above outlined and of the protection and help given them, nearly all of the Bukidnon people have left the mountain fastnesses through which they have until recently been scattered, and are voluntarily taking up their residences in towns which in their way are models.

Could the Filipinos keep them in the towns where we have settled them? No; and they would not if they could. They would chase them back into the forests as they were doing when we made them stop it. Furthermore, they could not if they would. In September, 1912, I heard the people of eastern Bukidnon tell Governor Reyes of Misamis that if their territory were put back into his province, they would take to the hills and live with the Manobos.

One of the most important factors in winning and retaining the good will of the non-Christian peoples has been the extension to them of protection from the impositions of their Filipino neighbours. The following is a fair sample of the sort of thing to which they have in the past been subjected.

During my last trip through Bukidnon I learned that a long-haired mountaineer who had been encouraged to plant coffee and Manila hemp had acted on the suggestion, working very hard and establishing an excellent plantation which had prospered. When he had products ready for market he had taken them to the coast town of Balingasák. He did not speak the language of the Visayan Filipino inhabitants of that place, so fell into the hands of one of them who knew his dialect. This rascal helped him to sell his produce, but took a heavy commission for this service. The hillman was nevertheless delighted with the result, whereupon his "commissioner" suggested that what he really needed was a partner in town to sell his crops, so that he could spend his whole time in cultivating his fields and not have to go to market. This struck the hillman as a good idea. The Filipino made out what purported to be articles of partnership and the hillman signed them with his mark, in the presence of witnesses.

A few months later he sent a valuable shipment of coffee and hemp to his "partner." When weeks had passed without his hearing from it, he went to Balingasák to find out what was wrong, whereupon his "partner" stated that he was greatly obliged to him for his trouble in cultivating and harvesting the products of the farm. The hillman demanded his share of the returns and the "partner" calmly assured him that he had no share, having sold his farm at the time of his last visit. Investigation proved that this ignorant man had signed a bill of sale for his place.

Lieutenant-Governor Fortich interested himself in the case and caused suit to be brought against the rascally "partner" for stealing the hillman's produce. The *fiscal*, or public prosecuting, officer was a bright young Filipino who had recently graduated from an American university. Nevertheless, he had the suit thrown out of court because the "partner" of the hillman claimed that the farm was his, and a question of property ownership could not be conveniently determined in connection with a criminal suit.

At this stage of events I took a hand and brought the matter to the attention of the Honourable Gregorio Araneta, secretary of finance and justice. The *fiscal* had suggested that the wild man could bring a civil suit for damages against his "partner." How could this helpless barbarian have gone to Cagayan, hired a lawyer and lived there while his case was pending? He was absolutely helpless. Naturally, I was not. Another suit was brought and the "partner" was sentenced to pay a fine and was given a term in jail.

This is no isolated case. The wild men are constantly deprived of their crops or their lands; cheated in the sale of their products and in their purchases; arrested and fined on trumped-up charges; compelled to work for others without compensation; charged by private individuals for the privilege of using government forests or taking up public lands; and badgered and imposed upon in a thousand and one other ways.

If the Filipinos were put in control, would there rise up among them unselfish men who would check the rapacity of their fellows, and extend to the helpless peoples the protection they now enjoy?

At all events, those who have made it their business to protect the people of the non-Christian tribes have not been popular among the Filipinos. As a precautionary measure, I warned every man appointed governor of, or lieutenant-governor in, a special government province that he must expect sooner or later to be accused of many of the crimes recognized by existing laws. Every such man who does his duty eventually has false, and usually foul, charges brought against him. A common, and indeed the favourite, complaint is that he has been guilty of improper relations with women. The Filipino is an expert in framing up cases of this sort, and seems to take special delight in it, partly no doubt because such charges are so excessively difficult to disprove.

Cruel abuse of the wild men, or their families; falsification of public documents; misappropriation of public funds; adultery; rape, — these are all common charges, while more than one of my subordinates has been accused of murder, and one has actually been brought into court on such a charge. It is certainly no sinecure to be an officer of a special government province.

A potent means of winning the undying regard of the wild man is to cure him when he is sick, or heal him when he is injured. Hospitals have already been established in two of the special government provinces and are doing untold good. Practically every officer of these provinces carries a set of simple remedies with him when

MAKING FRIENDS WITH THE MANDAYAS.

The people of this tribe are very fond of beads, a teaspoonful of which make a most acceptable gift.

he travels, and treats the sick without compensation as opportunity offers, but this work is as yet in its infancy.

The Filipinos have not doctors enough to heal their own sick. Would they remember to heal the wild men? Hardly.

Several of the wild tribes have progressed much more rapidly during the brief period since the American occupation than have any of the Filipino peoples, and if given adequate protection and friendly assistance they will continue to progress. Their splendid physiques and high intelligence, no less than their truthfulness, honesty and morality, certainly make them well worth saving.

Under Filipino rule the more helpless of these tribes would speedily come under the control of their former oppressors, but people like the Ifugaos, Bontoc Igorots, Kalingas and wild Tingians would fight to the death before submitting to them, and there would result a guerrilla warfare as endless and disastrous as that which has lasted so long between the Dutch and the Achinese. There is every theoretical reason to believe that the Filipinos would adopt toward such hostile primitive peoples the policy of extermination which the Japanese have been so vigorously carrying out in dealing with the hill people of northern Formosa, who do not differ in any important respect from the hill people of northern Luzón, with whom such helpful and friendly relations have now been established.

We have encouraged the primitive Philippine peoples to stand up for their rights. We have promised them our protection and help if they would do it, and thus far we have kept our promise. To break it now, and turn them over to the tender mercies of the Filipinos, who have never ceased to make threats as to what they will do when they get the chance, would in my opinion be a crime against civilization.

The Moros openly boast that if the Americans go they

will raid the Christian towns, and this is no idle threat. They will most assuredly do it.

Were American control to be withdrawn before the civilization of the wild tribes had been effected, their future would be dark indeed. Under continued American control they can be won over to civilized ways, and will in the end become mentally and morally, as they now are physically, superior to the lowlanders.

No man has been blessed with better subordinates than I have had to assist me in the work carried on under my direction for the non-Christian tribes of the Philippines. I wish it clearly understood that it is to the loyalty and efficiency of these men that the results which have been obtained are due. Fearlessly, tirelessly, uncomplainingly, they have borne their heavy shares of the white man's burden, finding their greatest reward in the respect, gratitude, and in many cases the affection, of those whom they have so faithfully and effectively served.

Think of Pack, weakened by illnesses which twice brought him within a hair's breadth of death, wearing himself out riding over the Mountain Province trails, many of which he himself had laboriously built, in order to keep the little handful of men who control its 400,000 non-Christian inhabitants up to the high-water mark of efficiency, when he could have gone home any day and spent his remaining years in leisurely comfort; of Bryant, wandering for weeks on end through the trackless forests of Nueva Vizcaya in order to get in touch with Ilongot savages who were a good deal more than "half devil" with the balance not "half child" but peculiarly treacherous, vicious and savage man; of Offley, packing the bare necessities of life on his own back while he struggled out to the coast from the centre of Mindoro, where his frightened carriers had deserted him; of Kane, burning in the heat of the lowlands or soaked and shivering on chilly mountain crests, while building new roads and keeping old ones open for traffic; of Lewis, trying to cover a territory large enough to tax the energies of three men, and in his efforts to do so riding until so weary that at night he fell from his horse unable to dismount; of Fortich, a Filipino lieutenant-governor, faithfully carrying out the white man's policy and protecting the Bukidnons from his own people who charged him with murder because he drove them from their prey; of Gallman, risking his life a thousand times in a successful individual effort to bring 125,000 head-hunting savages under effective control and to establish relations of genuine friendship with them; of Hale, turning tattooed Kalinga devils into effective officers for the maintenance of law and order, or making a bundle of the lances thrown at him and sending them back to the people who threw them with a mild suggestion that it was impolite to treat a would-be friend in such an unceremonious way; of Johnson, tramping through the reeking filth of the Butuan swamps with a cancer eating away the bone of his leg, and referring to it as "a little swelling" when asked what made him lame; of Bondurant, spending the last afternoon of his life in pursuing Moro outlaws through that worst of all tropical infernos, a mangrove swamp, when burning with pernicious malarial fever and fighting for the very breath of life; of Miller, faithful unto death!

We are wont to quote with feeling the familiar words, "Greater love hath no man than this, that he lay down his life for his friend," but what shall we say of the love of duty of men like Miller and Bondurant, who in doing their country's work cheerfully laid down their lives for an alien people?

While in the United States in 1910 I read Rudyard Kipling's "If" and thereafter did not rest until I had sent a copy of it to each governor and lieutenant-governor employed in the special provincial government service of the Philippine Islands. Kipling wrote for these men of mine up in the hills without knowing it. They understand him and he would understand them.

There is not one of them who has not learned to

"... fill the unforgiving minute
With sixty seconds' worth of distance run ";

not one whose personal experience has left him deaf to
the appeal of the lines : —

"If you can keep your head when all about you
    Are losing theirs and blaming it on you;
If you can trust yourself when all men doubt you,
    But make allowance for their doubting too;
If you can wait and not be tired by waiting,
    Or being lied about don't deal in lies,
    Or being hated don't give way to hating,
        And yet don't look too good, nor talk too wise."

Furthermore, each of them has again and again finished
on his nerve. Did not the words, —

"If you can force your heart and nerve and sinew
    To serve your turn long after they are gone,
And so hold on when there is nothing in you
    Except the Will which says to them : 'Hold on !' "

run through Bondurant's mind that last afternoon when
he was following Moro outlaws through a foul mangrove
swamp, while his senses reeled with the fever which was
so soon to end his life ?

In his wonderful quadruplet of stanzas Kipling has
fixed one criterion of manhood which it is hard indeed
to meet : —

"If you can bear to hear the truth you've spoken
    Twisted by knaves to make a trap for fools,
Or watch the things you gave your life to, broken,
    And stoop and build them up with worn-out tools."

I beg my fellow-countrymen to remember that the
non-Christians of the Philippines constitute an eighth
of the population ; that the work undertaken for their
physical, mental and moral advancement has succeeded
far beyond the hopes of those who initiated it ; that its

results would go down like a house of cards if American control were prematurely withdrawn. Shall the men who have devoted their lives to these things be forced to watch them broken, and then be denied the poor privilege of building them up again? If the splendid results of so much efficient, faithful, self-sacrificing and successful effort were to be lost, would not the dead who gave their lives for them turn in their graves?

The greatest of the non-Christian tribe problems in the Philippines at present is, "Shall the work go on?"

There is one satisfaction which no man can take from those of us who have worked for the advancement of these backward and hitherto neglected peoples. We have shown what can be done!

CHAPTER XXV

SLAVERY AND PEONAGE

CHATTEL slavery existed in the Philippine Islands when Magellan discovered them in 1521. It exists there to-day. Morga, who was in the Philippines from 1595 to about 1608, and is admittedly the most reliable chronicler of the events of those early days, has given the following interesting account of the conditions then existing : [1] —

"There are three classes of persons among the natives of these Islands, by which the commonwealth is divided: *principales*, of whom I have spoken before; *timawa* which is the same as plebeians, and slaves, of *principales* as well as of *timawa*. These slaves were of various classes: some are in entire servitude and slavery, like those which we have, and these are called *sagigilir;* they served in the interior of the houses and so also the children descended from them; others, who have their own dwellings, which they inhabit with their family, away from the house of their master, and these come in at times to help the latter in their fields and crops, as also aboard the vessel when they embark, and in the construction of their houses whenever they erect such, and they also serve in their houses whenever there is a guest of some distinction, and they are under obligation, whenever the master has them called, to come to his house and to serve him in this ministry without pay or other stipend; these are called *namamahai*, and their children and descendents are slaves of the same condition. Of these slaves *sagigilir* and *namamahai* there are some who are slaves entirely, and others who are only half slaves, and others who are slaves only for a fourth part. This originates thus: if either the father or the mother was free and they had a single child, the latter was half free and half slave. If they had more than one child, the children were distributed in this way: the first followed the condition of the

[1] Rizal's 1890 edition of Morga's "Sucesos de las Islas Filipinas," p. 297, *et seq.*

676

father, be he free or a slave, and the second that of the mother;
and if the number was uneven, the last child was half free and
half slave; and those descended from such child, if they had
a free father or a free mother, remained slave only for a fourth
part, because they were children of a free father, or mother,
and of a half slave. These half or quarter slaves, *namamahai* or
sagigilir, serve their masters only every second month, respectively, in proportion to their condition as slave.

"Among the natives the ordinary price of a slave *sagigilir*
used to be, if much, ten taes of good gold, worth 80 pesos, and
if he is a *namamahai* half of that, and thus in proportion the
others, taking into account the personality and age.

"It cannot be established as a principle from where these
classes of servitude among the natives arose, for they are all of
the islands and not foreigners; it is understood that they
made them in their wars and differences; and the most certain
is that those who were most powerful made and took as slaves
the others for slight causes and occasions, and most often
through loans and usurious contracts current amongst them, the
payment, risk and debt increasing with the lapse of time until
they became slaves; and thus all these forms of servitude have
their violent and unjust origin, and it is about them that there
arise the greater part of the lawsuits that exist among the
natives and with which they keep busy the judges in the forum
of the court, and the confessors in that of the conscience."

To the last of the preceding paragraphs Rizal makes
the following annotation, which, *mutatis mutandis*, should
give leading Filipinos of to-day matter for reflection : —

"This class of slaves exists even now in many parts, and
before all in the province of Batangas, but it must be confessed
that their condition is very different from that of a slave in
Greece, or Rome, from that of the negro, and even of those
made in later times by Spaniards. . . .

"Filipinas, in spite of so many centuries of christianiza-
tion, in spite of the efforts of some few noble minds, priests
as well as civilians, continues still, and is desired to continue,
almost in the same state as formerly, for those who direct
the country look more to the present than to the future, and
because they are guided not by confidence, but by fear. The
efforts of the religious corporations to improve this state of
things have never been as efficacious, nor as strenuous, as
might have been expected from them."

Morga continues : [1] —

"These slaves are the greatest wealth and capital which the natives of these islands possess, because they are to them very useful and necessary for their labors and farms; and among them they are sold, exchanged, and made objects of contract, like any other merchandise, from one pueblo to the other, from one province to the other, and likewise from one island to the other. For which reason, and in order to avoid so many lawsuits that would arise, if the question of these servitudes, their origin and beginning, were taken up, they [the slaves, Tr.] are retained and kept as they were kept formerly."

Rizal comments on this passage as follows : —

"Thus catholicism not only did not liberate the poor class from the tyranny of the oppressive, but with its advent in the Philippines increased the number of tyrants. Time alone, and instruction, which with it brings suaver customs, will ultimately redeem the Pariahs of the Philippines, for we see that the apostles of the peace did not find in themselves sufficient valour to battle with the oppressors, and this in times of great faith; on the contrary, they rather contributed indirectly to their misery, as we see from the foregoing."

· The most frequent cause, already mentioned above, from which these conditions of servitude arose, is again pointed out by Morga in the following passage : [2] —

"Loans with interest were in very common practice, excessively high rates of interest being current, so that the debt doubled and multiplied all the time during which the payment was deferred, until there was taken from the debtor what he possessed as capital, and, when ultimately nothing more was left, his person and his children."

Of these statements Rizal says : —

"This is the sad truth, and so much the truth that it subsists until now. In many provinces, and in many towns, there is taking place, word for word, what Morga says, it being to be lamented that at present not only Indios [Filipinos, Tr.] continue this usury, but also the *mestizos*, the Spaniards, and even various priests. And it has come to this that the Govern-

[1] "Sucesos," p. 300.   [2] *Ibid.*, p. 305.

A MANDAYAN BOY.

ment itself not only permits it, but in its turn exacts the capital and the person in payment of the debt of others, as occurs with the *cabeza de barangay*."

It would be easy to compile passages similar to the preceding from other authors, but those given are explicit and authoritative enough to make it clear, first, that slavery existed in the Philippines at the time of the conquest as a general tribal institution of social and economical character and in minutely regulated form; and, second, that although it lost, with the advent of the Spaniards, the character of an institution, and indeed was formally abolished by early edicts from Spain, it continued to exist as an unauthorized practice, so that Rizal, writing at the close of the nineteenth century could say that slaves still existed in many parts of the country.

In a statement recently published in the *New York Evening Post*, Señor Quezon, Resident Delegate from the Philippines to Congress, has said : —

"Since there is not, and there never was, slavery in the territory inhabited by the Christian Filipinos, which is the part of the Islands subject to the legislative control of the Assembly, this House has refused to concur in the anti-slavery bill passed by the Philippine Commission."

Whom will the American public believe, Morga, the historian, and Rizal, the Filipino patriot, or Quezon, the Filipino politician?

While I entertain no doubt as to the answer, I shall nevertheless discuss at length the more recent history and present status of slavery and peonage in the Philippines, because of the vital importance of full knowledge of the facts to intelligent consideration of the claim that the Filipinos have arrived at a stage of civilization comparable with that of the more advanced nations of the world, and are capable of establishing and maintaining a just and humane government.

The Spanish Penal Code did not prohibit or penalize slavery, or the purchase or sale of human beings. It did contain provisions against forcible detention of individuals and the abduction of minors, but in the Philippines at least they were more honoured in the breach than in the observance during the Spanish régime.

The Moros raided the towns of the peaceful Filipino inhabitants of the Visayan Islands and of Luzón until within quite recent times. An unhappy fate awaited the prisoners whom they took. Men were frequently compelled to harvest for their captors the crops which they themselves had planted, and were then mercilessly butchered. Women, girls and boys were carried away into slavery, the former to serve as household drudges or as concubines, and the latter to be brought up as slaves pure and simple. Some men met a similar fate. The only reason that more were not enslaved was that it was usually considered too much trouble to make full-grown individuals work. Slaves were held as chattels if it suited the convenience of their masters to retain them, and otherwise were sold, bartered or given away. Zamboanga was at the outset largely populated by escaped Moro slaves who had sought the protection of the Spanish garrison there. Coming originally from widely separated parts of the archipelago, these unfortunates had no common native dialect, hence there arose among them a Spanish patois now known as *Zamboangueño*.

The American occupation brought many and brusque changes in political conditions. The attitude of Americans toward slavery and peonage was very different from that of the easy-going Spaniards, who had never sanctioned it but had never made any determined effort to break it up.

From the effective establishment of United States sovereignty in 1899 until July 4, 1901, the Philippines were under military rule, which has one great advantage : its methods usually bring quick results.

Doubtless the majority of the slaves then held in the islands were too timid, and too suspicious of the character and purposes of Americans, to appeal to them for protection ; but there were not a few whose lives had become so unbearable that they were prepared to take almost any risk on the chance of securing release. People of this class ran away from their masters and sought the protection of army officers. I am glad to say that in every such instance which has come to my knowledge it was promptly given. Not only were they advised that they could not be held in bondage, and were free to go where they pleased, but when practicable their masters were warned against attempting to regain control over them. It is probable that the large majority of such cases were never officially reported. Most of the army officers concerned were in some doubt as to their legal status in the premises, but they knew that the constitution of the United States prohibits slavery ; their sympathies went out to the wretched human beings who appealed to them for aid, and they decided to be a law unto themselves.

After the establishment of civil government some army officers continued to exercise arbitrary powers in dealing with such cases of slavery as came to their attention, while others contented themselves with reporting them to the civil authorities.

The conditions which prevailed in the Moro Province in 1902 are concisely described by its military governor, General George W. Davis, in a report written on August 25 of that year. He said : —

"With a people who have no conception of government that is not arbitrary and absolute ; who hold human life as no more sacred than the life of an animal ; who have become accustomed to acts of violence ; who are constrained by fear from continuing the practice of piracy ; who still carry on slave trade ; who habitually raid the homes of mountain natives and enslave them ; who habitually make slaves of their captives in war — even when of their own race ; who not uncommonly make delivery of their own kindred as slaves in satisfaction of a debt for liquidation of which they have not the ready money; who habitually observe the precepts of the Koran, which declares that female slaves must submit to their masters, — it is useless to discuss a plan of government that is not based on physical force, might, and power."

Señor Quezon, in describing conditions in the Moro country, has said : [1] —

"American authorities made treaties with the Sultan of Joló whereby slavery was legalized and recognized among the non-Christian Moros and received the protection of the United States army and civil authorities. This state of things continued for a long time under official recognition and even after the treaties in question were abandoned it was allowed to go on despite the protests of Filipino and American students of the question."

It is true that General Bates attempted to negotiate a treaty with the Sultan of Joló, in which he felt himself compelled to recognize slavery as an existing Moro custom. This action was unauthorized and was disapproved by his superiors. It did not legalize slavery. Neither Moro nor any other kind of slavery was ever protected by the civil authorities.

The act providing for the organization of the Moro Province was passed on June 1, 1903, and hardly had the civil officers therein provided for been appointed when, on September 24, 1903, the legislative council passed an act entitled "An Act defining the crimes of slaveholding and slavehunting and prescribing the punishment therefor," [2] which was promptly approved by the Philippine Commission and thus came to have the force and effect of law. Under it active measures were adopted to

---

[1] "The Filipino People," Vol. 2, No. 1, p. 15, September, 1913.

[2] On July 15, 1913, I published an official report, as secretary of the interior, on "Slavery and Peonage in the Philippine Islands." It is hereinafter referred to in foot-notes under the title of "Slavery and Peonage." Beginning on p. 84 of this document will be found extracts from court records showing convictions obtained under this act, which is quoted in full on p. 83 of the same document.

break up slavery in the Moro Province. They have resulted very successfully, and persons who have captured others to be held or sold as slaves, as well as persons who have actually sold, bought or kept slaves, have been convicted and punished.

Señor Quezon's statement relative to the attitude of the civil authorities in this matter is therefore recklessly false.

The existence of slavery in the Moro Province was well known from the outset, hence the immediate enactment of legislation to meet the special conditions which prevailed there.

Little by little the commission learned that slavery was by no means confined to Moro territory, and that peonage was general throughout the islands.

Before going further, I wish to make clear the sense in which I use these terms.

I define slavery as the condition of a human being held as a chattel and compelled to render service for which he is not compensated. As food and clothing are necessarily furnished by the slave owner, they are not considered to constitute compensation.

Peonage I define as the condition of a debtor held by his creditor in a form of qualified servitude to work out a debt.

On April 28, 1903, the senior inspector of constabulary in Isabela wired the first district chief of constabulary, Manila, as follows : —

"In this province a common practice to own slaves. These are bought by *proprietarios* [property owners. — D. C. W.] from Igorrotes and Calingas who steal same in distant places from other tribes. Young boys and girls are bought at about 100 pesos, men 30 years old and old women cheaper. When bought, are generally christened and put to work on ranch or in house, and I think generally well-treated. In this town a number sold within last few months, and as reported to me, Governor has bought three. Shall I investigate further? Instructions desired.

(Signed) "SORENSON."

Senior Inspector Sorenson was instructed to make a thorough investigation of, and a detailed report on, the slave question.

On May 2 he complied with these instructions,[1] describing the conditions under which slaves were taken by the neighbouring Kalingas and Ifugaos, whom he wrongly calls "Igorrotes," the methods employed in selling them, and the treatment subsequently given them by their purchasers.

He also furnished a list of "Igorrotes" sold in the province during the past year, with names of the purchasers and prices paid. The ages of these unhappy individuals varied from eight to twenty-seven years, the prices paid for them, from one hundred and ten to two hundred and fifty Mexican dollars.

This report led Governor Taft to write to Governor Dichoso of Isabela, who was charged with owning a slave, asking him for a frank statement of the facts as to the prevalence of slavery in his province.

Governor Dichoso's reply, dated September 9, 1903, will make interesting reading for those who claim that slavery does not exist, and has never existed, among the Filipinos. I give it practically in full, omitting only the titles of the governor : —

"Having noted the contents of the official letter of the Honourable the Civil Governor in the Philippine Islands, Mr. W. H. Taft, dated the 8th of August, last, and of the copy of the report annexed thereto, which were received yesterday, I have the honour to respectfully reply that during the 21 years, more or less, that I have resided in this provincial capital (Ilagan), I have never thought of buying a member or a child of the race mentioned in the report, or of any other tribe, to serve as a slave in my household, not for the reason that this is prohibited and punished by section 484 and the following sections of the Spanish Code now in force, relative to the crime of kidnapping, but because it goes against my nature to treat in this

[1] For the full text of this interesting and important report see "Slavery and Peonage," p. 85.

manner a person who, like all human beings alive, is a likeness of the Highest. This I prove by means of the documents annexed hereto.

"I could easily have done so in time of the late Spanish Government, because I had good opportunities for doing so, and could have afforded to do so on account of my social position from that time on up to date, during which period I held successively the following public offices : —

* * * * * * *

"This having been my status, and considering the power and the opportunity which I had for obtaining slaves, I might not have had only one, but enough to harvest the tobacco on my plantation, and the other crops which I had planted.

"Under the past Government there existed slaves in this province, but only a small number, for only wealthy families could afford to keep them. The same was the case in the neighbouring Provinces of Neuva Vizcaya and Cagayan ; in the former they also used to have slaves of the Ifugao tribe, and in the latter Negritos, but very few of these.

"Since the glorious Star-Spangled Banner has been unfolded over the Province of Isabela, the slaves existing in the same, which had been purchased in that time and recently, are very well treated and seem to be members of the family, because the military authorities prohibited their masters from ill-treating them as they were wont to do. Since then many of the slaves have run away from their owners and have sought new masters who treat them well, as it happened in the case of an Igorrote woman of the Ifugao tribe, who was about 40 years of age, and who had been in the service of a lady in the pueblo of Echague for many years. When, in the year 1900, the military enforced the prohibition of ill-treatment of slaves in the said pueblo, this Igorrote woman ran away and presented herself at my house, I being at this time justice of the peace of this provincial capital, and asked me to employ her as servant. My principle not to have slaves preventing me from complying with her wishes, I directed her to apply to Mr. Andres Claraval and his wife, Filomena Salinas. They accepted her, and a short time afterwards they had her baptized and christened Magdalena Claraval. She is being treated like an adopted daughter by them.

"The gentlemen who are mentioned in the report as having purchased slaves really acquired Igorrotes by purchase and keep them in their house, some of them having died since. Some of these transactions were made in the Spanish times, as in the case of the late Mr. Policarpo Gangan, who bought 6 or 7 Ifugaos, whom on his death he left to his children, Mr. Pedro Gangan, Mrs. Susana Gangan, Miss Maria Gangan, and Mrs. Rufina Gangan, and others were made recently and secretly, while I was absent from town on official business in the pueblos of this province.   Mr. Thomas Gollayan, the late provincial secretary, bought two Igorrotes while I was in Manila in December and January, last.   They were well aware of the fact that I prosecuted kidnapping with tenacity, my object being to put a stop, if possible, to this abominable practice, which has since some time prevailed in the pueblos of this province. . . .

"In order to prove that I endeavoured to make the proper investigation for the purpose of proving whether slavery really existed in this province, I have the honour to annex an affidavit by Agapito Telan, a resident of Ilagan, in which it appears that he sold Igorrotes of the Ifugao tribe to several residents of this town.   I was unable to ascertain the numbers of Igorrotes of the same tribe sold by Modesto Sibal, Lorenzo Montevirgen, Lorenzo Montalvo, Andres Castro, and Cosme Ferrer, who are engaged in the same business as Agapito Telan, as it appears from the deposition of the latter, for the reason that these persons did not appear before me, although in 1902 I had on several occasions verbally requested the late municipal president, Mr. Pascual Paguirigan, to cause them to appear in an unofficial manner.   I was not surprised that they did not appear before me, as Paguirigan was involved in the investigation, as it happened in the case of the aforesaid Agapito Telan, who appeared before me when I asked the acting municipal president to have him do so.

"I was afraid to direct those persons to appear before me by means of written orders, because I had not document or complaint whereon to base them, as required by the procedure now in force, and feared that on account of the unlawful nature of the summons they might proceed against me for coaccion, and sue me besides for damages.

"According to my personal observation and to what I have seen in the other pueblos of this Province of Isabela, but principally in the provincial capital, the Igorrotes who are said to be slaves cannot be considered as such since the times of the military government, as they are considered and treated as members of the family of the chief of the household.   Nevertheless, I am and shall continue to be inexorable in the prosecution of slavery, as it is a crime and should be prosecuted as such, in order to prevent at least that the persons engaged in this business commit this crime again.

A GROUP OF BAGOBOS.

These people have, until within a short time, made human sacrifices in order to propitiate their divinities. They live in Mindanao, near the Gulf of Davao.

"It is my humble opinion that an act should be passed to the end of eradicating this practice which has become general throughout the Cagayan Valley.[1] Otherwise, as I have seen in my continual efforts, the provincial authorities cannot do anything to check the evil, however they may try. It is necessary that some one should be made to feel the rigour of the act suggested and suffer the punishment designated by it.

"As a rule the inhabitants of this province already understand personal liberty and know that a person is entitled to go wherever he pleases, which liberty has given birth to the humane treatment of the fellow-men which now prevails.

"Caciquism is still existing in parts of this province, but I am confident that with the coöperation of sensible persons in my continuous efforts it will be completely eradicated, and personal liberty will reign supreme, as in every republic where the laws assure complete and real liberty, the liberty from slavery."

As supporting evidence Governor Dichoso forwarded with his letter a number of statements from persons resident in the capital of Isabela to the effect that during the twenty-one years that he had lived there he had never purchased, intended to purchase, or kept in his house any Igorrote of the Ifugao or any other tribe.

In addition he forwarded a somewhat unique document in the form of a sworn statement by a slave dealer which is of such interest that I give it in its entirety : —

"I, Agapito Telan, a resident of this provincial capital (Ilagan), certify : On the 19th of June, 1903, I was summoned by the provincial governor, Mr. Francisco Dichoso y Reyes, and when I was with him in the office of the provincial government, he and the secretary took my sworn deposition, as follows : —

"Upon being asked to state the number of children of the infidel tribe of the Ifugaos sold by me to several residents of this provincial capital, the approximate age of these children, the names of the persons to whom they were sold, the number of children bought by these persons, the value of each of the said children, their sex, and the year, month, and day on which the said sales were made, deponent replied that in the year

[1] This valley includes the Provinces of Cagayan and Isabela.

1902, in the month of September, and on a day which he cannot remember, he sold to the late Policarpo Gangan two Ifugao boys, of the ages of 8 and 9, respectively, for the sum of 360 Mexican dollars, another boy, 9 years of age, he sold to Juan Dauag for the sum of 180 Mexican dollars, and another boy, 8 years of age, he sold to Seferino Malana for the sum of 160 Mexican dollars, the latter two being sold on the same month and year aforementioned, and in Ilagan also.

"In the year of 1903 the deponent sold a boy and a girl of the Ifugao tribe, who, judging by their physical development, were about 6 and 8 years old; the boy, six years of age, he sold to Pascual Paguirigan, late municipal president, and the girl to Doña Rufina Gangan, for the sum of 180 Mexican dollars each. This was in January, but deponent does not remember the day.

"In February he sold a boy and a girl of the same tribe, 8 years of age, the former to Cirilo Gantinao and the latter to Salvador Aggabao, for 180 Mexican dollars each. The purchasers are residents of this town.

"Upon being asked who are the other persons who, like deponent, are engaged in taking Ifugao children from the settlements of the infidels and then selling the same to whomever wants them, and that he state where they reside, deponent replied that the persons who are engaged in the same business as he, are Modesto Sibal, Lorenzo Monte-Virgen, and Lorenzo Montalvo, residents of the pueblo of Gamú, and Andres Castro and Cosme Ferrer, residents of this provincial capital.

"Upon being asked whether he knew if these persons are like him engaged in the purchase of minors and what was the number of children taken by each during the year of 1902 and 1903, and if so, to state to whom they were sold, and at what price the deponent replied that he is completely ignorant of the matter in regard to which information is requested, but that it was possible that they had taken more children, as they are living nearer to the settlements from which they are taken, and as they are able to make the trip three times to the defendant's once.

"Asked what methods they employ for the purpose of getting children from that tribe, deponent says that all they do is to enter into a contract with those whom they consider their dattos or chiefs, and who come down from the mountains with the children, which are purchased from them by the persons engaged in this trade.

"Asked to state the price of the children bought at the accustomed places for these transactions for the purpose of reselling them, the deponent states that the children are sold at the same price at which they are purchased at that place.

"He having thus stated, the foregoing was read to him, and he agreed to it, signing it after the Provincial Governor, which I, the secretary appointed for this act, attest.

"FRANCISCO DICHOSO,
"Provincial Governor.
"AGAPITO TELAN,
" FERNANDO DOMINGO.
" Secretary appointed.
(Sgd.) "AGAPITO TELAN.

"Subscribed and sworn to before me this 10th day of September, 1903.

(Sgd.) "FRANCISCO TAUAD,
"Clerk of the Court, Ilagan."

The existence of slavery in Misamis, a regularly organized province, had been disclosed at a still earlier date.

In May, 1902, its Filipino governor, Sr. Manuel Corrales, was asked to report, and did report, on slavery in that province, under the following circumstances : —

On May 2, 1902, General George W. Davis telegraphed the Adjutant-General, Manila : —

"Following telegram respectfully repeated: 'Zamboanga, May 1, 1902, via Malabang, to Wade. Commanding Officer, Misamis, reports April 30, that *Presidente* notified him that he was going to send armed party to capture two Moro slaves which have escaped from their Filipino master whose names were not given. Says there are many Filipinos who own slaves. *Presidente* was told that the troops had nothing to do with civilian affairs. I have no doubt but that the Filipinos on the north coast here have many slaves. At Butuan I saw one in November that had been recently purchased.'"

Governor-General Wright referred a copy of this telegram to Governor Corrales with an indorsement —

"calling his attention to the within communication. Information is desired as to whether or not the within facts are true as stated, and also whether there are any persons held in involuntary servitude other than convicts within the province, and if so, that full particulars be given."

Governor Corrales himself has none too good a record in connection with the treatment accorded the non-Christians of his province, and would certainly not paint a darker picture than was called for by the facts, yet in his reply [1] he gives the names of six towns in which "one still finds a few slave servants, most of them acquired many years ago." He adds : —

"At the present time, there are but few sales of slaves proceeding from the mountain tribes, which are now relatively civilized. In Iligan and Misamis, I have heard that such sales were more frequent, for two reasons: (1) the Moro race is more despotic and more numerous; (2) the weekly market in Iligan gives them an opportunity to carry on that sort of business, although they have to do it by stealth, on account of the watchfulness of the authorities.

"I will call your attention to the fact that the slaves proceeding from the Moro district constitute, in the Moro villages, an inferior social class, the slave family, whose origin is due to the prisoners taken by the Dattos on their expeditions; when they are transferred to the Christians in Iligan or Misamis, because their masters wish to make money, or are hard pressed by the famines which are so frequent in the region of the Lanao, their condition is considerably improved by the good treatment and the better and more abundant food which they obtain in their new situation, by the mere fact that they live with a more civilized people.

"Those who come from the mountain tribes are not born slaves; with few exceptions, the chiefs and principal men of these tribes do not own slaves which they use for their service or for agricultural work, as the Moros do. Slaves are generally obtained in the following way : —

"It happens that a chief with bellicose and sanguinary instincts, who leads a nomad life and does not belong to the peaceful class which is given to farm life, organizes a gang of men of his sort, makes incursions in the wildest parts of the woods and raids the lone huts inhabited by savage and nomad families; he kills by treachery the grown-up people and carries off the children, which he can easily master; he then sells them to the peaceful farm dwellers, who sell them in their turn to the Christian pueblos.

[1] For the full text of this document see "Slavery and Peonage," pp. 12–14.

"As I have already said, such cases are happily rare. In Iligan and Misamis, which are far from the capital of the province, and therefore from the Court and the provincial authorities, the slaves have had less opportunity to claim their rights, and it is not astonishing that neither the slaves nor their masters have a true notion of what is meant by individual liberty, although the former are at least sure of their lives since they left the jurisdiction of the Moros, at whose absolute mercy they were, and are much better treated among the Christians.

"I intend taking all necessary measures within my jurisdiction in order to put an end to such a hateful trade, and wait for any further instructions which you may deem it convenient to give me."

Unfortunately neither the measures taken by Governor Corrales nor those adopted by his successors have sufficed to end this "hateful trade" in the province of Misamis.

In July of the present year,[1] a man accused of holding two Bukidnon children in slavery did not deny the charge, but set up the defence that he was a resident of Misamis, where there was no law against this crime. He had been proceeded against under an anti-slavery law passed by the commission for the provinces under its exclusive jurisdiction, on the theory that he resided in Agusan. He won his case, proving that his house was about a hundred yards over the line.

The revelations contained in the reports above mentioned naturally called for action. Inspector Sorenson's report was referred to the commission with the following indorsement : —

"OFFICE OF THE CIVIL GOVERNOR,
"MANILA, August 13, 1903.

"The Senior Inspector of Constabulary in the Province of Isabela reports that there is quite a slave trade in the Cagayan Valley. The report of Sorenson, the Inspector, is submitted to the Commission and I suggest a reference to Commissioner Wright in order that he may include in the Criminal Code some clauses which will enable us to reach this abuse.

(Signed) "WM. H. TAFT,
"*Civil Governor.*"

[1] 1913.

The report was, by direction of the commission, referred to Commissioner Wright as suggested by Governor Taft for consideration in connection with a proposed new Criminal Code which was being prepared, under his general supervision, for enactment. An immense amount of work was necessary on this code, and it was never completed and enacted. Various matters needing attention have since been reached through the medium of special laws, and it is obvious that it was intended to pursue this course in this instance, as is shown by the fact that Governor Dichoso's reply was forwarded to General Wright on October 19, 1903, with the following indorsement : —

[First Indorsement]

"EXECUTIVE BUREAU,
"MANILA, October 19, 1903.

"Respectfully referred to the Secretary of Commerce and Police, for his information and consideration in connection with the proposed Act denouncing slavery and kidnapping and kindred offences as crimes.

(Signed) "WM. H. TAFT,
"*Civil Governor.*"

Why such an act was not drafted and passed I do not know. I was then absent on leave, and did not even learn of the existence of any of the above-quoted documents until years afterward. My personal attention was forcibly drawn to the existence of slavery outside of the Moro territory when I first inspected Nueva Vizcaya in 1905. The territory occupied by the Ifugaos, since separated as a sub-province of the Mountain Province, was then a part of Nueva Vizcaya, which had been organized as a province under a special act and was, in a way, subject to my executive control.

Its governor, Louis G. Knight, called my attention to the fact that Ifugao children were frequently enslaved by Filipinos of Nueva Vizcaya and Isabela. I asked him to get specific data so that we might prosecute the offenders.

Moro Boats coming out to meet the Philippine Commission at Jolo.

He soon sent to the Executive Secretary a report [1] which gave full details of a number of recent cases of the buying and selling of Ifugaos as slaves, contained a statement that Governor Knight, who was himself a lawyer, could "find nothing whatever in the penal code defining or punishing as a crime the buying or selling of human beings," and recommended that "this crime be defined and punished in the proposed new penal code."

The report was referred to me by the executive secretary on September 20, 1905, and on September 22 was by me forwarded to the Honourable Luke E. Wright, governor-general, with an indorsement —

"inviting attention to the inclosed statements from the Governor of Nueva Vizcaya, relative to the traffic in Igorrote children in his province.

"The undersigned has reason to believe that Negrito children and children of other non-Christian tribes are occasionally bought and sold by civilized natives, and is strongly of the opinion that in case the Penal Code does not provide adequate punishment for such offences, it should be so amended as to make it possible to inflict severe penalties upon those who buy and sell human beings in this Archipelago.

(Signed) "DEAN C. WORCESTER,
"Secretary of the Interior."

The papers were referred by Governor-General Wright to the Attorney-General —

"for an opinion as to whether there is not some provision in the present Penal Code which will provide adequate punishment for such offences as are related herein."

The opinion of the Attorney-General rendered in response to this request [2] encouraged me to believe that something could be done under existing law.

[1] For the full text of this document see "Slavery and Peonage," pp. 23–25.

[2] "Respectfully returned to the Honourable the Governor-General of the Philippine Islands, with the following opinion:

"The acts given in the attached letter of the Provincial Governor of Nueva Vizcaya, dated September 14, 1905, in so far as they refer

I returned the papers, together with the opinion, to the governor of Nueva Vizcaya and three test suits were brought as promptly as possible.

One of them has become historic. It was brought against Tomás Cabanag, a well-known slave dealer who made a business of buying and selling Ifugao children.

to the purchase and sale of human beings, are not provided for or punished under the existing Penal Code; but such actions are punishable under that Code when they constitute either the kidnapping of a minor, illegal detention or serious threats, according to sections 481, 484 and 494 thereof.

"Therefore, in accordance with the fourth paragraph of the letter of the said Provincial Governor, I am of the opinion that not only the Igorrotes who stole the Igorrote boy, but also those who received and sold him, as well as the woman who bought him for forty pesos, are guilty of illegal detention. The latter is furthermore guilty of grave threats, inasmuch as she threatened to kill the purchased Igorrote if he tried to escape from her service.

"With reference to paragraphs 5, 6, 7 and 8 of the attached letter, I believe that those who stole the little Igorrote and also the woman Antonia, who sold him when knowing him to have been kidnapped, are guilty of the offence of illegal detention.

"If the boy who was stolen and sold, referred to in paragraphs 9, 10, 11, 12 and 13 of the enclosed letter, was under seven years of age, then those who stole him are guilty of the offence of kidnapping a minor, and the Igorrote woman, Antonia, and the wife of Señor Arriola, the Clerk of the Court, are accomplices in the crime. But if the child was over seven years old, then the offence would be illegal detention. The same may be said of the case recounted in paragraphs 14 and 15 of this communication. The parties who stole, sold and bought the little Igorrote are guilty of kidnapping a minor or of illegal detention according to the age of the victim.

"The acts committed by Captain Vicente Tomang, referred to in paragraph 16 of this letter, are punishable both as a serious threat and as illegal detention, because he unlawfully deprived the two Igorrote women of their liberty when they desired to leave his service, for which purpose he threatened to kill them.

"Although not asked for in the indorsement to which this is a reply, I venture to suggest that the Igorrotes who armed themselves and formed a band for the purpose of kidnapping persons for subsequent sale, be punished under Act 1121, which penalizes as *bandolerismo* the abduction of persons for any purpose, even though there may be no extortion or ransom demanded, if the abduction be done by an armed band.

(Signed)   "L. R. WILFLEY,
            "*Attorney-General.*"

He was charged with illegal detention in connection with the admitted sale, by him, of an Ifugao girl named Gamaya.[1]

He was convicted in the Court of First Instance. I quote the following extract from the decision of the court :

"The Congress of the United States has declared that human slavery shall not exist in these islands and while no law, so far as I can discover, has yet been passed either defining slavery in these islands or affixing a punishment for those who engage in this inhuman practice as dealers, buyers, sellers, or derivers, the facts established in this case show conclusively that the child Jimaya was by the defendant forcibly and by fraud, deceit and threats unlawfully deprived of her liberty and that his object and purpose was an unlawful and illegal one, to wit, the sale of the child for money into human slavery. This constitutes the crime of *Detencion ilegal* defined and penalized by Article 481 of the Penal Code and this Court finds the defendant guilty as charged in the information."

The case was promptly appealed to the Supreme Court and was there lost on March 16, 1907.

Gamaya, a thirteen-year-old Ifugao girl, had been purchased from her mother for pigs, hens, rice and a cloak, under the absurd pretext that the object of the purchase was to keep her at home, where she would, of course, naturally have remained in any event. She was allowed to stay with her mother during a period of some three years. In this manner the purchaser was saved the cost of boarding her while she was growing up. Having now reached what the Igorots consider a marriageable age, she was sold to a man who was engaged in the business of buying in Nueva Vizcaya children to sell in the lowlands of Isabela ; in other words, to a slave dealer. He sold her to an inhabitant of the town of Caoayan, in Isabela, who had instructed him to buy a girl. Caoayan is distant many days of hard overland travel from this girl's home. When taken there she was among an alien

---

[1] Also written "Jamaya."

people of another tribe and another religion, and although, as stated by the Supreme Court, she was not kept under lock and key and although that court held that : —

" . . . There can be no unlawful detention under article 481 of the Penal Code without confinement or restraint of person, such as did not exist in the present case."

and held further that : —

"Under the complaint for this crime it is possible to convict for *coacción* under proof of the requisites of that offence . . . but among those requisites is that of violence through force or intimidation, even under the liberal rule of our jurisprudence . . .; consequently the charge of *coacción* against the accused cannot be sustained upon the evidence."

it is nevertheless true that this child, who had been thrice sold, was detained just as effectively in Caoayan as if chained to a post in the house of the man who bought her, and was required by him to perform menial labour without compensation. It would have been utterly impossible for her to escape and to make her way back through Isabela and Nueva Vizcaya to her own people, no matter how strenuously she might have endeavoured to do so.

It is extremely difficult to prove forcible detention in connection with most cases of slavery in these islands. Negrito slaves are usually purchased when mere babes and later have no recollection of their parents or of their former wild life in the hills. Babes or very young children bring a better price than do older children, for the reason that they are less likely to run away.

Adult Negritos, and adult members of other tribes held in slavery, have, as a rule, been made to feel the heavy hand of the oppressor and are so afraid of their lives that they will not testify. Only under very exceptional circumstances will they admit that they are being held against their will, although they are quick to make their escape when a favourable opportunity presents itself.

The difficulty involved in protecting these simple people is illustrated by the following case which came to my personal attention : —

An eleven-year-old Bukidnon girl was carried away from northern Mindanao to Bohol by a Filipino school-teacher who had been discharged from the insular service. Her parents gave every indication of bitter grief and begged to have their daughter restored to them. This was finally accomplished, to their great joy, as a result of my efforts. The kidnapper was ultimately brought into court, but before the case came up for trial the parents had been subjected to such "influence" that when called to the witness-stand they swore that the kidnapper had taken their daughter with their full knowledge and consent.

In order to be reasonably effective, laws in these islands must be so framed as to make it possible to protect people too ignorant, or too timid, to protect themselves.

Returning now to the Supreme Court decision, the court also held that : —

". . . the defendant appears to have engaged in the business of buying in Nueva Vizcaya children to sell in the lowlands of Isabela."

But it further held that : —

"Not even the abhorrent species of traffic apparently carried on by the accused justifies a sentence not authorized by law."

More important still, the court held that : —

"The judge below quotes the Bill of Rights of the Philippines contained in the Act of Congress of July 1, 1902, declaring that 'neither slavery nor involuntary servitude, except as a punishment for crime whereof the party shall have been duly convicted, shall exist in said Islands.' This constitutional provision is self-acting whenever the nature of a case permits and any law or contract providing for the servitude of a person against his will is forbidden and is void. For two obvious reasons, however, it fails to reach the facts before us : —
"First. The employment or custody of a minor with the consent or sufferance of the parents or guardian, although

against the child's own will, cannot be considered involuntary servitude.

"Second. We are dealing not with a civil remedy but with a criminal charge, in relation to which the Bill of Rights defines no crime and provides no punishment. Its effects cannot be carried into the realm of criminal law without an act of the legislature,"

and also that : —

"To sum up this case, there is no proof of slavery or even of involuntary servitude, inasmuch as it has not been clearly shown that the child has been disposed of against the will of her grandmother or has been taken altogether out of her control. If the facts in this respect be interpreted otherwise, there is no law applicable here, either of the United States or of the Archipelago, punishing slavery as a crime."

In view of the facts above cited the necessity for legislation seemed obvious.

The commission in its capacity as sole legislative body for the territory inhabited by Moros or other non-Christian tribes might have passed an act prohibiting and penalizing slavery, involuntary servitude and peonage in that territory ; but such an act unless supplemented by a similar one applicable to the neighbouring Filipino territory where most of the slaves are actually held would obviously have been ineffective, while the desirability of having uniform legislation throughout the Philippines was evident.

The Philippine Assembly was about to meet for the first time. The work of drafting a proper bill was duly provided for and I am sure that no member of the commission for a moment entertained the belief that there would be any difficulty in securing the concurrence of the assembly in the passage of a reasonable act prohibiting and penalizing slavery, involuntary servitude, peonage and the sale and purchase of human beings. The gentleman charged with drafting the bill encountered difficulty in so framing it that it would accomplish the desired end without unduly interfering with the rights of parents over their children. Long delay ensued.

I myself finally drafted a bill entitled: "An Act prohibiting slavery, involuntary servitude, peonage, or the sale of human beings in the Philippine Islands," and introduced it in the commission.

It was passed, in slightly amended form, on April 29, 1909, and sent to the Philippine assembly, where it was introduced on May 6, 1909. On May 7 it was referred to the Committee on Revision of Laws, and on May 17 it was returned by that committee with the following report : —

"May 17, 1909.

"MR. SPEAKER: The committee concurs with the Commission in the approval of Bill No. 100 with the following amendments :

"(a) That the word 'slavery' be stricken out of the title of the Act, because it does not exist in the Philippines.

"(b) That from section 1, page 1, lines 7 and 8, the following words be stricken out: 'take the fruits of his labours, compel him to deliver to another the fruits of his labours,' since the acts contained therein constitute other crimes that may be *robo*, *hurto*, or *estafa*.

"(c) From line 11 in the same section the words: 'less than six months nor;' and from line 12 the words: 'less than one hundred pesos and not;' because the acts penalized in section 1 may be of such slight importance that they should not deserve a punishment of imprisonment for six months or a fine of one hundred pesos.

"(d) From line 22 (p. 2), the word: 'peso,' substituting for it: 'two pesos and a half.'

"With these enactments Commission Bill No. 100 is drawn up, according to the one attached hereto.

"For these reasons the committee submits for the consideration of the Assembly Commission Bill No. 100 and recommends its approval with the amendments introduced.

"Respectfully submitted.

(Signed) "AGUEDO VELARDE,
"Chairman, Committee on Revision of Laws.

"To the Honourable,
"The SPEAKER OF THE PHILIPPINE ASSEMBLY."

This report, if adopted, would have emasculated the bill by striking out the minimum penalties, but it was not adopted. On May 19 the assembly laid the bill on the table without discussion.

So began a long struggle to secure the coöperation of the assembly in the enactment of legislation on this important subject.

I did not feel that the assembly ought to be allowed to make a joke of the provision of the Act of Congress of July 1, 1902, that "Neither slavery, nor involuntary servitude, except as a punishment for crime whereof the party shall have been duly convicted, shall exist in said islands," and inserted a frank statement of the case in my annual report. During my absence it was cut out by the governor-general acting on the cabled suggestion of General, then Colonel, McIntyre, speaking for the secretary of war. The Secretary, it is understood, based his decision on the statement of alleged facts and the argument in the above-mentioned memorandum prepared by General McIntyre, and signed by General Edwards, then chief of the bureau of insular affairs. Various of these statements of alleged facts were incorrect, and much of the argument was fallacious, but the *toute ensemble* was plausible, and likely to mislead any one not thoroughly familiar with local conditions in the Philippines. I did not see this communication until three years later, and so had no opportunity seasonably to discuss it, or to present my side of the case.

On learning that all reference to slavery had been cut out of my report, I sent the following memorandum to the governor-general : —

"BAGUIO, February 28, 1909.
"Memorandum for the Honourable the Governor-General.

"Practices in the matter of purchasing and practically enslaving the children of wild people, and holding wild people in the state of peonage, closely approaching slavery, are more grave and more common than is ordinarily understood here;

AMONG THE MOROS.

This photograph shows Governor Taft and Secretary Arthur W. Ferguson with Dato Utto, and other famous Moro chiefs, at Cotobato. Utto is sitting to the left of Governor Taft.

and, in my opinion, as stated in my report, ought to be brought to the attention of the Congress of the United States if the situation is not dealt with effectively by the Philippine Legislature at its next regular session.

"I do not object to the omission from my report of the matter treating on this subject, with the understanding that a strong effort will be made here to secure legislation which will, at least, penalize the sale for cash or other valuable consideration of human beings.

"As things stand at present, we should be placed in a somewhat embarrassing situation if any one thoroughly acquainted with the facts were to ask us what we had done to make effective the provisions of the Act of Congress prohibiting slavery.

"DEAN C. WORCESTER,
"Secretary of the Interior."

The following year I introduced in the commission the bill which the assembly had rejected. Action upon it was postponed, pending the receipt of information which was requested from the assembly as to the reason for the failure of that body to pass it the preceding year. Shortly after this was obtained in the form of the above-quoted extract from the minutes of that body I was called to the United States and no further action was taken in the matter at that time, although the Governor-General in his message to the Legislature had included the following recommendation : —

"There is no express provision of law prohibiting slavery or involuntary servitude in the Philippine Islands. While the law provides certain methods of punishing the practice of slavery, as for example, the law for illegal detention, yet it does not seem right that an enlightened and modern country should have no way of punishing the purchase or sale of human flesh. It is recommended that this be remedied by appropriate legislation at the coming session."

I had also again attempted to discuss this important matter in my annual report.

I myself reached Washington at about the time this document arrived there, but that part of it dealing with slavery and peonage was cut out without either consulting me or giving me a hearing. I was advised by General McIntyre that the secretary had disapproved it.

In writing to me under date of January 11, 1913, Mr. Dickinson said: —

"I have read with much interest the copy of your communication of October 28, 1912, with the Acting Governor-General in regard to the law prohibiting slavery. The whole matter interests me very much and is very enlightening to me.

"I note what you say in regard to the matter coming up during my administration and the memorandum made by General Edwards. My memory may be badly at fault, but I really cannot recall that this matter ever came to my personal attention. I may have forgotten it among the many hundreds of things that came before me, but I certainly have no recollection in regard to it."

I am quite prepared to believe that the matter was never allowed to come to his personal attention!

On January 31, 1911, I again introduced this bill in the commission. It was amended in minor details and passed on that date and was duly forwarded to the assembly. There it was introduced on February 2 and on February 3 was laid on the table. I here give the full record. It is significant as showing the lack of interest displayed by the assembly in this important subject.

"AN ACT PROHIBITING SLAVERY

"*The Speaker.* Commission Bill No. 88 is submitted to the House for consideration. Read the bill.

"*The Secretary.* [*reading*]. . . .

"*Señor Sotto.* The Committee on Revision of Laws proposes that this bill be laid on the table.

"*The Speaker.* Is there any objection?

"*The House.* None.

"*The Speaker.* On the table."

In my report as secretary of the interior for the fiscal year ended June 30, 1911, I again took up this subject.

After this report had been submitted to the commission I myself cut out all mention of slavery at the request of Governor-General Forbes, who urged that we make a last effort to get the assembly to act before appealing to Congress.

In spite of the desirability of having uniform legislation on such a matter as this in adjacent provinces, the commission felt that it could no longer with propriety delay action for the territory under its exclusive jurisdiction, and on August 7, 1911, passed the bill for Agusan, Nueva Vizcaya and the Mountain Province.

The same act was again passed by the commission for the territory under the jurisdiction of the legislature, when that body reconvened. The assembly referred it to committee on October 27, 1911, and tabled it without discussion on February 1, 1912.

In my annual report for 1912 I included the following recommendation : —

"That for the adequate protection of the non-Christian tribes a final and earnest effort be made to secure the concurrence of the Philippine Assembly in the passage for the territory under the jurisdiction of the Philippine Legislature of an Act identical with, or similar to, Act No. 2071, entitled 'An Act prohibiting slavery, involuntary servitude, peonage, and the sale or purchase of human beings in the Mountain Province and the Provinces of Nueva Vizcaya and Agusan, and providing punishment therefor,' and that in the event of failure, the attention of Congress be called to this important matter to the end that it may pass adequate legislation if it deems such a course in the public interest."

This time I sent the copy for the report to the printer without awaiting further possible requests or orders to remain silent, for I was thoroughly convinced that it was useless to expect action from the assembly and that nothing remained but to appeal to congress to pass suppletory legislation making effective the provision of the Act of July 1, 1902, prohibiting slavery and involuntary servitude in the Philippine Islands.

At the next session of the legislature the commission
again passed the bill. The assembly referred it to committee on October 26, and tabled it without discussion on
January 8, 1913.

From the above record it will be plain that, beginning
in 1909, the commission passed laws prohibiting and penalizing slavery and peonage annually during four successive
years, and that the assembly tabled each of the four
measures without deigning to give any of them one
moment's discussion. Much less have they ever asked
for any information as to the necessity for such legislation.

While no member of the assembly had ever made any
official statement on the subject, the Filipino press had
on various occasions denounced me as a liar or an igno-
ramus, and an enemy of "the Filipino people," for saying
that slavery existed.

In preparation for what I deemed to be a probable request from Congress for a detailed statement of facts, I
now proceeded to get together the information on file in
government offices and courts, called upon various officers
of the government for data in their possession which had
never been made of record, and initiated new investigations, using for this purpose the police of Manila, the
Philippine constabulary and various other agencies.
Drawing on the abundant material thus obtained, I
began the preparation of a report to the commission,
recommending that the necessity for legislation be called
to the attention of Congress, and supplying abundant
data relative to the existence of slavery and peonage in
the Philippines.

Before this report was completed there occurred a most
unexpected event.

Dr. W. O. Stillman, President of the American Humane
Association, had written me months before asking about
the power of the Philippine Legislature to enact humane
legislation, and further inquiring what laws of this sort,
if any, had been enacted. In my reply I had called his

attention to the act of the commission prohibiting slavery
and peonage in certain provinces, and to the fact that
the attitude of the assembly had prevented the enactment of similar prohibitive legislation for the remaining
territory. My letter, which furnished no supporting
data, was eventually published by this gentleman and
was read in the United States Senate by Senator Borah.
On May 1, 1913, the senate passed the following resolution : —

"RESOLVED, That the Secretary of War be, and he is hereby,
directed to send to the Senate any and all facts bearing directly
or indirectly upon the truth of the charge publicly made that
human slavery exists at this time in the Philippine Islands and
that human beings are bought and sold in such Islands as
chattels."

The reply addressed by the secretary of war to the
president of the Senate on May 6, 1913, contains the
following statement : —

"There is not in this Department, to the knowledge of the
Secretary thereof or of the head of the Bureau having charge
of insular affairs, a record of any facts bearing directly or indirectly upon the truth of the charge, publicly made, that
human slavery exists at this time in the Philippine Islands and
that human beings are bought and sold in such Islands as
chattels."

This was a most peculiar statement. The passage cut
out of my 1909 report was certainly on file there, and it
explicitly stated that slavery existed in the Islands.

The similar passage from my 1910 report should have
been on file there, and last but not least, when finally,
after the lapse of years, I saw the so-called "Edwards" memorandum, in reality written by General
McIntyre, on which the Secretary of War had based his
action in ordering all reference to slavery cut out of my
1910 report, I had made a full reply to it, containing a
specific statement that slavery and the sale of human
beings were common in certain parts of the islands and

citing certain specific cases. I had specially requested that this communication be filed in the bureau of insular affairs, and General McIntyre, the chief of that bureau, who acknowledged its receipt, could hardly have forgotten its existence.

The war department reported on this matter without seeking any information from Manila. I can only conclude that Secretary Garrison was deceived by some irresponsible subordinate.

As promptly as practicable I completed my report and sent it to the commission, which read and considered it on May 17, 1913, immediately passing the following resolution: —

"*Whereas* the Act of Congress passed July 1, 1902, 'temporarily providing for civil government of the Philippine Islands and for other purposes' provides that 'neither slavery nor involuntary servitude except as a punishment for crime whereof the parties have been duly convicted shall exist in said Islands,' and

"*Whereas* the Supreme Court of the Philippine Islands in the case of the U. S. *vs.* Cabanag (Vol. VIII, p. 64, Phil. Repts.), decided on March 16, 1907, decided that 'there is no law applicable here either of the United States or of the Archipelago punishing slavery as a crime;' and

"*Whereas*, in order to remedy this condition in accordance with the above-mentioned provisions of the said Act of Congress, the Philippine Commission in its exclusive legislative jurisdiction over all that part of the Philippine Islands inhabited by Moros or other non-Christian tribes passed Act No. 2071, and as a branch of the Philippine Legislature has in four successive sessions passed an act prohibiting and penalizing slavery, involuntary servitude, peonage, or the sale of human beings, and

"*Whereas* during each of said sessions the Assembly has failed to concur in the passage of such Act; now, therefore, be it

"*Resolved*, That the Honourable the Governor-General be requested to send to the Honourable the Secretary of War a copy of the proposed law entitled 'An Act prohibiting slavery, involuntary servitude, peonage, or the sale of human beings in the Philippine Islands' as passed by the Commission in the last

A MORO CHIEF WITH HIS WIVES AND DAUGHTER.

session of the last Legislature, but which failed of passage in the Assembly, with the recommendation that a copy of the law be sent to Congress with the request that the necessary legislation be enacted to render fully effective the above-mentioned provisions of the Act of Congress of July 1, 1902."

I was subsequently requested by the governor-general to address the report to him rather than to the commission, to the end that the Filipino members of that body might be spared the embarrassment which would otherwise result from the necessity of voting either for its acceptance or for its rejection, and I very willingly made the requested change.

The printing of the report was delayed until July 19, 1913, and I brought it up to that date, as evidence continued to pour in.

In this document I gave specific cases of chattel slavery in the provinces of Nueva Vizcaya, Isabela, Tarlac, Zambales, Pampanga, Batangas, Palawan, Agusan, Ambos Camarines, the Moro province, the Mountain province and Manila itself, describing quite fully the conditions under which Ilongots, Ifugaos, Negritos, Tagbanuas, Manobos, Mandayas, Moros and Filipinos are bought, sold and held as chattel slaves.

I will here only briefly summarize them.

The Negritos are savages of low mentality, and most of them lead a nomadic or semi-nomadic life. They constantly get the worst of it in the struggle for existence and to-day are found only on the islands of Mindanao, Palawan, Tablas, Negros, Panay and Luzón, where for the most part they inhabit very remote and inaccessible mountain regions. Owing to their stupidity and their extreme timidity it is comparatively easy to hold them in slavery, and they are probably thus victimized more than are the people of any other tribe. They are constantly warring with each other in the more remote of the mountain regions which they inhabit. It would be going too far to say that their moral sense has been blunted. It is probably nearer the truth to say that they never had any. It is therefore a simple matter for Filipino slave dealers to arrange with Negritos for the purchase of their fellow-tribesmen. The latter then proceed to obtain captives by raiding some hostile group of their own people, killing ruthlessly if occasion arises.

They are more ready than are the people of any other Philippine tribe to sell their children or other dependent relatives, and do this not infrequently when pressed by hunger, a condition apt to arise because of their utter improvidence. Unfortunately, the matter does not end here. It is by no means unknown for Filipinos to join in their slave-hunting raids, or even to organize raids of their own, killing Negrito parents in order to get possession of their children. I submit the following case to illustrate this latter procedure : —

"CAMP STOTSENBURG, PAMPANGA, P. I.,
"September 26, 1910.

"THE ADJUTANT,
"CAMP STOTSENBURG, PAMPANGA, P. I.

"SIR : I have the honour to inform you that a report has this day been made to me that a party of hostile Filipinos, about 15 in number, armed with 1 rifle, 1 revolver and the remainder with bolos, presumably ladrones, entered a small Negrito barrio situated about one and one half miles directly southeast from the Post during the forenoon of Tuesday, September 20, 1910, and killed three men and carried away two small children. I have visited the barrio and the body of one man showing frightful mutilation, both head, feet and hands completely severed from the body, was found. This settlement is situated in a dense jungle and the other bodies were presumably carried away or hidden, so that they could not be found.

"But one person can be found who witnessed the affair, an aged Negrito woman, who can scarcely walk from the treatment she received at the hands of these outlaws. She states that she would be able to recognize and identify some of the party. I am informed by Negritos living in the vicinity that this party of outlaws has a rendezvous a short distance east of Solbac where they might be apprehended.

"The killing took place without the reservation, but the

LIEUTENANT-GOVERNOR MANUEL FORTICH OF BUKIDNON.

Lieutenant-Governor Fortich is a Filipino. Various criminal charges, including that of murder, have been brought against him, because he protected the Bukidnons from their Filipino neighbors in Misamis.

matter is of sufficient importance, since all the Negritos living in the vicinity of the post are greatly excited and disturbed, to warrant the recommendation that it be referred to the Senior Inspector of Constabulary, San Fernando, Pampanga, P. I., for such action as he may desire to take.

"Very respectfully,

(Signed)   "KYLE RUCKER,

"*1st Lieut. and Squadron Adjutant, 14th Cav. Intelligence Officer.*"

The subsequent fate of these Negrito children is made plain by the following letter : —

"PHILIPPINE CONSTABULARY,
"SAN FERNANDO, PAMPANGA, P. I.,
"October 4, 1910.

"MY DEAR HOLMES: We have a case up here of murder committed near the town of Angeles in which several Negritos are mixed up.

"We managed to locate two Negrito children who had been sold by the man who killed their father. They were in the possession of a man named Ambrocio David who says he paid sixty pesos for them and says they are his property.

"I think that we can convict the murderer of the children's father, if we can catch him, but this sale of Negritos has gone such a pace that almost every family in Pampanga has at least one as a 'Companion' of their children, they say, but really as a slave.

"The Fiscal says there is no law against the sale or purchase of Negritos and I cannot find it, although I seem to remember a law, but whether it alludes to Negritos or only Moros I am unable to say.

"If there is a law, what number is it, and if not, can you get me an opinion of the Attorney-General or some ruling so as to show us how to act in this and future cases of this kind.

"Yrs.

"W. S. NORTH,
"S. I."

In this case one of the kidnappers was convicted of murder, but nothing could be done to him for selling the Negrito children nor could anything be done to Señor Ambrocio David for buying the children or for claiming that they were his property.

Like many primitive peoples, the Negritos are inordinately fond of strong alcoholic drinks. It is strictly against the law to give or sell any of the white man's liquors to them, but this naturally does not restrain slave hunters, who frequently get adults deeply intoxicated and then trade with them for their children or kidnap the drunken persons themselves and drag them away. Negritos are held to-day in bondage, in considerable numbers, in provinces like Zambales, Pampanga, Tarlac, Pangasinan and Cagayan. While they are not displayed for sale in any market in Pampanga, they can be readily negotiated for in several different public markets of that province; and if none happen to be available at the moment, the would-be purchaser is assured that the supply in the mountains is inexhaustible and that his needs can soon be met.

The publication of my report has caused consternation among slave owners in many provinces. Some slaves have since escaped and little effort has been made to recapture them. Others have been voluntarily set free by their masters, but in Pampanga the trade still goes merrily on. Until recently Negritos have been peddled around the country adjacent to Manila like carabaos or horses, and it is but a short time since their purchasers have in some instances refused to give them up, stoutly asseverating that they were their property. Now, however, warned by experience, owners make no such claim, but advance various more or less ingenious explanations of the fact that they have Negritos in their possession and deny that they are slaves. Some of them insist that it is a Negrito custom to kill orphan children, and that they have taken orphans out of kindness in order to save their lives. Patient investigation has failed to show the existence of any such custom among the Negritos.

Perhaps the commonest procedure of all is to claim that Negrito slaves are "adopted children" or "members of the family." The presumption against a Filipino's taking into his family one of these little woolly-headed, black, dwarf savages is strong. In no single case have I been able to obtain evidence of real, legal adoption. The following document illustrates the procedure which seems invariably to have been followed : —

"On the 25th of December, 1912, I, the authorized curate of this district, Lubao, Province of Pampanga, baptized solemnly, and put on the blessed *Oleos* in this church in my charge on one Negrita ten and eight years of age (18), and have given the name of Juana, daughter of a father poor and unknown. The foster mother, Doña Pia Vitug, married in this town received the charge as a parent to care for the spiritual welfare and other obligations.
"I for the truth sign,
"FRIAR PEDRO DIEZ."

(Girl given the name of Juana de Jesus Vitug.)

A document of this sort imposes no legal obligation whatever on the owner of a slave, and makes no change in the status of the slave, but merely serves as a basis for the claim that he or she "is treated as a member of the family."

This is a cheap and easy method of securing a slave, and the child thus "adopted" may be compelled to labour for a lifetime without compensation, or turned over for a consideration to be similarly "adopted" by some one else.

Other Filipinos who do not claim that their Negrito slaves are members of their families find complete justification for purchasing them in the allegation that they have taken them to Christianize, thus preventing their going to hell !

In the provinces of Agusan and Surigao the slave-taking raids of the Mandayas and Manobos are historic. In the more remote parts of these provinces they continue from time to time up to the present day. While one of them lies within the territory for which the commission has been able to legislate, what shall we say of those who contend that slavery does not exist in the

Philippine Islands in the face of such occurrences as have taken place there? The same query holds for the sub-province of Ifugao in the Mountain Province and for Nueva Vizcaya. The Ifugaos have been especially victimized. The following kinds of servitude are recognized by them: —

Jim-bút. This is the name applied to real slaves. The *Jim-bút* becomes an article of commerce and often changes owners several times before reaching the country of the *Ba-li-uon* (Christians).

Nij-cóp. This is the name applied to children who have been really adopted under a formal contract made with their parents or nearest relatives in case the parents are dead. The *Nij-cóp* acquire certain property rights from their new parents-by-adoption.

Baj-ál. This is the name given to orphan children who have been formally taken in charge by some well-to-do Ifugao and who are unable to support themselves. The *Baj-ál* is a tentative *Nij-cóp*, for if he turns out to be bright and industrious, he may become a member of the family and acquire property rights.

Ta-gá-la. This is the name applied to servants who receive regular compensation.

It is a matter of common knowledge throughout the sub-province that there are living to-day in Isabela hundreds of Ifugaos who have been sold to Filipinos as slaves.

In Nueva Vizcaya it has been possible to deal with the more flagrant cases since the passage by the commission of the law above referred to, but the commission is powerless to pass a law effective in Isabela.

The holders of slaves now seek to evade the law by nominally hiring them at a monthly salary which is not paid. The promulgation of Act No. 2071 prohibiting and penalizing slavery enabled Lieutenant-Governor Jeff D. Gallman of Ifugao to liberate some forty boys and girls held by Filipinos in Nueva Vizcaya. In no single case, however, could it be proved that the child had been sold.

The persons who held them testified in each instance that they were "hired servants."

When they learned of the provisions of the above-mentioned act they were easily prevailed upon to pay "salaries" long overdue to their "servants" and the latter were allowed to return to their homes.

It was found that some of the persons originally sold into slavery in Nueva Vizcaya had run away from their masters and become vagabonds. Few really wanted to return to their parents, whose language in many cases they had almost forgotten.

I wish this were the worst, but the worst is yet to come. Not only do the Filipinos buy, sell and hold the wild people as slaves, but Filipino children have been kidnapped, or enticed from their homes, by other Filipinos, and sold as slaves to their own kind. Young girls have been sold outright to Chinese who purchased and kept them for immoral purposes. They have been sold to panderers and keepers of houses of prostitution and compelled to enter upon lives of shame. Filipino children and young women have been sold to Chinese who have taken them to China. God only knows what fate may have befallen them there. In such cases the victims disappear from these islands, never to return.

Some slaves are well treated. Others are half starved, brutally beaten, injured or even killed. The Manobos and Manadayas of Agusan and Surigao, and the Bagobos of the Moro Province, have been accustomed to sacrifice slaves to appease their heathen deities. The Manobos on occasion even have their boys take lances and try the effect of different thrusts on slaves tied to trees or posts.

Those who desire long lists of specific cases of slavery will find them in my report. I think that I have here abundantly demonstrated the fact that genuine slavery exists in the Philippine Islands. It can never be successfully checked until there is a law of general application throughout the archipelago penalizing the sale, barter, or purchase of human beings. What reason has the Philippine Assembly for refusing to pass the necessary act?

Without hesitation I assert that, apart from false and foolish pride which makes the persons concerned unwilling to admit the fact of the existence of slavery, their chief reason for objecting to this law is that it would not only prohibit and penalize slavery, but would prohibit and penalize peonage, which is so common and widespread that it may properly be called general. Indeed, I have no hesitation in asserting that it prevails in every municipality in the Philippine Islands.

Slavery is a serious matter, but peonage is far more serious because of the very much larger number of persons involved. It lies at the root of the industrial system of the Philippines.

Much has been said relative to the probable attitude of large American landowners toward Filipino labourers. Thus far their attitude, and that of all other classes of Americans, has been infinitely better than has that of the wealthy Filipinos themselves. The truth is that peonage is repugnant to the average American. One of the complaints persistently made against us by the Filipinos is that we have raised the daily wage throughout the islands, and this is true. When I was there in the Spanish days, it was possible, in many regions, to obtain abundant labour at five cents per day with food, and ten cents with food was the general rule. Now the same class of labour costs at least twenty-five cents per day with food, and in some provinces it costs fifty cents or more. It must be frankly admitted that Americans are responsible for this sad condition of affairs! American landowners who desire to pay their employees regularly a living daily wage encounter difficulty in doing so, for the reason that the labourers have become accustomed to the old system, the evils of which they know, and are afraid of a new

GOVERNOR FREDERICK JOHNSON OF AGUSAN.

He is holding up the butt of a huge hemp stalk. Governor Johnson continued at his post for a year while a cancer was destroying the bones of his leg, without letting any one know of his trouble. His heroism cost him his life.

one, fearing that it may involve worse evils of which they know nothing.

Incidentally, Americans have learned that their labourers are worth more if well fed, and this is another grievance held against us in certain quarters.

With many of the Filipinos it is a different story.

The rich and powerful man, commonly known as a *cacique*, encourages the poor man to borrow money from him under such conditions that the debt can never be repaid, and holds the debtor, and frequently the members of his family as well, in debt servitude for life. One might fill a score of volumes with records of cases and I can here do no more than to select a few typical illustrations of the workings of this vicious system.

The Filipinos are born gamblers. Gambling is their besetting sin. The poor are usually glad to get the opportunity to borrow money, and will do this on almost any terms, if necessary, in order to continue to indulge in their pet vice. They are thoughtless about their ability to repay loans, and thus readily fall into the power of the *cacique* money-lenders, who thereafter use them as house servants or labourers, under conditions such as to render their escape from debt-servitude practically impossible.

Indeed, if they seek to escape, the *caciques* often threaten them with the law, or actually invoke it against them, while if they endeavour to homestead public land and thus better their condition, the *caciques* only too often cause opposition to be made to their claims and keep it up until they become discouraged.

The following facts have been furnished me by Hon. James A. Ostrand, judge of the court of land registration.

"In 1907 a woman, whose surname, I think, is Quintos, asked me to lend her twenty-five pesos with which to 'redeem' her daughter who had been mortgaged for that amount to a Chinese merchant, whose name at present I do not recall, but who had his establishment on the ground floor of the house of Ubaldo Diaz in Lingayen. The woman stated that the Chinaman was corrupting the morals of the girl, and that this was the reason why she wanted to make the redemption. I told her that under the circumstances no redemption was necessary, but that I would see that the girl was allowed to leave the Chinaman, who, on proper representations, was induced to let the girl go home. She stayed with her mother for a couple of weeks but, by adding ₱75 to the mortgage debt, the Chinaman got her back and shortly before I left Lingayen I learned that the girl, though scarcely fifteen years old, had given birth to a child."

"In 1907 a woman from the town of Balincaguin in Pangasinán came to my office and stated that she, about six years before had 'mortgaged' [the terms 'salda' in Ilocano and 'sanla' in Pangasinán are usually translated *mortgage*, but also imply *pledge*, as the creditor generally takes possession of the mortgaged property] her twelve-year old son for some twenty pesos to Don Cirilio Braganza, the member of the second Philippine legislature for the district in which I was then living; that her son had been working for Braganza ever since, and that, according to her reckoning, the debt had already been paid, but that Braganza had unjustly charged the loss of a carabao to her son's account, thus adding ₱120, if I remember correctly, to the debt. She further stated that she had asked Braganza to release the boy, but that he refused to do so. I informed her of the provisions of the Philippine Bill in regard to involuntary servitude, and advised her that her son was free to leave Mr. Braganza's services if he so desired. She said that if the boy should leave, she was afraid something might happen to him as Braganza was very influential in that locality. I then gave her a note for Braganza requesting him to let the boy go. Shortly afterwards Braganza came to me and gave me his version of the case, stating that he had always treated the boy well, and that the loss of the carabao was entirely due to the boy's negligence, and that he, Braganza, would not consent to the boy's leaving him before the carabao was paid for. At last reports the boy was still with Braganza and may be there yet. I may add that I believe Braganza told the truth, and that the boy was guilty of negligence in connection with the loss of the carabao."

The net result in this case was that a boy was "mortgaged" for a ₱20 debt and after six years the debt had very largely increased, probably in part as a result of the carelessness of the boy.

In a letter to Judge Ostrand I had defined peonage as "the condition of a debtor held by his creditor in a form of qualified servitude to work out a debt." Of its prevalence the judge says : —

"While practising law in the Province of Pangasinán, during the years 1905 to 1909, hardly a week passed but what cases of involuntary servitude, as defined in the within communication, came under my observation."

He also calls attention to the fact that interference with the system does not increase one's popularity : —

"Interference by third parties in cases of involuntary servitude is not looked upon with favour, and is generally considered highly reprehensible. I remember, for instance, a case where Mr. Pedro Sison [not the member of the Legislature], then a prominent resident of Lingayen, was, as he himself regarded it, made the victim of unwarranted interference. A woman bought a small parcel of land from Mr. Sison, agreeing to work out the purchase price, forty pesos. She worked with Mr. Sison for six years, at the end of which period the debt had increased to over sixty pesos, according to Mr. Sison's accounts. In the meantime the woman became a Protestant, and Rev. E. S. Lyons, the Methodist missionary in Pangasinán, advised her to leave Mr. Sison's service. Upon her doing so Mr. Sison became very indignant not only at her, but also at Mr. Lyons, and for some time thought seriously of having the latter criminally prosecuted. He appeared to be very much surprised when he found that there was no penal provision covering Mr. Lyons's action. Mr. Sison was otherwise a very estimable and good-natured man, but he never until his dying day, which occurred a couple of years afterwards, got over his bitter resentment toward Mr. Lyons."

Judge Ostrand summarizes the results of his observations as follows : —

"Nearly all the involuntary servitude cases of which I have any knowledge have arisen from the practice of mortgaging half-grown children. The sum advanced is usually some twenty or thirty pesos. As the money seldom draws interest at a lower rate than ten per cent a month, and the creditor furnishes the child food and such clothing as it may need, its services are ordinarily not considered worth more than the amount of the interest, and the debt instead of being reduced usually increases as the years pass. I venture to say that among the Filipinos in some sections of the Islands the majority of house servants are obtained and employed in this manner."

It would indeed seem that with interest at the rate of 120 per cent per year and the creditor in a position to fix his own price for food, clothing and other necessaries furnished his debtors while they were trying to work out their debts, they would not be likely to succeed in doing so!

In this connection I call attention to the fact that in the course of the discussion recently caused by requests for the resignation of certain public officials who had been loaning money at usurious rates of interests, several of the native papers took the attitude that 18 per cent per year was a very moderate rate of interest.

If the unfortunate peon finally rebels, the rich *cacique* often invokes the law against him by having him prosecuted on some false criminal charge.

In this connection the following letter is of interest: —

"Philippine Constabulary,
"Office of the Senior Inspector,
"PAMPANGA, SAN FERNANDO, September 26, 1912.

"THE SUPERINTENDENT, INFORMATION DIVISION, P. C.,
"MANILA, P. I.

"(Thru' Adjutant, District of Central Luzón.)
"SIR: Reference to the prosecution of Maria Guzman before the Justice of the Peace of Apalit for 'Infraction of Law 2098' (your file No. 8634–75) I have the honour to attach copy of decision in the case, and remarks: —
"About three (3) years ago Simeon de los Reyes, by and with the consent of his wife Maria Guzman, borrowed and signed receipt for fifty pesos (₱50) to Maria Santos of Apalit, contracting that his wife work out the debt moulding earthen jars — that for every hundred jars made Maria Guzman received

₱1, 25 centavos of which was to go on the debt. The woman states she could make about fifty jars per week, so that her actual wages were 50 centavos per week, or $.005 per jar. This without board, as the woman states that any money she got for food was charged on original debt.

"By the first part of this year the debt had 'decreased' to ₱70, when another receipt for that amount was signed by the husband, de los Reyes, and the old receipt for ₱50 destroyed. In the month of August ultimo the Santos woman refused to advance Maria Guzman more money, so Maria Guzman left and joined her husband, who was working in Manila. The debt at time of trial amounted to ₱79 and a fraction.

"Warrants of this nature are being continually sent from Pampanga, either by messenger or mail, direct to the Superintendent Information Division, without passing through my hands. The reason is evident.

"It is respectfully requested that in the future all warrants reaching your office in this way be referred back to me before execution.

"Very respectfully,

(Signed)   "L. T. ROHRER,
"Senior Inspector."

This woman, if she succeeded in making fifty earthen jars per week, received wages amounting to twenty-five cents against which her creditor charged her food and doubtless also her clothing. In other words, she was in effect charged for the privilege of making fifty jars per week for her master. The interest on her debt was meanwhile piling up while the principal steadily increased, and when she grew weary of her hopeless task and ran away, her taskmaster prosecuted her.

The following letter presents a typical case of peonage:

"ROSALES,
"March 26, 1912.

"CHIEF OF THE SECRET SERVICE DEPT., MANILA:

"DEAR SIR: On behalf of Garegorio Almario a young girl residing at my house I write to ask you if you cannot have this matter attended to.

"Six years ago a man named Tomas Almario, living at present in Rosales, borrowed some money (twenty pesos only).

This man was unable to repay this money so he sold this girl
named Inocencia Almario to a Mr. Galban.   I think he is the
President of Bautista.   Her sister has been to Bautista to take
this girl away but she has been rebuked by these people in my
presence.   They state she owes ₱60 the extra ₱40 being interest
on the ₱20 borrowed 6 years ago.   They have got this girl and
another girl working as slaves and to-day I heard that the girl escaped in a carromatta but they sent an automobile after her and
took her into Bautista beating her all the way.   In the interest of
justice I hope you will have this girl released and hand her
over to her sister in my house here out of the hands of those
wretches.   I also found out that this girl is being sent from
place to place amongst men who take girls to cover debts.   If
you send a man here to Rosales I have the proof and will show
you where this girl is and will get the evidence against these
people.   I understand that the President of Bautista is the
man who is at the bottom of the whole affair.   I hope you will
put a stop to this slavery.   I have the man here who owes the
money and sold the two girls to this man.   I have the sister
here ; also the other relatives to prove that this girl has worked
as a slave for 6 years to cover a debt of twenty pesos and now
they want 60 before they will release her.   Please release my
sister and oblige
            "Yours truly,
                     " ↓[her mark] GAREGORIO ALMARIO.
                     Witness : (Signed)   "W. A. COLE.
"Address GAREGORIO ALMARIO,
    "c/o W. A. COLE, Rosales, Pang."

I have not made the slightest effort to get the peonage
records of Philippine assemblymen, but have taken cases
as they came, yet three of the limited number here discussed concern members or ex-members of the assembly.
Is it any wonder that that body refuses to consider a law
prohibiting and penalizing peonage ?

My investigation of this matter has developed some
interesting phases of human nature.   Knowing the certain unpopularity which would result from telling the
truth, not a few persons who might have given valuable
testimony refused to tell what they knew, or even denied
that they knew anything.   Others made written statements which I was unable to use, as they insisted that

their names be withheld, and I wanted testimony only from witnesses who had the courage of their convictions. Fortunately there was no lack of people unafraid to tell the truth. Among witnesses to the existence of chattel slavery were army officers, constabulary officers, the Manila chief of police and many men of the police force of that city, judges, Catholic priests, the mother superior of a convent, the insular auditor and a number of his deputies, provincial governors, both Filipino and American, provincial treasurers, the director of education, school teachers, an ethnologist, newspaper men, business men and women both English and American. I accepted only written and signed statements. The long list of cases in my official report was a sample list, not an exhaustive one. I stand ready to furnish specific instances of chattel slavery, *ad nauseam*, giving names of slaves, their vendors and purchasers, prices paid and dates of transactions. I hold more than a thousand typewritten pages of evidence, and it continued to come in up to the day of my departure from Manila.

The attitude of the Filipino politicians toward this great mass of data and the witnesses who furnished it is a most interesting study, from which may be deduced logical conclusions of far-reaching importance. Let us examine it.

In the issue of the *Boston Herald* for June 24, 1912, Sr. Quezon, resident delegate from the Philippines to Congress, published an article entitled "The Filipinos as Legislators," [1] attacking Governor-General Forbes for referring in a public speech to the attitude of the assembly on the slavery question. I will quote and comment on its essential statements : —

"The fact that the Assembly has refused to approve of the bill referred to by Governor Forbes, bespeaks the legislative ability of our Assemblymen, while, on the other hand, the pas-

[1] Republished in "Slavery and Peonage," pp. 37–39.

sage by the Commission of said bill indicates either the incompetency or the negligence of the Commissioners. Do we have slavery and compulsory service in the Philippines or not? If we do not, the bill to abolish it is unnecessary. If we do, it is also unnecessary, because the Act passed by Congress, creating the present Philippine Government, which serves as our constitution, already prohibits slavery and compulsory service, and, therefore, no act of the Philippine Legislature is needed to declare it illegal."

This is a puerile quibble. The act referred to prohibits slavery, but does not penalize it.

"If there is slavery and compulsory service in the Philippines, the Governor-General as the Chief Executive, and the members of the Philippine Commission, who, with the Governor-General, compose the executive department of the Islands, are all of them guilty in not enforcing and executing the constitution of the Archipelago."

False. The Supreme Court of the Philippines has held that the "constitution" here referred to is non-enforceable without exactly such suppletory legislation as the commission passed and the assembly tabled.

"If there is anything in the Philippines akin to slavery or compulsory service, it can not be found in the provinces to which the legislative jurisdiction of the Assembly extends."

Utterly false.

"Should there be such a thing in the territories inhabited by the few non-Christian Filipinos, which are under the exclusive control of the Philippine Commission, I am sure the slaveholders can only be the Government officials, who are appointed by the Secretary of the Interior, the Honourable Dean C. Worcester, the head of the executive department in charge of said territories."

False and absurd. The larger majority of existing slaves are held by Christian Filipinos. Not a single official in the territory in question was subject to appointment or removal by me. Not one has ever owned a slave,

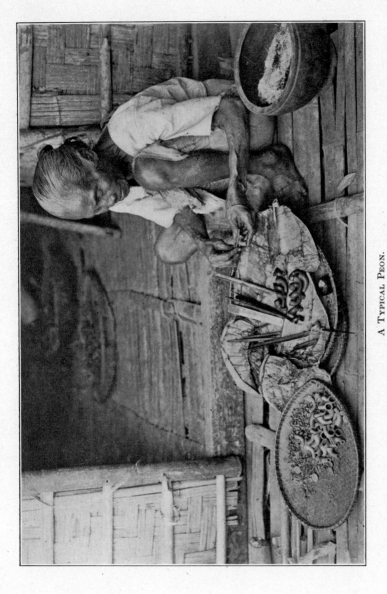

A Typical Peon.

Helpless and hopeless, she toils at her endless task, receiving in return a pittance that does not pay the interest on her constantly growing debt.

to my knowledge. This statement illustrates Quezon's disregard for the truth.

"It will not be out of place to indicate here the reason wherefor the Philippine Commission has passed the bill alluded to by Governor Forbes. The members of the Philippine Commission are sternly opposed to Philippine independence. Moreover, they are opposed to allowing the Filipino people to have a legislature wholly constituted of natives for reasons too apparent to be mentioned. One of their everyday arguments is 'that the premature withdrawal of the United States would result in the establishment of an oligarchy composed of small and favoured ruling classes who would oppress the masses.'

"The passage by the Philippine Commission of the anti-slavery bill placed the Philippine Assembly in a very awkward position (as it was perhaps intended to do); to concur in the passage of the bill was to admit that there is such a thing as slavery and compulsory service in the Philippines, which is not a fact. To reject the bill would be construed as indicating that the members of the Assembly were advocates of slavery. The moral courage of our Assemblymen was shown when they took the former course, that of truth. The members of the Commission denounce the attitude of their colegislators as proof of lack of sympathy for the masses of the people."

False, interesting, and important. There were four Filipino members of the commission at this time, all of whom were in favour of ultimate independence, and one of whom was a leading advocate of immediate independdence. All voted for the anti-slavery laws which the assembly refused to pass.

The Filipinos were not wholly to blame for the existence of slavery at the time of the American occupation, but the politicians are unable to grasp the fact that the way to deal with a cancer is to cut it out, not to deny its existence, and by their refusal to legislate have now made themselves fully responsible for the continued existence of slavery and peonage in the regularly organized provinces of the Philippines. The Filipino newspapers have even gone so far as to claim that there could be no slavery until a law defined it, hence to enact such a law would create slavery.

Resident Commissioners Earnshaw and Quezon were prompt and emphatic in their denials of the existence of slavery when Senator Borah read in the Senate Chamber my letter to Dr. Stillman. Sr. Earnshaw did not know any better. Sr. Quezon claims to know the facts. He himself has said : —

"As a Filipino familiar with the facts in the case, I do not hesitate to qualify the letter of Secretary Worcester as being at once false and slanderous. It is false, because there does not exist slavery in the Philippines, or, at least, in that part of the country subject to the authority of the Philippine Assembly. It is slanderous because it presents the Philippine Assembly, by innuendo, if not openly, as a body which countenances slavery."

He was unquestionably familiar with the facts, or many of them. Did he know of the report of the Filipino Governor Dichoso, describing slavery in Isabela ; of that of the Filipino Governor Corrales, describing slavery in Misamis ; of that of the Filipino Governor Pimentel, describing the sale of Filipino children into slavery to Chinese ; [1] of that of the American Governor George Curry, describing slavery in Isabela ; [2] of that of the American Governor Knight, describing slavery in Nueva Vizcaya ; [3] of that of the Filipino Governor Sanz,[4] describing the enticing from their homes of numerous Filipino children of Romblón and the disposal of them as peons or slaves ; of the reports of army, constabulary and police officers ; and of the records of courts on slavery and peonage ? Under the circumstances explanation or retraction would seem to be in order, but we have had from him only two more puerile quibbles. In a published statement he has said that slavery does not exist as an institution in the Philippines. Who ever said it did ? It exists there as a demonstrated fact, and it ought to be made a crime. In another published statement,[5]

[1] " Slavery and Peonage," pp. 14–15.
[2] *Ibid.*, p. 21.   [3] *Ibid.*, pp. 23–25.   [4] *Ibid.*, pp. 17–19.
[5] " The Filipino People," Vol. II, No. 1, p. 15, September, 1913.

Quezon says : —

"The allegation is a most serious one and we think it desirable to meet the charge directly without hesitation by asserting that it is unqualifiedly false and that the accusations made in the report are not only not sustained, but cannot be sustained by any evidence tending to show that such a 'system' exists."

The placing in quotation marks of a word not used by me fairly illustrates one of the typical methods of the Filipino politician, and for this reason alone I refer to it and to the following statements from the same editorial, which will serve a similar purpose : —

"There is a very serious aspect of this report of Commissioner Worcester's. If the system he speaks of exists and is known to him — indeed has been known to him for a long time — why did he never correct it ? He says that the Philippine Assembly has blocked action. The truth is that he and his fellows had absolute power long before the Philippine Assembly ever came into existence.

". . . Mr. Worcester now practically admits that he knew of similar conditions elsewhere than among the Moros, but that he never had anything to say about them and allowed them to go on until, it would seem, he thought that he could make some political capital out of a controversy with the Philippine Assembly regarding anti-slavery legislation."

It did not lie in my power to correct it. On the Philippine Commission rests the full responsibility for failure to enact anti-slavery legislation from the time when it first learned of the existence of this crime among the Filipinos until it passed its first act prohibiting and penalizing it on April 29, 1909. As I have already shown, the matter was dealt with, in 1903, by directing the inclusion of proper legislation in a proposed new Penal Code never completed. Valuable years were then lost in testing the adequacy of existing law, and when it proved inadequate further time was, in my opinion, needlessly wasted in drafting the necessary act. To this extent, and to this extent only, the commission shares responsibility for

existing conditions. Since April 29, 1909, that responsibility has rested on the assembly alone.

I have given two of the reasons for its refusal to act.
There is another, but I should have hesitated to give it,
as it would have been hard to prove, had not Speaker
Osmeña furnished the necessary evidence. He is commonly considered to be the leading Filipino statesman of
the day, so special importance attaches to his utterances
and he, if any one, can speak with authority concerning
the attitude of the assembly. The ominous rumble from
the United States which reached these distant shores led
him to give out a newspaper interview explaining the in-
activity of that body. He said : —

"Never has Mr. Worcester attempted to furnish us with
the facts which he has placed before Congress. The bill itself
was sent to the Assembly for action but on account of the
unfriendliness of the members for the secretary of the interior
and the lack of sympathy between the Assembly and him, it
was not given the consideration that it would have received if
Mr. Worcester had at the same time sent us the facts which
he has sent on to the United States.

"Mr. Worcester as the secretary of the interior, and not as
commissioner was in duty bound to furnish the Assembly with
the facts that he claims to have found. It is the duty of all of
the administrative officers of the government to enlighten the
legislature and to furnish it with information gained officially
by them. As a matter of fact, Mr. Worcester showed that he
was not anxious for the Assembly to consider the matter by
never once even mentioning the subject to me, as is customary
with other matters for legislation which the secretaries have
wished taken up by the Assembly."

If this were not so pathetic it would be very, very
funny. The assembly is now made up of 81 Filipino
delegates representing 34 provinces. An unfeeling American secretary of the interior, residing at Manila, is
charged with having failed to inform them of what was
going on under their very noses. All information deemed
by the commission necessary to justify legislation was

transmitted by me to that body when we lost our slavery case in the Supreme Court.

Never during all the years that this matter has been pending has there been the slightest suggestion that the assembly desired to receive information concerning it. If its members were to tell the half of what they themselves know about slavery and peonage the facts which I have been able to gather would fade into insignificance, but this is not the important thing in this interview.

The important thing is that dislike of the person who happened to introduce in the commission a bill prohibiting slavery and peonage in the Philippines is considered a valid reason for the refusal of the assembly to consider it during four successive years.

Shall thousands of suffering human beings be allowed to go on sweating blood for such a reason?

It is my earnest hope that as a result of the publicity which has now been given this matter there will be speedy action, either by the Philippine Legislature or by the Congress of the United States.

I hope that every right-minded person who reads these lines will insist that we have done with concealment of the truth and suppression of the facts; have done with boggling over hurting the feelings of the Filipino people; and will demand that those who have power to end the disgraceful conditions which now exist in the islands shall promptly and effectively exercise it.

The native press has naturally bitterly opposed any investigation of the truth or falsity of my statements. The following extract from a recent editorial is typical of its attitude: —

"Slavery is not slavery unless it has the characteristics of frequency and notoriousness. Is there here, or has there ever been, at least since Christian civilization has reigned, anything that resembles it? Where is, or who has seen previous to now, such characteristic slavery? Mr. Worcester? Let him point it out, let him give a detailed account of it,

let him define it. What will you bet that he will not do so?
How is he going to do it if it does not exist! It was enough
for him to say: "There is slavery in the Philippines" for
men, press, government officials and every stripe of public
elements in America to admit the possibility of the affirmation
and even an investigation of its likelihood to be ordered.
"That is simply absurd.   The mere investigation is an offense.
The proof must come solely from, and must be demanded solely
of, him who imputes the charge.   If he does not demonstrate
it, if he does not make it patent, further investigation is not
needed.   All that there was to investigate is investigated: it is
that he has lied."

Nevertheless aroused public sentiment in the United
States has forced action here.   Governor-General Harrison called the matter to the attention of the assembly
in his first speech, and that body is now [1] investigating it.
Unfortunately there is grave reason to doubt its good
faith.

It allowed me to leave Manila without the faintest
suggestion that it desired to hear me, and then had the
governor-general cable me an invitation to testify and
to assist in the investigation when I was halfway home
and could not possibly return.

Assemblyman Sandoval, defending in the public press
a friend charged with buying a Tagbanua slave who had
been thrice sold, says that the several purchasers did not
buy the unfortunate man but bought his debt.   A debt
is not ordinarily purchased for itself and it is admitted
that in this instance the man went with it.

The Filipino politicians have hardly approached this
matter in a judicial spirit, and the timid and the politic,
who refused to give me the information they might have
furnished, had some reason for their fears.

The removal of Judge Ostrand and Director of Education Crone, who gave valuable testimony, was loudly demanded on the ground that they were "traducers of the
Filipino people."

[1] November 1, 1913.

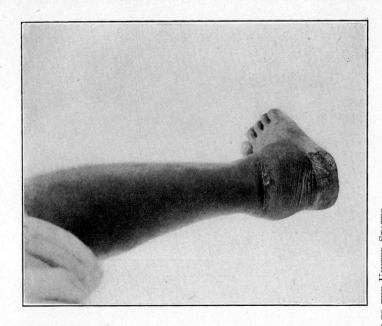

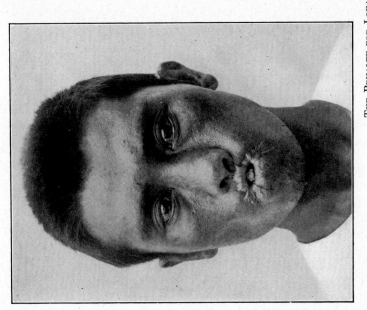

THE PENALTY FOR LOYALTY TO THE UNITED STATES.

This man had his lips cut off and was hamstrung, by order of the bandit chief Felizardo, because he was suspected of giving information to Americans.

The people were urged to "get together" and disprove my statements.

I have been denounced as an enemy of "the Filipino people."

It has been claimed: —

That my charges were false, and without foundation.

That, if they were true, I myself was to blame for the continued existence of slavery.

That I published my report when I did in order to hold my position.

That I published it when I did in anger because I had lost my position.

That I had been removed because I published it.

In just one instance, so far as I know, has a Filipino considered the possibility that the motive which actuated me was a desire to help many thousands of unfortunate human beings.

Good old Arcadio del Rosario, at one time insurgent governor of Benguet, who has a kindly feeling for the wild-men and was glad to note certain immediate results which followed the publication of my report, has said: "Would that Sr. Osmeña[1] might have had the glory of doing what Sr. Worcester has done."

What is needed to end slavery and peonage is congressional legislation enforced by Americans.

Without hesitation I assert that their existence in the Philippine Islands is the greatest single problem which there confronts the government of the United States, in its effort to build up a respectable and responsible electorate and establish representative government.

Is it reasonable to suppose that the hand which to-day crushes down the Filipino servant, the Filipino labourer, and the wild-man of the hills, will to-morrow raise them up and point them on the way to freedom?

[1] Speaker of the Assembly.

CHAPTER XXVI

MURDER AS A GOVERNMENTAL AGENCY

In discussing the prevalence of slavery in the Philippine Islands, Sr. Manuel Quezon has stated that it has never existed there as an institution. This is true, to the extent at least that it has never been recognized as a legal institution, nor directed nor authorized by order of any competent governmental authority. The same statements cannot be truthfully made with reference to murder, as I shall conclusively show by the records of the Insurgent government.

I wish at the outset to draw a sharp line between acts of barbarity or ferocity, committed without authority by ignorant and irresponsible Insurgent officers or soldiers during the heat of battle or as the result of passions aroused by armed strife, and those which I now discuss. The former must be regarded as breaches of military discipline. Aguinaldo sought to protect his government from their consequences by issuing endless orders in Spanish strictly forbidding them.

His troops were ordered again and again to respect American prisoners and treat them with humanity.

So far as concerns his own people, however, he displayed a very different spirit from the outset.

As we have already noted there exists among the Insurgent records a document written in Tagálog by him, and therefore obviously not intended for the information of Americans, which contains the following: —

"Any person who fights for his country has absolute power to kill any one not friendly to our cause." [1]

---

[1] P. I. R., 206. 1.

Aguinaldo armed not only ignorant and irresponsible people, but thieves, outlaws and murderers, and turned them loose on the common people with blanket authority to kill whomsoever they would, and they promptly proceeded to exercise it. *"Dukut"*[1] stretched out its bloody hand even in Manila, under the very eye of American officers, and as often as not struck down wholly innocent victims.

Aguinaldo was not alone in his views on the subject of murder. Felipe Agoncillo, long secretary of the Hong-kong junta, and official representative of the Insurgent government in Europe and the United States, wrote him on August 1, 1898, from Hongkong, suggesting that he kill the Spanish prisoners "if the country requires" that this be done, and adding, "if you deem it wise you should secretly issue an order to kill the friars that they may capture."[2]

Obviously Aguinaldo did not deem it wise to order the murder of the Spanish prisoners as a whole, nor that of the friars as a whole.

The following letter, marked "confidential," addressed to his cousin Baldomero Aguinaldo, for a time the Insurgent secretary of war, tells a significant tale of the course finally decided upon: —

"FILIPINO REPUBLIC,
" OFFICE OF THE MILITARY GOVERNOR,
" MALOLOS, February 17, 1899.

" SEÑOR SECRETARY OF WAR : —

"Referring to your note in regard to an unhealthy town or place in the province of Nueva Ecija fit for the concentration there of the friars; beside the town of Bongabong there is

[1] *Dukut* means secret assassination.

[2] "I was informed that some Spanish prisoners have succeeded in escaping. It is necessary to redouble vigilance upon them, especially upon the officers of rank and upon the friars, because said prisoners might be of great use to us later on. They should, however, be well treated, but without giving them liberty, and confined within prison walls. If the country requires that they should be killed, you should do so. If you deem it wise, you should secretly issue an order to kill the friars that they may capture. They should be frightened." — P. I. R., 471. 4.

no good place except the town of La Paz in the province of Tarlac, because, according to my observation, even the persons born there are attacked by malarial fever and ague and if they are strangers very few will escape death.

"Your always faithful subordinate,

(Signed) "ISIDORO TORRES.

"17th February, 1899." [1]

Evidently General Torres' recommendation was favourably acted upon, for among the papers of the Insurgent government is a memorandum,[2] apparently in Aguinaldo's handwriting, stating that —

"there were 297 Spanish friars held prisoners in Luzón, and that on February 17, 1899, those in Nueva Ecija, Tarlac, and Pampanga, 111 in all, had been ordered by him to be concentrated in La Paz"!

In many instances other prisoners were murdered outright. This hard fate befell three Spaniards, of whom one was a friar, and two were shipwrecked Englishmen, who were butchered in Zambales in December, 1899, upon the approach of the American troops, apparently by the order of the governor, Vicente Camara.[3]

On February 15, 1900, an expedition under the immediate command of Brigadier-General J. M. Bell sailed from Manila under the personal supervision of Major-General Bates. This was composed of troops detailed to take possession of North and South Camarines and Albay, to which provinces Insurgent troops, having many Spanish prisoners in their possession, had been forced to retire as a result of the operations in Tayabas Province. In compliance with these instructions the town of Daet was occupied after some resistance and the Insurgents in that quarter were driven to the northeast, taking with them a number of Spanish prisoners. A large proportion of these were murdered by command of the officer in charge of the guerilla band guarding them, probably because he was not able to force them to move as rapidly as his own men.

[1] Taylor, Ex. 833.   Spanish A. L. S. 32–2.   [2] Taylor, 46 AJ.

[3] Ibid., 15 HS.

On November 15, 1900, Simeon Villa, of evil fame, issued a circular letter[1] to chiefs of guerillas in the Cagayan valley, recommending that they all "learn the verb 'Dukutar'[2] so as to put it into immediate effect," and adding "it is the most efficacious specific against every kind of evil-doer, and most salutary for our country." This, too, under the "Filipino Republic" before the outbreak of war with the United States, and at a time when we are assured that "profound peace and tranquillity" prevailed in this region.

This villanous order was approved and made general in its application by Aguinaldo himself, on November 15, 1900.[3]

Aguinaldo's orders were not always couched in such general terms as the one above quoted. Among the most interesting of the captured Insurgent documents is the following : —

"OUR HONOURABLE PRESIDENT: We, the signers, who subscribe the declaration appended; by these presents protest against the American proclamation ; we recognize no authority but that of God and the Revolutionary Government, and we offer our lives and property for the independence of our country.

"MANILA, SAN MIGUEL, January 12, 1899.

"FELICIANO CRUZ
"SEVERINO QUITIONGCO."

(25 signatures follow.)

(On the back is written in the handwriting of E. Aguinaldo) :
"Leberino Kitionko:
"Feliciano de la Cruz : Commissioned to kill General Otis."[4]

---

[1] "TO CHIEFS OF THE PHILIPPINE GUERILLAS :

"The undersigned, Chief of the General Staff in the office of the Captain General, recommends that all chiefs of guerillas, provided that, in their judgment, there is no obstacle in the way, should kindly order their subordinates, down to the lowest, to learn the verb 'Dukutar,' so as to put it immediately in practice.

"It is the most efficacious specific against every kind of evil-doer, and most salutary for our country. "SIMEON S. VILLA.

"KAGAYAN VALLEY, November 15, 1900."

Extract from letter-sent book in Spanish of E. Aguinaldo, captured with him. — P. I. R., 368–3.

[2] *Dukutar* means to assassinate. [3] P. I. R., 1281 and 368. 3.

[4] P. I. R., 1199–1.

The difference in the spelling of the name Severino Quitiongco is doubtless due to the fact that Aguinaldo wrote it down as it sounded to him.

When the Insurgent government began to be pinched for funds, failure to pay taxes became, in many cases, sufficient ground for murdering the delinquent.

The method of procedure is set forth in the testimony of a tax collector, published in General Orders, No. 259, 1901, Division of the Philippines: —

"I carried a letter of authorization to act as special agent, which means authority to commit murder. Each time a murder was ordered a letter was sent to one of four men (named above) by one of the chiefs (naming them). Afterward the letter was taken up and burned. If a man did not pay his contributions to the insurgent collector he was ordered to be killed."

The chief cause for murder was friendliness toward the Americans. As time passed and the common people had an opportunity to contrast the brutality of their own soldiers with the kindly treatment usually accorded them by the American troops, they welcomed the latter. Weary of danger to life and property, the better men in the towns became very desirous to see the reëstablishment of local governments, and ready to assist in the work. The answer of the Insurgent leaders took the form of wholesale orders for the murder or assassination of all persons friendly to the Americans. I shall cite enough such orders to show that this policy was duly provided for throughout the length and breadth of the Insurgent territory.

Many of the Visayans were friendly toward the Americans from the outset. On March 24, 1900, "General in Chief" Maxilom, of Cebú, issued an order providing for the execution, after a most summary trial, of the presidentes of all towns which subscribed to and recognized American sovereignty. This rule was to apply to Filipino citizens, including even the wealthy, a most unusual arrangement! Failure to be "subject to the will of the Honourable President Señor Emilio Aguinaldo" spelled death.[1]

Outside the Cebú towns occupied by the Americans the guerillas commanded by Maxilom were able to collect tribute by the employment of such methods as were provided for on June 22, 1900, by Maxilom's order fixing the duties of the *magdudukuts*, or secret avengers, who were empowered to "execute without remorse all notorious traitors."[2] This was, in practice, a general warrant to commit murder.

Pursuant to these instructions Pablo Mejia, a Filipino of high character and conspicuous ability, was assassinated in a street of Cebú in August, 1899. The Visayans had reason to be proud of him and to execrate his assassins.

On January 31, 1900, Pio Claveria, delegate to the Military Government of Iloílo province, Panay Island, wrote

[1] " 1. The *presidentes* of all towns who subscribe to and recognize American sovereignty, shall be pursued by all the revolutionists without mercy and when captured shall be sent to these Headquarters for a most summary trial and execution as traitors to the country.

" 2. All Filipino citizens, including the wealthy, of the towns, are subject to the preceding regulation.

" 3. It shall be the duty of the revolutionary armies with regard to the towns which shall recognize or intend to recognize such sovereignty, to destroy the town or towns and without any consideration whatsoever to kill all males, even the poorest, and set fire to all the houses, without respecting any property excepting that of foreigners. And in order that hereafter such misfortunes may not occur, as chief of this province, I warn all the *presidentes* and wealthy people of each town to help us as Filipinos as we are your brothers fighting here in the field to give liberty to our mother country and woe to the traitor who falls into the hands of this revolutionary government, which will strictly carry out all the prescriptions above-mentioned.

" As the government which the invaders are endeavoring to establish is always provisional, if all the inhabitants of this province are true Filipinos, they can easily and simply answer that we are subject to the will of the Honorable President Señor Emilio Aguinaldo, whom we follow and recognize in this new born Republic as the President of the Nation."

[2] Taylor, 80 HS.

the presidente of Tigbauan, that if it was true that he and
various other residents of that town had taken an oath
recognizing American sovereignty and did not retract it
the town would be razed to the ground, and they would
be "deserving of the terrible penalties prescribed by the
laws of the revolution!" [1]

On April 3, 1900, General Leandro Fullón, who signed
himself "Political and Military Governor" of Antique,
and was one of Aguinaldo's emissaries, wrote a circular
letter, to be sent "by the fastest carriers from one town
to the other," imposing sentence of death and confiscation of property on people who had taken out certificates
of citizenship issued by the Americans, together with
annihilation of their towns.[2]

[1] "January, 1900.

"To the Local Presidente, Tigbauan (Iloílo).

" It is with profound regret that I have to state to you that in accordance with reliable information this military delegation has heard that
you and various residents of that town have as electors already taken
an oath recognizing the American sovereignty. If this news is true,
you still have time to retract the oath, as otherwise we will raze that
town to the ground without any hesitation whatever, and you and
your companions who have taken the oath shall be considered as pro-
scribed, and consequently deserving of the terrible penalties prescribed
by the laws of the revolution. This is not a threat: it is loyal and
sincere advice for your own good and that of the town in general.

" May God keep you many years.

"Pio Claveria,
" *Delegate of the Military Government.*

"31st, 1900."   — P. I. R., 1054–8.

[2] " April 3, 1900.

" To the local chiefs mentioned in the margin.

"I have heard with great sorrow that some of the towns of the
southern district of this province have taken out the certificates of
citizenship issued by the North American enemy, and have also complied with all the orders issued by them; this is exactly opposed to
the conduct of the northern district of the province and shows little
love for the country and an implied assent to the Government established by them, for which reason I see myself obliged to impose the
severest punishment which is a sentence of death and confiscation of
property of all those who shall submit to said Government, from the
Chief and his local Cabinet to the lowest citizen, and annihilating their
towns. For this purpose I have ordered the Commanders of Zones
to watch in their respective districts the towns which may show weak-

On July 11, 1900, Fullón issued a more sweeping order, containing the following provisions : —

"1. Any meeting or assembly of a popular character, held at the instance of the Officers of the United States, for the purpose of recognizing the liberty and independence of the towns of this province, is absolutely forbidden.

"2. The person arranging such meeting shall be shot at once without trial or court martial, unless forced to do so by majeure.

"3. Any Filipino filling any office in the name of the United States shall be considered a traitor to his country, and in addition to the penalties imposed by the Penal Code of Spain, provisionally in force, all his property shall be confiscated, and if this should not be possible, the authorities of the Philippine Republic shall endeavour to . . ." (remainder of sentence unintelligible).[1]

In Samar General Vicente Lucban ordered, on February 1, 1901, that persons who collected food for the enemy be killed, as well as those who "finding themselves in our camp pass to the enemy without previous permission from this government." [2]

In Leyte, Honesto Ruiz warned all his "soldiers and bolo-men that whenever a real Americanista, like the police and volunteers, is caught he will be killed." On August 11, 1900, he reported to General Moxica that "the result is that every day they are killing traitors to our country." [3]

The following is a sample order for the assassination of an obnoxious individual : —

ness before said Government, and to impose the punishment which I have mentioned above. This circular is to be published three consecutive nights for general information of all, a report that this has been done being made to these Headquarters. Send it by the fastest couriers from one town to the other, the last one returning it with the endorsements of the preceding ones.

" Headquarters of Tierra Alta, April 3, 1900.
" LEANDRO FULLÓN,
" General and P. M. Governor."
—P. I. R., 1047. 2.

[1] P. I. R., 1047. 2.   [2] Ibid., 824. 1.   [3] Ibid., 1204. 3

"October 4, 1900.
"Confidential.
"To the Local Chiefs of Sogod, Kabalián, Anajauan, Hinun-
dayan, and Hinunangan (Leyte):
"Immediately upon the appearance in the town under your
jurisdiction of the traitor to the Mother Country, Severino
Komandao, you will secure his person and send him to these
headquarters under the proper guard; or if that person should
come into the town followed by an American force, you shall try
to have him killed by treachery (traidoramente), by 'Dukut'
(assassination), for this is what a Filipino deserves who does
not know how to respect his own land and proceeds to injure
the beautiful ideal that we have in view.
"Return the present communication, treating it as confiden-
tial.   Health and fraternity.
"Maninging, October 4, 1900.
"M. Pacheco,
"*Military Commander.*"
"The Military Commander:
"The undersigned, Local Chief, notes the orders contained
in the present circular and will strictly comply therewith.
"Kabalián, October 6, 1900.
"B. Veloso,
"*Local Chief.*"[1]

In Negros, the Tagálogs long failed to effect a lodge-
ment. Ultimately, however, they managed to stir up
trouble, and to secure the help of "Pope" Isio, a noted
outlaw. On May 19, 1900, he suggested the advisability
of punishing "by decapitation all those who go with the
Americans" and ordered that "if it should appear that
they are real spies of the enemy they must be beheaded
immediately without any pretext whatsoever against
it." To be considered a "real spy," it was necessary
only to be seen talking to Americans.

The letter from which I quote was addressed to Señor
Rufo Oyos, General of Operations.[2]

[1] P. I. R., 981. 5.
[2] "You and Captain Antonio must take the field this week without
any pretext whatsoever, and must follow out my instructions very
carefully. We have had patience enough, and now it becomes necessary for us to assert our authority.

The Philippine Assembly in Session.

Evidently he obeyed orders, for he was still alive in November, 1901, at which time "Papa" Isio wrote him again, directing that there be an uprising of all the towns on December 20.

Towns which did not rise on the appointed day were to be "reduced to ashes and all their inhabitants killed, men, women, children and old people." Any presidente who had not collected the taxes of his town before the arrival of Isio was to be "hung without any hesitation whatever."[1]

"It is advisable to punish by decapitation all those who go with the Americans; but it is necessary first to ascertain the existence of the crime, and if it should appear that they are real spies of the enemy, they must be beheaded immediately without any pretext whatsoever against it (being accepted).

"You, Captain Antonio and Judge Cornello must perfectly understand what this order says: when the wealthy are Americanistas, you must seize all their money, clothing and other property belonging to them, immediately making an inventory of the property seized, and you may remain in the place where the seizure is made as long as may be necessary to make said inventory, even though a great amount is spent for maintenance.

"Know furthermore that if the soldiers take any of the property seized, they will speedily be put to death and will surely go to hell; therefore when it becomes necessary to enter a town to make a seizure, you must direct the soldiers not to touch the goods seized, even the most insignificant, in order to avoid consequence of character.

"I have heard, Rufo, that Judge Cornello is opposed to your father-in-law, and I want you to know that Judge Cornello is of my blood; therefore, tell your father-in-law to be very careful because he will have me to treat with shortly, and will be made to pay for those threats which he is making against the people without good cause.

"You will publish this order in the town hall, in order that the evil-minded may see it.

"You, Captain Antonio and Judge Cornello, who are the three comrades who are to take the field, will acquire some happiness if you comply with this order.

"Health and Fraternity.

"DIONISIO PAPA.

"Calibon, May 19, 1900." —P. I. R., 970. 4.

[1] "Make it evident in that circular that the towns which do not rise up in arms on the day fixed, shall be reduced to ashes and all their inhabitants killed, men and women, children and old people.

"The circular is to emanate from me, and you will sign it only by my order.

Obviously Isio's order was not without effect, for we learn that sometime during August, 1900, a man had just left the camp "with the head of the infamous Juan Carballo to hang it in a public place with a label saying 'Juan Carballo, a man pernicious to the revolution. May he rest in peace.'" [1]

Isio's agents collected blackmail according to a regular tariff, based roughly on the value of estates, threatening that those who did not pay up would be regarded as spies of the heretics.[2]

And now let us briefly review conditions in Luzón. Here many of the common people were at first hostile to the Americans, but flesh and blood could not endure what they had to suffer at the hands of vicious Insurgent officers and ignorant soldiers, and ultimately, having learned by experience that Americans were not the incarnate fiends which they had been led to expect to find them, they began to turn to them for help. And the answer of the Insurgent leaders was everywhere the same,—death. On March 20, 1900, Tinio ordered the killing of all officials who did not report to the nearest guerilla commander the movements and plans of the American troops.[3]

"Communicate also to the presidents of Cagayán and other towns that they collect the taxes of their respective towns, as soon as possible; and a president who shall not have collected the taxes on my arrival in the respective town, shall be hung without any hesitation whatsoever.

"I desire that the Presidents meet there soon and await my arrival."
— P. I. R., 970. 5.

[1] P. I. R., 1102. 7.   [2] *Ibid.*, 970. 11.

[3] "March 20, 1900.

"MANUEL TINIO Y BUBDLOC,

"Brigadier General and Commander in Chief of operations in the region of Ilocos.

"Considering that a sufficient time has passed and various means of having been employed as benignant as humanity counsels, to inculcate in the minds of many misguided Filipinos the idea of the country and to check in the beginning those unworthy acts which many of them commit, and which not only redound to the prejudice of the troops but also to the cause they defend, and having observed that such ac-

It has been claimed that there was no opposition to the Katipúnan Society, and that the Filipinos everywhere joined it gladly. This was not the case. At different times there were a number of similar organizations opposed to it, and most important of these was the "Guards of Honour." [1] Its members were ruthlessly murdered. On April 18, 1900, a guerilla chief in Union Province found it necessary to order that all towns in which members of the "Guards of Honour" lived should be burned with the property of the members of that association; that their fathers, mothers, wives and sons should be beheaded, while the men themselves should receive that punishment or be shot. All grown men in every town, and the Sandatahan, were to proceed immediately to aid in the attack upon the Americans and Guards of Honour under pain of being shot or beheaded. [2]

tion does not produce any favourable result on this date, in accordance with the powers vested in me, I have deemed proper to issue the following : —

"PROCLAMATION

" First and last article. The following shall be tried at a most summary trial, and be sentenced to death :

" 1. All local presidentes and other civil authorities, of the towns as well as of the barrios, rancherias and sitios of their respective districts, who as soon as they find out any plan, direction of the movement or number of the enemy shall not give notice thereof to the nearest camp.

" 2. Those who give information to the enemy of the location of the camp, stopping places, movements and direction of the revolutionists, whatever be the age or sex of the former.

" 3. Those who voluntarily offer to serve the enemy as guides, excepting if it be with the purpose of misleading them from the right road, and

" 4. Those who, of their own free will or otherwise, capture revolutionary soldiers who are alone, or who should intimidate them into surrendering to the enemy.

" Issued at General Headquarters on March 20, 1900.

(Signed) " MANUEL TINIO."
— P. I. R., 353. 8.

[1] Guardias de Honor.

[2] " So then dear brothers, be like those of Bacnotan who have not allowed their honour to be sullied, for when they saw the Guards of Honour enter their town they drove them off at once with blows [of bolos? — TR.] and cudgels and to the end that you may not have cause

In July, 1900, General J. Alejandrino ordered : —

"1st. That the Commanders of Columns proclaim as traitors all those in their respective Zones who in obedience to personal interests or from weakness under pressure of the enemy, accept civil positions and they shall be treated as such when they fall into our hands.

"2nd. The commanding officers of columns will concentrate their forces so as to fall upon the towns where exist individuals who favour the formation of such unpopular and despotic Governments and will use every means to arrest the said traitors." [1]

Nowhere is the policy which was being carried out set forth with more brutal frankness than in the following letter : —

"August 3, 1900.

"This letter is folded in envelope shape and addressed: Sr. Teodoro Sandico, Colonel, 1st Military Chief of Staff in Santo Domingo.

*   *   *   *   *   *   *

"MY RESPECTED CHIEF AND DEAR BROTHER: I have received your respected order, regarding the organization of the

to repent of what without doubt I shall be obliged to do, comply with this order, listen to the following :

"First. Whenever the Presidente of the town, Cabezas and Cabezillas of barrios shall have knowledge of the presence in their barrios of Guards of Honour, be they many or few, and do not cause their disappearance or death, they will be immediately shot or beheaded.

"Second. Every barrio or residence of the Guards of Honour where they are going about persuading the inhabitants to follow them in their noxious work — that we may be slaves forever — will be burned and all their property together with their houses; and their sons, their fathers, mothers and their wives will be shot or beheaded to pay for their treason.

"Third and last. All the grown men in the barrios, territorial militiamen or those called 'sandatahan' (bolomen), corporals, sergeants and privates, and everybody who is a Filipino will go immediately to help in the fight against the Guards of Honour and our enemy, the Americans; and those who pay no heed to this or hide themselves will incur the penalty of being shot or beheaded.

"This proclamation will be read in the barrios and will be passed from hand to hand so that it may be copied to the end that nobody may have an excuse when the time comes to put into execution what has been set forth." — P. I. R., 168. 9.

[1] Taylor, Exhibit 1083.

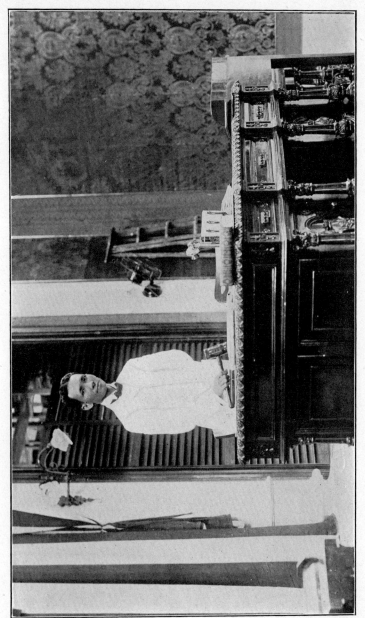

Señor Sergio Osmeña, Speaker of the Philippine Assembly.

Committee in the towns of Zaragosa, Aliaga, and Licab; (Nueva Ecija) from the movements and actions of these towns, I don't believe it possible to organize immediately. Before we can, it will be necessary that four or five lives be taken in each town. I believe that what ought to be done to those towns is to make a new conquest of them, especially the town of San Juan de Guimba; it is difficult there to set straight the Tagálogs and Ilocanos of importance, as they are badly inclined and they care to do nothing but pervert our soldiers.

"This is what I am able to inform you, in fulfilment of the respected order of the Chief.

"God guard you many years.

"SAN CRISTOBAL, August 3, 1900.

(Signed) "C. GONZALES." [1]

The organization of municipal governments by the Philippine Commission, in towns north of Manila, especially aroused the ire of Insurgent leaders, one of whom issued an order declaring traitors all persons who accepted municipal office under the Americans.[2]

[1] P. I. R., 509. 2.

[2] "September 11, 1900.

"To the local Presidents of Malolos, Bulacan, Guiguinto, Bigaa, Bocaue, Marilao, Meyauayan, Polo, Obando, Santa Maria, San José, Angat, Norzagaray, Bustos, San Rafael, Baliuag, Pulilan, Quingua, Santa Isabel, Barasoain, Paombong, Hagonoy, Calumpit, and the military commanders Pablo Tecson, Bonifacio Morales, Maximo Angeles and Colonel Simon Tecson Libuano, Colonel Rosendo Simon, and also Major Dongon.

" CIRCULAR

"As the American Civil Commission has taken charge of the government of the archipelago from the first of the present month and from that date will proceed to establish municipal government in the pueblos to take the place of the municipal councils which at present rule them; in order to duly execute the orders of the Commanding General of the Centre of Luzon, I give you the following instructions: —

"1st. You will arrest and send to these headquarters with the proper precautions to prevent escape, all inhabitants of these pueblos who accept offices in the municipal governments about to be established by the Americans, as they have been declared traitors to the country by the order I have referred to as issued by these headquarters.

"2d. You will employ the same method of procedure with those who favour the establishment of municipal government by the Ameri-

In October, 1900, we find General Vito Belarmino ordering that Filipinos in Ambos Camarines who accept office
under Americans "be treated as traitors," and that "commanders of columns and detachments will cause their
forces to fall on those pueblos in which there are individuals who are in favour of the organization of such unpopular
and therefore despotic governments."[1] One Tuason,
an American adherent, is notified that he and two other
persons, who are named, will be shot and their bodies
hung on the cathedral tower as a lesson to the inhabitants.[2]

In La Laguna province Cailles, who was now in command there, found himself compelled not only to fight
the Americans in the field, but to combat their growing
popularity in the towns, and he promptly inaugurated
a reign of terror, ordering the death of any person whom
he considered an undesirable. His victims were shot,
bayoneted or boloed. If they took refuge within the
American lines, they were followed and assassinated.
In his book of letters sent,[3] there appear the names of
thirty-one men whom he ordered killed between August

cans. You will not show them the slightest consideration, even if
they are your brothers. You are responsible under the severest penalties for the performance of this. God keep you many years.
   "MALOLOS, September 11, 1900.
                                   "I. TORRES,
                                        General."
                                   — P. I. R., Books C–3.

   [1] P. I. R., 341. 9.
   [2] "Two weeks ago a court-martial was held at these headquarters
presided over by Colonel Aréjola, on you, Tuason, and other civil
authorities of this capital, the decision being that you will be shot
when we get there, which will be very soon.
   "You as well as Tuason and Santachia, after having been shot,
will be hung on the cathedral tower to be seen by the inhabitants in
order that you may serve as a lesson . . . I tell you this only as a
companion and nothing more. Your obedient servant, who kisses
your hand.
                                   "EL MONTERO."
                                   — P. I. R., 2007. 1.
   [3] P. I. R., 716. 2.

20, 1900, and April, 1901. Some of these men were described as highwaymen or assassins, and probably deserved their fate, but others were classed as "spies" or "traitors," and certainly did not, unless in this country where it is claimed that Aguinaldo had his people a unit at his back it was an offence worthy of death to prefer peace and order under American rule to conditions such as Insurgent rule fostered.

Cailles did not hesitate to report the results of his orders for the assassination of individuals, giving full and grewsome details. The following is a sample circular letter on this subject, sent out by him : —

"To the local Chiefs and Commanders of Columns, of the province : —

"On this date I have received a communication from the Presidente of Santa Cruz which is as follows : —

"Sr. General : . . . I am pleased, much pleased my General, to inform you with much satisfaction of the end in this world of the villain, of the great traitor, Salvador Reyes, in the following manner : —

"This morning at 8 o'clock, according to the reports of Srs. Lázaro Alfonzo and Modesto de los Reyes, who would gladly give their lives for our honour and glory, your coachman told them that the traitor was proceeding to the northern part of the town. They followed him and upon coming to the front of the house and shop of Cabezang Jacinto Talcon, the aforementioned Sr. Modesto attacked him with a bolo like a tiger, with all the strength of his body and soul, hitting by chance his left jaw, when the other, that is to say, Sr. Lázaro Alfonso, followed the first, catching the traitor by the throat with his right hand and with the other fired three pistol shots at him, one of which missed and the other two took effect in the traitor's shoulder, from the effects of which he fell like a stone upon his face.

"Lastly, Sr. Modesto stabbed him with a bolo, and upon seeing that he was dead, took away his revolver, and carrying the traitor by his belt to Calle de Maria Christina, threw the body down. This was done in plain daylight and in plain view of everybody. . . ." [1]

[1] P. I. R., 716. 5.

"On January 6, 1901, 'the lieutenant-general of the Philippine Islands' ordered that all persons who disobeyed the orders of the Katipúnan were to be tried and sentenced. A member of the organization who found that any person was contemplating taking action opposed to the purposes of that venerable society was authorized to kidnap him, and when the Katipúnan laid hold upon a man he was henceforth seen no more among the living." [1]

The organization of the Federal Party caused an outburst of fury among the Insurgent leaders beside which that aroused by the organization of municipal governments was mild.

Throughout the islands the murdering of officers, members and agents of this party was ordered, and even those who sympathized with its ends were to be shot.

The following is a sample of the orders sentencing to death the adherents of this truly patriotic organization : —

" March 22, 1901.

"Señor Emilio Zurbano y Kajigal,

"Lieutenant Colonel and Military Governor of the Province of Tayabas.

*   *   *   *   *   *   *

"2nd. In view of the preceding section, the Local Presidentes and Commanders of the columns of this province, will carefully watch their respective jurisdictions in order that not one agent of the enemy nor of the Federal Party, may be secretly able to obtain any signatures of the residents, they shall seize any one who may do it and send him to me with all the possible safeguards for the execution of what is ordered in the foregoing section.

"3rd. All persons who may show themselves to be inclined to the Federal Party, will also be captured and shot on being arrested prior to the proceedings and legal formalities, because being inclined towards this party, is the same as declaring oneself a traitor to the country.

"4th. The commander of a column or local presidente who shall tolerate the existence of the Committees of the Federal Party in his jurisdiction, being able to avoid it, will be tried and in case he is found guilty, will be discharged from' his duty and will also be shot, as a traitor to his country.

[1] Taylor, 35 HS.

"5th. The presidentes of the popular committees, will furnish detailed information to the local presidentes and commanders of columns of persons within the towns occupied by the enemies who are engaged in the propagation of the Federal Party or in getting adhesions in any way, either directly or indirectly, to the said party, and the presidente of the popular committee who may fail to accomplish so sacred a duty, will also be punished with the penalty of death.

"6th. When any of the representatives of the federal party, or any of its adherents cannot be captured on account of remaining constantly with the enemy or being protected by him, the local presidentes and commanders of the columns will procure by all means the execution of the said representative or adherent within the line of the enemy through persons of known decision and of patriotism worthy of all commendation.

"7th. All the citizens living in the province of Tayabas who may be representatives or adherents to the Federal Party, aside from the criminal liability which he incurs personally, will be deprived of the benefits of his property, which will be seized by the Government, who will take charge of the profits of the same.

"8th & last. The Local Presidente of the pueblo in which exists any Committee of the Federal Party and the Commander of the column to whose protection the pueblo is entrusted on pain of incurring the punishment detailed in section third of the present proclamation, will proceed to the total destruction of the pueblo in which there is a federalist committee, if, after having been ordered to disband it, at the expiration of seven days the same continues in its traitorous and criminal functions.

"Issued at the Military Government, March 22nd, 1901.
"EMILIO ZURBANO,
"*Lieutenant Colonel, Military Governor.*" [1]

On March 3, 1899, Antonio Luna, general in chief of operations about Manila, directed that all persons who either directly or indirectly refused to aid the execution of his military plans were to be immediately shot without trial. Nothing could have been more sweeping than was his order, and the commanders of detachments of insurgents found in it an authoritative statement that the lives and

[1] P. I. R., 650. 8.

property of the inhabitants of the Philippines were theirs
to do with as they chose.[1]

Mabini made this vicious and cruel order the subject
of bitter protest, writing to Aguinaldo, on March 6, 1899,
a letter in which he says that Luna has grossly exceeded
his powers, and making the very pertinent inquiry
"if an educated man [2] can hardly understand his duties,
how will the uneducated one understand his?" He suggests that it would be better to remove Luna.[3] It does
not appear that this order was ever modified.

[1] "PROCLAMATIONS

"March 3, 1899.

"For general information, since it concerns everybody, we publish
the two important proclamations lately issued by the Chief of Military
Operations of Manila.

"Antonio Luna y Novicio, General of Division of the Army of the
Philippine Republic and General-in-Chief of Military Operations about
Manila.

"In order to prevent any act opposed to the military plans of these
headquarters and consequently to the ideals of the Filipino Republic,
I order and command (only one article). From this day any person
or individual whatever who either directly or indirectly refuses to give
aid to these Headquarters in the prosecution of any military plans, or
who in any manner whatever interferes with the execution of orders
dictated for that purpose by the General in Chief, commanding operations upon Manila will be immediately shot without trial. Communicate and publish this order.

"Given at the General Headquarters of Polo on the 3rd of March,
1899.

"Antonio Luna,
"*General-in-Chief of Operations.*"
— P. I. R., 214–2.

[2] That is, Luna.

[3] "March 6, 1899.

"Señor Presidente: Many complaints have been received here on
account of the abuses committed by General Luna. It is said that he
has lately published a decree in which he warned the people that those
who disobey his orders shall be shot to death without summary trial,
and he made his decree cover the whole province of Pampanga.

"To be shot to death without summary trial is a punishment which
can be inflicted on soldiers; but a chief cannot enforce it in a civilized
community, except among savages. Besides, he has only jurisdiction over Polo, where the General Headquarters is, and over the towns
of the zones of Manila.

I might furnish many similar data, but enough of orders. Any one who is not convinced by these extracts from the official Insurgent records that murder was a duly authorized governmental agency under the Philippine "Republic" is not amenable to reason or influenced by incontrovertible facts.

But were these brutal instructions carried out? They were, indeed, with a ferocity and a cold-blooded barbarity which make one shudder. Fortunate indeed was the man who was really shot, like the presidente of Nagcarlan,[1] and it made no difference if innocent bystanders were wounded or killed as well.

One of the common methods of procedure with victims

"I am very much surprised that these things are not well understood by General Luna. He has no executive power over Bulacán and Pampanga; he must have issued his orders through the military chiefs thereof.

"During such time as he is the commander-in-chief of operations of Manila he is not the director of war, and even if he is, he has no power other than to conduct his office and to take the place of the secretary in his absence.

"If an educated man can hardly understand his duties, how will the uneducated one understand his?

"Please make him acquainted with all of this in order to prevent any encroachment.

"I am at your orders.

(Signed) "AP. MABINI.

"P.S. — It would be better, I think, to remove him from his post.

"A. M."

— P. I. R., 512a–2.

[1] "April 6, 1901.

"Cailles Brigade. Flying column of Rizal and Nagcarlan.

"In conjunction with Captain Macario Dorado, I believed it my duty to attack the town of Nagcarlan, for the principal purpose of killing the American local presidente, as was done during the procession last Holy Thursday. The Presidente was killed and one of his sons, and two residents were wounded, probably by stray bullets, while taking part in the procession.

"Which I have the honor to communicate to you for your information and consequent effects.

"God preserve you many years.

"Nagcarlan, April 6, 1901."

(Illegible signature.)

"To the General in Chief and Superior Politico-Military Commander of This Province." — P. I. R., 1142. 8.

of "dukut" was to bury them alive. A number of individuals suffered this fate at Taytay, near Manila. They were taken out at night, made to kneel beside graves already dug, hit over the head with an iron bar and knocked into their last resting places and the earth was shovelled in on to them. They were confessed by a native priest, and people of the town were required to stand by and see them meet their end.

An American lawyer who afterward defended some of their murderers when the latter were apprehended and brought to trial, told me that among other grewsome details furnished by his clients, who shamelessly admitted to him their guilt, were the following : —

A victim who watched the murder of others, while awaiting his turn, did not want to be struck on the head and begged that as a special favor the blow from the iron bar be omitted in his case. His request was granted, whereupon he climbed into his grave, lay down, covered his face with his handkerchief, and directed his murderers to proceed. I could cite numerous specific cases in which persons were buried alive, and will do so if my word is called in question.[1] If not, enough of this !

[1] The Insurgent leaders did not hesitate officially to report the commission of this ghastly crime. The following is such a report : —
                                            "June 24, 1900.
    In Margin, stamp : "Headquarters First Column, Laguna.   No. 144.
    "I have the honor to transmit to you the enclosed letter from a resident of the town of Pila who had just returned from Manila, in which he gives me news of our present political situation, and as such news are satisfactory to our cause I send you said letter for your information.
    "It is known from very trustworthy information that General del Pilar is under arrest in Manila and he has been substituted in the command of his forces by Colonel Macanca, who was his second in command, and is at the present time repressing with a firm hand the bandits who swarm about the outskirts of the zone under his command, as one of the celebrated bandits named Major Eusebio de Rateros, who had previously been in Pagsanján was buried alive in the cemetery of Taguig by Captain Simplicio Tolentino who is at the present time a member of that brigade.

THE MANILA HOTEL.

The ground on which this fine building stands was redeemed from the bay, by using a part of the dredged material, when the new harbor was built.

Burning alive was occasionally resorted to.[1] More frequently, the victims had their eyes put out, their tongues cut out, and were then turned loose to shift for themselves. Justice Johnson,[2] of the Philippine Supreme Court, has described to me a case in which four policemen of a town which had received him in a friendly manner, were served in this way, and the procedure was a comparatively common one.

Taylor gives the following account of certain incidents which occurred in Ilocos Sur : —

"On page 154 is a record of part of the murders of a body of men in the town of Caoayan, Ilocos Sur Province, who, in July, 1900, calling themselves 'Sandatahan,' appointed a chief executioner, assistant executioners and a requisite number of grave-diggers, and then, with set purpose, proceeded to assassinate all persons who manifested reluctance to join them or to contribute to their support or to the support of the insurgents in the hills whom their leader claimed they were serving. They operated secretly at night, the leaders usually selecting their victims one at a time; and when they were secured they were conducted to a lonely beach covered with tall grass where the grave-digger had already dug the requisite number of graves and where the executioners were already assembled. There in the presence of the assembled band, men and women, bound and

"The news is also confirmed of the execution of Major Espada ordered by General del Pilar. I send you this news for your information.

"God preserve you many years.

"HEADQUARTERS, June 24, 1900.   — P. I. R., 605. 4.

"JULIO HERRERA,
"*Lieutenant Colonel, Commanding 4th Column.*
"To the General and Politico-Military Commander and of
Operations of This Province, *General Camp.*" — P. I. R., 605. 4.

[1] "A commissioner of the Katipúnan society at Ibung, Nueva Vizcaya Province, compelled the inhabitants to take the oath of allegiance to that organization, and issued orders that all who should refuse to follow the dictates of the same should suffer death; and, in pursuance of such orders, was proved to have had, in February, 1901, two men beaten to death, one man buried alive, and two women burnt alive." — Taylor, 38 HS.

[2] At the time of this event he was a judge of first instance.

helpless, were placed upon the brinks of their opened graves, their bodies were run through with swords and bolos and then buried. The band then dispersed, each man going to his own home. These operations were continued with industrious persistency through two months or more until the lengthening row of graves reached, in the language of one of the witnesses, 'about thirty, more or less.'" [1]

The Insurgent leaders themselves reported in a most businesslike manner their orders for assassination and the results of their activities in this direction.

The following are sample communications of this sort:

"HEADQUARTERS CAMP No. 6.
"TIERRA LIBRE (Free Soil), SALUYAN (Laguna Province)
"November 18th, 1900.
"GENERAL JUAN CAILLES,
"Military Governor of La Laguna :

* * * * * * *

"In Nagcarlang it appears that there will be soon a spy, one Juan, a native of Biñang, for he has already commenced to disobey the committee, and so I with much prudence have ordered his eternal rest. The inhabitants have left the town and no one will serve either as barber or laundry-man to the Americans.

* * * * * * *

(Signed) "JULIO INFANTE." [2]

"PROCLAMATION OF LIEUTENANT COLONEL EMILIO ZURBANO,
"MILITARY GOVERNOR OF TAYABAS, TO HIS FELLOW-CITIZENS.

"HEADQUARTERS AND MILITARY GOVERNMENT,
"TAYABAS, April 23, 1901.

"FELLOW-CITIZENS : The holiness, purity and elevation of purpose of us who fight for our independence has caused the execution of five of our fellow-citizens on the 18th instant at five o'clock in the afternoon. They were shot on the plaza of the town of Sampaloc. . . .

"Vivencio Villarosa, for assassination of eleven foreigners and for disloyalty; Pedro Cordero, for disloyalty and spying; Remigío Aviosa, for improper exercise of authority, for many assaults and robbery in a band; Segundo Granada, for many assaults and stealing many animals, and Rufino Sabala for

[1] Taylor, 35-36 HS.   [2] P. I. R., 653. 10.

being addicted to and a disseminator of the doctrines of the
Federal Party have fallen on the plaza of Sampaloc at the
very moment when the twilight of the happy triumph of our
ideal began to advance over the horizon of our country until
now hidden in clouds of blood. May they rest in peace.

* * * * * * *

(Signed) " EMILIO ZURBANO." [1]

After reporting to his subordinates that the local chief
of Bay had, under his orders, arrested Honorato Quisum-
bing, an *Americanista* who had never served as a spy,
and that his captor had killed him when he called to
American troops who were near to help him, Cailles adds :
"His companion was likewise duly executed as a spy and
guide for the enemy. Let us offer up a prayer for their
eternal rest." [2]

Blount has made the following statement : —

"I have heard, so far as I now recollect, of comparatively
few barbarities perpetrated by Filipinos on captured American
soldiers. Barbarities on their side seemed to have been reserved for those of their own race whom they found disloyal
to the cause of their country." [3]

One may well doubt whether he himself wrote the book
which goes under his name, for in it he is made constantly
to contradict himself. Relative to this matter he has also
said : —

"He [4] can never forget the magnificent dash back into the
wide, ugly, swollen stream, made by Captain Edward L. King
of General Lawton's staff, as he spurred his horse in, followed
by several troopers who had responded to his call for mounted
volunteers to accompany him in an effort to save the lives of
the men who went down. Their generous work proved futile.
But it was inspired partly by common dread of what they
knew would happen to any half-drowned soldier who might
be washed ashore far away from the column and captured.
If an army was ever 'in enemy's country,' it was then and
there." [5]

[1] P. I. R., 332. 9.   [2] *Ibid.*, Books A–1.   [3] Blount, p. 203.
[4] *Ibid.*   [5] *Ibid.*, p. 244.

As a matter of fact, not only did the Insurgents repeatedly torture and murder American prisoners, but they poisoned soldiers. Lucban and others directed that this should be done, described the procedure to be followed, and furnished the poison.[1]

Directions for poisoning soldiers were included in a letter written on August 21, 1900, to the Brigadier General Superior Military Commander of the Province of Leyte as follows: —

"It would also be well, in my humble opinion, for you to find out from the old men and quack doctors the kind of poison that can be mixed in alcoholic drinks and in cocoanut wine (tuba), as our enemies now drink these liquors; and after this poison has been known and tried, let it be used in such a way as to undermine the constitution of the man, until some day death occurs; for which purpose you ought to have persons, wherever there are Americans, to poison them. These things are now being done in Luzón, Cebu and Panay.

"There is a tree here in the province whose leaves inflame the body of a man considerably, once applied; for I have seen about Manila the leaves converted into powder, rolled in pellets of paper and shot in the faces of Americans. This causes the parts to swell and become completely useless; and I believe it would be well to do this within the towns, and

[1] "June 5, 1900.
" Sr. Local Presidente of Katibug:
    " I send you a little of the poison known as 'dita' that you may put it on the points of the 'balatik' and 'sura' (spears and traps) admonishing you to take care that none of our people are wounded with the said poison, and if by misfortune any one is wounded, immediately apply the stem of the 'Badian' mixed with that of the 'lingaton' in the wound, as this is the most efficacious means of neutralizing and removing the effect of said poison. Be active and place many of the spears, etc., in all the roads and trails where the enemy must pass, and as soon as you know of his next expedition, inform me immediately by despatch, both by day and night.
    " It is very necessary that the people detailed to place the poison on the points carry always the 'badian' and 'lingaton' so that in case of mishap some one may apply the remedy to neutralize the destructive ingredients of the poison at once.
    " Headquarters of Matuguinao, 5th of June, 1900.
                                    (Signed) " Lukban, General.
(Seal)   " Military Headquarters of Samar." — P. I. R., 502. 7.

especially to the drunkards asleep along the roads and to the fellows making love." [1]

Various other orders for the poisoning of soldiers or the use of poisoned arrows or spears were issued.[2] Furthermore, they were faithfully carried out,[3] and the results were duly reported.

[1] P. I. R., 2035. 3.

[2] The following issued by Col. R. F. Santos in Albay Province is a sample: —

"October 14, 1900.

"In view of the present exceptional state of affairs in our beloved mother country, the Philippines, considering the straits we are in, and in compliance with the order of the General of Division and Chief of Operations for his campaign plans, I trust that upon receipt of the present communication you will kindly order the captains of territorial militia of that barrio, Apud, Pantao and Macabugos, to have all the soldiers of their respective companies provide themselves with at least fifty arrows apiece and a sufficient quantity of the well-known poison called *dita* to apply to the points of the arrows, and to have their bolos well sharpened. I must remind you that as repeated practice is essential in order to secure the best results in the use of these weapons, you will endeavour to have at least twice a week, according to the convenience of the residents, said exercises take place in secluded spots, far from all danger of being surprised by the enemy.

"For the purpose indicated above you will likewise order that all the residents of your respective barrios have ready in a safe place a supply of the fruit commonly called *Ydioc*, putting it in water to decay, and to also have in readiness a squirt gun, that is to say, a 'Sumpit,' in order to use it in case of any invasion or attack of the enemy." — P. I. R., Books B, No. 113.

[3] The following is a sample report: —

"February 4, 1900.

"Lieutenant-Colonel C. Tinio:

"My Dear and Esteemed Uncle:

*   *   *   *   *   *   *

"I am now carrying out a scheme here in this town for the purpose of killing some American sentries, whose bodies will be buried in the woods near the town, where they cannot be traced and found by their comrades, in order to avoid any investigation by them. They will believe that these soldiers have deserted. I have just sent to Gerona for a supply of wine, which, mixed with a strong, sickening stuff, will be sold to them; once they drink of it, the effect will soon tell on them, and then we will seize their rifles.

"I feel that I should advise you of this matter, in order that you may know the reason if, perchance, it should happen that we lose the confidence of the inhabitants of the town on account of this scheme.

The murder of sentries and of soldiers who straggled was often ordered, practised and reported.[1]

As damnable as any of these horrible documents was the order of General Antonio Luna for the massacre of all Americans, foreigners and "disloyal" Filipinos in Manila.

Blount has alleged that Taylor "obtained no evidence convincing to him," relative to the authorship of this order [2] and that "a like investigation by General MacArthur in 1901 had a like result." Whether he is ignorant

However, we will be satisfied if we can seize some rifles without resorting to violent means or to a scandal.

"This is the purpose of your devoted nephew, who always prays God for your health and life, and who sends you his kindest regards.

"SAN JUAN (Tarlac Province?), February 4, 1900.

      (Signed) "LEONCIO ALARILLA,
         " Captain of Guerillas."
           — P. I. R., 480. 5.

[1] The following is a sample report. It will be noted that its author was a civilian, not a soldier: —

            "January 19, 1900.

"SR. LIEUT. COL. A. TECSON:

"With due respect I address you to inform you that yesterday at 10 A.M., I was in the barrio of Bagonbaulat and I saw one of the enemy's soldiers who was lagging behind his companions, and what I did was to order the man in charge of that place and three men to be called whom I ordered to capture the said soldier, and when a prisoner I ordered him to be led to the woods and there they killed him and buried the body; the rifle he carried and ninety cartridges I left with the people and continued my march to San Isidro; on my return when I was to get the rifle mentioned I could not find it and they told me they had sent it to Major Manolo. I inform you of this in compliance with the order.

"God guard you many years.

"ENTABLADO, 19th January, 1900.

      (Signed) "ROMAN I. TORRES,
         " Commissioner."
           — P. I. R., 573. 2.

[2] "At page 1890 of the same volume, Captain J. R. M. Taylor, 14th U. S. Infantry, a gallant soldier and an accomplished scholar, who was in charge in 1901 of the captured insurgent records at Manila, states that he was 'informed' that the document was originally 'signed by Sandico, then Secretary of the Interior' of the revolutionary government. Captain Taylor made an attempt to run the matter down, but obtained no evidence convincing to him. A like investigation by General MacArthur in 1901 had a like result." — Blount, p. 200.

MAYON VOLCANO.

This beautiful volcano, which in the recent past has destroyed many lives and much property, has now been quiescent for some ten years.

of the facts as to the authentication of the authorship of
this very important document, or chooses to ignore them,
I do not know. Taylor in the end conclusively settled
the matter, and so reported. Luna's order,[1] which was

---

[1] *"Luna's Order:*

"'MALOLOS, February 7, 1899.
" 'To The Field Officers of the Territorial Militia :

" 'By virtue of the barbarous attack made upon our army on the
fourth day of February without this being preceded by any strained
relations whatever between the two armies, it is necessary for the
Filipinos to show that they know how to avenge themselves of treachery
and deceit of those who, working upon our friendship, now seek to
enslave us.

" ' In order to carry out the complete destruction of that accursed
army of drunkards and thieves, it is indispensable that we all work in
unison, and that orders issued from this war office be faithfully carried
out.

" 'As soon as you receive this circular, measures will be taken for
strict compliance with the following orders :

" ' (1) Such measures will be taken that at 8 o'clock at night the
members of the territorial militia under orders will be ready to go into
the street with their arms and ammunition to occupy San Pedro street
and such cross streets as open into it.

" ' (2) The defenders of the Philippines under your orders will
attack the Zorilla barracks and the Bilibid guard, and liberate all the
prisoners, arming them in the most practical manner in order that
they may aid their brethren and work out our revenge ; to this end
the following address shall be made to them :

" 'BRETHREN : The Americans have insulted us and we must revenge ourselves upon them by annihilating them.

" 'This is the only means for obtaining justice, for the many out-
rages and infamies of which we have been the object. All the Filipinos
in Manila will second us. May the blood of the traitors run in torrents ! Long live the independence of the Philippines !

" ' (3) The servants of the houses occupied by the Americans and
Spaniards shall burn the buildings in which their masters live in such
a manner that the conflagration shall be simultaneous in all part of
the city.

" 'The signals for carrying this into effect — shall be to send up two
red paper balloons and the firing of rockets with lights and firecrackers.

" ' (4) The lives of the Filipinos only shall be respected, and they
shall not be molested, with the exception of those who have been
pointed out as traitors.

" 'All others of whatsoever race they may be shall be given no
quarter and shall be exterminated, thus proving to foreign countries
that America is not capable of maintaining order or defending any of
the interests which she has undertaken to defend.

issued on February 7, 1899, provided for the massacre of all Americans and foreigners in Manila. The lives of Filipinos only were to be respected. All others, of whatsoever race, were to be given no quarter, but were to be exterminated, "thus proving to foreign countries that America is not capable of maintaining order or defending any of the interests which she has undertaken to defend."

This effort to massacre all white persons in the city fell through, partly because the plan leaked out, and partly because Cavite Insurgent soldiers did not obey orders.

I consider it important that the authenticity of this much-discussed order should be placed beyond reasonable doubt, and so give Taylor's findings in full. He says: —

"A synopsis of this order was telegraphed to Washington by General Otis on February 21st, 1899, as having been 'issued by an important officer of the insurgent government at Malolos,

" '(5) The sharpshooters of Tondo and Santa Ana shall be the first to open fire and those on the outside of the Manila lines shall second their attack, and thus the American forces will find themselves between two fires. The militia of Trozo, Binondo, Kyapo (Quiapo), and Sampalok shall follow up the attack. All must go into the streets and perform their duties.

" 'The militiamen of Paco, Ermita, Malate, Santa Cruz, and San Miguel shall attack when firing has become general everywhere, which will be approximately about 12 o'clock at night; but if they see that their comrades are in danger before that time they shall give them the proper assistance and go into the streets whenever it becomes necessary.

" 'The Spanish militia enlisted as volunteers in our army shall go out at 3 o'clock in the morning and attack Fort Santiago.

" 'Brethren, the country is in danger and we must rise to save it. Europe sees that we are feeble, but we will demonstrate that we know how to do as should be done, shedding our blood for the salvation of our outraged country. Death to the tyrant! War without quarter to the false Americans who wish to enslave us! Independence or death!

" 'A. LUNA.

" 'MALOLOS, February 7, 1899.

" 'COLONEL JOSÉ: By order of General Luna, have several copies of this made, in order that these instructions may be communicated to all.' " — Senate Document 331, part 2, p. 1912, Fifty-seventh Congress, First Session.

February 15th, 1899, for execution during the evening and night in this city' of Manila. Page 157, Senate Document 208, Fifty-sixth Congress, First Session. On March 2, 1901, a Senate resolution called for all information in the possession of the Secretary of War 'relating to, or tending to show, the authenticity and genuineness of the alleged order for the massacre of the foreign residents of Manila, P. I., on the evening and night of February 15, 1899;' and, further, whether the original of that order was or ever had been in the possession of the War Department, and whether it had ever been seen by such a person. This order required a search in Manila, which was made. As a result of this it was ascertained that the synopsis which was telegraphed by General Otis was brought to Maj. F. C. Bourns,[1] an officer of the provost marshal general's office, by a rather prominent Filipino [2] who had given a good deal of information which on the whole had proved to be correct. He stated that the paper which he handed him was a copy of the original which had just been sent to officers of the bolo organization, the sandatahan, of Manila, but that he had not time to copy the whole of it; yet as far as it went the paper was an exact copy of the original order, which was signed by Sandico. Major Bourns said that at the time the paper was received there was no reason to doubt 'the man's statement that it was an exact copy of the original order, for we knew that some such order was under consideration, that this bolo organization existed, and it was under the orders of Sandico, who, in turn, was entirely under the influence of Luna. Since my return to the Philippines, however, several little things have occurred which have caused me to question whether or not the paper was an exact copy of the original order. That in the main it was correct, I do not doubt; but I am just a little inclined to think the man may have "stretched" things a little.'

"The search was continued, and finally one of the original orders, a translation of which immediately precedes this note, was produced by Dr. Manuel Xeres y Burgos who was then a surgeon employed in the Bilibid prison in Manila and who had been an officer in the territorial militia of that city. Doctor Burgos wrote in July, 1901, to Colonel Crowder, military secretary to the Military governor of the Philippines, that if he gave him all the details in regard to the means he had employed in obtaining the document, it would require many sheets of paper, and the story would seem like a novel to those who

---

[1] Major F. S. Bourns. [2] Dr. Manuel Xerez Burgos.

only superficially knew the customs of the Philippines. He said that 'a few days after the beginning of hostilities we were given to read an order of a mysterious character; we were not allowed to take a copy thereof or to keep it in our possession, probably from fear of some treachery. However the bearer told me that several copies had been made which were to be sent to all the districts in which the " Filipino militia" had been distributed. The chief of the latter were the men called upon to execute said order. You know that, thank God, it was not executed, not only through lack of arms, but also because most of the chiefs who were in Manila felt a repugnance to execute such a barbarous and foolish order, which, had it been attempted, would have been the cause of the extermination of all the Filipinos who were within the American lines as a just reprisal for such an atrocious order.

"' Luckily, not only the savage measure prescribed was never carried into execution, but it was impossible to attack the American army, the men who had been detailed to do it in Manila having only a few hundred bolos as arms, and the chiefs of the militia understood that with such arms they could not think of resisting the rifles and cannon of the Americans.

"' Up to the middle of April, 1899, several Filipinos who came from the lines declared that General Luna had sentenced us to death for having disobeyed that terrible order. We were 14 who were considered as traitors to our country, and we were precisely those who had worked for the release of the prisoners in whom we had the greatest confidence, answering for them to the authorities and exposing ourselves to get into trouble if they had broken their word.

"'We had decided to collect all papers which referred to certain facts, in order to show some day who were those who had lent real services to the country, and we resolved to try and find the document which was the principal cause of the danger which had threatened us at that time.

"' We would have had the paper in our possession since August last if it had not been for the terror inspired by the secret police with its unjustified arrests, and our emissaries fled from Manila and did not come back until after the end of the persecution.

"' On the 25th of February, 1901, our friend Benito Albey, who had been lieutenant of the militia and had distinguished himself in the war against Spain, began, on our advice, a new investigation, which was crowned with success.

"'The document was found among the baggage left by

Colonel Leyba to Teodoro de los Santos at Malolos, and which the latter had remitted to a certain Tolo Quesada at Alava, Pangasinán.

"' I am sincerely happy that said document, which is the clear proof of General Luna's iniquitous methods, should have been found so that it may serve as a voucher to the thoroughness of General Otis' investigations; although I would have liked to keep it among my papers, I have more satisfaction to be useful to the American General, who has obtained the sympathy of the Filipinos by his kind treatment.

"' And I hope, General Crowder, that you will say as much to General Otis, as I wish him to know that there are Filipinos who have kept a grateful recollection of him, and that all Filipinos are not ungrateful.

"' Very respectfully,
"' MANUEL XERES BURGOS.

"' GENERAL CROWDER.'

"On June 30, 1901, the original of this order, signed by Luna and produced by Burgos, was shown to Aguinaldo, who, after examining it, stated that the signature was that of General Antonio Luna, with which he was well acquainted. He furthermore stated that he had no personal knowledge of such an order, and had hitherto been unaware of its existence. He was then asked whether General Luna's authority, as Director of War, was of sufficient scope to authorize him to issue such an order without express authority from the insurgent government. He declined to answer this question.

"A photographic reproduction of the original of the order of Luna, dated February 7, 1899, a printed copy in Spanish, the translation which preceded this note, and the correspondence upon which the foregoing statement is based, is given beginning on page 1903, Senate Document No. 331, part 2, Fifty-seventh Congress, First Session, 'Hearings before the Committee on the Philippines of the United States Senate.'

"There does not seem to me to be the slightest reason for doubting the authenticity of this order. It was an atrocious one, but that argument is not sufficient to prove that the order delivered up by Dr. Burgos was a forgery in whole or in part.

"The facts of the case seem to me to be the following: In January, 1899, Doctor Burgos was employed in Bilibid prison by the Americans, and as an officer of Sandatahan was deep in the plotting for a general massacre of the foreigners in Manila. Sometime that month he wrote to Aguinaldo that the uprising in Manila should begin in Bilibid prison, and that the

Sandatahan should be posted on San Pedro street and the adjacent thoroughfares in preparation for an attack upon the Zorilla theatre, where the Pennsylvania regiment was quartered across the way from the prison (Exhibit 349). His suggestion was adopted as part of the plan for the uprising. Burgos, like the majority of the Filipinos in Manila, believed that Aguinaldo would win, and was doing what he could to aid his cause, but without giving up his position under the American government. The plan embodied in Luna's order was to be carried out as part of the attack upon Manila; but that attack was delivered prematurely, and it was found impossible to carry out the uprising in Manila which was to have preceded the attack upon the American lines. After February 5, 1899, the majority of the Filipinos in Manila ceased to believe that Aguinaldo was going to beat the Americans, and Burgos, who was known to have taken part in the movement in Manila headed by Sandico, found it expedient to ward off any investigation of his conduct by giving information. He wanted to stay out of prison, and he wanted to remain surgeon of Bilibid prison. He was well aware that Sandico was known by the Americans to have organized bodies of sandatahan in Manila, and he therefore delivered to the provost marshal general a partial copy of Luna's order which, if it was not then in his possession, he had seen; and he saw no reason for telling more than seemed expedient for the attainment of his immediate purpose, he said that it had been issued by Sandico, who he well knew the Americans would believe was the man most likely to have issued it. He naturally desired to avoid having to make too many explanations. In 1901, Luna being dead, and Burgos being safe from his vengeance, he found no great difficulty in delivering up the original document, which was probably, as he said, in the papers of Colonel Leyba, or Leiva, a native of Manila whose family lived there and whose house had probably been a centre of insurgent intrigue. In 1899 or 1900 Colonel Leyba, a trusted and confidential aid of Aguinaldo, had been murdered by 'The Guards of Honour' in Pangasinán Province, and Burgos seems to have had access to his papers. This, at least to me, seems a plausible explanation of the incomplete form in which this first order appeared, and why it appeared at all. It is true that I have found no record of it among the record-books kept at Malolos; but this order was not of a character to be written out in full in any letter-sent book; and, furthermore, the record-books of the government at Malolos show that almost no records were kept there for a week after the outbreak of hostilities. The clerks and officials were probably busy in preparing to defend the place against an advance of the Americans, whom they had hitherto looked upon with contempt.

"JOHN R. TAYLOR." [1]

In reality there was nothing novel about the issuing of such an order in the Philippines.

Alfonso Ocampo, who was to have led the attack in an attempt to massacre all Spaniards in Cavite at the outbreak of the revolt of 1896, testified as follows concerning the proposed movement : —

"It was to be carried out in conjunction with the towns of Imus and others of the province; the people were to enter by the Porta Vaga (the main gate of Cavite) and uniting into groups, were to assault, kill and rob all the Spaniards. The deponent was in charge of this affair. The jailer of the prison was to distribute daggers among the prisoners and then release them. When the plot was discovered, some of these arms had been distributed. The object of the rebellion was to assassinate all the Spaniards, then to rape the women, and cut their throats, as well as those of their children, even the smallest." [2]

On June 26, 1896, there was issued an order for an uprising in Manila, which contained the following provisions, among others : —

"Fourth. While the attack is being made on the Captain-General and other Spanish authorities, the men who are loyal will attack the convents and behead their infamous inhabitants. As for the riches contained in said convents, they will be taken over by the commissioners appointed by this G. R. Log. for the purpose, and, none of our brothers will be permitted to take possession of that which justly belongs to the treasury of the G. N. F. [Grand Philippine Nation ?–TR.].

"Fifth. Those who violate the provisions of the preceding paragraph will be considered malefactors, and will be subjected to exemplary punishment by this G. R. Log. [Grand Regional Lodge ?].

[1] This is the "note by compiler on exhibit 816," which is Luna's order.

[2] Taylor, 96 FZ.

"Sixth. On the following day the brothers designated will bury the bodies of all the hateful oppressors, in the field of Bgumbayan, as well as those of their wives and children. Later a monument commemorating the independence of the G. N. F. (Grand Philippine Nation?) will be erected on that site.

"Seventh. The bodies of the friars will not be buried, but will be burned in just payment for the crimes which during their lives they committed against the noble Filipinos, for three centuries of hateful domination." [1]

As much is said, in the very numerous orders for assassinations, of trials by courts of most summary procedure, especial importance attaches to Taylor's statement that there is an almost complete absence of records of trials or legal proceedings among the two hundred and fifty thousand documents on which his work was based. He says that "there are probably less than twenty-five records of trials among these papers, and not above one or two records of military courts of summary procedure. Law was the will of the official who would force obedience to his desire. If he wanted to kill he killed." [2]

General MacArthur is credited by Blount with the following statement: —

"The cohesion of Filipino society in behalf of insurgent interests is most emphatically illustrated by the fact that assassination, which was extensively employed, was generally accepted as a legitimate expression of insurgent governmental authority. *The individuals marked for death would not appeal to American protection, although condemned exclusively on account of supposed pro-Americanism.*" [3]

As a matter of fact, plenty of people appealed to the Americans for protection and got it. I have seen document after document each recommending some individual to American officers everywhere as worthy of protection, and as needing it on account of services rendered to Americans. Relative to this matter, Taylor says: —

[1] Taylor, 99 FZ.
[2] *Ibid.*, 44 HS.
[3] Blount, p. 313.

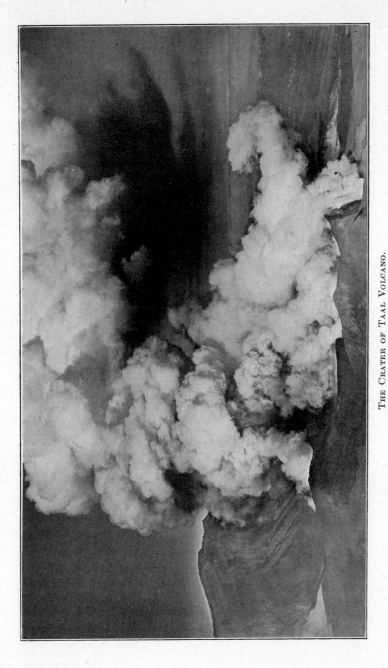

THE CRATER OF TAAL VOLCANO.

This photograph was taken a few hours before the destructive eruption of January 29, 1910, which killed some 1400 people in a few moments.

"Among the papers of the insurgents there are a few letters to American officers asking for protection against the insurgents. They represent a protest against conditions which were rapidly becoming unbearable; but most of them must have been sent without copies, for in case they fell into the hands of the guerillas they would have served as death warrants for the men who signed them. From early in 1900, they were much more frequent all over the archipelago than the number which have survived, either in the official records of the American army in the Philippines, or among the papers of the insurgents, would lead the investigator to believe. Those which were sent to the commanders of American detachments were not kept as a rule, for a small detachment has few records. As early as March, 1900, the head of the town of Passi, Panay, asked American protection against robbers and insurgents." [1]

General MacArthur had a fixed idea that all Filipinos were against us, but he was wrong.[2]

In very many cases our efforts to furnish protection were necessarily futile. It is easy enough to protect a town from an open attack. It is often excessively difficult to protect an individual against an assassin who proffers him one hand in assumed friendship and stabs him with the other.

We shall never know how many men were murdered in accordance with the orders which I have cited, and other similar ones.

On February 10, 1900, General P. García wrote to General Isidoro Torres advising him to inform the inhabitants of Bulacan, among whom it was understood that the Americans were about to establish municipal governments, "of what occurred in the Island of Negros where two hundred men have been shot and forty more have

[1] Taylor, 70 HS.
[2] "In December, 1900, the people of the town of Santa Cruz, Ilocos Sur, seized the guerilla commander of the town because he had raped some women, and then burnt their acts of adhesion to the insurgent government. They declared themselves adherents of the Americans, proceeded to give them all possible aid and assistance, and captured and delivered to them all the guerillas who dared enter the place (P. I. R., Books C–13)." — Taylor, 45 HS.

been cast into the water for having accepted the American sovereignty, and because they were suspected of not being adherents of the cause of the independence of our country." [1]

In reviewing the sentence of the Taytay murderers, General Adna R. Chaffee, who, as the ranking military officer in the Philippines, was closely in touch with the situation, made the following statement : —

"The number of peaceful men who have been murdered in these islands at the instigation of the chiefs, while impracticable of exact determination, is yet known to be so great that to recount them would constitute one of the most horrible chapters in human history. With respect to these chiefs, the commanding general has, therefore, no other recourse than to invoke the unrelenting execution of the law upon them and to appeal to the intelligent and educated among the Filipino people to aid him by renewed efforts to end a reign of terror of which their own people are the helpless victims." [2]

Taylor has made the following summary of the facts : —

"The justice of the United States was slow in its course ; witnesses had to be examined, and before a notorious criminal could be punished it had to be proved that he had committed some particular crime. Unless the crime was proved to the satisfaction of a military commission by witnesses, the greater part of whose testimony had to be translated into English from some native language by an interpreter, who was almost never an American, the man whom a whole village knew to be an assassin would escape punishment and would return to avenge himself upon those who had denounced him. The justice of Aguinaldo was a different matter. The Americans might hang for murder, but he would bury alive for serving them. The Americans might send a man to prison for burning a town, only to release him when an error was found in the proceedings. There were no errors in the proceedings of the guerillas. There was usually no summoning of witnesses, no slow taking of testimony and no careful search for laches which would invalidate the finding of the court and inure to the benefit of the accused. It was sufficient for some native to be denounced as in the employment of the Americans, or

---

[1] P. I. R., Books A–9, No. 39.   [2] Taylor, 37 HS.

as an agent, or as a civil officer under the United States, for a summons to be issued for his appearance before a court of summary procedure, which was a court in name only; or for a mandate to be sent ordering that 'the serviceable method of *dukut* was to be employed in his case.' That meant that he was kidnapped and murdered, usually after a priest had received his confession; or that he was sent back to the town hamstrung and with his tongue out, as a warning to the people that the justice of Aguinaldo was sharp and that his arm was long." [1]

The blood of these men cries out against those who would deceive the American people into believing that the Filipinos were ever united in loyalty toward the Filipino Republic or the leaders who made murder a governmental agency in the Philippine Islands.

Most of the men who wrote the orders and perpetrated the acts which I have cited are alive and active to-day. Were independence granted, they would rule again the country that they ruled before. Is there any reason for believing that their warped intelligences have straightened, or their hard hearts softened? Would the United States care to assume responsibility for any government which they could set up or would maintain?

[1] Taylor, 28-29 HS.

CHAPTER XXVII

THE PHILIPPINE LEGISLATURE

FROM September 1, 1900, to October 16, 1907, the Philippine Commission was the sole legislative body. The Act of Congress of July 1, 1902, temporarily providing for the administration of the affairs of civil government in the Philippine Islands, had provided for the taking of a census after the insurrection should have ceased and a condition of general and complete peace should have been certified to by the commission. It had provided further that two years after the publication of the census, if such condition of peace had continued in the territory not inhabited by Moros or other non-Christian tribes, and was certified to the President by the commission, the President should direct the commission to call, and the commission should call, a general election for the choice of delegates to a popular assembly to be known as the Philippine Assembly, and that after said assembly should convene and organize all the legislative power theretofore conferred on the commission in all that part of the islands not inhabited by Moros or other non-Christian tribes should be vested in a legislature consisting of two houses, the Philippine Commission and the Philippine Assembly.

The first of the certificates required of the commission was issued on September 8, 1902. President Roosevelt on September 23, 1902, issued an order for the taking of the census.

On March 28, 1905, Governor-General Wright proclaimed the publication of the census. On March 28, 1907, the commission issued the second of the certificates required of it.[1]

[1] The essential part of the resolution reads as follows: —
"*Whereas* since the completion and publication of said census there

768

The following day a cablegram was received from the President directing the commission to call a general election for the choice of delegates, and on March 30, 1907, the commission adopted the necessary resolution calling such election to be held on July 30, 1907, in accordance with an election law previously passed on January 9 of the same year. This law provided for eighty-one delegates proportioned among thirty-five provinces according to population, except that each province entitled to representation was allotted at least one delegate, no matter how few people it might have. Cebú, the most populous of all, was given seven. The Mountain Province, the Moro Province, Nueva Vizcaya and Agusan were left without representation because of the predominance of Moros or other non-Christians among their people. On April 1,

have been no serious disturbances of the public order save and except those caused by the noted outlaws and bandit chieftains Felizardo and Montalón, and their followers in the Provinces of Cavite and Batangas, and those caused in the Provinces of Samar and Leyte by the non-Christian and fanatical pulajanes resident in the mountain districts of the said provinces and the barrios contiguous thereto; and

"*Whereas* the overwhelming majority of the people of the said Provinces of Cavite, Batangas, Samar, and Leyte have not taken part in said disturbances and have not aided nor abetted the lawless acts of said bandits and pulajanes; and

"*Whereas* the great mass and body of the Filipino people have, during said period of two years, continued to be law-abiding, peaceful, and loyal to the United States, and have continued to recognize and do now recognize the authority and sovereignty of the United States in the territory of said Philippine Islands: Now, therefore, be it

"*Resolved* by the Philippine Commission in formal session duly assembled, That it, said Philippine Commission, do certify, and it does hereby certify, to the President of the United States that for a period of two years after the completion and publication of the census a condition of general and complete peace, with recognition of the authority of the United States, has continued to exist and now exists in the territory of said Philippine Islands not inhabited by Moros or other non-Christian tribes; and be it further

"*Resolved* by said Philippine Commission, That the President of the United States be requested, and is hereby requested, to direct said Philippine Commission to call a general election for the choice of delegates to a popular assembly of the people of said territory in the Philippine Islands, which assembly shall be known as the Philippine Assembly." — Journal of the Commission, Vol. I, pp. 8–9.

1907, the governor-general issued a proclamation embodying the resolution of the commission.

The election was duly held, and on October 16, 1907, the first session of the Philippine Legislature was opened, under authority of the President, by Mr. Taft, then secretary of war, who had returned to the Islands for this and other purposes.

The action of the commission in issuing its second certificate has been criticised on account of conditions which arose subsequent to the publication of the census, in Cavite, La Laguna and Samar. These conditions were referred to in the commission resolution. There was no desire to conceal or misrepresent them. As we have already seen, the trouble in Samar was stirred up by abuses among the hill people. It has been claimed that they were not members of any non-Christian tribe. There are a limited number of genuine wild people in Samar, but the great majority of the so-called *pulájanes* were in reality *remontados*[1] or the descendants of *remontados*.

In La Laguna and Cavite disorder caused by wandering *ladrone* bands at one time had become so serious that it was deemed advisable temporarily to suspend the writ of habeaus corpus and to authorize the reconcentration of the law-abiding inhabitants of certain regions to the end that they might be adequately protected and to make it easier to distinguish between good citizens, and thieves and murderers.

Whether these occurrences were or were not to be considered as of such a nature as to render it impossible to certify that a condition of "general and complete peace, with recognition of the authority of the United States" had continued to exist in the Philippine territory not occupied by Moros or other non-Christians, was a matter

---

[1] A designation applied by the Spaniards to people who had taken to the hills to avoid paying taxes or to escape abuses, or punishment for crimes.

of judgment, and the commission exercised the best judgment it possessed.

During the Spanish days ladronism had always been rampant, affecting every province in the islands and being especially bad in the immediate vicinity of Manila. When we issued our certificate we had little hope of promptly ridding the archipelago of ladrones, as has since been done. On the contrary we expected that a certain amount of ladronism would continue for many years. We did not think that it should be considered public disorder within the meaning of the act of Congress. Furthermore, we were all anxious to encourage the Filipinos and to give them a chance to show what they could do. I for one hoped that by this act of liberality we might win the good-will, and secure the real coöperation, of many of the Filipino politicians. It is always easy to look back and see one's mistakes. I now know that nothing could have been more futile than the hope of gaining the good-will of the men with whom we were dealing by any concessions whatsoever, yet the attempt was worth making. It is the wild men in the hills and the good old taos [1] in the lowland plains who appreciate and are grateful for fair treatment when they realize that they are receiving it.

The politicians of the present day are a hungry lot. The more they are fed, the more their appetites grow, and the wider their voracious maws open. Most of them are without gratitude or appreciation, and regard concessions as evidences of weakness on the part of those who grant them. Philippine officials and lawmakers might as well make up their minds to do what is right because it is right, and let it go at that. By the same token they should refrain from doing what is questionable in the hope that the good-will resulting will more than counterbalance the possible evil effect of doubtful measures.

[1] A Tagálog designation applied to the common people, and especially to field labourers.

It cannot be denied that the issuance by the commission of its certificate of March 30, 1907, was a somewhat doubtful measure, involving a rather strained construction of the words "general and complete peace, with recognition of the authority of the United States" in the Act of Congress of July 1, 1902. I am now firmly of the opinion that in thus giving the Filipinos the benefit of the doubt we erred, with the result that the Philippine Assembly came at least ten years too soon. Its creation in 1907 has resulted in imposing a heavy financial burden on the country for which there has been no adequate compensating return.

In the Philippine Legislature neither house enjoys any special privileges, and either may originate any bill which the legislature is authorized to pass. The assembly has been characterized as "a harmless little debating society" and the government of the Philippines has been called "a toy government" because it was claimed that no real powers were given to the lower house. The commission has exclusive power to legislate for certain non-Christian territory. In all other legislative matters the assembly and the commission have equal power. The passage of legislation requires affirmative action by both houses, a condition which is certainly sufficiently common in legislative bodies composed of two houses, and one that does not ordinarily evoke criticism.

Of late the assembly has claimed for itself the exclusive right to initiate appropriation bills, but there is not a vestige of legal authority for such a claim, and even the so-called "Jones Bill" does not confer such right on the lower house. It shares, with the upper house, one power of deadly effectiveness. It can prevent legislation on any subject whatsoever. It has not hesitated to employ this power, when occasion arose, to obstruct the passage of many important and desirable measures, either in the hope of being able in the end to make a trade and thus securing the passage of acts of more than doubtful utility, or be-

A Bit of the Pagsanján Gorge.

cause of a purpose to prevent the enactment of laws dealing with the matters in question.

The most striking instance of the blocking of important legislation by the assembly is afforded by its action in tabling four anti-slavery acts passed by the commission at successive legislative sessions. This matter has already been fully discussed.[1]

The history of the Cadastral Survey Act affords an example of the holding up by the assembly of a measure of undoubted and undenied utility in order to attempt to force the passage of positively vicious acts.

The case of the would-be landowner who has occupied land for years under such conditions that he could have completed an unperfected title to it, and who finally desires for one reason or another to do so, has been a rather hard one, as the cost of the necessary survey is chargeable to him and when a survey party has to be sent a long distance to measure a little tract of land the ratio of such cost to the value of the land is often very high. Cost of surveys can be materially reduced if all the privately owned land parcels in a given area are surveyed consecutively, and this procedure has the further great advantage of effectively delimiting the public domain in the area in question.

In the interest of small property owners, advantage has been taken of provisions of the Public Land Act which make it possible to compel the survey of private lands under certain conditions in cases of doubt as to ownership. As soon as the people concerned could be made to understand our object in doing this they became enthusiastic about it, but the legal procedure authorized was by no means adequate or satisfactory, and there was great need of the passage of a carefully drafted Cadastral Survey Act providing the necessary legal machinery for accomplishing the desired end with the least possible delay and at the lowest possible ex-

[1] See p. 699 *et seq.*

pense, and providing further for the distribution of such expense between the insular, provincial and municipal governments and the property owners. All are interested parties, the insular government because it learns what land in a given region belongs to the public domain ; the provincial and municipal governments because the collection of taxes is facilitated, and accurate maps of towns and barrios are made.

Such an act was passed by the commission. It was clearly and indisputably designed expressly for the benefit of poor Filipinos. No legitimate objection could be made to it. The treatment accorded it by the Philippine Assembly conclusively demonstrates the irresponsibility of that body, and its unfitness to deal with great questions which vitally affect the common people. Realizing that the commission, and especially the governor-general, were earnestly desirous of securing its passage, the assembly refused to pass it. It was duly reintroduced at the next session of the legislature.

I was a member of the commission conference committee appointed to meet a similar committee from the assembly and discuss it. The assembly committee informed us at the outset that a *sine qua non* for the discussion of the bill was that we should agree to an amendment which would admit, without examination, to the work of making public land surveys Filipino so-called surveyors, known to be utterly incompetent, who could not make correct surveys under the most favourable circumstances. But this was not all. It was generally understood that an additional requirement was to be an amendment to the Judiciary Act providing for a number of new judges. The commission committee believed that they were unnecessary, and were asked for with a view to making places for political appointees. Needless to say, the Cadastral Survey Act failed in conference. In the session of 1912–1913 it finally passed, with practically all of these objectionable features eliminated, but it is at present much less useful than it might be for the reason that an act amending the Judiciary Act so as to provide more judges in the Court of Land Registration, where they are badly needed, instead of for courts of first instance, where no such necessity exists, was killed in the assembly.

As it will take the Court of Land Registration something like three years to finish hearing the cases already in hand, the preparation of a large additional number for it, as a result of the application of the Cadastral Act, will not materially help the present situation unless the number of its judges is increased. There is reason to fear that future attempts to bring this about will be met by demands that there be more judges of first instance, and that they be given jurisdiction in land cases, which should be decided by specially trained and qualified men.

One who examined only the laws actually passed by the legislature might gain the impression that the assembly had done good work. It should be remembered that 312 acts passed by that body have been disapproved by the commission. Had they become laws there would have been a very different story to tell. One hundred and seven acts passed by the commission have been disapproved by the assembly. A careful study of these two groups of acts will be found worth while, but in order to make the picture complete it should be supplemented by detailed consideration of the amendments to assembly bills made by the commission before they have been passed, which have sometimes involved the striking out of everything after title, and the insertion of practically new provisions. It should further be remembered that many really good measures, which have apparently originated as assembly bills, have been drafted by members of the commission, or under their direction, and then first presented in the assembly in order to facilitate their passage.

Had some one of the several gentlemen who have made

brief visits to the Philippines and then expressed their views as to the fitness of the Filipinos for early independence devoted himself to the line of study above outlined, he would have gained valuable information on their present fitness to legislate, and we should perhaps now be profiting by the practical results of an experiment already made, instead of embarking on a new and dangerous one.

I cannot here do more than briefly call attention to the nature of a few of the bills killed by the commission and the assembly respectively. For convenience of reference, I refer to these bills by session and number.

FIRST LEGISLATURE

Inaugural Session

Assembly Bill 117 was "An Act to extend the period within which provincial boards organized under the Provincial Government Act may remit the collection of the land tax in their respective provinces."

This was the first of a very long series of assembly measures designed to abolish or reduce existing taxes, or indefinitely to postpone the time for their collection. Provincial boards, with a majority of their members elective, were very amenable to influence in the matter of "postponing" the collection of the land tax.

The per capita rate of taxation is lower in the Philippines than in any other civilized country. Money is badly needed for education, health work and the improvement of means of communication, and all of these measures were ill-advised.

First Session and Special Session of 1908

Assembly Bill 23 provided for the appointment of jurors in courts of first instance and justice of the peace courts. Under it the provincial boards were to select the eligibles from a list of names submitted by the municipal councils of the provincial capitals. This would in effect have put the administration of justice in the hands of the political party in power.

Assembly Bill 104 was entitled " An Act amending Act numbered fifteen hundred and thirty-seven of the Philippine Commission on horse-races in the Philippine Islands."

Gambling is the besetting sin of the Filipinos, and in the city of Manila gambling in connection with horse racing had grown to be such a scandal that the commission had been compelled to take action limiting the days on which it was permitted to legal holidays and one Sunday per month. The evil had reached large dimensions. Several race-tracks were maintained in one small city, and the money that went through the totalizer, or gambling machine, had reached the enormous sum of $3,500,000 per year. Even poorly paid clerks were leaving their work to bet on the races, and then stealing in order to recoup themselves for their losses. The morals of the community were being rapidly undermined. The act passed by the commission interfered with the business of conducting daily crooked races. It certainly left plenty of opportunity to indulge in horse-racing as a legitimate sport. The amendment proposed by the assembly permitted horse-racing on all Sundays, on three days prior to Lent and on all legal holidays except Memorial Day, Rizal Day and Thursday and Friday of Holy Week. If passed it would have protected certain vicious interests and opened the way to a prompt extension of the gambling business.

Assembly Bill 134 reduced the tax on distilled intoxicating liquors one-fourth. The tax was already low. The rate proposed by the assembly was a concession to the demand of powerful interests and its attitude was worthy of severe condemnation.

Assembly Bill 136 abolished provincial boards of health, substituted therefor district health officers and took important powers away from the director of health and gave them to provincial boards. Substantial progress had been made in improving provincial sanitary conditions through provincial boards of health, under the control of the director of health. As was to be anticipated in a country like the Philippines, many necessary health measures were unpopular. This bill, vitally affecting one of the most imperative needs of the islands, would if concurred in by the commission have resulted in widespread disaster.

Assembly Bill 148 provided for the teaching of the local native dialects in the public schools. This would have had the effect of doing away with the teaching of English, or preventing its inauguration, in many places; would have emphasized and perpetuated the different native dialects; would have helped to keep the people speaking these several dialects apart, and would thus seriously have hampered progress toward national unity. One of the most important and useful things that the American government is doing is to generalize the knowledge of the English language, which not only gives the several peoples of the archipelago a common means of communication, but opens up new fields of knowledge to them and makes it easy for them to travel. Even during the days of the Filipino "republic" Mabini advocated making English the official language.[1]

[1] Mabini's "True Decalogue," published as a part of his constitutional programme for the Philippine Republic (P. I. R., 40. 10) contains the following among other remarkable provisions: —

"Elementary instructions shall comprise reading, speaking and writing correctly the official language which is Tagálog, and the rudimentary principles of English and of the exact physical and natural sciences, together with a slight knowledge of the duties of man and citizenship." — Taylor, 19 MG.

Also the following: —

"Whenever the English language is sufficiently diffused' through the whole Philippine Archipelago it shall be declared the official language." — Taylor, 20 MG.

Assembly Bill 197 abolished the Bureau of Civil Service and organized in its stead a division attached to the Bureau of Audits. This bill, ostensibly an economy measure, was designed to minimize the usefulness of one of the most important bureaus of the government. In the early days of the American régime Filipinos who had served the government were often deeply offended that appointments were not given to members of their families or to their near relatives, absolutely irrespective of their fitness for office. Naturally they disapproved of the civil service law when they found that it prevented such appointments.

Second Session

Assembly Bill 201 prohibited the employment of foreigners as engineers or as assistant engineers on vessels in the Philippine Islands. There were at this time an extremely limited number of Filipinos capable of filling such positions, which were largely held by Spaniards and other Europeans who had married native women and had lived in the islands for years. This measure would have crippled shipping companies and would have been a grave injustice to the men above referred to.

Assembly Bill 278, which heavily reduced taxes on distilled spirits and cigarettes, was another attempt to make concessions to certain large tobacco and liquor interests, which could perfectly well afford to pay at the rates then prescribed. It would have decreased the annual insular revenues about $1,000,000 at a time when it was anticipated

Of this language matter Taylor says : —
"Mabini's plan of having English the language of the state is odd. He wanted independence and he wanted the recognition of the right and of the ability of the natives to govern themselves; and yet he wanted them to adopt a foreign language. By the time this pamphlet was published, or shortly afterwards, Tagálog had been tried and found wanting. The people of the non-Tagálog provinces did not know it and showed no desire to learn it, and indeed protested against its use. Spanish, and all things Spanish, Mabini was weary of, and would sweep them all away. Yet, when he wrote this he did not know English."

that free trade with the United States, resulting from the passage of the Payne Bill, would greatly reduce customs duties. Such a loss would seriously have crippled the administration of the islands.

Assembly Bill 352 exempted all uncultivated land, except land in Manila, from the payment of the land tax for a period of five years. The excuse given for its passage was the alleged lack of draft animals. Its real purpose was to exempt valuable property from taxation. It would have encouraged the continued holding of great tracts of uncultivated land and was in the interest of large landowners whose land taxes were likely to be burdensome if they did not come to a reasonable agreement with their tenants and bring their holdings under cultivation.

Assembly Bill 360, "specifying the responsibility in a publication and amending certain sections of the existing libel law," would have rendered that law abortive by making it possible for a newspaper to employ as a "libel editor" some irresponsible person who would be glad to go to jail upon occasion for a consideration.

The Philippines has a fairly good libel law and it was imperatively needed, for in oriental countries especially, the tendency of a public press which has been subjected to the strictest censorship is to run to license when complete liberty suddenly comes.

Assembly Bill 370, creating the new province of Zamboanga, embodied an attempt on the part of that body to legislate for territory inhabited by Moros and other non-Christian tribes, over which it had no jurisdiction. If passed, it would have led to bloodshed between Moros and Filipinos.

Assembly Bill 433 was an act prohibiting the use of lumber imported from foreign countries in the construction of public buildings. It was not then possible to get enough native lumber to erect the public buildings authorized and needed. The passage of this act under the circumstances showed lack of business sense.

A GIANT TREE FERN.

Assembly Bill 487 provided for compulsory school attendance. It was so worded as to make it largely inoperative, and if operative it would have been impracticable, as there were something like 1,200,000 children of school age in the islands and there were neither teachers enough to instruct them, schoolhouses enough to hold them, nor funds available with which to pay for new buildings and additional teachers. Its passage showed lack of business sense.

Assembly Bill 547 amended the so-called *"bandolerismo"* [1] act." Up to the time of the American occupation brigandage had been a crying evil throughout the islands. The amendment proposed would not only have greatly weakened the act under which it had been very successfully suppressed, but would have turned loose 1156 criminals, many of whom were desperate and hardened, seriously disturbing the tranquillity of the country and necessitating the early hunting down of many of them.

Assembly Bill 567 was "An Act empowering the Secretary of Commerce and Police to make contracts with silk producers, insuring them the purchase of their silk at a price not to exceed $9 per pound." The Bureau of Science had conclusively demonstrated the possibility of establishing a silk industry in the Philippines. This extraordinary measure would have made it possible for an executive officer to provide for the expenditure of all the revenues of the government in case of a great development of the silk industry. Its passage showed lack of business sense.

Assembly Bill 558 was "An Act to provide for a permanent annual appropriation of $15,000 to reward the inventor of a steam plough or any mechanical engineer who shall perfect a ploughing machine." It was a foolish measure, as there were various successful steam ploughs and other motor-drawn ploughs then in use, and there was no

[1] Brigandage.

good reason for offering a reward for the invention of a thing which already existed.

Assembly Bill 395 was a most extraordinary and dangerous measure. The Spanish law fixed the age of consent of women at twenty-three, which is about ten years after the time when young girls in the Philippines begin to turn their thoughts toward marriage. Whenever a man had sexual relations with a woman under twenty-three he was liable to go to jail for rape unless pardoned by the parents, grandparents or guardian. This provision of law was continually taken advantage of in blackmailing persons. Suit would be brought and the necessary proof provided. Pardon would be offered for a consideration. The crime was known as a private crime, not a crime against the public. The commission had amended the Penal Code, making it a public crime so that once complaint was made no pardon on the part of the interested persons could stop the proceedings. There had been a consequent noticeable falling off in the number of cases brought for the purpose of extorting money. Assembly Bill 395 was designed to change this state of affairs and restore the old conditions. It was a vicious measure.

Special Session 1910

Assembly Bill 396 authorized the use of certain kinds of sledges on improved roads, although it had been abundantly demonstrated that they were veritable road destroyers. The commission had passed a law prohibiting their use and the natives had been compelled to substitute for them carts with wide-tired wheels that turned freely on their axles, and improved the roads instead of ruining them. This bill was an effort to authorize a return to the road-wrecking practices which had previously prevailed.

Assembly Bill 481, "An Act prohibiting the admittance of women and of minors under eighteen years of age into cock-pits established in the Philippine Islands," was a measure encouraging vice, masquerading in the guise of a reform. By inference it permitted the entrance of women and minors more than 18 years of age to cock-pits for the purpose of gambling, and it provided that women and minors could go as sightseers!

Assembly Bill 491 authorized certain classes of people to have firearms irrespective of their individual characteristics. The presence of firearms in the hands of irresponsible people had been a source of great trouble and the granting of gun licenses was then restricted to persons in whom the government had entire confidence. This had been an important factor in suppressing brigandage and highway robbery, and the proposed change in the law was highly undesirable.

Second Session

Assembly Bill 141, "An Act repealing the last paragraph of Act Numbered 1979," took away from the governor-general authority to approve suspension of the additional cedula tax for road purposes, and gave it to provincial boards. The need of improved highways was very great as the inadequate system which had existed under the Spanish régime had gone to pieces during the war. A comprehensive plan of highways for the islands had been worked out and was being put into effect as rapidly as possible. This act would have allowed provincial boards to determine whether funds should be collected for road construction and maintenance, thus bringing this fundamentally important question into the domain of local politics.

Assembly Bill 168 provided that "the Spanish language shall continue to be the official language of the courts until such time as the Philippine Legislature shall provide otherwise."

The reasons why the generalization of English was

desirable in the Philippines have already been stated. Under then-existing provisions of law it was to become the official language of the courts in 1913. Assembly Bill 168 would have had the effect of leaving Spanish the official court language for an indefinite time, thus discouraging the use of English and discriminating against young lawyers who had made every effort to obtain a good knowledge of it because of its supposed certainty of usefulness to them.

A novel and objectionable feature of Assembly Bill 947, which appropriated $375,000 for the construction of roads and bridges, was that it made executive action of the secretary of commerce and police subject to the approval of a committee of the legislature.

First and Special Sessions of 1913

Assembly Bill 91 was "An Act prohibiting the exhibition of inhabitants of the non-Christian tribes, and establishing penalties for its violation."

This act grew out of the desire of the assembly to conceal the fact of the existence of wild peoples in the Philippines. It prohibited the publication of indecent photographs of non-Christians, and the appearance at any fair or carnival of a member of a non-Christian tribe clothed in such a manner as to offend against public morals. The commission committee which had this Act under advisement stated, as a part of their report on it, that : —

"It is obvious that no indecent or immoral picture should be published, irrespective of whether the person or persons depicted are Christian or non-Christian. It is equally evident that no person should be allowed to appear at any exposition, fair or carnival in a costume which offends against morality, whatever may be his religious beliefs or his tribal relationships. Your committee is of the opinion that there now exists on the statute books adequate legislation properly penalizing the one offense and the other."

This act also attempted to limit the right of non-Christians to enter into contracts.

Assembly Bill 130, "An Act declaring invalid the confession or declaration of a defendant against himself, when made under certain circumstances," provided that courts should not give any value to a confession or declaration, oral or written, of any defendant against himself made before the agents of the constabulary, municipal police, judicial or executive officers, or before any other person not vested with authority, during his preventive detention, or while in their custody, unless ratified by the defendant himself in proper style before a competent court.

Only persons familiar with the extreme timidity of many Filipino witnesses, and with the frequency with which they deny in court true statements previously made by them, can appreciate the dangerous character of this measure.

Assembly Bill 170, "An Act obliging manufacturing, industrial, agricultural, and commercial enterprises in the Philippine Islands to provide themselves with a duly qualified physician and a medicine chest for urgent cases of accident and disease among their laborers, and for other purposes," would have had the effect of forcing the employment of a large number of incompetent Filipino physicians for the reason that no one else would have been available to fill many of the positions in question.

Assembly Bill 172, "An Act protecting the plantation of the cocoanut tree," prohibited the damaging, destroying, uprooting or killing of any cocoanut plant or plants without the owner's consent. There was then going on a large amount of highway construction and widening. This bill would have strengthened the position of certain persons disposed to ask exorbitant prices for land needed for rights of way. At about this time the Manila Railroad Company was compelled to pay a large sum for orange trees on a piece of land through which its road was to pass. On investigation the orange trees proved to be cuttings from branches, or young seedlings, recently stuck into the ground, many of them being already dead.

Assembly Bill 250 would if passed have had the effect of depriving agents of the Society for Prevention of Cruelty to Animals of the power to make arrests, and of compelling the payment of all fines imposed and collected through the efforts of the society into the insular treasury, so that the society would have been dependent upon direct appropriations for funds with which to prosecute its work. For three successive years there had been no appropriation bill. The Filipinos have little sympathy with the work of this society, and this was a scheme to kill it. Under the existing law one-half of the fines in question go to it for use in promoting its objects.

Assembly Bill 251, "An Act to create rural guards in all the municipalities organized under Act No. 82, and for other purposes," would seriously have interfered with the maintenance of a proper state of public order. The duties which it proposed to vest in rural guards are now performed most satisfactorily by the Philippine Constabulary. The effect of the bill would have been to restrict the administrative authority of the director of constabulary over the movements of his force, and to interfere with the administrative authority of municipal presidents to utilize their police as in their judgment the public interests require.

Assembly Bill 262 contained the following : —

"*Provided:* That the Director of Agriculture or his agents shall not adopt quarantine measures in provinces organized under Act No. 83 without previous agreement with the Provincial Boards concerned."

For many years no more serious problem has faced the insular government than that of stamping out the contagious diseases which were decimating the horses and cattle of the islands and threatening to render agriculture almost impossible. The director of agriculture was necessarily given wide authority in the matter of establishing proper quarantines. This act would have taken necessary powers from him and vested them in provincial boards. Quarantining was very unpopular with the very people who were benefited most by it, hence the passage of this act.

Assembly Bill 282 was designed to do away with the public improvement tax in the provinces of Palawan, Mindoro and Batanes, and to substitute therefor the so-called double cedula tax. This would have resulted in decreasing by one-half the amount of money available for the construction of public works in those provinces and increasing in the same amount that available for paying salaries of officials and employees.

Assembly Bill 312, amending "The Philippine Road Law" "so as to punish the violent occupation of land on both sides of any public highway, bridge, wharf, or trail at present occupied by other persons, since prior to the passage of such Act," would have prevented the recovery by the government of highway rights of way where they had been encroached upon by abutting owners during the long period of neglect of road maintenance attendant upon war.

Assembly Bill 319, entitled "An Act to prohibit, and punish judges for the issuance of orders of arrest at hours of the night or on days other than working days," was a most extraordinary measure, the object and effect of which are apparent from merely reading its title. There are 365 nights and 63 legal holidays in the year, so that the time during which judges could issue orders of arrest without exposing themselves to punishment would have been somewhat restricted.

Assembly Bill 324, entitled "An Act amending certain articles of the Penal Code of the Philippine Islands," had for its object the reduction of the age of consent of women to the crimes of abduction and seduction.

Assembly Bill 348 provided for the formation of a "poor

list," and regulated "gratuitous medical attendance at public dispensaries and hospitals in the city of Manila and the municipalities, or public hospitals in the provinces."

One of the great things which the American government has done for the Philippines is to bring medical and surgical service of a high order within the reach of a very large number of poor persons. By the proposed bill free service to Filipinos was limited to those who declared themselves to be paupers. Many of the deserving poor would have preferred to perish miserably rather than make such a declaration. Most of the self-respecting poor of the islands are not paupers. Free service could be rendered to foreigners only on presentation of certificates of poverty from their consuls, usually residing in Manila, which would have worked great hardship on such persons living in remote parts of the islands and in need of immediate attention. Charitable free service furnished by the government was objected to by certain Filipino physicians, who hoped to get paid for attending the persons thus relieved. The practical result of the bill would have been to force the poor to depend on these people, and to pay their charges, which are frequently very exorbitant.

COMMISSION BILLS DISAPPROVED BY THE ASSEMBLY

SECOND LEGISLATURE

Commission Bill 55, amending "The Philippine Administrative Act by including vessels within the provisions of Sections 322 and 323 of said Act," was designed to make vessels responsible for the transportation of contraband cargo, or for smuggling merchandise, in the same degree that attached to vehicles for land transportation, the attorney-general having held that the word "vehicle" used in the existing law could not be construed to include vessels. This measure was important in connection with the suppression of opium smuggling.

Commission Bill 59 amended an act providing for the

SCENE ON A BIRD ISLAND.

punishment of perjury "by changing the punishment for perjury and by punishing persons who endeavour to procure or incite other persons to commit perjury." Its object was to remedy a defect in existing law under which there is no punishment provided for subornation of perjury in official investigations.

Commission Bill 60, "An Act defining habitual criminals and providing additional punishment for the same," had for its object the breaking up of petty thieving, the records of the Bureau of Prisons showing that one hundred twenty-nine persons had been convicted twice, twenty a third time and one as high as thirty-two times. It would unquestionably have been a very useful measure.

The Supreme Court of the United States had found that certain punishments of the Spanish Penal Code, particularly with reference to the falsification of public and private documents, were cruel and unusual, and under its decisions a number of criminals, who should have served moderate sentences, were turned loose because the sentences actually imposed were admittedly too severe. The Penal Code fixed the penalties in such cases and gave no option to the judge to impose lesser ones. This decision of the Supreme Court of the United States had the practical effect of making it impossible to penalize certain crimes at all. Commission Bill 61 remedied this situation by providing moderate penalties. The bill was asked for by the secretary of finance and justice, who is a Filipino, and by the president of the code committee, but the assembly would not pass it.

THIRD LEGISLATURE

First Session and Special Session

Commission Bill 59 provided "more severe punishment for illegal importers and dealers in opium."

Great difficulty has been experienced in endeavouring to check the use of opium in the islands.

Commission Bill 70 provided for gradually restricting cock-fighting by decreasing from year to year the number of days on which it was allowed. It imposed annual license fees of $5 on each fighting cock or cock in training, prohibited persons under 18 years of age and women, except tourists, from entering cock-pits, and forbade all games of chance of any kind on the premises of a cock-pit.

This very cursory review of some of the acts which have failed of passage will serve to show, in a general way, the attitudes of the two houses toward a number of important questions.

Had the commission not prevented the passage of much dangerous and vicious legislation approved by the assembly the public service would have suffered seriously, and public order would have been endangered.

Heretofore the commission has prevented the enactment of really vicious legislation. By giving the Filipinos a majority in this body a very important safeguard has been removed.

Another serious result will follow. It was undoubtedly the will of Congress, when its Act of July 1, 1902, was passed, that Americans should control legislation for the Moros and other non-Christians; hence the power to legislate for the territory which they inhabit was reserved by Congress for the commission. Under the new arrangement Filipinos will control in this matter also, and so the will of Congress will be defeated, although the letter of the law is not violated. The outlook for the backward peoples of the islands, under these circumstances, cannot fail to arouse grave apprehension among all who are genuinely interested in them.

The elections for delegates to the assembly have caused endless trouble in many of the provinces. Neither the people at large nor the candidates themselves have as yet learned cheerfully to accept the will of the majority, and the number of protested election cases is out of all proportion to the number of delegates.

In many towns, like Cuyo, these elections have given rise to serious feuds which have brought their previously rapid social and material progress to a standstill, divided families against each other, and in general have produced very disastrous results. Many of the best people of Cuyo are now begging to have the right to elect an assemblyman taken from their province, on the ground that otherwise there is no hope for the restoration of normal conditions.

The assembly is the judge of the qualifications of its members. It has seen fit to admit a number of very disreputable characters. In my opinion neither the character of its members nor that of the legislation passed by it has justified its establishment, much less the "Filipinization" of the commission.

CHAPTER XXVIII

The Picturesque Philippines

HAVING now devoted a good deal of time to the consideration of political conditions in the Philippines, let us turn our attention to the islands themselves and consider their physical characteristics, their climate and their commercial possibilities.

There has been much discussion as to the number of islands in the archipelago. The United States Coast and Geodetic Survey has counted them. Big and little they number thirty-one hundred forty-one, of which ten hundred ninety-five are large and fertile enough to be inhabited.

The total land area is a hundred fifteen thousand twenty-six square miles. The Philippines lie between 5° and 22° North Latitude and 117° and 127° East Longitude. It follows that the lowlands throughout the archipelago have a tropical climate, and in the past those two words have been very generally considered to spell danger for people of the white race. In this connection it should be said, first, that the Philippines have one of the most healthful tropical climates in the world, and second, that the results of sanitary work both there and within the limits of the Panama Canal zone have largely eliminated the tropical climate bugaboo. There is plenty of malaria in some portions of the archipelago, but that is a matter of mosquitoes, not of climate, and there is no difficulty in freeing any given region from this disease if drainage is practicable.

The two great drawbacks to life in the tropics are admittedly heat and humidity. Curiously enough the heat in most parts of the Philippines is never extreme. We do not have in Manila anything approaching the high temperatures sometimes experienced in New York or Boston. Humidity in the atmosphere makes heat trying, and is responsible for what we call "sultry" days. The dry-bulb thermometer shows how hot one is, but it takes an instrument with a wet bulb to show how hot one feels. Fortunately, the periods of greatest heat and greatest humidity do not coincide in the islands. April and May are the hottest months, while August and September have the highest humidity.

It must be remembered, however, that very extreme heat for a few days, followed by cool weather, is not so debilitating as is a lower temperature which is nevertheless continuously high. There are often many days in succession during May when the thermometer stands in the nineties, but there is usually a cool northeasterly breeze at that season, and throughout the Philippines, except in the Cagayan valley and in one or two other inland regions of the larger islands, hot nights are almost unknown. Indeed, it is doubtless due to the fact that the land area is broken into myriad islands, and is therefore swept by the cooling sea breezes, that it has such an exceptionally healthful climate. The heat is never trying when the monsoons blow, and they blow much of the time.

Speaking of the islands in general one may say that they have a wet season from July to October and a dry season from December to May, the weather during June and November being variable. On the Pacific coast, however, these seasons are reversed, and in the southern Philippines they are not well defined, the rainfall being quite uniformly distributed throughout the year. During the months of November, December, January and February weather conditions are usually ideal, with bright, clear days and cool and decidedly invigorating nights. Comfort throughout the year is largely dependent on oc-

cupying well-ventilated houses from which the winds are
not shut off.

The following table shows for each month the highest
temperature, the lowest temperature and the average
temperature recorded at Manila from 1885 until 1912 : —

Month	Highest ° F.	Lowest ° F.	Average ° F.
January	93.0	59.0	76.8
February	96.1	60.3	77.5
March	97.2	61.2	79.9
April	99.9	64.4	82.8
May	100.9	68.7	83.3
June	99.7	70.9	82.2
July	95.4	70.0	80.8
August	95.4	69.1	80.8
September	95.5	69.6	80.4
October	95.2	67.3	80.2
November	93.0	62.2	78.6
December	92.3	60.3	77.4

The highest temperature ever recorded at Manila is
103.5° Fahrenheit, in May, 1878 ; the next highest, 101.9°
in May, 1912.

It should be remembered that there are no abrupt
changes either between day and night or from season to
season, and that one can therefore wear light, cool clothing throughout the year.

Far from being oppressive, the tropical nights are, as
a rule, delightful. I know of nothing more satisfying
in its way than a stroll in the moonlight on a hard beach
of snow-white coral sand bordered by graceful cocoanut
palms on the one hand and by rolling surf on the other.

The vegetation in the provinces is a constant delight.
Unfortunately, in the immediate vicinity of Manila it is
less attractive than in most other parts of the archipelago,
but by crossing the bay to the Lanao forest on the slopes
of Mariveles Mountain, or by taking an automobile ride
to Atimonan, one may see it in all its magnificence.   No

word painter, however skilled, can convey any adequate idea of it.

Everywhere, both on land and at sea, one sees matchless greens and blues, — greens in the vegetation and in the water, blues in the water and in the sky. The cloud effects are often marvellously fine. I had begun to think that perhaps my prolonged residence in the Philippines had made me forget what was to be seen in other countries, but in 1913 I took the distinguished English vulcanologist, Dr. Tempest Anderson, on a trip with me, and his enthusiasm over the cloud views knew no bounds.

Philippine sunsets are unsurpassed and unsurpassable. I have repeatedly noted one remarkable effect which I have never seen elsewhere, namely the complete reflection in the east of the western evening sky. On the occasion when I first witnessed one of these extraordinary sights I could hardly believe my senses. I was at sea, and had taken a late afternoon siesta. When I awoke familiar landmarks showed me that I was looking due east, and yet I saw a magnificent sunset with wonderful beams of rays radiating from a dark cloud behind which it seemed that the sun must be hidden. A glance to the westward furnished the explanation of the mystery, for the view was duplicated there. I have seen similar wonderful sights several times.

A typhoon, or tropical cyclone, is often dreadfully destructive but is a most imposing thing to watch from a safe viewpoint, and the weather service in the Philippines is so excellent that if one observes such a storm from an unsafe viewpoint it is usually one's own fault. The rush of the mighty waves at sea and their thunder on the shore, where they may dash up the cliffs for hundreds of feet, are awe inspiring. The resistless sweep of the wind, which sometimes attains a velocity of a hundred twenty miles an hour, or even more, makes one feel one's insignificance. If one chances to be in the region over which the centre of the storm passes, there comes a sudden lull in the

terrific gale, followed by a dead calm.   Often the sun shines
for a brief interval, and then, without warning, the wind
renews its relentless assault, coming from a direction dia-
metrically opposed to that from which it was blowing
before the lull.   The rainfall is often enormous.   At such
times rivulets are converted into roaring rivers, valleys
into lakes.

If one is near buildings with galvanized roofs which
may fly through the air in pieces, or trees which may blow
down, it is best to keep under cover, but after the storm
there are always to be seen curious and interesting freaks of
wind and water.   When the northern district of Manila is
flooded, as not infrequently happens during severe typhoons, the people turn out for a regular water *fiesta* as
soon as the wind moderates, and go paddling about the
streets in dugout canoes, wooden tubs, or on rafts extemporized from old barrels, pieces of bamboo, or the
stems of bananas which have been blown down.

Due warning of the approach of a typhoon is given by
the Weather Bureau at least twenty-four hours in advance,
so that the damage done may be reduced to a minimum.
Houses of light materials are apt to suffer severely, but
serious damage to strongly built houses is comparatively
rare, as they are constructed with a view to meeting just
such conditions.

Waterspouts are among the most imposing and picturesque of nature's phenomena in the Philippines.   I have
repeatedly had the good fortune to watch them form, and
start on their stately march across the sea, but to my
everlasting regret have never had a camera available on
such occasions.   They sometimes produce a rain of fishes.

The scenery is never monotonous.   At sea one views a
constantly changing panorama of islands, many of which
are picturesque in the extreme.   On land one may travel
over long stretches of level, fertile plains, but there are
always fine mountains in the background, and once among
them what pleasures await one !   Some are grass-covered

A Day's Catch.

These fish were taken in Malampaya Sound in a day by four fishermen working from two boats with only three rods.

to their very peaks; others are buried from base to summit in the rankest tropical growth. On yet others, pine forests begin to cover the slopes at four thousand feet, and are in turn replaced by oak forests at five or six thousand feet. The numerous rushing streams and waterfalls are a joy in themselves. In one short day one may go from the tropics to the temperate zone, and come back again.

Active and extinct volcanoes form a striking feature of many Philippine landscapes. Of the former, Mayon, in the province of Albay, is the delight of the vulcanologist and of the layman alike on account of its exquisite form, which is that of the theoretically perfect volcano. It rises to a height of seventy-nine hundred sixteen feet from an almost level plain, and the extreme outer periphery of its base measures approximately a hundred twenty miles. An excellent automobile road extends completely around it, well within the peripheral line above mentioned, and the trip, which has no equal in its way, may readily be made in half a day.

Mayon is a storehouse of titanic energy which has frequently broken forth in the past with destructive violence. During the last eruption, which occurred in 1900, lava flowed into the sea at a distance of some fourteen kilometres [1] from the crater. During previous eruptions whole towns have been destroyed by lava flows or by falling volcanic ejecta. Mayon is quiet at present and has been repeatedly climbed of late. The trip is dangerous because of the steepness of the slopes and the unstable nature of the material composing them. It takes two days.

Taal Volcano, situated on an island in Bombon Lake, and distant but thirty-nine miles from Manila, is of special interest on account of its destructive eruption on January 30, 1911, which killed some fourteen hundred people within the space of a few moments. It is very easily climbed, the elevation of the lowest point of the crater rim

[1] $8\frac{3}{4}$ miles.

above the lake being only 369 feet, and the ascent gentle.

Other important active volcanoes are Apo, in Mindanao; Catarman, on the island of Camiguin; Canlaon, sometimes also called Malaspina, on Negros; Caua, in northeastern Luzón; and Claro Babuyan, on the island of the same name. A considerable number of the volcanic peaks of the Philippines, including the one last named, have never been ascended.

It goes without saying that in a country where there are so many active, dormant and extinct volcanoes hot and mineral springs are of common occurrence. On the slopes of Canlaon there are three of the former, known respectively as "the chicken killer," "the hog killer" and "the carabao killer," on account of the supposed destructive powers of their waters. The Tivi Spring, near the base of Mayon Volcano, is famous. The water of Sibul Spring, in Bulacan Province, has medicinal properties of undoubted value, as do the waters of various other mineral springs, including those at Itogon and Daklán in Benguet. The scenic surroundings of some of them are most attractive, and doubtless important watering places will be established in their vicinity in the course of time.

Gigantic limestone cliffs are among the most striking features of many of the more mountainous regions, and in some parts of the islands, especially along the coast of Palawan, rise directly out of the sea. They take on wonderfully beautiful, and sometimes very weird, forms and are often full of caves in which may be found the famous edible birds' nests, so highly prized by the Chinese.

A range of limestone mountains ends at St. Paul's Bay on the west coast of Palawan. The bay takes its name from a majestic peak, with a wonderful limestone dome, which looks like a cathedral. Near it is another remarkable mountain called Liberty Cap, on account of its peculiar form. Beneath this range lies the scenic wonder of the Philippines, the famous Underground River, up which a ship's launch can run for more than three miles to what is called the "stone pile," caused by the falling of a great section of the roof. One may climb this obstruction, and utilizing native boats dragged over it by my party in August, 1912, may continue for a distance of half a mile, to a point where the roof of the cave drops to the level of the surface of the water, and further progress becomes impossible.

A trip up this river is an experience never to be forgotten. There is no danger of getting lost, as the three short side passages which run off from the main cavern all end blindly. The channel has been mapped by the Coast and Geodetic Survey and is plainly marked at all critical points.

One's launch should be provided with very powerful acetylene lights so arranged as to give a general illumination. Stalactites and stalagmites occur in every conceivable form. There are vaulted chambers which are full of them, and there are long straight passages which lack them and have roofs and walls resembling those of a New York subway. In places the cavern is full of edible-nest-building swifts and of bats. The air in the main passage is fresh. During the rainy season water runs from the roof in many places, and one must expect an occasional shower bath, but this is the only discomfort attendant upon the trip.

Unfortunately, the mouth of this river is quite fully exposed to the heavy seas stirred up by the southwest monsoon, which heap up sand, forming a bar on which the surf breaks heavily; but during the northeast monsoon the current often opens up a wide and deep channel through this bar.

There are several other underground rivers in the Philippines. An adventurous soldier embarked in a *banca* on one in Samar, and passed completely under a large mountain. Judging from his description of his experiences, this trip would be remarkably well worth taking.

In the limestone caves we may some day find remains which will throw light on the history of the early inhabitants of the Philippines, as many of them have been used for burial purposes in bygone times.

Pleasurable river navigation is by no means confined to underground streams. In Mindanao there are two rivers which offer strong attractions to tourists. One may ascend the Rio Grande de Cotabato through fertile plains, to a remarkable series of lakes swarming with great tame crocodiles and with a wonderful variety of waterfowl. On this trip one will see the Moros at home. The Agusan River, which rises near Davao Gulf and empties on the north coast of Mindanao, is the largest navigable stream in the islands. During ordinary weather it is strictly confined between well-marked banks. The dense forests which cover them have been cleared in a few places to make room for Manobo villages. Exquisite orchids and beautiful ferns abound. After ascending the river for one hundred twenty miles one comes to a remarkable submerged forest in a region which subsided a few years ago during a great seismic disturbance. Formerly it was very unsafe to enter it without taking an experienced guide, as the original river bed was completely destroyed and the many small streams flowing through the sunken area formed a very complicated maze. Now, however, two clearly defined canals have been opened up, both terminating in the immediate vicinity of the town of Veruela, and a trip through either of them will not soon be forgotten, for here tropical vegetation is seen at its very best.

During a portion of the year one may ascend the Rio Grande de Cagayan, the great river of northern Luzón, in a good-sized stern-wheel steamer for a distance of one hundred twenty miles, passing through a sparsely settled but potentially very rich agricultural district which now produces the best tobacco grown in the islands.

It is a common thing for temporary residents in the

Philippines to quote the foolish saying that the flowers are without odour and the birds without song. There is no more delicious fragrance than that given off in the evening by the shrub known as *dama de noche*.[1] The perfume made from ilang-ilang flowers goes all over the world. That extracted from the blossoms of the champaca brings fabulous prices. Jasmine is produced in abundance. If one wishes a heavier odour, tuberoses furnish it, while many species of trees make the whole forest fragrant when in flower.

Some of the birds are sweet singers, while others brighten the landscape with their vivid colours. A row of snowy egrets, perched on the back of a carabao, presents a striking picture. One constantly hears by day the plaint of the *limócon*, a wood pigeon which exercises a most extraordinary influence over the lives of many of the wild people, for they believe that the direction and the nature of its notes augur good or ill for the enterprises which they have in hand. The crescendo shriek of a great black cuckoo, called by the natives *bahów*, commonly heard at night, is likely to cause alarm to one not cognizant of its origin, and has led many a sentry on a wild goose chase into a mangrove swamp in the belief that he was hastening to the rescue of some human being undergoing dreadful torment.

One of the most interesting of the feathered denizens of Philippine fields and forests is the inconspicuous tailor bird, which carefully unwinds the silk from cocoons, and using it for thread, stitches together the edges of living leaves and then builds its nest in the green pocket thus formed.

The insects are as varied and interesting as are the birds. There are very numerous species of ants, and the manifestations of their extraordinary intelligence are well worth careful observation. The work of the huge flocks of locusts which sometimes devastate the fields is worth seeing, although the sight is not a cheering one. There

[1] Lady of the night.

are butterflies and moths of great size and of the most brilliant and varied hues. Some of the very gaudily coloured species disappear as if by magic when they alight, because the under surfaces of their wings, exposed when they close them, perfectly resemble dead leaves. Other protectively coloured insects look marvellously like green leaves or dead twigs.

After all is said and done, the most interesting study of mankind is man, and man in most varied form is to be found in the Philippines, beginning with Manila itself, where the mixture of Chinese, Japanese, Spanish, English, German and American blood with that of the original Malay invaders has produced a wonderfully varied series of types.

Many of the women are bravely decked out in the gayest of colours, which harmonize well with their raven black hair and brown or yellow skins.

Manila is a very interesting city. North of the Pasig River are several native residence districts which have changed comparatively little in a century. Old Manila, lying just south of the river, is one of the best remaining examples of a walled town, and it has many buildings which have withstood typhoons and earthquakes for centuries. Its churches are of especial interest. The acoustic properties of the cathedral are excellent, and if an opportunity to hear fine music there presents itself it should not be missed.

At the University of Santo Tomás and at the Jesuit convento there are good museums. The insular government has a museum on Calle Anloague, where may be seen very interesting ethnological collections and an important and striking exhibit of the products of the Philippine forests.

In the botanical and zoölogical collections of the Bureau of Science specialists will find a wealth of material.

The Philippine General Hospital richly repays a visit. It is the largest and most complete institution of its kind

in the Far East, and within its walls American and Filipino physicians, surgeons and nurses work side by side for
the relief of suffering humanity.

I have only hinted at a few of the interesting sights
which may be seen without leaving the city limits. The
open country and the provincial towns are made readily
accessible by splendid automobile roads. To the north
one finds great mango trees with their solid hemispheres
of beautiful foliage, and endless rice-fields in the cultivation of which the people still employ the methods of
bygone centuries. The good sanitary condition in many
of the towns shows that American and Filipino health
officers have not been idle.

To the south the automobile road runs straight away to
Atimonan on the Pacific coast, distant one hundred twelve
miles. It passes near Banájao, one of the most beautiful
extinct volcanoes of the Philippines; is bordered for
long distances by cocoanut groves, and extends for many
miles through a most beautiful forest.

No visit to the Philippines is complete without a trip
to Baguio, the summer capital. It is reached by train and
automobile in less than a day. Here one is just at the
edge of the wild man's country and may go to villages of
the Benguet Igorots in an automobile.

Starting at Baguio, one may take one of the most wonderful horseback journeys in the world over the "Mountain Trail" to Cervantes in the neighbouring sub-province
of Lepanto and thence to Bontoc, the capital of the
Mountain Province. Here dwell the Bontoc Igorots, who
were famous head-hunters until brought under American
control. Four or five days more will suffice to make a trip
north to Lubuagan, the capital of the sub-province of Kalinga, inhabited by another most picturesque tribe of
head-hunters. They are physically a wonderfully developed people, and their personal cleanliness, brightly
coloured clothes, and striking feather ornaments make
them especially attractive.

On the way one is sure to see women clad in skirts extemporized from banana leaves, *camote* tops, or ferns, of a type popularly but wrongly supposed not to have been in style since the days of mother Eve.

From Bontoc one rides to the eastward over the Mount Polis range and descends along the wonderful terraced mountain sides of the Ifugaos, finding everywhere abundant evidences of the extraordinary industry displayed by the people of this head-hunting tribe. At Quiangan the traveller will be amazed to see beautiful buildings of cut stone, and when informed that they have been erected by Ifugao schoolboys under an American foreman will doubt the possibility of such a thing unless he is fortunate enough to see the boys at work.

From this point one may return to Baguio by way of Sapao, and the Agno River valley, or may continue his journey to the eastward, coming out on the fertile plains of Nueva Vizcaya. Before the return to the lowlands of Pangasinán from this province one may make a short side trip of half a day into the country of the Ilongots, but I do not recommend such an expedition to persons not familiar with the ways of savages who are sometimes inclined to be a bit treacherous. The Ilongots have harmed only one white man, but they still occasionally murder each other, and it is hard always to know what they will do next.

There are comfortable rest houses at frequent intervals along the excellent horse trails over which one rides in making this trip, so that all one really requires is a good horse and saddle and necessary clothing. Baggage is transported by Igorot carriers or pack ponies. It is always well to take one's own blankets. Good thick ones will be needed, for the Mountain Trail reaches an elevation of seventy-five hundred feet, and at this height the nights are cold.

Until within a short time it has been impossible for tourists to travel with comfort in the Philippines. There was no good hotel even at Manila. This latter difficulty

After the Hunt.

has now fortunately been remedied. The old carriage and cart roads were impassable during much of the year. Their place has been taken, in many provinces, by heavily surfaced automobile roads serviceable at all times. Accommodations on the inter-island boats were atrocious. They are still far from first-class, but are rapidly improving, and on a number of the steamers are now very fair. There is good prospect that a number of new and up-to-date steamers will be put on inter-island routes in the near future.

Meanwhile it can safely be said that the world does not afford more attractive ground for yachting than that to be found in the Philippines. The scenery among the Calamianes Islands and in Bacuit Bay and Malampaya Sound is beautiful beyond description. That of the famous Inland Sea of Japan does not compare with it. Safe, quiet anchorages are to be found at frequent intervals, and the weather during the winter months usually leaves nothing to be desired.

CHAPTER XXIX

Rod, Shotgun and Rifle

THE Philippines offer strong attractions to the devotees of the shotgun and the rifle, and they are a fisherman's paradise.

Having in my earlier days spent some four years in collecting natural history specimens in the islands I did not need to be enlightened as to the pleasure which might be had in hunting ducks, snipe, shore birds, jungle fowl, and wild pigeons; nor as to those afforded to the hunter of large game by bringing down wild carabaos, hogs, and deer, bagging an occasional man-eating crocodile, or trying to outwit the wily tamarau of Mindoro, which is one of the most difficult of all forest-inhabiting ruminants to track down and kill, and has an uncomfortable habit of hunting the hunter when molested; but now, in view of my neglected early opportunities, I must confess with shame and confusion of face that it remained for Governor-General Forbes to show me, after I had resided in the islands for sixteen years that I had been missing a sport fit for kings by not sooner taking up fishing in the sea.

To one who has been even temporarily attached to a hundred-pound barracuda through the medium of a split bamboo rod, a tarpon reel, three hundred yards of line, and a good strong spoon hook, or has fought a sixty-pound tanguingui, or even a thirty-pound pampano, to a finish, it seems strange that any one should ever have characterized fishing as a "gentle art."

If good old Sir Izaak Walton had struggled with a big tuna until his fingers and thumbs were blistered or skinned, and every muscle in his body was tired and sore, only to see a huge shark bite his finny prey off back of the gills when it was almost ready to gaff, it is possible that his language in discussing fishing would have been less mild, and his general attitude toward the subject less gently philosophic.

Verily, Sir Izaak missed much by not having been born after modern fishing tackle had been invented and employed in taking the denizens of deep tropical seas. Let no one be unduly dismayed over the diminution of big game fish in the vicinity of Catalina Island, or off the Florida coast, for among the myriad islands of the Philippine Archipelago one may fish to one's heart's content, visiting grounds already well known, or seeking new ones for himself, in the assurance that the supply of marine game fishes will not be perceptibly diminished for many a long year to come.

Soon after his arrival, Governor-General Forbes began to inquire about the opportunities for sea fishing. He received little reliable information and less encouragement, but undeterred, proceeded to find out for himself when and where to fish and what tackle to use in order to obtain the best results. At the outset his efforts netted him few fish or none, but he kept at it as opportunity offered, and, thanks to his perseverance, the sport is now firmly established on a sound basis.

One must have rod, reel, line and gaff suitable for tarpon fishing, and an abundant supply of good spoon hooks, wire leaders and swivels. Live bait and cut bait are as useful here as elsewhere, but game fish are so abundant, and spoon hooks have proved so successful in taking them, that comparatively little use has as yet been made of other lures. One should fish from a power boat which can be slowed down to four miles an hour without stopping, and will safely ride a moderately heavy sea.

When thus equipped, if the fisherman hies him to the edge of a coral reef where the bottom slopes steeply downward, runs the boat so that he sees green water on one side and black water on the other, and pays out fifty to a hundred yards of line, he will not have long to wait before his reel sings the merry tune so dear to the heart of his kind, and he finds himself vainly striving, with both thumbs on the brake, to lower the pitch of that insistent high note by slowing down the speed of the barracuda which has grabbed the spoon, hooked itself securely, and started for the coast of China with the obvious intention of getting there before dark.

A big barracuda may take fifty yards of line in his first rush and he may take two hundred, but one can be certain that when he is finally stopped he will jump clear of the water, and then will jump again just to show that he means it. After that, as he is reeled in, he will jump some more to keep up the interest. Ultimately, having acquired the habit of coming toward the boat, he will continue to practise it until he sees that craft, whereupon he is likely to start off at a rate which makes his first rush seem slow and deliberate. Now and then he will run down on the line for variety's sake, and then is the time for the boatmen to get into action, for if he gets slack line nothing remains but to bid him good-by as cheerfully as possible.

The largest specimen yet taken in the Philippines and actually weighed was a hundred ten pound monster caught on a trolling line trailed behind the coast guard cutter *Polillo*, on which I was making an inspection trip along the west coast of southern Palawan.

The largest specimen yet taken with rod and reel weighed fifty-two and eight-tenths pounds. It was brought to gaff in Biobican Bay by Governor Leo J. Grove of Nueva Vizcaya.

Very numerous individuals weighing between twenty and forty-five pounds have been captured, and the only reason why numbers of much larger specimens have not been taken is that tackle was not strong enough, or the skill of the fishermen was not sufficiently great. Big barracudas have teeth that would do credit to small sharks, and have sawed through or broken many a wire leader.

In the Philippines, as in other civilized countries, there are not lacking narrators of good "fish stories." From Filipino residents of San Juan, Siquijor, I recently heard a tale of a barracuda which towed a native dugout boat all day, jumping frequently, and was finally cut loose after dark by its disgusted would-be captors who found themselves unable to tire it out!

Of tanguingui, or sail fish, there are at least two species. The smaller commonly attains a weight of twenty to forty pounds. In the open sea off the coast of Leyte I took a specimen which measured sixty-four inches in length and weighed sixty-five pounds. It proved to be of a species new to science. This magnificent fish, when fresh from the sea, was a sight calculated to cheer a graven image.

Tanguingui fight much as do barracuda, except that they seldom jump out of the water after being hooked unless pursued by sharks. This seems strange, as under normal conditions they leap for the pure joy of the thing, attaining heights which I hesitate to specify lest I be held to have qualified for the Ananias club. I know of nothing more startling in its way than the shock one gets when his eye has missed the upward leap of a big tanguingui but catches the fish as it is dropping back toward the sea, apparently from the clouds.

While barracuda and tanguingui may be taken throughout the year, there seems to be a time when the fish of the latter species "run." At all events they are found in great numbers during April and May in the vicinity of Fortune Island, a short distance south of Manila Bay, but are very scarce, or entirely absent, there during the remainder of the year. I once visited the famous fishing grounds around Tanguingui Island, north of Cebú, in August, only to be assured by a light-keeper that I would find no fish at that season. He said that the barracuda would return in November and the tanguingui in February. His prediction as to the fishing in August promptly came true.

Pampano rank high among the game fish of the Philippines. What will California coast fishermen, accustomed to taking little fellows weighing a pound or two, say to fifty-pound individuals? I can imagine what they would say if not confronted by hard facts, but the truth is that a number of such pampanos have already been taken with rod and reel in the Philippines, and that there are plenty more waiting to be caught. During a trip to Palawan in December, 1911, Captain Tornroth of the coast guard cutter *Polillo* took a forty-nine-pound specimen. The same evening Dr. Victor G. Heiser, Director of Health, took an individual weighing thirty-two pounds. The following August the record was raised first to fifty-three pounds and then to sixty-three and a half pounds, the latter fish being caught by Mr. Frank W. Sweitzer.

The pampano takes the hook with a rush and seldom misses his strike. He never leaps while being played, but helps himself to line very liberally at the outset and runs deep at once. A large specimen is never satisfied until almost directly under the boat with several hundred feet of line out, and will get bottom, snag the line on a sharp point of rock or a branch of coral, and break away, if such a thing is materially possible. A pampano never quits fighting until he is in the boat, and is an adept at turning up his broad side after being hooked and swimming in a circle, resisting to the utmost all efforts to raise him. Under reasonably favourable circumstances it usually takes from twenty minutes to half an hour to land a twenty-five-pound individual. Pampano run in schools and when they once begin to bite the fun is fast and furious.   ·

The sergeant fish is one of the gamest fighters for his weight to be met with in Philippine waters. He keeps up his determined rushes until brought to the side of the boat and leaps frequently while being played, at the same time making vigorous efforts to shake the hook. None of the specimens so far taken have exceeded twenty pounds in weight.

Ocean bonito are often met with in great schools and present a wonderful sight when one drives one's boat among them and sees them leaping high into the air, close at hand, on every side. The largest specimen yet caught with rod and reel is a sixty-pounder taken by Governor Forbes. I have seen numerous individuals which must certainly have weighed a hundred pounds or more.

Red snappers weighing five to twenty pounds also occur in great schools. They are usually caught with bait by sinking in deep water, but at times take the spoon freely. The larger individuals make a game fight. Annually during November and December these fish run in very large numbers from Naujan Lake in Mindoro to the sea. Whether or not they can be captured with rod and line while in fresh water remains to be determined.

The lapu-lapu, or "groupers," of which there are twenty-four known species in the Philippines, do not attain very great size, but are much prized on account of the delicious flavour of their especially tender flesh. Dr. Heiser has taken one weighing twenty-two pounds and I have seen the dried flesh of one which must have weighed approximately forty pounds. The colouring of a number of the species is extraordinarily beautiful. Some are light gray with round blue spots; others carmine red with blue spots over the body and blue lines and bars about the head; others are dark blue with carmine spots. There seems no end to the variety and beauty of the colour patterns, and each new one appears for the moment more wonderful than those which one has seen before.

Lapu-lapu have a special fondness for crevices in the rocks, and for holes in coral reefs, and in consequence are responsible for the loss of much good tackle. One must fight them from the moment they strike and give them no slack. The penalty for any carelessness in this regard is a broken line.

Leather jacks, commonly called *dorados* in the Philippines on account of their beautifully coloured yellow bellies, are extraordinarily abundant at certain seasons of the year when they run into the shallow waters at the heads of bays and sounds, apparently to spawn. When encountered at all they afford good sport for their size, fighting well and frequently making splendid leaps out of the water even after they are brought close to the boat and are apparently tired out. They commonly run from five to fifteen pounds in weight, but occasionally reach eighteen or twenty pounds.

The Philippine giant sea-bass, or jewfish, belongs to the same family as does the California species. While I was on shore at Mæander Reef in August, 1911, numerous hand lines with which sailors were fishing from the *Polillo* were carried away by jewfish. With the permission of the captain, the ship's log line was then pressed into service. I returned to the steamer just in time to assist in landing a hundred-and-thirty pound specimen. A steam trawler, which operated for a short time in the Philippines, took a specimen seven feet three inches in length, which weighed three hundred thirty-four and a fourth pounds.

In Coron Passage during July, 1911, I fought a very large fish, probably a jewfish, for an hour and twenty minutes, at the end of which time his dead weight broke my line when Governor Forbes, who was with me, attempted to lift him by it after he had indulged in a prolonged sulk in deep water. Although I had fought him steadily, I could not see that I had tired him in the least. In the course of the fracas the butt of my rod had made a two by three inch black and blue spot on my right leg and had worn the skin off over a similar area on my left leg, while my abdomen lacked a good deal of epidermis and I

TYPICAL SCENE AT THE EDGE OF A HARDWOOD FOREST.

was tempted to believe that it lacked some dermis as well. My companions who witnessed the fruitless fight christened this particular fish the "sea carabao." [1]

Belt and socket should, of course, be used in fighting fish of such size. Heavy cots for the thumb and first finger of the left hand and the thumb of the right hand are very essential. I once got a badly burned thumb because I thought that I was not likely to hook a fish which would make a quarter-inch-thick leather brake heat through. A big ocean bonito promptly undeceived me.

Very exciting sport may be had by harpooning the huge rays which come to the surface in great numbers at certain seasons of the year. Specimens thirty feet across have been taken in the vicinity of the island of Siquijor. When one of these great fishes is harpooned, Filipino fishermen make two or three large boats fast to it as soon as possible for the reason that a single boat might be dragged under. Even so the taking of giant rays is not unattended with danger, for they make most extraordinary leaps into the air, and were one of them to fall on a boat the result would be disastrous.

We have knowledge of the existence of other very large game fishes which we have not as yet so much as seen. One species is taken by the natives of Siquijor, who use a three-quarter inch Manila rope and fish in water of considerable depth. A number of boats work close together and as soon as a fish is hooked all flock to the assistance of the lucky fisherman. A tremendous struggle then ensues and we are assured that if the fish is landed, it makes a meal for a whole village. What this species may be we do not know.

One of the charms of fishing in the Philippines lies in the fact that one can never tell what one is going to strike next. At Mæander Reef I took the first yellowtail ever caught in the islands with rod and line. Doubtless there are plenty more where that one came from. Indeed,

---

[1] Carabao is the Filipino name for water buffalo.

yellowtails are common in the market at Zamboanga at certain seasons. Off the coast of Mindoro I took the first dolphin known to have been captured in these waters. On a recent trip I took a large porgy of a species new to the Philippines and likely to prove new to science. As yet we have hardly begun to explore the fishing grounds. What shall we find among the swift currents of the Batanes Islands, and what along the barrier reef of the unexplored east coast of northern Luzón? No one knows!

Although some 1400 species of fish have already been reported from the Philippines, new ones are constantly being added to the list, and it is rather a rare event when a returning party of fishermen fails to present the ichthyologist with one or more puzzles. On my first trip to Apo Reef, Dr. Heiser hooked a tremendous fish which leisurely went its way regardless of his efforts to control its movement. At one time it deigned to come under the bottom of the launch and within forty feet of the surface, where it could be seen with perfect distinctness. It was a long, slender, gamy-looking creature weighing perhaps one hundred fifty pounds, and it had vertical yellow bars on its sides. No such fish is known from these waters. Having viewed the boat to its satisfaction, it proceeded to go back to the reef and to take refuge under its overhanging edge. Vigorous efforts to dislodge it, lasting for half an hour, resulted only in sawing off a heavy wire leader.

One may tire for the moment of catching fish, but with a glass-bottomed boat at his disposal he will never tire of looking at them as he floats over the wonderful coral reefs for which the archipelago is famous. Certainly there are no "sea gardens" anywhere which can excel those of the Philippines. The powerful tropical sun penetrates the marvellously clear sea water to a great depth, revealing marine animal and plant life in endlessly varied and marvellously beautiful forms which beggar description. Former Secretary of War Dickinson is a rather serious-minded man, but when he gazed for the first time through the glass bottom of a boat into one of these wonder houses of nature, he shouted in his excitement and delight for all the world like a small and enthusiastic boy.

In a few moments one may see fish of the most amazing forms and extraordinarily bizarre colours : huge sharks ; enormous rays ; great sea-turtles ; clam shells big enough for children's bath-tubs ; sea-urchins ; starfish ; sea-anemones ; jellyfish in endless variety of form and colour ; sea-fans ; and many other varied forms of marine animal and plant life.

When one grows weary of the water, one may land on snowy coral-sand beaches, bordered by cocoanut palms, may visit old deserted Spanish forts rapidly being invaded by rank tropical vegetation ; may gather exquisite orchids ; or may for the time being substitute hunting for fishing. In the Sulu Sea he may visit wonderful bird islands where the feathered folk refuse to get out of his way and peck viciously at his legs if he comes too near.

All these delightful experiences may be had without suffering any discomfort from the Philippine climate, concerning which such absurd ideas prevail among the uninformed. From November to March the temperature is delightful, except during the midday hours of bright days, when fish do not bite well in any event, and when sensible people keep off the water.

Thus far I have referred only to those game fishes which I myself have taken, or concerning which I happen to have personal knowledge. I will now briefly summarize what is at present known about the game fishes of the Philippines.

The *albacore* is fairly common, especially during the cooler months.

Amberjacks, reaching a length of two feet or more, are also common.

There are *barracudas* of seven different species, some of which attain a length of six feet and weigh a hundred pounds or more.

Bonitos of four different species have been taken. The "ocean bonito" and the "true bonito" are both abundant and afford fine sport. The larger individuals sometimes attain a weight of a hundred pounds or more.

There are six different species of *croakers*, also called *roncadores*. Some individuals reach a weight of a hundred pounds.

Groupers, locally known as *lapu-lapu*, are found in great variety, no less than twenty-four species having been recorded.

Hardtails, reaching a length of three feet, are abundant.

Leather-jacks, commonly called *dorados*, are also very abundant. They take the spoon freely and fight well. In weight they commonly run from five to fifteen pounds.

There are several small species of *mackerel* which are excellent table fish and afford fair sport.

Pampanos are found in great variety, no less than thirty species having already been recorded. Individuals weighing as much as fifty pounds are not uncommon.

Porgies of twelve different species have been taken, and some of the individuals have weighed up to thirty pounds.

Of *snappers* we have thirty-four known species. The *red snapper* not infrequently attains a weight of twelve to fifteen pounds, and the larger individuals fight well. At times they take the spoon freely. The *gray snapper* runs up to forty pounds in weight and makes a good fight. The *rivulated snapper*, which takes its name from the form of its beautiful colour pattern, is a good game fish, and I have seen specimens which weighed up to twenty pounds.

Sea-bass of two distinct species are common. Specimens weighing fifty to seventy-five pounds are frequently seen in the markets. The largest specimen as yet recorded from the islands weighed three hundred thirty-four and a fourth pounds.

Spanish mackerel, or *tanguingui*, are common throughout the islands at the proper season. A very intelligent Filipino collector of natural history specimens in the service of the government, who saw my sixty-five-pound specimen landed, assured me that he had previously seen larger ones caught.

Swordfish, nine feet or more in length, may be taken during the cooler months.

Tarpons up to five feet in length may be taken at the proper season, off the mouths of large streams. The species is distinct from that found in Atlantic waters, and the young take the fly freely.

Ten pounders, commonly called *bid-bid* in the Philippines, are not uncommon, and in spite of their name often attain a weight of thirty pounds.

Tunas. The great, or leaping, *tunas* are met with in large schools during the winter months. The natives call them "*cachareta*." So far as I am aware, none have yet been taken with rod and line, but their capture is, of course, only a question of time.

I believe it certain that the Philippines will become a Mecca for deep-sea fishermen, and to the end that piscatorial pilgrims may not come in vain, reliable data are being gathered and compiled by the Division of Fisheries of the Bureau of Science. The exact locations where exceptionally good catches are made are being marked on a comprehensive series of charts which cover the entire archipelago, and an accurate card record is also kept giving full information as to the localities where, the seasons when and the weather conditions under which exceptional catches have been made. Fishermen seeking fine sport and novel experiences will surely not be disappointed if they come to the Philippines.

While it is possible to find sheltered waters at any season, and to take fish throughout the year, our experience thus far seems to justify the belief that the months from January to August are on the whole the most favourable ones.

Fishermen may establish themselves at some favourable point, such as one of the many excellent camping grounds on Malampaya Sound, and work from this as a base, with no other water transportation than the motor boats from which they fish. Those who wish to have a good movable base of operations and to explore for themselves may, by making seasonable application, secure the use of one of the government coast guard boats at a cost of $115 a day. These convenient little vessels measure one hundred forty-eight feet over all and draw nine to eleven feet of water, according to the amount of coal carried and its distribution. They are safe in all weathers. Most of them have four good staterooms for passengers, with berths for eight people; but as they are provided with good double awnings and have abundant deck room, a much larger number of persons can be made comfortable, if willing to sleep on deck, using the staterooms for dressing-rooms. As a matter of fact, people who have been long in the islands seldom think of sleeping inside. The coast guard boats readily carry four motor boats on their davits, and two more might be placed on deck forward. The *Negros* is especially fitted out, and has stateroom accommodations for twenty people. All of these vessels have electric light, refrigerating plants and distilling plants.

I know of nothing more delightful than to explore the shores and bays of this wonderful archipelago in such a vessel, fishing and landing when and where one pleases. With the certainty of fine weather during the winter months the nights under the deck awnings are a delight, and nothing will more promptly restore jangling nerves to a normal state, straighten out impaired digestion and bring back vigorous health, than will such a salt water fishing trip in the Philippines.

Ducks and snipe are the stand-bys for the hunters who love the shotgun. A few years ago magnificent duck shooting was to be had on the Laguna de Bay, as well as in the province of Bataan just across the bay from Manila. Unfortunately the ducks on the Laguna were educated by some stupid fellows who shot at them with a Colt automatic gun. The ideas which they then developed as to danger zones seem to have persisted ever since, and it is now difficult to get within range of the great flocks which still continue to frequent this the largest fresh-water lake in the Philippines.

Ducks have been shot in season and out of season around the water-holes in Bataan and in the Candaba Swamp, as well as in the vicinity of the fish pens in Bulacan. The shooting has fallen off rapidly here, and in Nueva Ecija and Tarlac, for the same cause. We are powerless to remedy this condition. Some years ago a law was passed authorizing the secretary of the interior to provide regulations governing the seasons during which game might be shot, but through oversight no penalty was provided for the infraction of these regulations, and the assembly has persistently refused to amend the law in this respect.

On Naujan Lake in Mindoro, and elsewhere in the provinces, magnificent duck shooting may still be had. The whistling tree-duck and the Philippine mallard are the two species which afford the best sport, although pintails, bluebills, widgeons, and blue- and green-wing teal come in on migration as does a tiny goose, smaller than the ordinary duck. Several other species stray into the southern Philippines from the Celebes, while at least one Formosan species sometimes visits the Batanes Islands.

Jacksnipe come to the islands in enormous numbers from Asia, usually arriving about the middle of August in northern and central Luzón and gradually working their way south to Mindanao. The return migration commonly comes during February. The flight of the Asiatic jacksnipe is exactly like that of his American brother. In fact only an ornithologist can distinguish between the two species. A bag of one hundred birds to the gun is by no means unusual at the height of the season, and a strong sentiment is developing among Americans in favour of limiting the bag.

There are very numerous species of pigeons and doves in the Philippines. All of them are excellent table birds and several of them offer good sport. If one can take up his position under a fruit tree frequented by the great gray and green pigeons, known locally as *baluds*, about the middle of the afternoon he will get a wonderful series of shots at incoming birds flying fifty or more yards up in the air. They approach very rapidly, so that one must lead them a long distance, "pulling them out of sight" in order to bring them down. One may burn many a cartridge before he learns the knack of stopping these powerful, swift-flying birds. During certain seasons the larger pigeons roost, in countless thousands, in trees on little isolated cays remote from the larger islands, where wonderful shooting may be had during the morning and evening flights.

Junglefowl, the ancestors of all our domestic breeds of poultry, are to be found throughout the islands but only in a few places do they offer much opportunity for the sportsman who likes to kill his birds on the wing. Prior to the last eruption they were very numerous on the slopes of Taal Volcano.

A party which happened to visit Cavilli, a small isolated coral island in the Sulu Sea, once found it alive with junglefowl. No one else has ever seen any there. Obviously a great flock flew in and then flew away again.

Particularly fine sport may be had on Fuga Island by walking along the edge of the forest in the late afternoon. The birds which are then feeding in the open fly straight for cover and present difficult cross shots.

The larger hornbills are very good to eat, but as easy to hit on the wing as a fair-sized door sailing through the air would be, so do not offer much sport.

Wild hogs are abundant throughout the archipelago. Deer are found on nearly all of the islands, but there are

A Typical Forest Scene.

From the buttressed roots of great hardwood trees, like the one here shown, beautiful table tops are obtained.

several noteworthy exceptions, such as Palawan and
Cebú. The Filipinos are very fond of hunting deer.
Sometimes they run them down with dogs and drive them
into nets where they lance them — a most unsportsman-
like proceeding. The wealthier Filipinos like to take
up their stations at good strategic posts, and then have
the country beaten toward them. In this· way they
sometimes get fifty or more deer in a single drive. I have
never been able to see anything very exciting about this
method of hunting.

It is very good sport, on occasion, to still-hunt deer.
The best deer shooting I have ever had was at what is
called the *Cogonal Grande* in the center of the island of
Culion. It is a great circular valley sloping very gradually toward the center. Its higher portions are overgrown with *cógon* grass which gives the valley its name.
Probably it was once the bed of a lake. At all events its
centre is swampy at the present time and has grown up
into a hopeless jungle of pandanus, bamboo grass, etc.,
through which runs a maze of deer paths. Numerous
little cañons lead down from the neighbouring hills to this
valley and each of them has forest in it.

In the month of December, when the *cógon* is dry, if
fired it burns toward the centre on all sides until the blaze
reaches the wet swampy portion where the vegetation
is not dry enough to burn. If dogs are then put into the
little stretches of forest which run down the ravines toward
the open valley, they almost invariably drive out deer
which run straight for the tangle at its centre, necessarily
crossing ground which has been burned bare.

As a result one gets hard cross shots but has the advantage of seeing every bullet strike, as the soil is very
dry at this season. This makes interesting shooting.
One gets game enough to keep the camp in meat and not
enough so that he feels like a butcher.

Many hunters go out at night with bull's-eye lanterns,
shine the deer and fire at their eyes. This is not so bad

as jacking them from a boat, because a man who hunts on foot necessarily makes a good deal of noise, and they are apt to become alarmed and run away, whereas one can approach in a boat so silently that they do not hear the noise of the paddles or the rippling of the water.

Hunting at night in this way in the Philippines is very interesting. One sees all sorts of nocturnal animals which are never met with by day, and also gets a good opportunity to pick up owls, nighthawks and other birds which are not ordinarily taken except by accident. However, the ordinary hunter is not an ornithologist, and does not care for such opportunities.

Wild hogs are hunted much as are deer. They drive readily. On account of the habit of the old boars of turning and facing dogs when the latter molest them, it is easy to bring them down.

The common people kill wild hogs with spears after the dogs have brought them to bay. This is by no means a safe undertaking, as some of the old boars attain tremendous size, have very formidable tusks and are capable of killing a man in short order if able to come to close quarters with him.

The wild hogs of the Philippines are very cleanly beasts. They take daily baths whenever possible, and often build for themselves beds of clean, fresh brush. They are extremely intelligent animals, and it is therefore very difficult to still-hunt them. In view of their huge bulk and ungainly proportions the absolute silence with which they move through the forests cannot fail to impress one who sees them stealing quietly along. After being disturbed they make plenty of noise as they rush away.

One of the best ways to still-hunt them is to secrete one's self near a water hole which they frequent for bathing purposes, but their sense of smell is very keen, and if the wind happens to blow in the wrong direction they will not approach the place where a hunter is lying in wait.

Wild hogs are fruit eaters for the most part, and their flesh is delicious. They are enormously abundant on the island of Tawi Tawi, where the durian tree abounds. The Moro inhabitants will not touch them, and as food is very plentiful during much of the year the island swarms with them, and they attain the largest size. Moros say that during the fruit season they become so covered with fat that if pursued for any length of time they fall, overcome by the heat and the running!

When I was in Tawi Tawi in 1901 with Dr. Bourns and a Filipino helper, one of us took a rifle along each morning when we went out to collect birds and in a few moments, after finishing his bird shooting for the day, was able to kill hogs enough to keep not only our party but the local Spanish garrison in meat, while the lard which our servants tried out lasted us for more than a year thereafter.

There are two animals in the Philippines which can with propriety be dignified by the name of "big game." These are the wild carabao, which is still to be found in various parts of the archipelago, and the tamarau, a true buffalo of a species which occurs nowhere in the world except on the island of Mindoro.

The wild carabao is a formidable antagonist, hard to stop and a vicious fighter after he is once wounded. Under ordinary circumstances he is very wary and difficult to approach. It is highly important in hunting him to use bullets with great stopping power. A number of men have been killed in the Philippines by wild carabaos which they had severely wounded. The most recent case which has come to my knowledge was that of a Mr. Barbour, in Mindoro. He was an old hand at the game, and had killed fifty-odd specimens. He shot a bull three times and it dropped apparently dead. Walking close up to it he dropped the butt of his rifle to the ground between his legs, and held the barrel with his knees while trying to light a cigarette. Without the slightest warning the injured bull sprang to its feet and drove a horn completely through him, killing him instantly.

There is an interesting and unsettled question as to whether the wild carabaos of the Philippines are indigenous to the islands or are merely the descendants of imported animals which have made their escape from captivity. My own opinion is that both beliefs are true or, in other words, that we have both a native wild race and other carabaos just as wild and just as fierce which are the descendants of tame individuals. The ordinary wild bulls have comparatively short and thick horns, while the bulls of the species found in Nueva Ecija and in northern Luzón generally have long, slender, very sharp, strongly curved horns. I believe that the latter animals belong to the true native race.

Wild carabaos are found not only at various points in Luzón, but abundantly in Mindoro and the Calamianes Islands. They appear in considerable numbers in Masbate, Negros and elsewhere in the archipelago.

To the inexperienced hunters who are inclined to try to bring them down my advice is "Don't!"

Few indeed are the men who have killed so much as a single specimen of the tamarau of Mindoro. It is a small jungle-inhabiting ruminant. Its color, when adult, is precisely that of the carabao. It is, however, a much smaller and more active animal. The bulls lose no opportunity to attack carabaos, both domesticated and wild, and in spite of their own inferior size kill them with apparent ease.

The tamarau is extremely muscular and when it charges, which it is prone to do on very slight provocation, bores a hole through the jungle vegetation, coming on with the speed and recklessness of a rhinoceros. Under such conditions it is excessively hard to stop, and when it pushes its charge home, woe be to the unlucky hunter. With rare exceptions it attacks when wounded if it so much as catches sight of a human being. Even when unmolested it not infrequently charges, without warning, when one gets unduly near. It feeds at night, and never lolls around in the water as does the carabao.

At the time I first came to the Philippines to collect natural history specimens in 1887, this animal was known only from travellers' tales and from what purported to be a stuffed individual in the Dominican museum. It was certainly *stuffed*, being about as shapely as a kerosene barrel. Its skin looked so exactly like that of a carabao that uncharitable persons had suggested that it was an artifact.

At this time the most absurd tales about the tamarau were in circulation. I was solemnly assured by one group of persons, who claimed to have seen it, that it had only one horn which grew out of the top of its head. Others were certain that it had two horns and but a single eye.

We did not anticipate the good fortune of discovering either a unicorn or a cyclops, but thought that there must be something behind all of these remarkable stories.

After undergoing many hardships and performing much hard work, our party succeeded in taking five individuals, the first ever killed and properly preserved.

The best way to hunt these wary and dangerous animals is to pick up a fresh trail early in the morning along some water course where they come to drink during the night, and follow it as noiselessly as possible. One is liable to jump the game at any moment. I shall never forget my astonishment when, on climbing up a steep river bank and diving into a tunnel through *runo* grass, I nearly fell over an old bull. Ordinarily, however, no such luck awaits one. It is frequently necessary to trail the quarry five or ten miles before one comes up with it, and then the usual reward, after crawling through underbrush and wriggling along on the ground, bitten by ants and mosquitoes, torn by thorns and covered with pestiferous land leeches, is to hear a terrific crash in the brush and never so much as catch a glimpse of the animal which makes it. The tamarau sleeps during the day, almost invariably lying down in the densest of jungle growth, facing back upon its own trail. Furthermore, it is uncommonly likely to put a bend in that trail before lying down, so that while one is still a mile or two from it by the line which it followed, it may in reality be not more than fifty or a hundred yards away.

A very skilful tracker is necessary if one is to have much hope of success, and one should not fire, even after the game is in sight, unless he can get a brain shot or can be certain of breaking the spinal column; otherwise, he endangers his own life by shooting, if the tamarau is at moderately close quarters.

I believe that no other ruminant is harder to kill outright. Certainly there is no other approximating the tamarau in size which is so tough. I refrain from chronicling my own experiences, as I am certain that my statements would not be believed, and prefer to leave hunters to find out for themselves how much shooting it takes to put one of these extraordinary beasts out of commission.

There is one place in Mindoro called Canturai, where tamarau may be taken with comparative ease. It was described to me, in Spanish days, as an extensive open area with a conical hill near its centre, and I was told that by burning the grass and sleeping on the hill one could readily get early morning shots at tamarau which came out to lick up the ashes.

But various other stories had also been told me, and one and all had proved false. I had dug pitfalls for the wary beasts in vain. I had perched in trees, devoured by mosquitoes, and with hard branches cutting into my flesh, waiting for some pugnacious bull to come out and fight a tame carabao fastened at a convenient distance from my hiding place, all to no purpose. Under such conditions a tamarau once came and bellowed around in the bushes, but did not show himself. I had heard tales

OLD-STYLE ROAD ACROSS LOWLANDS.

Tracks of this sort become completely impassable during the rainy season.

NEW-STYLE ROAD ACROSS LOWLANDS.

Roads like this are passable at all times.

of men who rode tamarau down on horseback and lanced them, and these yarns I knew to be false. So I never took the trouble to look up the Canturai story, worse luck, for it proved to be true.

American soldiers occupied Mindoro for years before one of them succeeded in killing a tamarau. Finally a party of officers went to Canturai and the first morning they shot seven! Various other persons who have since gone there have had extraordinary luck, although several have narrowly escaped being killed, owing to their folly in following wounded animals into the *cógon* grass.

A tamarau pursued under such circumstances will almost invariably back off at right angles to its own trail, wait for its pursuers to come up, and charge them, giving them no time to fire.

Young calves are as wild as their parents, and I am credibly informed will often endeavour to attack female carabaos if an attempt is made to get them to regard these animals in the light of foster mothers.

It is a curious fact that calves, and in fact young animals up to a year or more of age, are of a light reddish colour closely resembling that of some Jersey cattle. Their coats turn dark later on. Their horns, too, are at first circular in cross-section. Later they become triangular.

When pursued, tamarau cows have a curious fashion of passing their heads under their calves, raising them with the horns pressed down in such a way as to hold them against their necks, with forelegs hanging on one side and hindlegs on the other, and running with them. All in all, they are very interesting beasts, and we still have much to learn about them. The man who attempts to hunt them with anything but a heavy and thoroughly reliable rifle is a fool.

Crocodiles of the largest size frequent many of the streams and most of the lakes in the Philippines. They are also to be seen occasionally on sandbars rising out of the sea. Doubtless they will some day be shot for their hides, but as yet they are left undisturbed, unless they display special proclivities for eating human beings, valuable horses or fat cattle. The Filipinos claim that with crocodiles the liking for human flesh is an acquired taste, and that it is only in comparatively rare instances that they become man-eaters, as do tigers. I believe that this is true. Certainly, I have seen a clear pool full of happy Tagbanua children with a big crocodile lying in plain sight at the bottom of it. On the other hand, I have known of individual crocodiles, of evil reputation, each of which have killed numbers of human beings. In one little pool crossed by a trail which I have had occasion frequently to use in Cagayan province ten persons were pulled down and devoured in three years. Most men who use the rifle sooner or later become interested in putting these vicious reptiles out of the way whenever opportunity offers.

Hunters and fishermen, in search of new and exciting experiences, will not fail to meet with them in the Philippines, and the tourist will find there much that is picturesque, strange or wonderful.

CHAPTER XXX

PHILIPPINE LANDS

ESPECIAL interest attaches to the subject of Philippine lands for three reasons: first, the very large majority of small landholders in the islands have no titles; second, there are enormous areas of unoccupied, unclaimed, uncultivated land which are doing no one any good at present and ought to be brought under cultivation as rapidly as possible; third, not only insular government officials, but Mr. Root and Mr. Taft have been very unjustly attacked for the land policy pursued in the Philippines.

As regards ownership, some 31,879 square miles may be considered to be private land to which owners have obtained titles or could have done so had they known how to assert their rights. Only about 8937 square miles of this total amount are estimated to be under cultivation at the present time.

Excepting only private lands and a few acres belonging to municipal or provincial governments or to the insular government as the case may be, the remaining land constitutes the public domain of the Philippine Islands which is the property of the government of the United States, but is administered by the insular government. It is made up of forest land, mineral land, agricultural land, and foreshore and land under water.

Fifty-four thousand square miles are estimated to be forest land. The rest is now provisionally classified as agricultural land for the reason that the mineral land and foreshore have never been segregated.

The condition in which private land titles were found at the time of the American occupation was very distressing. It had been a difficult matter to secure title under the Spanish régime and the very large majority of the common people had accordingly put it off until a mythical to-morrow which never came. Even those who had succeeded in obtaining formal documents had in many instances lost them as a result of the vicissitudes of war.

The Public Land Act of the Philippine Commission, passed under the provisions of the Act of Congress of July 1, 1902, became effective on July 26, 1904. It contained liberal provisions relative to Spanish grants and unperfected titles.

Any citizen of the Philippine Islands or of the United States or of any insular possession thereof over the age of twenty-one years or the head of a family can obtain a forty-acre homestead by five years of cultivation, two years of occupancy and the payment of $10.

The Public Land Act also provided for the issuance of a free patent to a tract not exceeding forty acres in extent to any native of the Philippine Islands then an occupant and cultivator of unreserved, unappropriated, agricultural public land who had continuously occupied and cultivated such land either by himself or through his ancestors since August 1, 1898; or who prior to August 1, 1898, continuously occupied and cultivated such land for three years immediately prior to such date, and who had been continuously since July 4, 1902, until the date of the taking effect of the Public Land Act, an occupier and cultivator of such land.

Most liberal provision was thus made for the small landowner, or would-be landowner, but neither Congress nor the commission reckoned with the ignorance of the common people nor with the opposition to the acquisition of land by poor Filipinos which developed on the part of their richer and more intelligent fellow-countrymen. This latter difficulty has proved to be a quite serious one. The *cacique* does not wish his labourers to acquire land in their own right, for he knows well enough that if they did so they would become self-supporting, and it would cease to be possible for him to hold them as peons, as is commonly done at present. Serious obstacles are therefore frequently thrown in the way of poor people who desire to become owners of land, and if this does not suffice, active opposition is often made by municipal officers or other influential Filipinos, who claim as their own private property land which poor men are trying to get.[1]

[1] Of the endless cases which might be given I cite the following as a fair sample : —

"Personally appeared before me the undersigned ——, this 24th day of July, 1913, W. A. Northrop, who first being duly sworn, deposes and says : —

"'1. That he is a duly appointed Public Land Inspector of the Bureau of Lands of the Government of the Philippine Islands and that acting in such capacity on the 3d day of June, 1913, he visited the sitio of Buyon, barrio of Maddelaro, Municipality of Camalaniugan, province of Cagayan and there investigated the complaint of homestead entrymen Pascual Valdez and Tomas Valdez whose applications for land in the said sitio of Buyon under provision of Act No. 926 as amended had been entered by the Director of Lands under No. 9253 and No. 9254 respectively, that they were prevented from occupying said homesteads and deriving the benefits therefrom by certain persons living in the barrio of Maddelaro :

"'2. That while so investigating the claim of the said entrymen and their opponents he was told by Placido Rosal, one of the opponents to the homestead entrys, that "it was immaterial to him what decision was made by the Director of Lands concerning the land as, if he (Rosal) lost the land he and others would burn the houses of the entrymen and if necessary kill them"; this in the Spanish language with which he is familiar.

"'3. That at that time he was accompanied by Mr. Blas Talosig of the barrio of Buyag, who was acting as his interpreter in speaking in the Iloco language and that these threats were made in his hearing and that he, W. A. Northrop, was informed by said interpreter that he not only heard them but that he heard similar threats made in the Iloco language by various other persons, henchmen of the Placido Rosal and his family.

"'4. That on the 9th day of June, 1913, said entrymen came to him in the City of Aparri and reported that on the night on the 7th day of June the granary of Eduardo Baclig, resident in the said sitio of Buyon and a son-in-law of Tomas Valdez had been burned and an attempt made to burn his house and that while the entrymen were not in position to prove that said Placido Rosal or his henchmen had started the fires they were sure they were of incendiary origin, as due to the direc-

The Bureau of Lands now interests itself actively and directly in protecting the public lands against such

tion of the wind the fires could not have originated from sparks from kitchen fires.'

"Further deponent sayeth not.

(Signed)   "W. A. NORTHROP.

"Subscribed and sworn to before me this 24th day of July, 1913, in Tuguegarao, Cagayan, Philippine Islands, the affiant first having exhibited his cedula, No. 1516, issued in Manila, January 3, 1913.

(Signed) "PRIMITIVO VILLANUEVA
"Notario Publico,
"Mi nombramiento expira el
"31 de Diciembre de 1913."

"Extract from a report of H. O. Bauman, chief of Bureau of Lands survey party No. 27.   Report dated June 30, 1913 :

"In 1905 the applicant (Fernando Asirit) entered an application for homestead and proceeded to clear the remainder of the land not already cleared. Sometime during the following year or two, this Catalino Sagon began to clear a piece of land included in the homestead application. When Fernando Asirit saw the man cleaning the land, he told the man that that particular land was included in the homestead and that the work he was doing was useless. Catalino admitted this to me personally. However, the applicant to show his good faith, paid Catalino a sum of ten pesos for the small area that he had cleaned and took a receipt therefor and Catalino left the land. Now when the private surveyor came in 1910, this Catalino appears and claims this land despite the fact that he never cultivated nor occupied the land and that he received payment in full for the work that he had done in clearing an acre of the land. When the land was surveyed in 1910, Catalino at the request of a politician of Ilagan, made a protest against the land and between the two they frightened the applicant into letting this Catalino have possession of the land. Since 1910, Catalino has not cultivated the land but loaned it out to another person, Frederico Mayer by name. Personally, Catalino did not ever cultivate or live on the land. The politician who has been stirring up this trouble is Gabriel Maramag, third member of the Provincial board. The applicant is an old man seventy years old and this Maramag had the old man fined ₱125.80 for refusing to let these two have his land. They also told him that if he persisted in refusing to let them have the land, they would fine him ₱500. As the old man has no such amount and being thoroughly bulldozed by these cheap politicians, he had no other course to pursue. The co-partner of the third member is the Sheriff Joaquin Ortega against whom the people are very bitter on account of his shady dealings. It might be noted here that these men are under investigation by the Constabulary now for accepting money illegally. Furthermore this Maramag has the plans of the land of a great many men in his house and thus has a hold on them and they cannot do anything without his consent."

spurious claims, and thus keeps large areas open to claim by the common people.

Absolute ignorance of the law was the commonest of all causes of the failure of the poor to take advantage of its very liberal provisions. Every known resource was exhausted in endeavouring to enlighten them. Pamphlets informing them of their rights were published in all important native dialects, and widely circulated. The schools coöperated in this good work. Provincial and municipal officials were instructed to inform the people of their rights, but in very many cases these instructions were disregarded.

Because of the complete illiteracy of practically all of the members of the non-Christian tribes in Benguet and Lepanto, I caused a survey party to be sent out from the Bureau of Lands to inform them of their rights and to assist them in making the necessary applications. It was from this territory that proportionately the largest number of applications were sent in.

The period within which applications might be made was extended from January 1, 1907 to January 1, 1909, yet it is undoubtedly true that when it finally expired the vast majority of those who might have profited by the free patent privilege had failed to take advantage of it because of ignorance that it existed.

With the rapid spread of the English language such a condition would not now arise. At its last session the Philippine Legislature passed an act to renew for a period of ten years the right to secure free patent, but this act, like the one which it amends, is subject to the approval of the President and of Congress. It is to be hoped that such approval will be given. In my opinion every reason which made it advisable to grant free patents in the first instance is still of full force.

The total number of homestead applications received since the Public Land Act took effect is only 19,313, and of these it has been necessary to reject 4811 because the provisions of law were not complied with. Forty-eight patents have been issued, and there are 8225 approved applications, while 6219 not yet approved by the bureau are pending.

The figures for free patents are as follows: Number of applications, 15,885; free patents issued, 722; cases still pending, 11,871; rejected for cause 3292.

One reason why so many of the free patent cases are still pending is that there never has been, and is not now, a sufficient force of surveyors to keep the work of the Bureau of Lands up to date, all efforts to secure the necessary additions to this force having failed.

Under the Land Registration Act provision was made for the issuing of so-called Torrens titles for which the government is virtually responsible, once they are given out, so all that is now necessary to make it possible rapidly and effectively to remedy the existing situation is the appointment of a sufficient number of judges in the Court of Land Registration.

Government lands of provinces or municipalities are chiefly those needed and utilized as sites for public buildings, plazas and the like. The insular government owns a similar class of lands, and has certain lands in trust, such as the San Lazaro Estate, which was set aside long ago as a source of income for the support of lepers, but the so-called friar lands, which have a history of their own, are its most important holdings.

Under the Spanish régime several of the religious orders acquired large wealth in the form of estates, most of which were brought under high cultivation, although several of the largest, like the San José Estate in Mindoro, and the Isabela Estate in the province of the same name, were nearly or quite uncultivated, and a number of the others contained large uncultivated areas.

Field labour was performed exclusively by tenants who were settled on the estates in large numbers and in a number of instances had built up large and well-organized towns. For various reasons bitter hostility arose between them and their landlords. In some parts of the islands the friars were detested by the populace on general principles. Furthermore, the Filipino becomes greatly attached to his home, especially if his fathers have lived there before him. Tenants on the friar estates could be, and not infrequently were, arbitrarily dispossessed, and the possibility that this might occur was a thorn in their flesh.

During the insurrection the confiscation of the friar estates was very seriously considered by the so-called Insurgent government, which nominally took over their administration. As a matter of fact, there was then no real administration of them, and the occupied lands passed under the control of the tenants, who remained in undisturbed possession for years and came to consider themselves the virtual owners of their holdings. We have already seen how hostility to the friars reached its climax at this time. Some were killed outright, and others imprisoned under such conditions as to make death probable, but the majority of those captured were in effect held for a long time for ransom, their liberty being offered on condition of a large cash payment.

Upon the inauguration of civil government and the reëstablishment of law and order the friars naturally endeavoured to reassert their rights. With few exceptions their former tenants absolutely refused to pay rent. The friars threatened action in the courts, and would have been abundantly justified in bringing it, but such a course would unquestionably have led to serious disturbances of public order.

Agitators and demagogues had succeeded in firmly convincing many of the tenants that they were the actual owners of their lands, and those of them who knew better were bright enough to take advantage of the peculiar situation.

Hostility between Filipinos and friars had become so

general that the return of the latter to their parishes, accustomed as they had been to the exercise of a large measure of control over their parishioners, and with the memory of grave abuses recently suffered fresh in their minds, was deemed to be undesirable, but their permanent withdrawal from the provinces was hardly feasible so long as they continued to hold very large estates there. It was believed to be in the public interest to encourage the several tenants to buy their individual holdings so that they might become responsible landowners rather than remain discontented and ready at any time to become *ladrones.* It was believed that without great difficulty they could be persuaded to attorn to the government, and that if the estates could be purchased at a reasonable price individual holdings could eventually be sold to their occupants. Because of the beneficial influence of such a course on public order and the probable resulting improvement in social conditions, the purchase of these estates was believed to be in the public interest.

Had there been sufficient funds in the treasury the insular government would have been within its right in making this purchase, but as the total sum involved was large, and a bond issue was required to raise it, it became necessary to get the consent of Congress. This was given in sections 63, 64 and 65 of the Act of July 1, 1902. Under the authority thus conferred the commission passed the so-called Friar Lands Act, which provided among other things for the temporary leasing and ultimate sale of their holdings to tenants as well as for the determination of values and the fixing of rentals and purchase prices.

Naturally the first thing to be done was to get tenants to acknowledge the ownership of the government. Until this could be brought about little could be accomplished toward assisting them to buy their holdings. With all possible promptness temporary leases were issued to them. No effort was made carefully to ascertain the real extent

TYPICAL OLD-STYLE COUNTRY ROAD.

TYPICAL NEW-STYLE COUNTRY ROAD.

Note the deposit of surfacing material. Also the *caminero*, or road tender, at work. During the rainy season, one man looks after each kilometer of road, keeping it constantly in repair. During the dry season one man cares for two kilometers.

or value of their holdings, and unless their statements were upon their face obviously very gravely in error they were accepted as a basis for the first leases issued. The amount of opposition which was encountered was, under the circumstances, surprisingly small, and the progress of the work was unexpectedly rapid.

Planimeter surveys were made as rapidly as possible, and it was soon found, as had been anticipated, that tenants in general had understated both the size and value of their holdings. While the rate of rentals as compared with values remained unchanged, there was a resulting general increase in their amounts, and this caused murmuring, but no really serious trouble resulted. There followed as rapidly as possible the completion of accurate surveys and the fixing of final values which necessitated further changes in rentals. The volume of work was simply enormous. Many of the estates were divided into an incredible number of small holdings with boundaries of the utmost irregularity. An effort was made to get the consent of the tenants to a readjustment of boundaries on a rectangular system, leaving the size of their holdings unchanged but straightening them out. It had to be abandoned. A tenant would be unwilling to part with a given clump of bamboo or a magnificent mango tree planted by his great-great-grandfather. The fact that these valuable possessions occupied salient angles in his boundary naturally did not worry him at all.

The definite right to purchase their holdings was from the outset conferred upon lessees so that from the time the first leases were issued the only possible reasons for the failure of a tenant to purchase his holdings would be unwillingness to do so or lack of funds.

In passing the Friar Lands Act, which they did during my absence on leave, the commission, none of whose members were posted on land matters, rather thoughtlessly made applicable to the sale of vacant lands the conditions and limitations of the Public Land Act.

We had been compelled to purchase some vacant estates and to forego the purchase of several which were thickly occupied, for the reason that the friars insisted on selling the one and absolutely refused to sell the other. We had to take the best bargain we could get. The vacant lands on certain of the estates could not be sold in small tracts.

The Friar Lands Act was accordingly amended by the Philippine Legislature, of which the Philippine Assembly was then the Lower House, and all restrictions on the areas of those lands which might be sold were removed, so as to make it possible to get rid of the vacant friar lands.

Interest was piling up on the purchase price of the latter, and obviously it was best for the government, which had to administer them, and for the people, who had to pay the bill, that they should be disposed of as soon as possible.

Ultimately an opportunity presented itself to sell the San José Estate of some fifty-eight thousand acres in its entirety to an individual, and it was thus sold after consultation with the attorney-general of the Philippines and the attorney-general of the United States as to the rights of the government in the premises, and with the approval of the secretary of war and of President Taft first had. The buyer acted as an agent for Messrs. Welch, Havemeyer and Senf, who were all heavily interested in sugar growing and desired to establish a modern sugar estate in the Philippines. This fact, when it became known, was the beginning of trouble.

Two very distinct classes of men were interested in imposing the existing legislative restrictions relative to the sale of Philippine lands. The first were influenced by the most honourable of altruistic motives. They feared the monopolization of agricultural lands and the evils of absentee ownership. The other class were the representatives of certain important sugar interests in the United

States who wished to keep out Philippine sugar at all
hazards and had shrewdly figured out that the simplest
way to do this would be to prevent its production on a
commercial scale. They therefore sought to restrict the
sale of public land so as to make it impossible for an
individual or an association to buy enough to establish
a modern sugar estate. This they succeeded in doing.
They even went further, and by limiting the land which
a corporation might own and control made it impossible
for a corporation to purchase enough land of any sort
for such an estate. But that is another story with
which we are not here concerned.

They built a fence around Philippine lands which
they deemed to be "pig-tight, horse-high, and bull-strong,"
but we unwittingly cut a small hole through it. The
limitations on the sales of land did not apply to land
belonging to the insular government which had first imposed certain restrictions on the size of the areas of
vacant friar land which might be sold and had then removed them, having the same right to do the one thing
that it exercised in doing the other.

The San José Estate was sold to an individual. By
him it was sold in part to other individuals who had the
undoubted right to acquire as much land as they could get,
and in part to a corporation not authorized to engage in
agriculture which acquired only such land as it needed to
conduct its legitimate business and was therefore within
its legal right. The transaction was a perfectly legitimate
one from every view point. It spread consternation
among the beet-sugar men, and Congressman Martin of
Colorado, a state which has extensive beet-sugar interests,
made upon the floor of the House a scurrilous attack
upon President Taft, Secretary Root and the insular
government officials concerned in which he accused them
of violating the law and of having formed a gigantic
conspiracy with great corporate interests, more especially
with certain sugar interests, not only to deprive the friar

land tenants of their holdings but to prevent Filipinos in general from acquiring land and to turn the Philippines over to the trusts. Mr. Martin and his fellows insisted that section sixty-five of the Act of July 1, 1902, in itself imposed the restrictions of the Public Land Act on the sale of friar lands; that the commission in imposing these limitations in the first instance had merely voiced the will of Congress and that its act in subsequently withdrawing them was illegal and iniquitous. They apparently lost sight of the fact that if so, the iniquity was shared by the Philippine Assembly. Later they endeavoured to explain the action of the assembly by saying that it did not know what it was doing, and certain members of that body made a similar claim, for political effect. As a matter of fact, I myself explained to the members of the assembly friar lands committee the purpose of the bill with which they were then in full accord.

I requested an investigation. One was authorized by the House. It was made by the Committee on Insular Affairs. Its cost to the United States was very large. The secretary of the interior, the executive secretary, the attorney-general, the director of lands and other witnesses, were called to Washington from the Philippines and taken away from their work at a rather critical time. The result was a complete vindication of the several persons who had been attacked. Congressman Martin failed to make good his charges in any particular, and incidentally members of the committee and such other persons as cared to follow the proceedings were given a valuable demonstration of the manner in which the insular government transacts its business.

There was, however, one unfortunate indirect effect. In view of the difference of opinion among congressmen as to whether Congress had or had not intended to make the limitations to the Public Land Act relative to areas which could be sold applicable to friar lands the secretary of war issued an executive order providing that their sale should be subject to such limitations, pending an expression by Congress of its will in the matter. Congress has never acted.

There are large tracts of vacant friar lands which cannot be sold for years to come, if subject to existing restrictions, either because they are situated in very sparsely inhabited regions where there is no demand for them on the part of would-be small landowners, or because the price as fixed by law is materially in excess of that of equally good, adjacent, unoccupied public lands which can be had subject to identical conditions as to areas purchasable. As the Philippines are "land poor," the inadvisability of such a policy would seem to be sufficiently evident. The argument against large estates is without force, both because the amount of land concerned is relatively insignificant, and because there are already in the islands so many large estates, owned in many instances by Filipinos, that the addition of a few new ones more or less would not perceptibly change the existing situation.

The question might well be raised as to the authority of the secretary of war to suspend by an executive order the operation of a law duly enacted by the Philippine legislature pursuant to powers conferred by Congress, especially as Congress has power, and has had opportunity, to disapprove it. I think it possible that the director of lands could be compelled by mandamus to sell vacant friar lands in any quantity to an individual applicant.

The facts as regards forest lands are set forth in sufficient detail in the chapter on the Philippine forests.

The existing legislation relative to mineral lands is defective, or objectionable, in several minor particulars, but on the whole is reasonably satisfactory except for the provision that a person may locate but one claim on a given vein or lode. Such a provision would have very greatly hampered the development of the mining industry in the United States and it greatly hampers it in the Philippines.

Recommendations that Congress amend the law relative to mining claims have been persistently made by the commission and have been persistently ignored, probably for the reason that Congress is too busy with other matters to give much attention to such requests from the Philippines.

We now come to the subject of public agricultural lands. I have already called attention to the fact that little advantage has been taken of the liberal provision of the Public Land Act relative to free patents and homesteads. There has been some agitation in favour of a homestead of one hundred sixty acres instead of the forty acres now allowed. Personally I do not attach great importance to this matter. Five acres is as much as the average Filipino will cultivate[1] and if he has forty there is abundant room for him so to distribute his cultivated area as to let much of his land "rest," which he is very fond of doing. To increase the size of the homestead would help a very limited number of Americans, but a better way of accomplishing this would be to allow them to buy what they require, within reasonable limits.

No one who has not travelled widely in the Philippines can be adequately impressed with the insignificance of the areas now under cultivation as compared with those which would richly repay it. The country is failing to produce food enough for eight millions of people, yet if advantage were taken of the opportunities which nature so bountifully affords it could readily feed eighty millions.

Under such conditions the present restrictions on the

---

[1] The best evidence of what the average Filipino cultivates is found in the free patents. Of the 15,885 free patents applied for the average area is declared to be 7¾ acres; 4,025 Free Patents have been actually surveyed; their average area is only 5 acres.

sale of public lands, which make it impossible for an individual to buy more than forty acres, or for a corporation or association of individuals to buy more than twenty-five hundred acres, are simply absurd. What we want is not the indefinite preservation of our present vast trackless wastes of the richest public agricultural land, but productive farms.

Every opportunity should be extended to each native of these islands who desires to obtain land and cultivate it with his own hands.

The same statement holds for persons who wish to secure land and to employ others as labourers. Large estates on which modern machinery and modern agricultural methods are employed are greatly needed. The methods employed by Filipino owners of such estates are primitive. The natives believe what they see, and learn far better by example than in any other way. Absolutely no harm has resulted from the establishment of large sugar plantations on the San José Estate in Mindoro and the Calamba Estate in Luzón. On the contrary, both of these great farms have supplied abundant labour at increased wages to a very large number of needy people ; have taught labourers much about sanitary living, and have given them very valuable object lessons in agriculture. Both are frequently visited by intelligent agriculturists glad of the opportunity to acquire the practical knowledge which can there be so easily obtained by observation.

It may be a revolutionary statement to make, but if I personally controlled the public lands of the Philippine Islands, I would without hesitation give them to persons who would cultivate them, making the amounts conceded dependent strictly upon the ability of their would-be owners to cultivate, and restoring to the public domain any lands not promptly and properly utilized.

The money which the government now derives from the sale of public lands is a bagatelle compared with the benefit which would result to the country if cultivated areas were widely extended, and there is abundant labour here to extend them very rapidly. All that is needed is the introduction of modern machinery, modern agricultural methods and capital.

The existing provisions of the Public Land Act relative to leases are very liberal, but the average man wants to own land before he spends much money on it.

There are several serious omissions in the provisions of the act of Congress relative to the sale of public lands. No authority exists for their sale for residence purposes, business purposes, or cemetery purposes, except within town sites. The need of land for cemetery purposes became so acute that I deemed it wise to stretch the law a bit in meeting it. Many of the old cemeteries were situated in the midst of dense centres of population, or immediately adjacent to sources of public water supply. Their areas were usually grossly inadequate properly to accommodate the very large number of bodies requiring to be buried. Shockingly unsanitary conditions resulted, and it became necessary for the Bureau of Health to close many of them. Because of the trouble between the Aglipayan and Catholic churches, it was often impossible for representatives of the Catholic church to purchase private lands for cemetery purposes. Their old cemeteries were closed, yet they could not open new ones, although able and willing to pay liberally for the necessary land. Under these circumstances I ruled that public land could be sold to them, and that occupation by caretakers, and such cultivation as is ordinarily given in beautifying cemeteries, would be held to constitute occupation and cultivation within the meaning of the law, so that title could eventually pass.

In closing let me emphasize the fact that the only method of informing the common people of the Philippines relative to their rights in the matter of acquiring public lands thus far found practicable has been to send special

A Canga, or Carabao Sledge.

Sledges of this sort, which were formerly in common use, promptly destroyed good roads.

A new-style cart, with broad-tired wheels, which does not injure the roads.

land inspectors from house to house, to convey the information by word of mouth. A considerable number of such inspectors are now employed, and more are badly needed.

The total area of all public lands sold to Americans or foreigners since the American occupation is seventeen thousand acres; that of all public lands leased by such persons, seventeen thousand three hundred ninety acres. This is the answer to those who claim that there has been exploitation of the public domain.

The needs of the Philippine Islands in the matter of land legislation may be briefly summarized as follows: —

More judges in the Court of Land Registration so that the cadastral survey work may be expedited, and the poor man may be able to obtain title to his holdings promptly and at small expense.

The employment of more surveyors on public land work.

A renewal of the privilege of obtaining free patents on the old conditions during a period of at least ten years.

The employment of more public land inspectors to inform the poor and ignorant of their rights, and to assist them in obtaining them.

More liberal legislation relative to the size of the tracts of public land which may be purchased, and the number of mining claims on a given vein or lode which an individual may record.

Authorization for the sale of public agricultural lands outside of town sites for residence purposes, business purposes, and for cemeteries.

CHAPTER XXXI

The Philippine Forests

Would that I had adequate words in which to describe the wonders of the Philippine forests, through which I wandered almost daily for four years, and which I love to revisit whenever the opportunity presents itself! Their majestic stateliness and magic beauty defy description. I have seen them swept by hurricanes when huge branches crashed down and mighty trees thundered to earth, imperilling life and limb, and I have seen them in the still noons of the tropics when not a leaf stirred. At times they are vocal with songs of birds and ceaseless din of insects, and again they are as silent as the grave. Who could do justice to the endless variety and beauty of tree-trunk, leaf and flower; the exquisite drapery of vines, ferns and orchids which covers the older forest monarchs; the weird masses of aërial roots which lead superstitious natives to believe some trees to be haunted, and small wonder; the ever changing light and shade bringing out new beauties where one least expects to find them; the endless differences in the flora due to variations in altitude and in the distribution of moisture?

In Mindoro, Palawan and Mindanao we find tropical vegetation in its absolute perfection; in the highlands of northern Luzón we meet our old friends, the pine and oak, while beside them grow strawberries, raspberries, huckleberries, jacks-in-the-pulpit and other friends of our childhood days.

Surely the Philippine forests should be preserved, but not for their beauty alone! In them the people have a

846

permanent source of wealth, if they can only be made to realize it and to take proper measures to protect it.   Certainly no other country has a greater variety of beautiful and serviceable woods. Some of them are so close-grained and hard that they successfully resist the attacks of white ants, and prove almost indestructible even when buried in the earth. Others will not stand exposure to the weather, but last indefinitely under cover and are excellent for inside framing and finishing. We have the best of cabinet woods, such as ebony, *camagon*, *narra*,[1] *acle*, and *tindalo*. From some of our trees come valuable gums, such as *almaciga*[2] and gutta percha. Others produce alcohol, tan barks, dyewoods, valuable vegetable oils or drugs. The so-called "Singapore cane," so highly prized by makers of wicker furniture, grows abundantly in Palawan. Great areas are covered with a bamboo which makes an excellent paper pulp.

In short, the Philippine forests should be like money in the bank for the inhabitants of the islands. There are in this world wise people who under ordinary circumstances spend only the interest on their money ; and there are others who spend the principal while it lasts. To which class do the Filipinos belong?

It has been said that the civilization of a people may be measured by its forest practice, and in a sense this is true, for forestry as we know it to-day, and as the leading nations of Europe have known it for a long period, means the limiting of immediate gain in the hope of future reward, direct and indirect ; in fact, it means present-day sacrifice for the sake of an unborn posterity. A wise national forest policy therefore involves not only foresight, but statesmanship and patriotism, which in their most advanced degree are to be found only among the people of the most enlightened nations. The manner in which a people regards its forest resources may be taken as fairly indicative of its outlook in general. What then

[1] Frequently and wrongly called rosewood.   [2] Damar.

has been the policy of the Philippine government and what the attitude of the people, toward these resources?

There is little room for doubt that practically the entire land area of the Philippines from the plains at sea-level to the highest mountain-tops was originally covered with forest growth. At the time of the American occupation two-thirds of this wonderful heritage had ceased to exist. This would be all very well if any considerable portion of the vast deforested areas were cultivated, or put to any permanent profitable use, but such is not the case. According to the best estimates which it has thus far been possible to make, only about fifteen per cent of the land from which the original forests have been stripped is to-day under any form of cultivation. The remainder is covered with commercially worthless second-growth forest, and with several giant grasses which are collectively known as *cógon*.

The *cogonáles* [1] make up approximately sixty per cent of the deforested area, or forty per cent of the land area of the entire archipelago. They are not good for grazing unless fed down very closely. They are difficult to bring under cultivation because of the vitality of the grass roots and the acidity which they impart to the soil. *Cogonáles* are often the breeding places of swarms of locusts which devour growing crops in neighbouring fields. They have been produced by the shiftless form of agriculture known as *caiñgin* making.

A large majority of the inhabitants of the Philippines will not fight, for any length of time, the tropical weeds and grasses which invade their cultivated fields, and rather than attempt to do so prefer to clear forest lands, slaughtering the trees indiscriminately and burning them where they fall. An area so cleared is known as a *caiñgin*. It is usually planted with *camotes*, corn, rice or some similar quick-growing crop. Cultivation is carried on in a haphazard way, but is soon abandoned when a jungle growth

---

[1] An extensive open region covered with *cógon* is called a *cogonál*.

of grass, weeds and seedling trees begins to spring up. At the end of the first, the second or, at latest the third year the *caiñgin* maker abandons his clearing and starts a new one. Fires sweep over the abandoned areas, killing everything except the cógon grass which takes possession and holds it against all comers. The forest destruction thus wrought in the past is appalling. Within limits, it still continues, although unlicensed *caiñgin* making is now forbidden by law.

In cutting timber for domestic use and for the market, the Filipinos have in the past been absolutely indifferent to the matter of reproduction, making a clean sweep in those places where merchantable tree species could be readily and cheaply obtained.

Six weeks after the Philippine Commission became the legislative body of the islands, it passed an act for the reorganization of the Forestry Bureau, which had previously been created by military order, continuing as its chief Major George P. Ahern, who had held this position under the military régime, and who is to-day in length of service the ranking bureau chief of the insular government.

Major Ahern was thus intrusted with the management of some fifty-four thousand square miles of forest land, and was charged with the duty of investigating the forest resources of the Philippines, and of developing and protecting them. These two latter objects are by no means incompatible. Vastly more timber falls and rots in the Philippines than is cut and marketed, and the forest wealth of the islands may be developed in such a way as actually to improve the areas that are cut over by removing old trees, and thus giving light and air to younger ones which then rapidly grow up and take their places.

The stand of hardwood timber in the Philippines is now probably the finest in the world. The United States and Europe are ready to purchase every foot of the selected grades of lumber that we can ship. China offers a practically inexhaustible market for the cheaper grades. Stumpage charges are moderate. Yet in spite of all these advantages the islands do not, as yet, produce lumber enough to supply their own needs.

This condition is rapidly changing, however, and if adequate measures are not adopted for the conservation of the forests, we shall sooner or later be confronted with the danger of their devastation by the lumberman.

Under the direction of the Bureau of Forestry the trees which are to be felled are in many instances marked, and in any event care is taken to prevent the cutting of any which have not attained to certain prescribed diameters, while the leaving of enough adequately to provide for reproduction is obligatory.

Up to the time of the American occupation forest operations had been limited to a very small number of well-known species of demonstrated commercial value. The total number of tree species which had then been identified was about twelve hundred. The number identified up to the present time is approximately twenty-five hundred. A large amount of important work has been done in determining what ones of the commercially unknown species are valuable, and in what ways they may best be utilized.

One of the most important functions of the Bureau of Forestry has been to investigate unexplored and unknown forests, and ascertain definitely the stand of commercially valuable trees, at the same time giving proper consideration to the practicability of getting lumber from them to the market at reasonable expense. As a result of this work the bureau has been able to furnish much accurate and valuable information to persons desiring to engage in the lumber industry.

Some forests have been found to be very valuable, while others are practically worthless either on account of the absence of the better tree species or because of difficulties which render it impossible or unprofitable to transport lumber from them to a market.

At the time of the American occupation the methods employed in felling trees and converting them into lumber were primitive in the extreme. The small Malay axe, the edge of which is hardly wider than that of a good-sized chisel, was in common use. Once felled, trees were necessarily cut into short lengths, as all logs had to be hauled by carabaos. The logs were ultimately cut into lumber by hand with whip-saws operated, as a rule, by two men each. There was not a modern sawmill in the Philippine Islands. The few mills which existed were of the most antiquated type, and with one or two negligible exceptions were confined to Manila.

To-day there are about sixty steam sawmills in operation and orders have been placed for others, some of which will have a capacity of one hundred thousand board feet of lumber per day. The actual investment in logging equipment and sawmills runs into the millions of dollars.

Logging was formerly closely restricted to the most valuable species, so situated that they could be rolled into the water or hauled to the beach by carabaos. Large tracts are now being logged with modern machinery under conservative forest methods, and the logging railway and the skidding engine are rapidly coming into use.

Three forest reserves, similar in purpose to the national forests of the United States, have been set aside to insure a permanent timber supply in certain regions and to afford permanent protection to streams capable of furnishing irrigation water upon which may depend the prosperity of the inhabitants of neighbouring plains. One hundred and forty-nine communal forests have been created for as many municipalities, in order permanently to provide them with timber and firewood. The interests of the Filipinos themselves have been given first consideration, and the inhabitants of towns for which communal forests have not been set aside may freely cut and gather from any public forest, without license and without payment, all timber of the second and lower groups which they require for domestic use, while gratuitous licenses can be had for first-group timber to be employed in the construction of permanent houses.

Within recent years the revenue derived from forest products has steadily increased, in spite of the fact that the government charges have been materially reduced.

The public forests of the Philippines are not sold, but are developed under a license system. Small operators usually work under ordinary yearly licenses for definite small areas. Exclusive licenses, or concessions as they are popularly called, are generally in the form of twenty-year exclusive licenses to cut and remove timber and other forest products from certain specified tracts. The land itself is in no way affected by such licenses. Merely the timber and minor forest products are included. When a lumberman is seriously considering an investment in the Philippines, he himself, or an experienced representative, should state to the director of forestry approximately the extent of the investment he contemplates. He will then be given information about several tracts which promise to answer his needs, and arrangements can be made for an experienced forester to accompany him over the tracts in question so that he may size up conditions for himself. All maps, estimates and other detailed information which may have been collected on the tracts will, of course, be placed at his disposal, and he can count upon the heartiest governmental coöperation and assistance in making a success of his enterprise. It should be understood, however, that in no case does the director of forestry guarantee the correctness of the estimates or other data which he furnishes. These are given to the applicant for what they are worth, and in every case he is advised to take such steps as may be necessary to satisfy himself as to whether or not they are correct. If the

ROAD DESTROYERS AT WORK.

Carts of this type, with solid wooden wheels fixed on their axles, were admirably suited to destroy roads. Their use is now prohibited.

lumberman then decides to apply for a concession, he makes a formal application in writing to the director of forestry for an exclusive twenty-year privilege for the tract he has selected. His application is then forwarded by the director of forestry with recommendations to the secretary of the interior, who may approve the issuance of an exclusive license if he decides that such a course is in the public interest. For an area of more than a thousand hectares (approximately twenty-five hundred acres) proposals for bids to secure the desired privilege are published in the *Official Gazette* and other papers. At least six weeks intervene between the appearance of the first advertisement and the opening of the bids, but in order to give interested parties in the Philippines ample time to correspond with their principals in Europe or America, this period is usually extended to about four months. The advertisement also enumerates certain minimum requirements which principally specify the minimum amount of capital which must be invested within a certain given time and the minimum cut during the several succeeding years, together with certain requirements regarding logging and milling equipment.

Formal bids are finally submitted, and the license is ordinarily granted to the bidder who gives the best assurances of developing the tract most thoroughly and promptly. The right to reject any and all bids is expressly reserved.

In fixing the annual production there is taken into consideration, so far as possible, the amount of over-mature timber on the stand and the amount of the annual increment, with the object of rendering the investment a permanent one instead of merely permitting the operator to strip and abandon the area he holds. In preparing regulations under which the operator is required to work, first care is given to the future condition of the area, in order that the land after logging may be potentially as valuable as before, and no consideration of immediate profit is allowed to interfere. Nevertheless, the logger in the Philippines will find that in comparison with similar conditions elsewhere he will have few restrictions to contend with, and in practically no cases are these such as seriously to increase the cost of his operations. It is to permit such permanent use of the land that concessions are granted over such large areas, often consisting of a hundred square miles or even more.

As local residents are given the right to cut what lumber and firewood they may need for their private use in the territory covered by exclusive licenses, this system is not open to objection, especially as there are more than sufficient forest areas to accommodate all applicants desiring exclusive licenses. The director of forestry has the right to reduce cutting areas if outputs do not come up to requirements, so that a dog-in-the-manger policy is rendered impossible.

The local market takes about one hundred million feet per year. Only a few million feet are exported annually at present. A properly distributed cut of five hundred million feet per year would actually improve the forests.

It would seem that the policy which we have followed would meet with the almost unanimous approval of the Filipinos, but as a matter of fact it has been far from popular with them. The forest reserves have been set aside against the protest of the very people who will profit by the conservation of their resources, and would be the first to suffer from their destruction. The native press, and the Filipinos generally, have opposed the opening up of timber tracts by modern logging methods, despite the fact that such tracts are usually inaccessible to persons operating with old-fashioned equipment, and the further fact that the establishment of important lumbering enterprises means additional employment for well-paid skilled and unskilled labor, increase in the money in circulation, decrease in lumber imports and the ultimate development of a lucrative export trade. Fear of American capital can hardly be cited as an explanation of this phenomenon. Of three concessions granted last year only one, which was subsequently abandoned, went to American capitalists.

Thus far the Filipinos have made no attempt to share in the development of their forests on any save a very small scale. Of the total amount of lumber sawed in the islands only about ten per cent is produced in mills owned or controlled by them. It is useless to argue that the timber should be saved for future generations, for if not cut at maturity trees fall and rot.

So far as concerns conservation, the attitude of the Filipinos is even less satisfactory. There is abundant evidence on which to base a prediction as to the policy which they would follow in practice, if the compelling hand of an enlightened nation were withdrawn.

There is a singular indifference to the results of wanton forest destruction, not only on the part of the persons guilty of it but on that of the municipal, provincial and judicial officials who should prevent it by enforcing the law. Even when the employees of the Bureau of Forestry have laboriously gathered conclusive evidence against *caiñgin* makers it often proves excessively difficult, or impossible, to secure conviction. The existing opposition to forest protection springs from a desire on the part of the Filipinos to consume their capital as well as their interest, without thought of the morrow, or of the permanent advantage to their country as a whole which would result from conservation of its forest wealth. If they were left to their own devices the forests would once more blaze with *caiñgin* fires set by the poor peasant at the command of the influential *cacique*. Unfortunately that is now only too often the way in which *caiñgins* come to be made. The rich landowners compel ignorant dependents to make them, furnishing seed for the first agricultural crop. Under this arrangement the poor labourer runs all the risk of being prosecuted, does all the work, and often gives half or more of his crop to the *cacique* as a return for the seed loaned him. After the *caiñgin* is abandoned the *cacique* claims the land as his own, and through his influence in provincial politics can often succeed in delaying, or avoiding, prosecution even if detected in his wrong-doing.

What the result would be were all restraint withdrawn, and were the Filipinos permitted to destroy their forest resources at will, may easily be inferred from what has happened in the past, as well as from the difficulties encountered in enforcing the present law. Cebú, the most thickly populated large island in the archipelago, is already practically deforested, and until recently many other islands have been rapidly approaching the same unfortunate condition.

Under conservative forest management the existing annual output of lumber might be increased fivefold and the unfortunate results from reckless cutting, which have so frequently occurred in the past and which not infrequently still occur, might be completely avoided.

If these very desirable ends are to be attained, the force employed by the Bureau of Forestry must be materially augmented. It has been conclusively demonstrated that every increase in the number of its employees is promptly followed by a sufficient increase in the insular revenues derived from forest products to more than offset the expense involved in the payment of the additional salaries and travel expenses. For every extra peso that the government expends in this way it takes in about two, and if this can be done, and the enormous forest resources of the islands developed and conserved at the same time, there *ought* to be no trouble in securing the necessary legislation.

I long endeavoured to bring about the establishment of a fixed relationship between the amount annually collected on forest products and the amount allotted for the work of the Bureau of Forestry. Obviously the working force of the bureau must be increased as the lumber industry develops, or adequate supervision cannot be exercised.

Increasing the working force of the bureau makes possible investigations which stimulate the development of the lumber industry, and lead to a largely increased output.

The collection of revenue on forest products from government lands is made by the Bureau of Internal Revenue under the general supervision of the secretary of finance and justice. I have recently learned, to my amazement, that every large sawmill owner in the islands is allowed to make the statement of the output of his mill upon which collections are based; a procedure very like allowing importers to assess their own customs dues. The inevitable result is that the government is robbed right and left. Finding that an attempt was made to justify this procedure on the ground that it was impracticable to have lumber measured at the mills, as the Bureau of Internal Revenue has not sufficient employees for this purpose, I endeavoured to remedy this extraordinary situation.

Under existing law, timber may be measured in the round, in the square, or after it has been manufactured into lumber. Measurement in the round is quick and simple, and it has the further advantage that loss due to wasteful sawing falls on the lumberman, while if the sawed lumber only is measured such loss falls on the government. I therefore drafted and submitted to the commission a law providing that all timber should be measured in the round, with proper allowance for defects. Had the law passed, I could have had employees of the Bureau of Forestry measure the logs brought into each of the several mills which collectively turn out ninety per cent of the sawn lumber of the islands, and so could have effectively prevented frauds upon the government.

A system which practically allows the individuals interested to fix the amounts which they shall pay the government for its timber naturally meets with the unqualified approval of the lumbermen. I therefore expected that they would strenuously object to the proposed change in law. To my surprise there was no complaint while it was pending before the commission, which passed it.

Then, and only then, I learned that certain lumbermen had quietly done their work where they believed, rightly, that it would be effective, and that the bill would not pass the assembly. An effective lobby, headed by a Filipino representative of the largest Filipino lumbering concern in the islands, had been organized against it, and so a measure having no other object or effect than to prevent frauds on the government and increase its revenue, was killed, for the time at least, consideration of the bill being "deferred," by the assembly, with the result that a large number of foreign mill owners will be allowed to continue to make an illegitimate profit, and a very limited number of Filipino mill owners will do the same.

The commercial outlook for the Philippine lumber industry is very encouraging. No more greedy lumber market exists than Manila has offered during the past few years, this condition being due primarily to the stimulus given to all lines of industrial development by the economic policy of the insular administration.

Prices are high, and the supply is still unequal to the local demand. Forest products to the value of $696,407 were last year imported into the Philippines when we should have exported them in large quantities. A lumber company properly equipped and managed, and operating on a suitable tract, can place lumber in its Manila yards at a cost of half or even less than half the price at which the same lumber readily sells. The export trade, which should be very profitable, has as yet scarcely been

AN OLD-STYLE CULVERT.

Many a good horse has been killed by breaking through a structure like this.

inaugurated. Tan bark, dyewoods, valuable gums and rattans find a ready sale. It may reasonably be expected that the world's demand for forest products of all kinds will increase as the years go by, and that the resources of older countries will become depleted, or at least inadequate to supply steadily growing needs. Forest growth in the Philippines is rapid, and under suitable conservation methods reforestation comes about quickly. With continued enforcement of existing law, and with adequate supervision over cutting and reforestation, the cost of which should be paid by the lumber industry itself, the forests of the islands should become an important permanent source of revenue and wealth. Filipinos ought to become holders of forest concessions instead of labourers on the concessions of others. Whether any considerable number of them will care to do so remains to be seen, but at all events their forests should be conserved, so that the opportunity may be ever before them. At the present time *caiñgin* makers destroy far more timber in the course of a year than lumbermen use.

In the hope of awakening an interest among Filipinos in forest conservation and development, and of being able to train an adequate Filipino working force, a forest school has been started at Los Baños, in the immediate vicinity of one of our forest reserves, where practical instruction can advantageously be given. It is anticipated that the graduates of this school will be of great use in bringing about a radical change in the attitude of the Filipinos toward forest conservation.

It is an astonishing fact that the Bontoc and Lepanto Igorots have been the only ones of the very numerous Philippine peoples to see for themselves the benefits derivable from forest conservation.

When I first visited their country I noted that all the trees in certain pine forests were carefully trimmed of their lower branches, and on inquiry found that trees might not be felled until they reached a certain size, although branches might be cut for firewood. The prevention of fires, which are very destructive in pine forests, and the care of young trees, were also adequately provided for ! The Bureau of Forestry now employs Igorots as fire wardens in Benguet and Bontoc.

If the policy were adopted of appropriating annually an amount equivalent to sixty per cent of the forest revenues for the work of the Bureau of Forestry, the proper conservation and development of the great potential source of wealth intrusted to that bureau would be adequately provided for. The commission has agreed to such an arrangement; ten per cent of the total forest revenues to be expended in the provinces under its exclusive legislative control, and fifty per cent in the other provinces. Appropriations for the territory occupied by non-Christians are now made on this basis. No appropriation bill has been passed by the assembly since this policy was agreed to by the commission. It remains to be seen whether the former body will favour the expenditures necessary to support the work of forest conservation and development, with the reasonable certainty that such work will not only assure to them and to coming generations a permanent source of wealth, but will more than pay for itself in dollars and cents.

CHAPTER XXXII

IMPROVED MEANS OF COMMUNICATION

THE improvement in means of communication which has taken place in the Philippines since the American occupation is almost revolutionary. I well remember my tribulations in the Spanish days, resulting from the inadequacy of the mail system. There were long delays in receiving letters sent from Manila to the more important towns in the archipelago, but if, as was usually the case with us, one was living in a small and more or less isolated provincial town, he was fortunate to get his letters at all. They would be forwarded from place to place by irresponsible native carriers, and under the most favourable circumstances were likely to be greatly delayed in transmission. There was little respect for the privacy of letters. On one occasion I arrived at Joló, confidently expecting a large mail, only to be disappointed. A week later my companion, Dr. Bourns, was calling upon a German resident of that place. Lying in a waste-basket he saw a letter written in a hand which he recognized as that of one of my friends. He thereupon called upon the German to deliver any other letters he might have for me, and some were produced, but others had been thrown away! We found that our mail had begun to come prior to our arrival, and as the Spanish postmaster did not know any persons named Bourns or Worcester he turned it over to this man to see whether he could make out whom it was for. The latter opened the letters, read them, and threw them away.

But this was not the worst of it. There was a time when for months I received no letters, and my companion no newspapers or magazines. Then the arrangement was reversed. I got my letters but no papers or magazines, while he had papers but no letters.

Under the Spanish régime letter carriers in Manila received the munificent salary of $46 per annum, but were authorized to collect a charge of three-quarters of a cent on every article of mail delivered by them, except letters from foreign countries and letters passing between persons living in Manila.

The Spanish government did not admit general merchandise to the mails, but accepted only samples and medicine. We admit all classes of merchandise except certain objectionable things and certain articles dangerous to the mails or to those handling them. We have increased the maximum allowable weight of mail packages to eleven pounds, and on January 1, 1913, established a "collect on delivery" service under which merchants and others may send goods through the mails and have the charges thereon collected from the addressee before delivery. These are important and valuable extensions of the service, and greatly benefit the Filipinos as well as the merchants by bringing people throughout the islands into touch with shops from which they can order the goods they need.

It is difficult to determine the difference in the amounts of business done under the Spanish and American systems for the reason that the Spanish figures are in many cases obviously unreliable. The latest available statistics, for the fiscal year 1893, show an enormous discrepancy between the amount of mail matter claimed to have been transported and the revenue received, which should theoretically have been about twice as large as seems to have been collected. It is believed, however, that the following figures are fairly reliable.

The number of post-offices has increased from four hundred sixty-six to five hundred ninety. It is anticipated that one hundred fifty additional post-offices will be established in smaller municipalities and out-of-the-way places within the present year, and as it is these places are receiving postal service through the employment of competent letter-carriers, who are collecting and delivering their mails.

Only sixty-five of the Spanish post-offices were in charge of officials employed by the general government. The remaining four hundred one were looked after in a way by local municipal officials. All postmasters are now paid by the general government.

The mails are being carried with much greater frequency than ever before. During the last year there were 273 contract routes on which mails were carried a total of 873,957 miles at a cost of $40,440.75.

So far as can be judged from the figures available the mails despatched from the islands during the fiscal year 1912 were about five times those annually despatched during the late years of the Spanish régime.

In 1893 nine parcel post packages were sent to foreign countries. In 1912, 2640 such parcels went abroad. In 1893 the number of registered articles transmitted between Philippine post-offices was 29,078. In 1912 it was 535,137. The increased use of newspapers is shown by the fact that in 1893 the weight of the newspapers mailed for delivery within the Philippines was 121,070 pounds, while in 1912 it was 687,568 pounds. This difference is no doubt largely due to the severe restrictions imposed on the press under the Spanish régime as compared with the freedom which it enjoys to-day.

The Spanish postal administration paid little attention to complaints by Filipinos relative to losses of articles transmitted through the mails. Now the most trivial complaint is painstakingly investigated, and only in rare cases is there failure to recover the value of lost or stolen articles from the postal employee responsible. The sanctity of the mails which now prevails is an important factor in the increased use which the people make of them.

It is claimed that under the Spanish régime few matters of importance were intrusted to the mails by Filipinos because their letters were so frequently opened and inspected by government officials.

The Spaniards had four subsidized mail routes after 1897. We have nine subsidized routes, and six others which are maintained wholly at government expense by the Bureau of Navigation.

The Spanish government provided no postal money-order service whatever, and the transmission of money by mail with safety was impossible. We have 265 money-order post-offices and during 1912 issued 160,524 money-orders payable in the islands, the total sum of which was $5,592,205.85. We also issued 68,229 orders amounting to $1,764,608.02 payable in the United States, and 2607 orders amounting to $68,364.83 payable in other countries. These amounts were transmitted largely by Filipinos, who now do a considerable mail order business with merchants in the United States.

A further great convenience not furnished by the Spanish government is the payment of money-orders transmitted by telegraph. During the last fiscal year there were forwarded 8333 such orders, covering payments amounting to $1,128,229.79.

The improvement in the telegraph service has been quite as marked as that in the mail service. In 1897 there were only 65 telegraph offices in the islands, 49 of which were on the island of Luzón, 9 on Panay, 4 on Negros and 3 on Cebú. The total length of all telegraph lines was some 1750 miles. There were no cables or other means of telegraphic communication between the islands.

Practically all of the old lines were destroyed during the revolution which began in 1896, so that the lines now existing must be considered as having been built since the American occupation. There are 282 telegraph offices with 4781 miles of land line and in addition 1362 miles of marine cable and 7 wireless stations in operation.

Every provincial capital, with the exception of Basco in the remote Batanes Islands, and Butuan in Agusan Province, now has telegraphic facilities as does almost every other place of commercial importance in the Philippines. The advantage of prompt telegraphic communication with such outlying points as Puerto Princesa, Joló, Zamboanga, Davao, Suriago and the east coast of Samar is enormous, while the extension of the cable service to Catanduanes has been a great boon to the hemp growers of that island. The latest available figures relative to the telegraphic business conducted by the Spaniards are for the year 1889, during the second six months of which there were handled 33,697 commercial telegrams. During the fiscal year 1912 our business of the same class reached a total of 496,643 telegrams. This class of business has been increasing from 25 to 30 per cent yearly for several years.

The expenditures of the Spanish government for all postal and telegraphic service for the fiscal year 1895 amounted to $484,960.50. Those of the Bureau of Posts for 1912 were $1,072,684.48. No statement of the Spanish revenues can be found. Our revenues for 1912 were $627,724.70. The personnel of the Spanish service for 1895 shows only 31 positions paying salaries of more than $500 per year, most of which were filled by Spaniards. There are now 96 positions paying salaries of more than $500 per year filled by Filipinos. Filipino post-office employees receive salaries 50 to 100 per cent larger than those of employees of similar rank during the Spanish régime. Think how much these figures mean in increased opportunity for employment of Filipinos, and in increased communication not only between the people in the islands but between them and the outside world.

In a number of instances the telegraph lines which are controlled by the Bureau of Posts are supplemented by provincial telephone systems, which are of great value in maintaining quick communication with towns not reached

by telegraph wires. Such lines are especially useful in
the Mountain Province, Mindoro, Palawan, Nueva
Vizcaya, and the sub-province of Bukidnon, where messengers who travel by land have to go on horseback or on
foot.

The following table shows the growth of the postal and
telegraph business of the Islands : —

POST-OFFICE AND TELEGRAPH STATISTICS

FISCAL YEAR	MONEY ORDERS SOLD		POSTAGE RECEIPTS	TELEGRAPH RECEIPTS	
	Amount	Increase (+) or decrease (−)		Amount	Increase (+) or decrease (−)
		Per cent			
1900	$1,526,310	. . . .	$117,848	. . . . .	. . . .
1901	1,514,435	− 1	122,833	. . . . .	. . . .
1902	1,854,927	+22	126,375	. . . . .	. . . .
1903	2,842,587	+53	132,445	. . . . .	. . . .
1904	3,102,606	+ 9	121,714	. . . . .	. . . .
1905	3,444,053	+11	121,648	. . . . .	. . . .
1906	3,687,127	+ 7	198,583	[1]$56,351	. . . .
1907	3,229,446	−12	198,546	118,360	+110
1908	3,645,123	+13	220,306	136,138	+ 15
1909	4,008,678	+10	245,482	139,208	+ 2
1910[3]	4,890,835	+22	282,317	168,402	+ 21
1911	6,132,582	+25	313,549	184,555	+ 9
1912	7,425,173	+21	349,407	236,679	+ 28
1913[2]	8,272,858	+ 6	380,942	283,305	+ 4

As I have elsewhere remarked, the Philippines have a
coast line longer than that of the continental United
States. A very large percentage of the municipalities
are situated on, or close to, the sea and the maintenance
of adequate marine transportation is therefore a matter
of vital importance to the peace and commercial pros-

[1] First year for which statistics are available.
[2] Twice the actual figures for the first half of the year : $3,942,647 ;
$194,296 ; $123,339.
[3] First year after Payne Tariff Bill took effect.

perity of the archipelago.   In the early days of American
occupation conditions were most unsatisfactory.   Most
of the boats in the coastwise trade were antiquated, foul
and had no decent facilities for transporting passengers.
As the number of vessels was too small to handle the business of the country, ship-owners occupied a very independent position.   The freight rates on such things as lumber
and currency were practically prohibitive.   It was a
common thing for vessels to refuse to receive hemp, sugar
and perishable products that had been brought to the
beach for shipment, giving as an excuse the fact that
they were employed in the private business of Messrs.
Smith, Bell & Co., Warner, Barnes & Co., or whoever
happened to own them, and could not transport freight
for the public as the volume of their private business would
not permit it.   However, if the owners of the freight were
willing to sell it to the ships' officers for a fraction of its
value, they encountered no difficulty in transporting it !

Furthermore, there existed the danger of Moro raids,
the necessity for checking the operations of smugglers,
and that of preventing the ingress of firearms, which in
the hands of irresponsible persons might cause great
damage and expense to the government and the public.

In view of these facts it was decided to establish a fleet
of twenty coast-guard vessels, which were not only to
do police duty and to assist in the transportation of troops,
but were to carry freight and passengers when opportunity
offered.   Fifteen such vessels were ordered from Messrs.
Farnham, Boyd & Co., of Shanghai, and five from the
Uraga Dock Company of Japan.   The Japanese vessels
proved unsatisfactory, and only two were accepted, making the total fleet seventeen.   As the condition of public
order improved the coast-guard boats became available
to a constantly increasing extent for commercial service.

Prior to July, 1906, there were practically no established
steamship routes over which commercial vessels operated
on regular schedules.   With the exception of the service

between Manila, Cebú and Iloílo, vessels traded here and there without regular ports of call or fixed dates of arrival or departure. The policy which guided their owners was one of privilege and monopoly, and by agreement between them competition was rigidly excluded. Trade was discouraged and the commercial development of the islands seriously retarded.

In accordance with a plan formulated by Mr. Forbes, then secretary of commerce and police, the coast-guard vessels were placed on regular commercial routes and were operated on schedules which gave efficient service to all important islands of the archipelago. Ten routes were maintained and many isolated points, and small towns or villages which offered so little business at the outset as to make them unprofitable, and therefore unattractive as ports of call for commercial vessels, were put in close communication with the larger towns and distributing centres, so that the small planters could market their products with little trouble. This promptly led to increased production and trade, and greater prosperity through the islands.

Business increased to such an extent that in July, 1906, it proved practicable to withdraw the government vessels and turn these routes over to commercial firms which entered into a definite contract with the government to maintain an adequate service. Their vessels were allowed substantial subsidies, amounting in the aggregate to $100,000 per year, in order to assure the prompt despatch of mail, adherence to schedule, and efficient service. The ten old coast-guard routes were divided into fourteen new commercial routes which gave excellent service to all parts of the islands.

Secondary routes were then arranged and coast-guard cutters were placed on them. A number of these were in turn given over to commercial vessels after they had developed enough trade to be commercially profitable. Three such routes are now maintained by the Bureau of

THE OLD WAY OF CROSSING A RIVER.

THE NEW WAY OF CROSSING A RIVER.

Navigation, and it is planned to establish two more in the near future.

The importance of the change thus brought about by the government in transportation facilities can be appreciated only by those who have had actual experience with the intolerable state of affairs which previously existed. Meanwhile conditions on the inter-island steamers have been enormously improved by the enforcement of proper sanitary regulations, and insistence that staterooms be decent and food reasonably good.

Of the original cutters two were for a long time under charter by the military authorities for use as despatch boats and transports; two are employed as lighthouse tenders, and two have been assigned to the Bureau of Coast Surveys for coast and geodetic work; one collects lepers and takes them to the Leper Colony at Culion. The cable-ship *Rizal*, operated by the Bureau of Navigation, has succeeded in repairing and keeping in repair the marine cables throughout the islands. Such cables are especially subject to injury in Philippine waters on account of the strength of the currents between the islands, the frequency with which stretches of sea bottom are overgrown with sharp coral, and the common occurrence of earthquakes. When not otherwise engaged the *Rizal* carries commercial cargoes if opportunity offers. She has proved useful for bringing in rice when a shortage of this commodity, which is the bread of the Filipino people, threatened, and for handling cargoes of lumber of sizes such that regular inter-island steamers could not load it.

In addition to the vessels above mentioned, the Bureau of Navigation owns and operates a fleet of launches, some of which are seagoing, and a number of dredges which are employed in improving the harbours and rivers of the islands as funds permit. The bureau also owns and operates its own machine shop and marine railway, and repairs its own vessels.

A section of the machine shop is set aside for lighthouse

work, and in it lighthouse apparatus of every description
is fabricated and repaired.   While lighthouses and buoys
are not means of communication they are aids to it.

The thousand and ninety-five inhabited islands and approximately two hundred and fifty ports of varying importance, depending as they do entirely upon water transportation for communication with each other and with the
outside world, had no wharfage whatever available for
large vessels, and no publicly owned wharfage within ten
yards of which even the larger inter-island steamers could be
berthed.   Manila had no protected anchorage, and during
the season of southwest monsoons and typhoons vessels
were sometimes compelled to lie in the harbour for weeks
before they could unload, a fact which gave the port a
deservedly bad name.

The Spaniards had commenced harbour work at Manila
in 1892, twenty-five years after preliminary study began
and sixteen years after prospective plans had been submitted.   Their operations were stopped by the insurrection in 1896, at which time the present west breakwater
had been about half completed, but as the completed portion was at the shore end and in shallow water it afforded
no protection to ships.   There had been constructed
twenty-four hundred feet of masonry wall partly enclos-
ing one of the basins provided for in the Spanish plans,
and fourteen hundred eighty-five feet of wall lining canals
connecting the proposed new harbour with the Pasig River.
These also were temporarily useless, because there had been
no dredging in front of them, or backfilling in their rear.

Outside of Manila practically nothing had been done
to facilitate the loading and discharge of vessels, or to
protect them from the elements.

We now have at Manila a deep-water harbour dredged
to a uniform depth of thirty feet and enclosed by two
breakwaters having a total length of nearly eleven thousand five hundred feet.   Two hundred and sixty-one acres
of land have been reclaimed with the dredged material.

Two steel piers extend from the filled land into the deep-water harbour.   One of these is six hundred fifty feet long and one hundred ten feet wide, the other six hundred feet long and seventy feet wide.   Both are housed in, the sheds covering them having a total area of ninety-two thousand square feet.   These piers and sheds are practically fireproof, and the largest ocean-going steamers on the Pacific can lie alongside them.   Additional work planned, which should be undertaken when funds permit, includes two more piers; and bulkheads to connect the inner ends of the present piers, so as to give inter-island steamers opportunity to unload.

At Cebú the sea-wall has been completed to a length of two thousand sixty feet and the channel in front of it dredged in part to ten and a half and in part to twenty-three feet at low water.   Some ten and a half acres of land have been reclaimed with the material removed.   Streets and roadways have been built on the reclaimed area, and a wharf eight hundred twelve feet in length, designed as an extension to the wall, is now fifty per cent completed.   The harbour at Cebú should ultimately be dredged so as to give thirty feet of water along the piers.

At Iloílo the dredging of a fifteen-foot channel up to the custom-house was completed in March, 1907.   Seven hundred and eighty-three feet of river wall and twelve hundred ninety feet of reënforced concrete wharf, both to accommodate vessels of eighteen feet draft at low water, have been built along the south bank of the middle reach of the river.   The lower reach has been dredged to twenty-four feet at low water, the middle reach to eighteen feet and the upper reach to fifteen feet, while two hundred ten thousand square metres of land have been reclaimed and two hundred six thousand improved with the dredged material.   Wharves for ocean-going steamers should ultimately be constructed at this important port.

At Paracale, in Ambos Camarines, a reënforced concrete

pier four hundred ninety feet in length has been built. It extends out to a depth of fifteen feet at low water.

At Bais, Negros, a timber pier for vessels of sixteen feet draft, with a stone causeway approach a mile and a half in length, and a warehouse for the temporary storage of sugar, have been constructed.

Channels have been blasted through the coral reefs surrounding the islands Batan, Sabtang and Itbayat in the Batanes group, where the annual loss of life had previously been great, owing to the occurrence of sudden storms which often made it impossible for people to return to their towns through the surf. The port of Pandan, in Ilocos Sur, has been improved by means of a stone revetment twenty-nine hundred seventy-five feet in length along the north bank of the Abra River, thus maintaining the channel in one position and affording vastly better means of loading and discharging cargo for the important town of Vigan. A self-propelling combination snag boat, pile driver and dredge for the improvement of the great Cagayan River has been built, and is now in operation on that stream.

Very numerous other works of repair and construction have been carried out. Some 80 surveys have been made in minor ports to determine the feasibility of improvements, and in many cases plans have been prepared for proposed work.

The Spaniards had devoted much time and study to a project for coast illumination. At the outbreak of the insurrection in 1896 they had twenty-eight lights, fourteen of which were flashing and fourteen fixed minor lights, while four additional stations were under construction. Then all work was stopped, and when systematic inspection was made by American lighthouse engineers five years later, extensive repairs were found to be necessary. The repairs were made as promptly as possible, and new construction then began. To-day there are a hundred forty-five lights in operation, and the waters of the Philippines are among the best lighted in the world. One hundred and eleven buoys of various classes are being maintained.

The following table shows the progress made in the construction of lighthouses:—

Fiscal Year	Light-houses in Operation	Fiscal Year	Light-houses in Operation	Fiscal Year	Light-houses in Operation
1902	57	1906 . . .	105	1910 . . .	143
1903	66	1907 . . .	117	1911 . . .	142
1904	76	1908 . . .	129	1912 . . .	145
1905	89	1909 . . .	139	1913[1] . . .	145

In all nearly $7,000,000 have been expended in the improvement of ports and harbours, and about $750,000 in the construction of lights.

At the time of the American occupation, knowledge of the waters of the archipelago was in a most unsatisfactory state. There was not even an accurate chart of Manila Bay. Navigating officers followed certain well-known trade routes which experience had shown to be safe, but did not dare to leave them. Uncharted dangers were soon discovered at Iloilo and in other important ports, and the necessity for a systematic survey of the waters became immediately apparent.

On September 6, 1901, the Bureau of Coast and Geodetic Surveys was organized. The work is conducted under a joint agreement such that it is supervised by the superintendent of coast and geodetic surveys at Washington, who is represented in the Philippines by an officer called the director of coast surveys. The latter reports to the head of the insular government so far as concerns the expenditure of funds furnished by that government, which has the power of approval over his assignment to duty. There is a division of expenses between the two

[1] On March 1, 1913.

governments. The United States has paid approximately
fifty-five per cent of the total cost, and the insular government has paid the balance.

The Bureau is engaged in a systematic survey of the
coasts, harbours and waters of the Philippine Islands and
of the topography of the shore-line. It determines positions astronomically and by triangulation, investigates
reported dangers to navigation, and observes tides, currents and the magnetic elements. Five steamers are now
engaged in this very important work. It is estimated
that fifty-four per cent of the surveys of the coast and
adjacent waters have already been completed. When one
remembers that the coast-line of the Philippines is longer
than that of the continental United States, one realizes that
this is a remarkable achievement.

The Bureau has published one hundred twenty-four
charts covering the entire boundaries of the islands, and
six volumes of sailing directions which are kept constantly
up to date by additions whenever new facts of importance
to mariners are ascertained. The greater part of the information thus made available represents results obtained
by the Bureau, but these are supplemented by the most
reliable data that can be obtained from other sources.

The following table shows the number of miles of coast
surveyed at the end of each year, beginning with 1901 :—

NUMBER OF MILES OF COAST SURVEYED

FISCAL YEAR	MILES	FISCAL YEAR	MILES
1901	89	1908	6,109
1902	576	1909	7,126
1903	1,208	1910	8,763
1904	1,921	1911	9,992
1905	2,415	1912	11,308
1906	3,041	1913 [1]	11,748
1907	4,536		

[1] On January 1, 1913; increase of six months only.

Not only have all important waterways through the islands been surveyed and lighted, but travel and the transportation of merchandise on land have been enormously facilitated by the construction of additional railways and of a system of first-, second- and third-class roads and of trails.

Prior to 1907 the only railroad line in operation in the Philippines was the so-called Manila-Dagupan Railway, which was 122 miles long.

The following table shows the steady increase in mileage since that time and also the steady increase in railroad earnings : —

RAILROAD STATISTICS

Fiscal Year	Total Mileage in Operation	Earnings of Philippine Railway Co., Amount	Increase	Calendar Year	Earnings of Manila Railway Co.	
					Amount	Increase
1907[1] . .	122	. . . . . .	. . .	1907	$25,823	. . .
1908 . . .	221	. . . . . .	. . .	1908	961,936	16
1909 . . .	290	$74,815[2]	. . .	1909	1,023,812	6
1910 . . .	400	118,646	59	1910	1,233,794	21
1911 . . .	455	142,888	20	1911	1,919,244	56
1912 . . .	599	386,970	171	1912	2,304,436	20
1913 . . .	611[3]	([4])	. . .	. . .	. . .	. . .

The north line of the Manila Railroad Company, which is the successor to the Manila and Dagupan Railway Company, now extends to Bauaug in the province of La Union. It has laterals terminating at Camp One, on the

[1] Only railroad line in operation prior to 1907 was 122 miles of the main line of the Manila Railroad Company.

[2] First year of operation.

[3] On February 1, 1913; increase of six months only.

[4] The Philippine Railway Company has recently changed its accounting from the basis of the Government fiscal year (beginning July 1) to a calendar year basis. Figures are not therefore available for a complete twelve months subsequent to June 30, 1912. The figure for the first year on the new basis (ending December 31, 1912, and duplicating part of the last amount given above) is $376,512.

Benguet Road; Rosales in Pangasinan; Mangaldang in Pangasinan; Cabanatuan in Nueva Ecija; Camp Stotensberg in Pampanga; Florida Blanca in Pampanga; Montalban in Rizal, and Antipolo in Rizal.

The main south line of this road extends from Manila to Lucena in Tayabas. It has branches to Cavite in the province of the same name; to Naic in Cavite; to Pagsanján in La Laguna, and to Batangas in the Province of Batangas.

The Philippine Railway Company has built and is now operating a line on Panay which extends from Iloilo to Capiz, and a line on Cebú which extends north from the city of the same name to Danao and south to Argao.

The development of the road system is even more important than that of railroads.

The following tables show the mileage of first-, second- and third-class road, and the total number of permanent bridges and culverts, in existence at the end of each year, beginning with 1907 : —

PUBLIC WORKS STATISTICS

FISCAL YEAR	TOTAL MILEAGE OF ROADS IN EXISTENCE			
	First-class Roads	Increase	Second-class Roads	Third-class Roads
		Per Cent		
1907	303 [1]	—	—	—
1908	423	40	—	—
1909	609	44	—	—
1910	764	25	641 [1]	2,074 [1]
1911	987	29	664	1,837
1912	1,143	16	1,342.1 [2]	1,999
1913 [3]	1,187 [4]	—	1,305.3	1,967

[1] No accurate statistics before 1907 and 1910, respectively.
[2] Increase due to change in definition.
[3] On January 1, 1913.
[4] Increase of six months only.

Fiscal Year	Total of Permanent Bridges and Culverts in Existence		Fiscal Year	Total of Permanent Bridges and Culverts in Existence	
	Number	Per Cent		Number	Per Cent
1907 [1] . . .	3,280 [1]	—	1911 . . .	4,842	11
1908	3,631	11	1912 . . .	5,181	7
1909	3,865	6	1913 . . .	5,660	9
1910	4,372	13			

The old Spanish road system was quite extensive and very well planned, but the amount of really good construction was very limited. The system of maintenance was faulty, and the abandonment of maintenance during the insurrection against Spain and the war with the United States resulted in the almost complete destruction of many roads which were in fairly good condition at the time public order became seriously disturbed. The total value of Spanish work on existing roads is estimated at $1,800,000. The total value of all American work up to June 30, 1911, is estimated at $6,100,000.

The imperative need of better highways throughout the islands was brought home by the difficulties encountered by the army during the insurrection, and the first act of the Philippine Commission, passed on the twelfth day after the commission became the legislative body of the islands, appropriated $1,000,000 ($2,000,000 Mexican) for the construction and repair of highways and bridges.

Much of this money was very advantageously expended by the military, who contributed a large amount of transportation free of cost. Unfortunately, while the necessity for roads was at this time fully appreciated, there was failure to appreciate the extraordinary rapidity with which tropical rains and vegetation destroy good roads in the Philippines. We further failed to appreciate the absolute indifference of the Filipinos themselves as to whether roads once built are or are not maintained.

[1] No accurate statistics before 1907.

One of the first large pieces of work undertaken was a road from Calamba on the Laguna de Bay to Lipa, an important town in the province of Batangas, and thence to the town of Batangas itself. This road ran for its entire extent through a rich agricultural district. I passed over it when the dirt work had all been completed, and when all but two short stretches were surfaced. I certainly had vigorously impressed upon me the necessity of surfacing. Over that portion of the road which had been so treated an automobile could have been driven at sixty miles an hour. Over the remainder of it, built by the same engineer, shaped up in the same way, and as good a dirt road as could be constructed, four mules could not haul the ambulance in which we were riding without our assistance. We had to get out and literally put our shoulders to the wheel, or tug at the spokes, in order to enable the faithful beasts to extricate the ambulance from the morasses into which the two unsurfaced stretches had been converted.

Needless to say, the surfacing was completed as soon as possible, and then came what the Filipinos call a great *desengaño*.[1] I venture to say that from the time the road was finished until it was completely destroyed there was never a shovelful of dirt nor a basketful of gravel placed upon it. In 1908 I attempted to drive over it in one of the two-wheeled rigs known as *carromatas*, which will go almost anywhere. I was upset twice in as many miles and gave up the attempt.

For a considerable time the destruction of roads almost kept pace with their construction, and until 1907 the small amount of provincial funds available usually resulted in failure to attempt repairs until both surfacing and foundation had been badly injured or destroyed. The remnants of old Spanish roads still existing, and the new roads constructed by Americans, were in danger of being wiped out. It was then decided that further insular aid for road con-

[1] Literally "disillusion."

A TYPICAL OLD-STYLE BRIDGE.

A TYPICAL REËNFORCED CONCRETE BRIDGE.

struction should not be given until the indifference of provincial officials could be overcome, and funds provided for proper maintenance. It was further decided that roads and bridges should be considered as on a basis similar to that of other government property, and that maintenance must take precedence over new construction. Regulations providing for it were outlined and incorporated in a proposed resolution which was submitted to the several provincial boards with the information that further insular funds would not be appropriated for any province until its board passed this resolution, thereby agreeing to provide road and bridge funds by means of the so-called double cedula tax, and perpetually to maintain the heavily surfaced roads then in existence within its limits.

The cedula tax is an annual personal or poll tax. The amount originally fixed by the commission was one peso, but legislation was subsequently enacted empowering provincial boards to increase it to two pesos, the additional amount to go for road and bridge work.

Most of the provinces promptly took the suggested action, and the few which at first stood out were soon compelled by popular opinion to follow suit. It is not too much to say that real progress in permanent road and bridge construction in the Philippines dates from 1907 when the present regulation relative to maintenance was put into effect.

Provision was made for a yearly provincial maintenance appropriation of not less than $282 per mile of duly designated road. Stone kilometer posts were erected beside all improved roads.

During the rainy season one *caminero*, or roadman, is stationed on each kilometer section. During the dry season one *caminero* cares for a two-kilometer section. These men are constantly at work cutting the encroaching vegetation from the lateral banks, keeping drains clear, and immediately filling depressions in the road-bed as they appear, using for the purpose material stored in specially constructed bins placed at regular intervals and kept filled with broken stone and gravel. Heavy repair work which may be necessary after great typhoons or floods must be specially provided for.

The inspection of each kilometer of road is made as follows: daily, by the sub-foreman; bi-weekly, by the foreman; monthly, by the district engineer; and tri-monthly by the division engineer.

Under this system, in spite of unfavourable climatic conditions the reconstructed or newly constructed Philippine roads are to-day maintained far better than are most of the roads in the United States, and one may drive automobiles over them at top speed. Numerous freight and passenger automobile lines have already been established.

The average present cost of constructing heavily surfaced roads, including bridges which are apt to be numerous and expensive, is $8250 per mile.

Only first-class bridges, of concrete, masonry or steel, are permitted on main roads in the lowlands. Arbitrary enforcement of this rule is the one thing about the present road system which in my opinion affords grounds for legitimate criticism.

While no one can dispute the wisdom of constructing bridges of hard materials whenever this can be done, it is possible to carry too far the policy of limiting construction to such materials, and in my opinion it has been carried too far in a number of instances.

Years ago a good automobile road was constructed from Cagayan de Misamis to and beyond the barrio of Agusan, which is the point of departure for the main trail into the sub-province of Bukidnon. Numerous small streams on this road were bridged with reënforced concrete, but proper allowance was not made for their terrific rise during heavy rains in the highlands and almost without exception the bridges were destroyed during the first severe typhoon. Funds are not yet available for their reconstruction with strong materials. Meanwhile nothing has been done. The road is therefore impassable during heavy rains, as the streams cannot then be forded. Meanwhile, our "temporary" wooden bridges on the connecting trail system, constructed before the bridges on the coast road were built, remain intact, and render it possible always to cross streams much larger than any of those which intersect the coast road.

Of course if the hard and fast rule governing bridge construction in the lowlands is once departed from, its enforcement may become difficult. Nevertheless, I am of the opinion that existing regulations should be so modified as to authorize and encourage the construction of temporary bridges in such cases as that above cited.

The enormous change which road construction has produced in ease of travel, and in reduced cost of transporting farm products, cannot be appreciated by one unfamiliar with conditions in Spanish days. Then the ordinary country road was a narrow ditch sloping in on both sides toward the bottom, this condition being brought about by failure to provide proper drainage so that there was tremendous erosion during the rainy season, at which time these so-called roads became converted into deep quagmires by the action of very narrow-tired solid wooden cart wheels, most of which were fixed upon their axles. It was not unusual to see carts in mud up to their bodies, seeming to float on it while being pulled by floundering carabaos. Many of the roads were so bad that wheeled vehicles could not be used even during the dry season, and their place was taken by so-called *cangas*, or bamboo sledges, which also caused rapid road destruction. When all else failed, the Filipino mounted his faithful carabao, which could swim the unbridged streams if the current was not too swift, and could successfully negotiate deep quagmires, and thus he journeyed from place to place, leaving the transportation of his products until the coming of the dry season.

The use on improved roads of *cangas*, and of carts with

narrow-tired wheels or with wheels fixed on their axles, is now forbidden by law. The carts permitted to be used have broad tires that help to smooth the roads instead of cutting them to pieces.

As already stated, this road system is supplemented in the wilder parts of the archipelago, so far at least as the special government provinces are concerned, by a trail system which is rapidly being extended. The trails, which are at first built only wide enough to permit the passage of horses, are on grades such that they can be converted into roads by widening and surfacing, and are gradually widened in connection with the maintenance work so as to permit the passage, first of narrow-tired carts, and later of carts of ordinary width. Indeed one such trail extending from Baguio, in Benguet, to Naguilian, in the lowlands of the neighbouring province of Union, has already been sufficiently widened to permit the passage of automobiles, and the same thing can be done with any of the others when occasion requires.

It has been most interesting to note to what an extent the construction of good roads and trails and the cultivation of the land in their vicinity have gone hand in hand. The prosperity of the country has been enormously increased by the carrying out of the present sensible road policy for which Governor-General W. Cameron Forbes is primarily responsible.

The policy of the Forbes administration contemplated the steady continuance of road and bridge construction and maintenance until a complete system, which had been carefully worked out for the entire archipelago, should have been finished.

What would result if road and bridge work were turned over to a Filipino government? Judging from their absolute failure to maintain any roads until the insular government assumed control in 1907, and from the present neglect of municipalities to care for the sections of road for which they are responsible, we are justified in saying that new construction would promptly cease; maintenance would be neglected; existing roads would be destroyed; bridges would be left up in the air by the destruction of their approaches, and would ultimately go to pieces, and the whole system would come to rack and ruin.

To be sure, the Filipino politicians loudly assert that they are heartily in sympathy with the present road policy of the government, but this is largely because the securing of government aid for roads in their respective provinces increases their popularity with the people, and the probability that they will be reëlected. If it were left for them to determine whether money should be expended for this purpose or for some other which would more immediately inure to their private benefit, there can be no two opinions as to the result.

The continuance of American control for the present is absolutely essential, if proper means of communication and aids to navigation are to be established and maintained in the Philippine Islands.

CHAPTER XXXIII

Commercial Possibilities of the Philippines

If the commercial possibilities of any region are to be attractive to Europeans or Americans, it must have a just and stable government; a reasonably healthful climate; fairly good means of communication and transportation; forest, agricultural, mineral or other wealth, and labour with which to develop it. Proximity to main lines of travel and to markets is also an important consideration.

The present [1] government of the Philippines is highly effective and the state of public order leaves little to be desired. Doubt has been expressed as to the stability of the existing régime, but it is at the very least safe to assume that the United States will never withdraw from the islands without leaving behind a government which will assure to the residents of the archipelago, foreign and native, personal safety, just treatment and security of property rights.

Health conditions are now excellent, and the death rate among whites at Manila is lower than that in many European and American cities. If one will only vary the monotony of the continuous warmth by making an occasional trip to Baguio, and take reasonable precautions as to food, drink and exercise, there is no reason why one should not die of old age.

Means of communication by land are now fairly good and steadily improving. The seas are well lighted and the main lines of sea travel have been carefully surveyed.

The islands have many beautiful harbors and, as we have seen, at Manila, Cebú and Iloílo extensive harbour improvements have already been made. There are no

---

[1] Oct. 1, 1913.

special difficulties attendant upon the loading or unloading of ships anywhere in the archipelago. The rapid extension of highways, and the construction of additional railways, are facilitating and cheapening land transportation.

The natural resources of the country are unquestionably vast. I have already devoted a chapter to the discussion of the forests and their wealth.

As to the mineral resources, while we have much still to learn we already know that there are excellent lignite, some coking coal and extensive deposits of highgrade iron ore and of copper. One flourishing gold mine is now giving handsome returns, and several others seem to lack only the capital needed to develop them on a considerable scale in order to make them pay; dredges are operating for gold with great success in the vicinity of Paracale in eastern Luzón, and there are other gold placer fields in the islands which are worthy of careful investigation. The prospect of obtaining in quantity a high-grade petroleum with paraffine base rich in lowboiling constituents is very good.

Difficulties in the way of the development of the mining industry are to be found in the disturbances of geological formations which are inevitably met with in volcanic countries, in the dense tropical vegetation which in many regions covers everything and renders prospecting difficult, and in the unevenness of the rainfall which in some parts of the archipelago results in severe floods at one season and in the lack of sufficient water to furnish hydraulic power at another. But we are at least free from the troubles incident to freezing cold, and in my opinion a prosperous mining industry will ultimately be built up in the Philippines.

Agriculture has always been, and will doubtless long continue to be, the main source of wealth. In the lowlands may be found conditions of soil and climate favourable to the growing of all important tropical products. Owing to the position of the islands with reference to the northeast and southwest monsoons, practically any desired conditions as regard humidity and the distribution of rainfall can be found. There are regions which have strongly marked wet and dry seasons, and regions in which the rainfall is quite uniformly distributed throughout the year. In some provinces the heaviest rains come in January, while in others they come in July or August. The Philippine Weather Bureau has gathered an immense amount of very valuable rainfall statistics and is constantly adding to its present store of knowledge. Father José Algué, its distinguished director, can always be depended upon to furnish any obtainable information.

But this is not all. We are not confined to tropical products. In the highlands of Luzón and of Mindanao practically all the vegetables and many of the grains and fruits of the temperate zone may be produced.

When well fed, properly directed and paid a reasonable wage, the Filipino makes a good field labourer. Much of his so-called laziness is unquestionably due to malnutrition. A diet made up largely of rice, especially if that rice be polished, does not develop a maximum of physical energy.

When threshing machines were first introduced it was impossible to get Filipinos to handle the straw. The work was too strenuous for them. We soon discovered that by picking fairly strong men, and feeding them plenty of meat, we could make them able and willing to do it.

Some extraordinary misstatements have been made as to Manila's position with reference to main lines of travel and to markets. In this connection Blount says that it is an out-of-the-way place so far as regards the main travelled routes across the Pacific,[1] and adds that shippers would

[1] " Of course, the writer did not mention that Manila is an out-of-the-way place, so far as regards the main-travelled routes across the Pacific Ocean, and also forgot that, as has been suggested once before, the carrying trade of the world, and the shippers on which it depends, in the contest of the nations for the markets of Asia, would never take to the practice of unloading at Manila by way of rehearsal, before

A Collapsible Bridge.

Bridges of this type are employed in streams which are ordinarily narrow but become very wide during floods. The top of the bridge is not attached to the supports but is fastened to the bank by a strong cable. When the river rises, it floats off and can be readily replaced later.

not take to unloading cargo there before finally discharging it on the mainland of Asia.

With singular inconsistency he also says that Manila could never succeed Hongkong as the gateway to Asia.[1]

One might almost believe him ignorant of the fact that Hongkong is an island, separated from the continent of Asia, and that the very thing which he says would not happen at Manila, to wit the "unloading by way of rehearsal, before finally discharging on the mainland of Asia," is the thing which has made Hongkong harbour one of the busiest ports in the world.

Manila has numerous very definite advantages over Hongkong. Health conditions are vastly better, and there is far less danger that crews of vessels will become infected. Ocean going steamers come alongside piers and unload directly into great sheds which protect goods during storms. The pier sheds have direct connection with the electric railway system of the city, so that freight can be quickly and cheaply transported under cover. The Manila breakwater affords excellent protection during typhoons, whereas Hongkong harbour is periodically swept by storms which cause great damage to shipping and very serious loss of life.

Hongkong is a free port, but the construction of bonded warehouses at Manila for the reception of goods intended for reshipment would largely make up for the fact that Manila is a port of entry.

The reply to the claim that Manila is far from markets and established lines of travel is simple. Look at the map and compare it with Hongkong !

finally discharging cargo on the mainland of Asia, where the name of the Ultimate Consumer is legion." — BLOUNT, p. 49.

[1] ". . . Manila, being quite away from the mainland of Asia, could never supersede Hongkong as the gateway to the markets of Asia, since neither shippers nor the carrying trade of the world will ever see their way to unload cargo at Manila by way of rehearsal before unloading on the mainland ; . . ." — BLOUNT, p. 44.

Let us now consider more in detail the resources of the Philippines.

The first thing that impresses one who studies their agriculture is the extremely primitive state of development to which it has attained. Rice is the bread of the people and is produced in large quantities, but as a rule land is prepared for planting it by ploughing with what is little better than a crooked stick, which may or may not have an iron point, and by subsequent puddling with a muck rake, both instruments being drawn by carabaos. As the ground cannot be worked in this fashion until the rains come on, and the young plants should be set in the ground very shortly thereafter, the period during which the soil can be prepared is brief, and the amount brought under cultivation is correspondingly small. Rice is usually planted in seed beds and transplanted by hand, the object of this procedure being to give it a start over the weeds which would otherwise swamp it. It is a common thing to see a crowd of men, women and children setting it to the music of a small string band, with which they keep time. Organizations which have the reputation of maintaining a rapid rhythm are quite in demand because of the increased amount of rice set! Ordinarily, in the lowlands at least, comparatively little attention is paid to subsequent weeding, and when harvest time comes the crop is usually gathered by cutting off the heads one at a time. Threshing is frequently performed in the open air on a floor made of clay and carabao dung. Often the grain is trodden out under the feet of the owners themselves; sometimes it is stripped off by drawing the heads between the teeth of an instrument somewhat resembling an inverted iron rake; again it is beaten off against stones; a more advanced method is to drive horses, carabaos or cattle over the straw until the grain has been loosened from the straw. The *palay* [1] is usually winnowed in the wind, although crude fanning mills are sometimes em-

---

[1] Unhusked rice.

ployed for this purpose. The threshing takes much time, and while it is in progress great loss results from the depredations of rats and wild hogs, from unseasonable rainstorms, and from the carrying off of the grain by the threshers. A large part of the *palay* employed for local domestic use is husked by pounding it in wooden mortars and winnowed by tossing it in flat baskets. As a result of such methods the Philippines, which ought to export rice, are compelled to import it, the figures for the last 15 years being as follows: —

RICE IMPORTS

FISCAL YEARS	TONS (Metric)	VALUE
1899	58,389	$1,939,122
1900	109,911	3,113,423
1901	178,232	5,490,958
1902	216,403	6,578,481
1903	307,191	10,061,323
1904	329,825	11,548,814
1905	255,502	7,456,738
1906	138,052	4,375,500
1907	112,749	3,662,493
1908	162,174	5,861,256
1909	137,678	4,250,223
1910	184,620	5,321,962
1911	203,083	6,560,630
1912	260,250	10,569,949
1913	179,205	7,940,857

American influence has already made itself strongly felt on the rice industry and small steel ploughs, of suitable size to be drawn by single animals, are coming into very general use. A steadily increasing amount of rice is harvested with sickles instead of with small bladed knives. Modern threshing machines are rapidly discouraging the employment of the threshing methods of biblical days, and their operation in the large rice producing regions is a good business for persons with limited capital, as the returns are immediate and the investment is small. The customary toll taken for threshing is one-eighth of the output.

While under my direction, the Bureau of Agriculture began the introduction of modern threshing machines. The amount of grain obtained from a stack of given size when thoroughly machine-threshed before there had been time for waste was so much greater than that to which the Filipinos had been accustomed that they thought that there must be a *deposito* of grain hidden away somewhere within the machine, and insisted on sticking their heads into it in search of this supposed source of supply !

Many small, mechanically driven hulling machines are now in use and the number of regular rice mills, with up-to-date machinery for hulling and polishing, steadily and quite rapidly increases.

The rice industry has at present two great needs : the first is irrigation, the second, careful seed selection. The average Filipino depends directly on rainfall for irrigation water, and although there may be a stream close at hand, he does not trouble to turn it on to his land unless conditions happen to be exceptionally favourable. The result is that dry years cause a very heavy, and largely avoidable, loss to the islands. A dependable supply of irrigation water would make two crops a certainty where one is now more or less of a gamble. The insular government is spending considerable sums on irrigation work, and in my opinion it offers a wide field for profitable private investment.

There are in the Philippines many different varieties of rice, each with its peculiar advantages and disadvantages. There is no possible doubt as to the opportunity which lies before the skilled plant breeder to increase the crop, and shorten the time required for its production, by the methods which have been so successfully applied to wheat and other grains.

Finally, in the highlands of Bukidnon, in Mindanao,

there are immense areas which can be cultivated and planted with motor-drawn machinery. After taking off the first crop it would be readily possible to plough, harrow and seed in one operation, and here, if anywhere, modern harvesters and threshers can be employed to good advantage. In short, rice can be grown in Bukidnon as wheat is grown in the United States, and the company which goes into this business on a large scale should make money.

Abacá, commonly called Manila hemp, was for many years the most important Philippine export. The plants from which it is produced resemble bananas so closely that the uninitiated cannot distinguish them. They furnish the longest and strongest cordage fibre in the world. The Philippines have practically a monopoly on its production. Abacá culture is carried on in a very primitive way. The plants require well-drained soil and for this reason the Filipino often puts them out on steep mountain sides. The forest is felled, the timber is burned on the ground and the young plants are set before weeds have time to encroach. The bolo is usually employed for subsequent "cultivation," which consists in the occasional chopping down of weeds. Fortunately the shade in an abacá plantation is so deep that it materially impedes the growth of other plants. The fibre is obtained from the leaf petioles which make up the stem. At the present time practically all of it is stripped by hand. This is a slow and tedious process, involving very severe physical exertion to which the average Filipino is disinclined, and serious losses often result from inability to get the crop seasonably stripped. Stripping is greatly facilitated if the knife under which the fibre bands are drawn has a serrated edge, but in that case the fibre is not thoroughly cleaned, soon loses its original beautiful white colour, and diminishes in strength owing to decay of the cellular matter left attached to it.

The production of high-grade fibre or of comparatively

worthless stuff is chiefly a matter of good or bad stripping.

Abacá requires evenly distributed rainfall and constant high humidity for its best development, and should not be planted in regions subject to severe drought, which greatly reduces the crop and may kill the plants outright. Experience has shown that it richly repays real cultivation.

The trunks are heavy, and water makes up a large part of their weight, but they are full of air chambers, float readily and could be rafted or sluiced to a central cleaning plant wherever conditions are favourable for so transporting them. The one great desideratum of the industry is a really good mechanical stripper which will turn out clean, high-grade fibre in large quantity at small cost. At least one machine has been brought reasonably near perfection. In my opinion all that is now necessary is to put a skilled mechanic into the field with it under service conditions, and keep him there until such minor difficulties as remain have been successfully overcome. Stripping mills could readily be established in regions like that along the lower Agusan River, where climate and soil are ideal and water transportation is always available. A reasonable number of such plants in successful operation would go far toward revolutionizing the hemp industry, the development of which is at present greatly handicapped by the production of enormous quantities of badly cleaned fibre, which does not sell readily, whereas first-class abacá is without a rival and always sells at a high price.

The table on the opposite page shows the value and amount of hemp exports during a period of fifteen years.

Copra, or the dried meat of the coconut, has now become one of the most important exports of the islands, which lead the world in its production. The table on the opposite page shows the rapid increase in copra exports.

PREPARING RICE LAND FOR PLANTING.

PLANTING RICE.

HEMP EXPORTS

	To All Countries		To United States, including Hawaii and Porto Rico		
Fiscal Years	Tons	Value in U. S. Currency	Percentage Total Exports	Tons	Value in U. S. Currency
1899	59,840	$ 6,185,293	45.1	23,066	$ 2,436,169
1900	76,709	11,393,883	52.6	25,764	3,446,141
1901	112,215	14,453,110	34.6	18,158	2,402,867
1902	109,969	15,841,316	58.3	45,527	7,261,459
1903	132,242	21,701,575	54.7	71,654	12,314,312
1904	131,818	21,749,960	58.8	61,887	10,631,591
1905	116,733	22,146,241	59.6	73,351	12,954,515
1906	112,165	19,446,769	59.5	62,045	11,168,226
1907	114,701	21,085,081	61.7	58,389	11,326,864
1908	115,829	17,311,808	52.7	48,814	7,684,000
1909	149,992	15,833,577	51.0	79,210	8,534,288
1910	170,789	17,404,922	43.6	99,305	10,399,397
1911	165,650	16,141,340	40.5	66,545	7,410,373
1912	154,047	16,283,510	32.3	69,574	7,751,489
1913	144,576	23,044,744	43.3	63,715	11,613,943

COPRA EXPORTS

	To All Countries		To United States including Hawaii and Porto Rico		
Fiscal Years	Tons	Value in U. S. Currency	Percentage of Total Exports	Tons	Value in U. S. Currency
1899	14,047	$ 656,870	4.7	——	——
1900	37,081	1,690,897	7.8	——	——
1901	52,530	2,648,305	10.0	103	4,450
1902	19,687	1,001,656	3.6	——	
1903	97,630	4,472,679	11.2	61	9,173
1904	54,133	2,527,019	7.0	174	9,231
1905	37,557	2,095,352	5.6	205	14,425
1906	66,158	4,043,115	12.3	——	
1907	49,082	4,053,193	11.8	1,110	108,086
1908	76,420	5,461,680	16.6	2,968	228,565
1909	105,565	6,657,740	21.1	4,714	287,484
1910	115,285	9,153,951	22.9	5,538	447,145
1911	115,602	9,899,457	24.9	12,241	1,030,481
1912	169,342	16,514,749	32.8	24,160	2,339,144
1913	113,055	11,647,898	21.9	7,460	720,245

An extraordinary drought, which seems to have extended throughout the Far East, is largely responsible for the decrease in exports during the last fiscal year, its effect having been felt long after it had passed.

Coconut oil is very extensively used in making high-grade soaps, and is now also employed in the manufacture of butter and lard substitutes. Their quality is excellent, they keep well in the tropics, and being non-animal in their nature are not open to the æsthetic or religious objections which some people entertain toward oleomargarine and true lard. Lard made from coconut oil is of course especially appreciated in Mohammedan countries. There is a steady demand for the shredded coconut used by confectioners. The press-cake which remains after the oil has been extracted is a valuable food for fattening animals. A rich, palatable and nutritious "milk," on which "cream" rises in a most appetizing manner, is made by wringing out fresh shredded coconut in water. Whether or not it can be preserved and utilized as a commercial product remains to be seen, but the experiment would be worth trying.

Thus far coconut cultivation has been conducted in a very haphazard way. In fact, the existing groves are hardly cultivated at all. Nuts or young trees are put into the ground in whatever fashion seems good to the individual planter, and are invariably set too closely. There may be a little initial cultivation, but usually nothing is done except to cut down weeds and brush with a bolo, and often even this is neglected. The trees, once established, are left to shift for themselves, and are soon contending with each other for root space and air. The owner cuts notches in their bark in order to facilitate climbing. Water gathers in them and starts decay.

If under such circumstances coconut growing is so profitable that to-day plantations can hardly be bought at any price, what will happen when carefully selected seed nuts are put out at proper intervals and growing trees are given high cultivation? In considering the profits resulting from coconut culture, estimates are sometimes based on twenty nuts to the tree per year, while forty are considered a very liberal allowance. This number is even now largely exceeded throughout extensive areas in the Philippines under the unfavourable conditions above described. The effect of good cultivation can be determined, in a measure, by the condition of trees which chance to be so situated that the ground near them is kept clean. The results of fertilization can be estimated by observing the condition of trees standing near native houses. I recently endeavoured to have the nuts on a series of such trees counted from the ground. This proved impossible. In fact, it was necessary to cut out a bunch of nuts in order to make it possible for a climber to scramble over the great masses of fruit, and get among the leaves. I therefore bought the nuts on several trees and had them thrown down. The trees were in a little Manobo village, and the ground around them was cultivated. The two which seemed to be bearing most heavily could not be climbed, as bees had taken possession of them. The third best tree had three hundred ninety-seven nuts on it; the fourth only three hundred twenty-three, but its output had been reduced by tapping a number of its blossom stalks for tuba. All the nuts were very large. The meat from an average specimen was carefully dried and we found that one hundred fifty-six such nuts would make a picul of copra. A common estimate of the average number of nuts required for a picul is three hundred.

Of the whole number of nuts on these trees a few would have failed to develop, owing to lack of room, but it is fair to suppose that the first would have ripened three hundred fifty nuts and the second two hundred seventy-five. Actual observation has shown that it takes nuts two hundred thirty-eight to two hundred fifty-nine days to mature in Mindanao.

Coconut trees attain a great age, and a producing plantation in the Agusan valley would be a mine of wealth.

The time required for the trees to come into bearing varies from five to seven years with differing conditions of soil and climate, and with the altitude above sea-level. I have seen individual trees heavily loaded with nuts at four and a half years. The owner of a coconut plantation must wait for his returns, or grow something else meanwhile. Quick growing catch crops may at first be raised between the rows if soil conditions are favourable, but it must be remembered that coconut trees thrive on soil so sandy that it will produce little else of value. They require abundant water and plantations should be well open to the breeze. Such conditions are frequently found along the seashore, which doubtless explains the belief so common among natives throughout the tropics that the coconut will not grow where it cannot "hear" or "see" the sea. The trees do equally well on open inland plains.

They have few enemies or diseases in the Philippines, the bud rot which has caused such destruction in other countries being almost unknown there. They resist wind storms admirably, and even typhoons seldom uproot them, but violent gales injure the leaves and blow down the fruits, thus temporarily checking production. While coconut growing is profitable on suitable soil throughout the islands, it can be carried on most safely to the south of the typhoon belt.

At present practically all Philippine copra is either sun-dried or smoked. The latter process hardens the outer layer of the meat before it is thoroughly dried within, and also causes the deposit of more or less creosote. The resulting product moulds and decays readily, and has given Philippine copra an evil name, but this will not seriously interfere with the sale of a good article from the islands, as its quality will be readily determinable.

Until within a very short time the crudest and most

antiquated hand machinery has been used in the local manufacture of coconut oil. Soon after the American occupation a modern oil mill was established at Manila. It prospered until it burned, which it rather promptly did for the reason that it was constructed of Oregon pine, which speedily became soaked with coconut oil, and was ready to flash into flame at the touch of a lighted match or of a cigarette butt.

A new mill of iron, steel and reënforced concrete has now been erected. It is equipped with the latest machinery and labour-saving devices, and is reported to be operating on a wide margin of profit.

The market for coconut oil seems to grow more rapidly than the supply increases. There is abundant room for more oil mills in the Philippines, especially as the machinery used in extracting coconut oil is equally well suited to the milling of castor beans, peanuts and sesamum, all of which can be produced in any desired quantity.

Modern drying apparatus is just beginning to be imported for copra making.

Sugar and tobacco are the remaining principal agriculture products. Both can be very advantageously grown. All that has been said relative to primitive methods in rice, hemp and coconut production can be repeated with emphasis in discussing sugar culture. The machinery and methods employed might almost be called antediluvian, and it is a wonder that sugar could ever have been produced at a profit under such conditions as have prevailed. Deep ploughing was unknown. There was not an irrigated field of cane in the islands. The most modern of the estates was equipped with a three-roll mill, and with some vacuum pans which the owner did not know how to use. The soil was never fertilized, and no sugar grower dreamed of employing a chemist. Forty to sixty per cent of the sugar in the cane was thrown out in the bagasse, and that extracted was full of dirt and promptly began to deliquesce.

Philippine sugar could never have competed successfully in the world's market under such conditions.

Fortunately one modern central has already been
established, and several others are in process of construction. Up-to-date mills could well afford to grind cane
for Filipinos, giving them outright as much sugar as they
had previously been able to extract from it and making
a very handsome profit out of the balance. But as yet
most Filipinos have not learned the benefit of coöperation,
and are too suspicious to contract their crops of cane to a
mill. It follows that mill owners must control, in one
way or another, land enough to produce cane sufficient to
keep their mills in profitable operation. As we have seen
advantage has been taken of this fact by unscrupulous
sugar men in the United States who have secured legislation limiting the amount of land which corporations
authorized to engage in agriculture may own, with the
deliberate intention of thus crippling the sugar industry
in the Philippine Islands. It is iniquitous so to handi-
cap an important industry in a colonial dependency,
and this legislation should be stricken from the statute
books.

Fortunately there is no law limiting the right of individuals to contract their crops, nor is it apparent that
such a law could be enacted. Furthermore, there is no
law limiting the amount of land which an individual may
hold, nor is it likely that any will be passed. It would
therefore seem that while vicious legislation may interfere with the rapid development of the sugar industry
in the Philippines, it cannot destroy it.

The table on the opposite page shows the amount and
value of sugar exports for the past fifteen years.

It is said that the tobacco which now produces the
famous Sumatra wrapper originally came from the Philippines, which now have to import it. This condition of
things is mainly due to lack of system and care in tobacco growing. Seed selection is almost unknown;

SUGAR

	To All Countries		To United States, including Hawaii and Porto Rico		
Fiscal Years	Quantity (metric tons)	Value in U. S. Currency	Percentage of Total Exports	Quantity (metric tons)	Value in U. S. Currency
1899	57,447	$2,333,851	15.9	2,340	$143,500
1900	78,306	3,000,501	12.3	143	21,000
1901	56,582	2,293,058	8.6	2,153	93,472
1902	67,795	2,761,432	10.0	5,225	293,354
1903	111,647	3,955,828	9.9	34,433	1,335,826
1904	75,161	2,668,507	7.2	11,626	354,144
1905	113,640	4,977,026	13.4	57,859	2,618,487
1906	125,794	4,863,865	14.8	7,302	260,104
1907	120,289	3,934,460	11.5	6,610	234,074
1908	151,712	5,664,666	17.2	48,476	2,036,697
1909	112,380	4,373,338	14.0	21,285	881,218
1910	127,717	7,040,690	17.6	94,156	5,495,797
1911	149,376	8,014,360	20.1	128,926	7,144,755
1912	186,016	10,400,575	20.6	161,783	9,142,833
1913	212,540	9,491,540	17.8	83,951	3,989,665

worms are not picked; fertilization is not practiced; the system under which each labourer settles on the land, plants as much or as little as he pleases, and manages his crop in his own way, is in vogue, and it is an eloquent testimonial to the merits of soil and climate that the tobacco so grown is good for anything.

The domestic consumption of tobacco is very large. Practically every one smokes. Exportations are increasing. The tables on pages nine hundred and nine hundred one will give an adequate conception of the recent growth of the tobacco industry.

Bananas form an important part of the food of the people, yet there is not such a thing as a real banana plantation in the islands. The average Filipino has a few plants around his house, but with many of them even this is too much trouble, and they prefer to buy the fruit at a comparatively high price in the local markets. Good bananas sell readily in Manila at half a dollar a bunch,

TABLE SHOWING THE NUMBER OF CIGARS REMOVED FROM MANU-
FACTORIES FOR DOMESTIC CONSUMPTION AND FOR EXPORT DUR-
ING THE PAST EIGHT FISCAL YEARS

FISCAL YEAR ENDED JUNE 30	CIGARS MANUFACTURED AND			TOTAL
	Consumed in the Philippine Islands	Exported to Foreign Countries	Shipped to United States	
	Number	*Number*	*Number*	*Number*
1906 . . .	74,184,537	94,110,336	231,206	168,526,079
1907 . . .	79,476,459	117,684,485	82,175	197,243,119
1908 . . .	82,986,278	115,738,939	29,570	198,754,787
1909 . . .	86,800,520	116,981,434	867,947	204,649,901
1910 . . .	89,272,890	109,006,765	87,281,673	285,561,328
1911 . . .	96,115,525	104,604,170	27,531,596	228,251,291
1912 . . .	109,924,014	104.476,781	70,518,050	284,918,845
1913 . . .	96,193,811	106,563,541	102,894,077	305,651,429

TABLE SHOWING THE NUMBER OF CIGARETTES REMOVED FROM MAN-
UFACTORIES FOR DOMESTIC CONSUMPTION AND FOR EXPORT DUR-
ING THE PAST EIGHT FISCAL YEARS

FISCAL YEAR ENDED JUNE 30	CIGARETTES MANUFACTURED AND		TOTAL
	Consumed in the Philippine Islands	Exported to Foreign Countries	
	Number	*Number*	*Number*
1906	3,509,038,750	21,062,844	3,530,101,594
1907	3,509,999,575	158,349,812	3,668,349,387
1908	3,774,303,310	72,387,396	3,846,690,706
1909	4,122,385,209	53,250,328	4,175,635,537
1910	4,138,647,668	34,859,581	4,173,507,249
1911	4,058,603,123	35,425,865	4,094,028,988
1912	4,369,153,048	35,776,760	4,404,929,808
1913	4,449,340,088	51,431,838	4,500,771,926

TABLE SHOWING THE QUANTITY OF SMOKING TOBACCO EXPORTED
DURING EACH OF THE PAST FIVE FISCAL YEARS

COUNTRY TO WHICH EXPORTED	TOTAL EXPORTS DURING THE FISCAL YEAR				
	1909	1910	1911	1912	1913
	Pounds	Pounds	Pounds	Pounds	Pounds
Canary Islands	33,488	18,547	21,329	28,645	59,454
For consumption on high seas	14,490	17,655	22,610	24,488	29,257
France	4,740	6,182	11,334	3,091	11,433
China	2,233	1,586	7,938	6,077	9,569
All others	5,082	5,174	25,791	4,151	7,417
Total	60,034	49,145	89,004	66,452	117,130

TABLE SHOWING THE QUANTITY OF LEAF TOBACCO EXPORTED
DURING THE CALENDAR YEARS 1909, 1910, 1911 AND 1912

	CALENDAR YEAR			
	1909	1910	1911	1912
	Pounds	Pounds	Pounds	Pounds
Exported in the leaf [1]				
To the United States	13,503	12,269	4,946	93,928
To other countries	21,218,588	26,469,800	28,354,636	28,041,374
Total	21,232,079	26,482,069	28,359,582	28,136,302

and the best varieties bring even a higher price. The
latter may be bought at ten cents a bunch in the Agusan
River valley, where conditions are ideal for their successful cultivation. I recently measured a series of trunks
there which ran from forty inches to four feet in circum-
ference.

[1] There were also exported 423,877 pounds of cuttings, clippings
and waste during 1910, and 914,630 pounds of the same materials
during 1912.
NOTE. — All figures given above are for unstemmed leaf.

There are numerous varieties of bananas in the Philippines, and some of them are of unrivalled excellence, but fruit of uniform quality is unobtainable, if desired in any considerable quantity. In the course of a brief morning visit to the Zamboanga market I have seen fifteen to twenty different varieties of bananas on sale there, of which a considerable proportion were full of tannin and fit only for cooking.

A banana plantation gives returns at the end of a year from the time of planting, and the fruit ought to be grown on plantation scale for the markets of Cebú, Iloilo, Manila and Hongkong.

Throughout extensive areas conditions are ideal for rubber production, and Para, castilloa and ceara trees all thrive. Those of the latter species reach their most perfect development in Bukidnon, where they grow at an astonishing rate and produce hemispheres of foliage which look almost solid. A plantation of these trees should be not only beautiful to look upon but very profitable.

Conditions in the highlands of Luzón, in the subprovince of Bukidnon, and in other portions of Mindanao, are admirably adapted to the production of coffee. Indeed, one of the few known wild varieties is indigenous to the Philippines. The coffee at present produced is grown in violation of every accepted principle of coffee culture, but is nevertheless excellent in quality, and any surplus not required for local consumption is eagerly bought up for shipment to Spain. In Bukidnon the opportunity for growing coffee upon a large scale is excellent.

There is little doubt that tea could be advantageously produced in the Philippine highlands, especially in northern Luzón.

Throughout extensive regions the soil and climate are ideal for growing cacao, from which is made the chocolate of commerce. It has numerous insect enemies, and careful scientific cultivation is needed to obtain the best results.

A Three-year-old Coffee Bush.

Coffee thrives in the highlands of Mindanao, where this photograph was taken, and in those of Northern Luzon.

A determined and very successful effort is being made by the Bureau of Education to interest the Filipinos in raising corn, which is a far better food than is rice. They are being taught how to grind and cook it for human food, and its use, which has long been common in islands like Cebú, Negros, Siquijor and Bohol, is rapidly increasing. It can be grown to good advantage in the Philippines, and at existing prices its production upon a commercial scale for human consumption would be profitable, but there is another good use to which it can be put. The supply of fresh pork is not equal to the demand, and there would be a ready market, at a high price, for a largely increased amount. Corn-fed hogs are practically unknown in the islands. They ought not to be.

Both corn and *camotes* flourish in Bukidnon, where the former often attains a height of from twelve to eighteen feet and produces one to four ears to the stalk. Here, as elsewhere, careful seed selection rapidly increases the crop. *Camotes*, planted after the first ploughing, kill out all grass and weeds, but rapidly impoverish the soil. Planting *camotes* on a large scale and close subsequent pasturing of the land with hogs would leave the soil enriched and in excellent condition for planting with other crops. A little corn would put camote-fed hogs in splendid condition for the market. In this way it would be possible to raise them inexpensively and on a large scale.

The Philippines produce citrus fruits in considerable variety. Some of the native oranges and lemons are excellent. No care has as yet ever been given to their cultivation. They are never pruned or sprayed, nor is the ground around them kept clean. The larger Philippine towns and cities afford a good market for citrus fruits, and any surplus could be shipped to neighbouring Asiatic cities. Experiments in budding American varieties on to the native stock are now in progress.

In many parts of the islands climate and soil are perfectly adapted to the production of pineapples, which at

present usually grow uncared for. One pineapple plantation has already been established, and a factory for
canning the product is under construction. Others will
follow.

Roselle, from the fruit of which is made a jelly equal to
currant jelly in colour, and very similar to it in flavour,
grows luxuriantly and produces heavy crops of fruit.
An excellent fermented drink may be made from its leaves
and stems.

Mangos, commonly considered to be the best fruit
produced in the islands, can be successfully canned.

Guavas grow wild over extensive areas, and a properly
located factory could produce guava jelly in large quantity.

Briefly, there is every opportunity for the profitable
investment of brains, capital and energy in agricultural
pursuits along a score of different lines. Such investment would be of immense advantage to the Filipinos
themselves. They are neither original nor naturally
progressive, but they are quick to imitate, and would
follow the example set for them. Their country would
readily support eighty million people, and it has eight
million, so there is still room for a few foreigners.

If rice is the bread of the people, fresh fish is their meat.
Twenty or thirty thousand pounds of fresh fish are sold
daily in Manila, and the supply is inadequate to meet the
demand. A similar condition exists in many of the
larger towns throughout the archipelago. Dried fish
is extensively used, and sardines preserved in brine find
a ready sale. They may be taken in immense quantities
in the southern islands at certain seasons. The intelligent
application of modern methods to the taking, preserving
and marketing of fish would give immediate and large
returns.

Rinderpest appeared in the islands in 1888, and from
that time until the establishment of civil government
under American rule swept through the archipelago
practically unchecked, causing enormous losses to ag-

riculture.   For a time it was impossible to plough anything like the normal amount of land, because of the lack of draught animals.

Promptly upon their establishment, the Bureau of Science and the Bureau of Agriculture began a determined campaign against this the most dangerous pest of cattle. The fight has never ceased up to the present time. While the disease is not completely stamped out, its ravages have been reduced to insignificant proportions, and the natural increase of the surviving animals has rehabilitated agriculture.

Good draught animals still bring abnormally high prices. I well remember that in Spanish days an ordinary carabao cost $7.50, and an excellent one could be purchased for $12.50.   Similar animals to-day bring from $50 to $75 each, and in certain districts the best carabaos sell for $100 each.

There is still a great shortage of beef cattle. Refrigerated meat is imported in large quantities, but many of the Filipinos do not like it, and will not buy it unless compelled to do so by the lack of any other.

It has been found impracticable to remedy these conditions by importing Chinese cattle or carabaos for the reason that cattle disease is prevalent in the regions from which they would necessarily come, but a way out of the difficulty has now presented itself. Nellore cattle, one of the humped breeds of India, belonging to a distinct race known as *zebus*, are immune to rinderpest, and do not suffer from tick fever, which is prevalent throughout the islands. They flourish in the Philippines, and do especially well in Bukidnon.

They are much larger than the Chinese cattle now in common use, walk faster, are extremely gentle and make superior draught animals. Their flesh is excellent. Cattle raising in Mindanao on a large scale is certainly possible, and offers a most attractive field for investment.

The establishment of a great silk-growing industry is

dependent only upon the necessary capital and initiative. The Bureau of Science has laid the foundation for it by conclusively demonstrating that silk worms, and the mulberry trees on the leaves of which they thrive, flourish here. Worms have now been grown for six years, and have never suffered from any disease. Filipina women and girls, with their deft fingers, would make excellent help for silk culture. Indeed, the opportunity to engage in it would be a great boon to them in many parts of the islands where they now lack profitable employment.

Manufacturing is as yet in its infancy. There are a number of regions where very cheap power can be had by hydraulic development. That the Filipinos make good factory labourers has been abundantly demonstrated in existing tobacco factories, a hat factory, a match factory and a couple of small factories for the manufacture of tagal braid,[1] all in successful operation. With plenty of good labour, cheap power and abundant raw materials, important manufacturing industries should be developed.

I will not discuss at length the possibility of engaging profitably in trade. Such possibility exists wherever commodities are bought and sold, and here as elsewhere profits or losses largely depend on the abilities of individuals. But the question of the trade relations, present and possible, between the Philippines and the United States is one of very great importance.

In the next chapter I show the enormous increase in the total trade of the country since the American occupation, and the rapid growth of trade with the United States.

Next to rice, cotton goods form the most important element in the consuming markets of the islands, and the rapidity with which the United States is gaining control of this trade is well illustrated in the following table, showing by years the value of such goods imported since 1904 : —

[1] Made of Manila hemp, and used for sewing into hats.

A Ceara Rubber Tree.

Trees of this species grow particularly well in Bukidnon. The one shown was less than three years old.

IMPORTATIONS OF COTTON CLOTH

YEAR	UNITED STATES HAWAII AND PORTO RICO	ALL COUNTRIES
1904	$278,106	$4,919,840
1905	764,990	6,346,962
1906	278,796	6,642,329
1907	1,056,328	8,320,079
1908	604,742	7,909,395
1909	508,229	6,862,135
1910	2,043,000	8,444,453
1911	4,110,837	10,305,017
1912	4,143,067	9,246,595
1913	6,827,082	11,483,638
Total	$20,615,177	$80,480,443
Annual average		$8,048,044

From a proportion of slightly over five per cent of the total trade in manufactures of cotton in 1904, importations of the American product have increased until they supply fifty-nine per cent of the present local demand!

The following table is of especial interest. It shows in the first column the nature and amount of the total exports from the United States and in the second the nature and amount of United States exports to the Philippine Islands.

	To ALL COUNTRIES	To PHILIPPINE ISLANDS
Foodstuffs in crude condition, and food animals	7.48	2.25
Foodstuffs partly or wholly manufactured .	13.19	14.39
Crude materials for use in manufacturing .	30.10	.42
Manufactures for further use in manufacturing	16.84	7.19
Manufactures ready for consumption . .	32.04	75.73
Miscellaneous	.35	.02
Total	100.00	100.00

The most profitable class of exports is manufactures ready for consumption. It forms no less than 75.73 per cent of the United States exports to the Philippines. The least profitable exports are crude materials for use in manufacturing, which make up but forty-two hundredths of one per cent of the total exports to the Philippines.

Tropical and sub-tropical products are constantly increasing in popularity in the United States, which is able to produce them to so small an extent that although the classes included in this table comprise nearly forty per cent of the total United States imports for the year, there are but two on which duty is levied.

The following table shows the amount and value of tropical products imported into the United States during the year ended June 30, 1913 : —

PRODUCTS	AMOUNT	VALUE
Cocoa	140,039,172 lb.	$17,389,042
Coffee	863,130,757 lb.	118,963,209
Fibres	407,098 T.	49,075,659
Manufactures of fibres	——	76,972,416
Fruits and nuts	——	42,622,653
Goatskins	45,729,000 T.	24,790,417
Gums of various kinds	——	15,138,895
Rubber	214,000,000 lb.	101,333,158
Matting	——	1,651,813
Vegetable oils	——	38,112,883
Silk, unmanufactured	——	84,914,717
Spices	65,225,401 lb.	6,187,136
Sugar	4,740,041,488 lb.	103,639,823
Tea	94,812,800 lb.	17,433,688
Leaf tobacco	67,454,745 lb.	35,919,079
Manufactured tobacco	——	6,577,403
Cabinet woods	——	8,880,000
Rattans and reeds	——	1,800,000
		$751,401,991

The balance of trade with the more important countries from which we get these products is heavily against us, as is shown by the following table in which I have included Switzerland, not because we get tropical or subtropical products from that country, but because it furnishes us embroideries, etc., which could be very cheaply produced in the Philippines. The figures are for the fiscal year ended June 30, 1913 : —

	U. S. IMPORTS FROM	U. S. EXPORTS TO	BALANCE AGAINST U. S.
Brazil	$120,155,855	$42,638,467	$77,517,388
Cuba	126,088,173	70,581,154	55,507,019
British E. I.	116,178,182	15,108,956	101,069,226
Japan	91,633,240	57,741,815	33,891,425
China	39,010,800	21,326,834	17,683,966
Switzerland	23,260,180	826,549	22,433,631
Mexico	77,543,842	54,571,584	22,972,258
Colombia	15,992,321	7,397,696	8,594,625
Venezuela	10,852,331	5,737,118	5,115,213
Egypt	19,907,828	1,660,833	18,246,995
	$640,622,752	$277,591,006	$363,031,746

There is no such relationship with the Philippines, which during 1912 imported $20,770,536 worth of merchandise from the United States to offset the $21,619,686 worth shipped to that country.

The Philippines could readily produce all of these products in quantities sufficient to meet the demands of the United States if there were proper development of the resources of the islands, which have rich land, good labour and suitable climate, but lack capital and competent, skilled supervision.

The situation has been admirably summed up in the following statement issued some time since by the Manila Merchants' Association : —

"The Philippines will consume of imported commodities what they are able to pay for. Their purchasing capacity will always be measured by their production of export commodities. There is nothing that they produce, or are adapted to produce, that the United States is not at present under the necessity of buying from foreign countries whose import trade it does not, and never will, control. Thus it cannot hope for such advantages in other fields yielding tropical products as it already possesses in these Islands."

The Philippines should furnish the bulk of the tropical products imported into the United States. The commerce between the two countries should in the very near future increase to $100,000,000 per year each way and should go on increasing more and more rapidly thereafter.

CHAPTER XXXIV

PEACE AND PROSPERITY

UNEXAMPLED material prosperity has come to the islands, partly as a result of the establishment of peace, and the improvement in means of communication; partly from a very different cause.

Among other dire calamities which he says have befallen the Philippines Blount includes "tariff-wrought poverty," [1] and he roundly scores the Congress of the United States for its attitude toward the suffering Filipino.

As a simple matter of fact, tariff legislation enacted by Congress has been the commercial salvation of the islands. The tariff law of 1909, known as the Payne Bill, was passed August 5, 1909, and went into effect sixty days thereafter. In order to make the effect of this act more apparent, the figures from July 1, 1909, in the following statistical tables are printed in bold-faced type. These tables speak for themselves, very loudly.

INTERNAL-REVENUE STATISTICS

FISCAL YEAR	TOTAL COLLECTIONS	INCREASE	FISCAL YEAR	TOTAL COLLECTIONS	INCREASE (+) OR DE-CREASE (−)
		Per Cent			Per Cent
1906 [2] . .	$4,434,364	—	1910 . .	$7,160,810	+ 22
1907 . .	4,729,515	7	1911 . .	7,922,787	+ 11
1908 . .	5,542,022	17	1912 . .	8,389,929	+ 6
1909 . .	5,871,267	6	1913 . .	9,035,922	+ 8

[1] Blount, p. 571.　　[2] First year for which statistics are available.

911

TRADE WITH THE UNITED STATES

FISCAL YEAR	IMPORTS FROM THE UNITED STATES	EXPORTS TO THE UNITED STATES	TOTAL
1899	$1,150,613	$3,540,894	$4,691,507
1900	1,656,469	3,635,160	5,291,629
1901	2,666,930	2,572,021	5,238,951
1902	4,035,243	7,871,743	11,906,986
1903	3,944,082	13,863,059	17,807,141
1904	4,843,207	11,102,860	15,946,067
1905	5,839,512	15,678,875	21,518,387
1906	4,333,917	11,580,569	15,914,486
1907	5,155,478	12,082,364	17,237,842
1908	5,079,670	10,332,116	15,411,786
1909	4,693,831	10,154,087	14,847,918
1910	10,775,301	18,703,083	29,478,384
1911	19,483,658	16,716,956	36,200,614
1912	20,970,536	21,619,686	42,390,222
1913 (at the rate of) .	26,264,218	23,573,865	49,838,083 [1]

TOTAL TRADE, INCLUDING THAT WITH THE UNITED STATES

FISCAL YEAR	IMPORTS		EXPORTS		TOTAL CUSTOMS COLLECTIONS	FOREIGN TONNAGE CLEARED	
	Value	Increase (+) or Decrease (−)	Value	Increase (+) or Decrease (−)		Amount	Increase (+) or Decrease (−)
		Per Cent		Per Cent			Per Cent
1899 . .	$13,116,567	—	$14,640,162	—	$3,106,380	336,550	—
1900 . .	20,601,436	+57	19,821,347	+35	5,542,289	636,034	+89
1901 . .	30,276,200	+47	23,222,348	+17	8,982,813	987,094	+55
1902 . .	32,029,357	+ 6	24,544,858	+ 6	8,528,938	1,104,968	+12
1903 . .	32,978,445	+ 3	33,150,120	+35	9,540,706	1,542,200	+40
1904 . .	33,221,251	+ 1	30,226,127	− 9	8,493,868	1,542,138	—
1905 . .	30,879,048	− 7	32,355,865	+ 7	8,263,444	1,417,396	− 8
1906 . .	25,799,290	− 16	31,918,542	− 1	7,553,206	1,455,055	+ 3
1907 . .	28,786,063	+12	33,721,767	+ 6	8,194,708	1,293,266	− 11
1908 . .	30,918,745	+ 7	32,829,816	− 3	8,318,020	1,464,448	+13
1909 . .	27,794,482	− 10	31,044,458	− 5	8,539,098	1,392,333	− 5
1910 . .	37,067,630	+ 33	39,717,960	+ 28	8,286,073	1,715,268	+ 23
1911 . .	49,833,722	+ 34	39,778,629	+0.2	8,678,810	1,808,308	+ 15
1912 . .	54,549,980	+ 9	50,319,836	+26	9,363,296	1,939,079	+ 7
1913 . .	56,327,533	+ 11	56,683,326	+17	8,246,026	1,868,811	−4 [1]

[1] Twelve-sevenths of the actual figures for the first seven months of the year: $15,320,794; $13,751,421; $29,072,215.

Fiscal Year	Receipts from Percentage Tax on Business	Amounts of Business on which Percentage Tax is Collected	Increase (+) or Decrease (−)
			Per Cent
1906	$ 666,996	$ 200,098,983	—
1907	677,847	203,354,298	+ 2
1908	643,707	193,112,160	− 5
1909	631,877	189,563,361	− 2
1910	759,718	227,915,673	+20
1911	885,804	265,741,443	+17
1912	951,775	285,532,500	+ 7
1913	1,110,000	333,000,000	+17

The Philippine government collects as internal revenue one-third of one per cent of the gross business done by merchants and manufacturers in the islands. The fiscal year ending June 30, 1909, was the last before the opening of free trade with the United States. The figures for the four subsequent years therefore show the resulting stimulus to business.

The gross business on which the percentage tax was collected in 1909 was $190,000,000 (₱380,000,000). The increases over that year have been : —

Year	Increases over 1909		Percentage of Increase
	United States Currency	Philippine Currency	
1910	$38,000,000	₱76,000,000	20.0
1911	76,000,000	152,000,000	40.0
1912	96,000,000	192,000,000	50.5
1913	143,000,000 [1]	286,000,000	75.3
	$ 353,000,000 [1]	₱706,000,000	

The gross business increased by a fifth in one year; by two-fifths in two years; by more than a half in three years; and by more than three-quarters in four years.

[1] Estimate based on collections to March, 1913.

In the year 1909 the total exports and imports of the Philippine Islands amounted to $59,000,000 (₱118,000,000). The increases over that year have been : —

YEAR	INCREASES OVER 1909		PERCENTAGE OF INCREASE
	United States Currency	Philippine Currency	
1910	$18,000,000	₱36,000,000	30.5
1911	31,000,000	62,000,000	52.5
1912	46,000,000	92,000,000	77.9
1913	61,000,000[1]	122,000,000	103.4
	$156,000,000	₱312,000,000	

The total trade increased by nearly one-third in one year; by more than a half in two years; by more than three-quarters in three years; and more than doubled in four years.

	UNITED STATES CURRENCY	PHILIPPINE CURRENCY
Total increase of business as above	$353,000,000	₱706,000,000
Total increase of trade as above . .	156,000,000	312,000,000
Total increase of business and trade	$509,000,000	₱1,018,000,000

An attempt has been made to make political capital out of one of the heavy drops in hemp values.[2]

[1] Estimate made pro rata on the basis of the figures for the first seven months.

[2] "It is precisely these Americans, and their business associates in the United States, who have gotten through Congress the legislation which enables them to give the Filipino just half of what he got ten years ago for his hemp, and other like legislation, and the Filipinos know it." — BLOUNT, p. 118.

Also the following : —

"Apparently, Messrs. Roosevelt and Taft thought, in 1907, that granting the Filipinos a little debating society solemnly called a legis-

It is astonishing how fully Providence sometimes squares accounts with the falsifier. Whatever may be thought of the advisability or inadvisability of the hemp duty rebate, there is no escape from the conclusion that it does not determine the price of hemp. While it is true that there has been a time during the past two years when the hemp grower received half, or less than half, the price for his product which he obtained ten years ago, it is also true that during the latter part of this same period he has received very much higher prices than either he or any of his ancestors ever before obtained. This apart from the fact that the price ten years ago was quite abnormal, due to crop shortage resulting from a bad state of public order. It is a poor rule that does not work both ways. If the hemp rebate is responsible for the recent slump in prices, it must also be responsible for their having later "kicked the beam."

The facts set forth in the following tables are also significant of improved conditions : —

lative body, but wholly without any real power, was ample compensation for deserted tobacco and cane plantations, and for the price of hemp being beaten down below the cost of production by manipulation through an Act of Congress passed for the benefit of American hemp manufacturers. If we had had a Cleveland in the White House about that time, he would have written an essay on taxation without representation, with the hemp infamy of this Philippine Tariff Act of 1902 as a text, and sent it to Congress as a message demanding the repeal of the Act. But the good-will of the Hemp Trust is an asset for the policy of Benevolent Assimilation. The Filipino cannot vote, and the cordage manufacturer in the United States can. No conceivable state of economic desolation to which we might reduce the people of the Philippine Islands being other than a blessing in disguise compared with permitting them to attend to their own affairs after their own quaint and mutually considerate fashion, the Hemp Trust's rope, tied into a slip-knot by the Act of 1902, must not be removed from their throats. By judicious manipulation of sufficient hemp rope, you can corral much support for Benevolent Assimilation. Therefore, to this good hour, the substance of the hemp part of the Philippine Tariff Act of March 8, 1902, remains upon the statute books of the United States, to the shame of the nation." — BLOUNT, pp. 614–615.

BANKING

FISCAL YEAR	TOTAL RE-SOURCES OF COMMERCIAL BANKS	INCREASE (+) OR DECREASE (−)	FISCAL YEAR	TOTAL RE-SOURCES OF COMMERCIAL BANKS	INCREASE (+) OR DECREASE (−)
		Per Cent			Per Cent
1906 . . .	$15,351,690	. . .	1910 . . .	$22,856,455	+ 26
1907 . . .	17,054,358	+ 11	1911 . . .	24,557,697	+ 7
1908 . . .	17,454,214	+ 2	1912 . . .	35,885,728	+ 46
1909 . . .	18,138,425	+ 4	1913 . . .	31,210,177	− 13

POSTAL SAVINGS BANK

FISCAL YEAR	DEPOSITORS IN THE POSTAL SAVINGS BANK		TOTAL AMOUNT DUE DE-POSITORS AT CLOSE OF YEAR	
	Number	Increase	Amount	Increase
		Per Cent		Per Cent
1907[1]	2,331	. . .	$254,731	. . .
1908	5,389	131	515,997	102
1909	8,782	63	724,479	40
1910	13,102	49	839,123	16
1911	28,804	120	1,049,737	25
1912	35,802	24	1,194,493	14
1913[2]	38,075	. . .	1,252,189	. . .

COASTWISE TONNAGE CLEARED

FISCAL YEAR	TONNAGE	INCREASE (+) OR DECREASE (−)	FISCAL YEAR	TONNAGE	INCREASE (+) OR DECREASE (−)
		Per Cent			Per Cent
1899 . .	237,852	—	1907	899,915	+16
1900 . .	482,685	+103	1008	978,968	+ 9
1901 . .	676,307	+ 40	1909	1,045,075	+ 7
1902 . .	773,243	+ 14	1910	1,053,426	+ 1
1903 . .	832,438	+ 8	1911	1,303,606	+24
1904 . .	905,821	+ 9	1912	1,362,620	+ 5
1905 . .	840,504	− 7	1913 (at the rate of)	1,262,136[3]	− 7
1906 . .	774,032	− 8			

[1] First year of operation.

[2] On December 31, 1912; increase of six months only.

[3] Twelve-sevenths of the actual figure for the first seven months of the year: 736,246 tons.

IMPORTATIONS OF COAL (EQUAL CONSUMPTION VERY NEARLY) [1]

FISCAL YEAR	METRIC TONS (2205 POUNDS)	FISCAL YEAR	METRIC TONS (2205 POUNDS)
1899	30,812	1907	295,684
1900	87,238	1908	322,928
1901	126,732	1909	294,902
1902	236,332	1910	375,518
1903	268,650	1911	413,735
1904	295,716	1912	436,687
1905	269,666	1913 (at the rate of) .	408,118 [2]
1906	268,577		

If possible, let us have more of this same kind of tariff-wrought poverty and commercial distress! The country needs it.

This extraordinary story of rapid increase in commercial prosperity, as well as in the volume of commerce between the Philippines and the United States, is but a faint indication of what would come about under a fixed policy which assured future adequate protection to life and property in these islands.

Specific assurance that the United States would not surrender sovereignty over the archipelago until its inhabitants had demonstrated both ability and inclination to maintain a stable, just and effective government would be followed by a steady, healthful commercial development which would bring in its wake a degree of prosperity hitherto unknown and undreamed of. The Philippines have the best tropical climate in the world; soil of unsurpassed richness; great forest wealth; promising mines;

[1] The figures for coal importations are exclusive of the quantities imported from the United States by the federal government. These are excluded because they have been for the most part made in large quantities in alternate years, and would, therefore, while considerably increasing the average total amounts imported, give a false idea of the rate of increase of the more strictly domestic consumption.

[2] Twice the actual figure for the first half of the year: 204,094 tons.

and a constantly growing population willing to work for
a reasonable wage.   Give assurance of a stable government, and prosperity will increase by leaps and bounds.
Turn the country over now, or ten years from now, to the
Filipinos to govern, and the reputable business men,
mindful of Aguinaldo's demand for his share of the war
booty when Manila was taken; of the attempted confiscation of the lands of the religious orders and of Spanish
citizens generally,[1] of the proposal to tax foreigners[2] as
such, and of the torturing of friars, other Spaniards and
Filipinos as well, in order to extort money from them; of
the widespread brigandage, the raping, the officially
authorized and directed murdering and burying alive
which prevailed during the period of undisturbed Filipino rule, will fold their tents like the Arabs and quietly
steal away.   There will remain that peculiar class of
business men who, as the Filipinos put it, love to
fish in troubled waters.   They will not lack good fishing grounds.

Should we not stimulate the commercial development
of the islands by adopting liberal provisions as to the
sale of public lands, safeguarding the public interest by
imposing at the same time severe conditions as to cultivation?   And should not our anti-imperialist friends cease

[1] There were several different plans for the confiscation of the friar
lands.   The following shows the action taken in one instance, relative
to the property of Spanish prisoners: —
"On February 2, 1899, the secretary of the treasury informed the
governor of the province of Isabela that the property of all Spanish
prisoners should be confiscated as booty of war." — P. I. R., 1302. 6.

[2] The following telegram was sent to the cabinet by the director
of diplomacy, Manila: —

"December 21, 1898, P.M.

"Missed the train on account of government business.   Beg of
you to pardon my absence, and bear in mind my suggestion to look
up an easy method of abolishing the law imposing a tax of 100 to 5000
pesos on foreigners, as not only unjust but impolitic at this time, when
we seek the sympathy of the powers.   I represent to the cabinet that
such step is very urgent, because I have ascertained that members
of the chamber of commerce have reported this tax to their respective
governments in order to formulate a protest." — P. I. R., 849.

A Typical Cocoanut Grove.
Dried cocoanut meat is one of the principal exports of the Philippines.

to rail at those of their countrymen who are willing to
spend the money without which commercial development
is impossible? Can they not grasp the fact that the in-
flux of Americans and American capital sounds the death
knell of slavery and peonage? It was Americans whose
testimony enabled me to prove to the world the existence
in the Philippines of these twin evils, and to bring pressure to bear which resulted in prohibitive legislation. It
is Americans who are helping the poor Filipinos to become
owners of land. It is Americans who are encouraging
them to take contracts for cultivating cane, so that they
have a direct interest in the crop.

Increasing prosperity means more money for the maintenance of order, for schools, for hospitals, for sanitary
work and for public improvements. The diminution of
exports which would promptly follow any serious disturbance of the peace of the country would result in the
loss of much of the ground already gained.

The average business man is not a sentimentalist. So
long as he can safely carry on his work, and can be sure
of just treatment, he does not worry much over the na-
tionality of the government officials who maintain such
conditions, but he will not invest his money in a country
where it is not reasonably certain that such conditions will
continue to prevail.

The business men of the Philippines know by experience what American government of the archipelago
means. Some of them know, also by experience, what
Filipino rule means. The slump in real estate values and
customs receipts which so promptly followed Mr. Wilson's
expression of hope that the frontiers of the United States
might soon be contracted, conclusively demonstrated their
opinion as to the effect of Philippine independence on
the peace and prosperity of the country.

The number of Filipinos who thus far have demonstrated ability successfully to manage large commercial
enterprises is exceedingly limited. Must not commercial

prosperity coexist with political independence, if the latter is to be stable?

During the visit of the congressional delegation which accompanied Mr. Taft on his return to the Philippines in 1907, public sessions were held at which the Filipinos were given opportunity to make complaints. One fervid orator denounced the collection of customs dues, internal revenue taxes, the land tax and the cedula tax. A congressman asked him how he expected to get money to run the government after all taxes were abolished. He replied, "That is a detail which can be settled later."

Would it not be well to consider, at this time, one very important detail, namely, what would be the effect on the insular government of a marked falling off in the business from the taxes on which practically all of the insular revenues are at present derived?

CHAPTER XXXV

SOME RESULTS OF AMERICAN RULE

HAVING set forth at length what seem to me the more essential facts relative to the American occupation of the Philippines and the results of American rule, supporting my statements by a rather free use of documents chiefly drawn from the Insurgent records, I will briefly summarize some of the more important points which I have endeavoured to establish, lest my readers should not see the forest for the trees.

Independence was never promised to Aguinaldo or to any other Filipino leader by any officer of the United States, nor was there ever any effort to deceive the Filipinos by arousing false hopes that it was to be conceded.

The Insurgent force never coöperated with that of the United States. The two had a common enemy and that was practically all that they did have in common. Each proceeded against that enemy in its own way. Each ignored requests of the other relative to the manner in which it should proceed. The Insurgent officers planned from the outset to utilize United States soldiers in bringing about the termination of Spanish sovereignty in the Philippines, and then to attack them if practicable and necessary in order to oust the United States from the islands. If not, they planned to consider asking us for a protectorate or for annexation.

The temporary government established by Aguinaldo and his associates was not, in any sense of the word, a republic, nor was it established with the consent of the people. It was a military oligarchy pure and simple, imposed on the people by armed men and maintained, especially during its latter days, by terrorism and by the very free use of murder as a governmental agency. The conditions which arose under it were shocking in the extreme. Property rights were not respected; human life was cheap indeed; persons aggrieved had no redress, and there was hardly a semblance of a system for the administration of justice.

There were individual instances in which Insurgents and Insurgent sympathizers were treated with severity, and even with cruelty, by officers and soldiers of the army of the United States, but it is nevertheless undoubtedly true that never before have the officers and men of any civilized nation conducted so humanely a war carried on under conditions similar to those which prevailed in the Philippines.

Hostilities were deliberately provoked by the Insurgents, who had previously prepared an elaborate plan for a simultaneous attack on the American lines around Manila from within and without, and for the killing of all Americans, Europeans and American sympathizers among the Filipinos.

The war ended with a prolonged period of guerilla warfare, deliberately inaugurated by the Insurgents, which bred crime and struck at the very roots of good government.

At the earliest possible moment the Filipinos were given a share in the control of their own affairs when municipal governments were established, under military rule, by army officers. Many Filipinos who accepted municipal offices under the Americans paid for their courage with their lives, and a very large number saved their lives only by serving two masters. Because of the special conditions which prevailed, such persons were very leniently dealt with when their double dealing was discovered, and in the effort to afford adequate protection to those who had put their confidence in the United States, our armed forces were divided to an extent probably

A TYPICAL FILIPINO TOWN.

This photograph shows a part of Laoag, the capital of Ilocos Norte.

previously unprecedented in history, and more than five hundred separate garrisons were established.

The first Philippine Commission was appointed in the hope of bringing about a friendly understanding between Insurgent officers and the representatives of the United States, and for the purpose of gathering reliable information relative to people and conditions which might serve as a basis for future legislation for the benefit of all the inhabitants of the islands. As the result of the breaking out of hostilities before the commission reached its destination, its work was necessarily limited to the gathering of information and to efforts to promote the earliest possible establishment of relations of friendliness and usefulness between the two peoples.

The second Philippine Commission was endowed with far-reaching powers. Shortly after its arrival in the islands it became the legislative body, and proceeded gradually to establish civil government as rapidly as practicable in a country under military rule, many parts of which were in active rebellion.

This difficult undertaking was carried out with a minimum of friction between civil and military authorities. The latter were invariably consulted by the former before civil government was established in any given region, and their wishes in the premises were respected. The commanding general stated that the establishment of civil governments was a help to him in his work, and in accordance with his desires and recommendations they were established prematurely in three provinces, with the result that the temporary restoration of military government became necessary.

Under American rule there has been brought about in the Philippines an admirable state of public order, and life and property are to-day safe throughout practically the whole of an archipelago which, at the close of Spanish sovereignty, was harried by *tulisanes, ladrones* and Moros. There were also very extensive areas in undisputed possession of wild and savage tribes where governmental control had never been established, where a man was esteemed in proportion to his success as a warrior, and where property was likely to find its way into the hands of men brave enough to seize it and strong enough to hold it.

We have established friendly relations with the very large majority of the wild people and the numerous changes for the better which we have brought about in their territory have been effected practically without bloodshed except in certain portions of the Moro country. By effective legislation, strictly enforced, we have saved these backward tribes from the threatened curse of alcoholism.

Good order was established in Filipino territory through the admirable work of the United States Army, assisted toward the close of military rule by the second Philippine Commission, which did much toward securing the co-operation of the better element among the Filipinos.

Under civil control Filipinos and wild men have been utilized as police officers and soldiers in their respective habitats, and have been an important factor in bringing about present conditions. The Philippine Constabulary, recruited in part from Filipinos and in part from Moros and other non-Christian peoples, has not only proved a most efficient body for the performance of ordinary police work but has rendered invaluable assistance to other bureaus of the government; notably to the Bureau of Health and the Bureau of Agriculture for which it has effectively performed very important quarantine work. It has furthermore proved to be a reliable and most useful body in meeting great public calamities like those caused by the recent eruption of Taal volcano, and the Cebú typhoon.

Reforms of radical importance in the judicial system have been another important factor in making life and property safe, and have resulted in bringing even-handed justice within the reach of many of the poor and the weak.

We found Manila and numerous provincial towns pestholes of disease, while the death-rate of the archipelago as a whole was so high that its climate had gained an evil reputation.

We have given Manila a modern sewer system. We have supplied its people with comparatively pure drinking water from a mountain watershed in place of the contaminated water of the Mariquina River which they were formerly forced to use. We have steadily reduced the death-rate of the city, which is now a safe and healthful place of residence for all who will observe a few simple precautions.

In the provinces, some eight hundred and fifty artesian wells have brought pure water to hundreds of thousands who were previously compelled to depend on infected wells, springs and streams. By making many of the previously most unsanitary regions of the archipelago healthful we have conclusively demonstrated that the lack of necessary sanitary measures, not the character of the climate, was responsible for the conditions which formerly prevailed.

The islands were periodically swept by frightful epidemics of disease. We have eliminated smallpox, previously rightly considered an almost inevitable disease of childhood, as an important factor in the death-rate. We have practically stamped out cholera and bubonic plague. Years have now passed since there has been a wide-spread epidemic of disease among the inhabitants.

The United States Public Health and Marine Hospital Service has not only thrown its protective line around the archipelago but has sent its outposts to important neighbouring Asiatic centres for the dissemination of disease, thus facilitating the exclusion from the archipelago of dangerous communicable ailments and preventing the introduction of pneumonic plague, the most fatal of them all. It would unquestionably have entered the islands had it not been stopped at quarantine.

We are giving humane care to a considerable number of insane persons who were previously chained to floors or posts.

The lepers of the islands have been isolated and are being well cared for. A few have apparently been permanently cured.

The scientific work of the insular government has been coördinated in such a way as to insure maximum efficiency at minimum cost. Not only has an immense amount of routine work been economically performed but there has been a large amount of original investigation, some of which has resulted in discoveries of far-reaching importance to mankind.

We have found the cause of beri-beri, have eliminated this disease from government institutions and from among persons subject to governmental control, and have shown the Filipinos how they may rid their country of it, and save money at the same time, by a slight change in their food.

We have found a specific for that horribly disfiguring disease "yaws," and have cured large numbers of persons afflicted with it, thus earning their lasting gratitude.

We have made pure food and pure drugs purchasable throughout a country which was formerly a dumping ground for products not allowed to be sold elsewhere.

We have not only made long strides in the improvement of sanitary conditions in the provinces but have brought skilled medical and surgical service within the reach of very large numbers of persons who formerly had none at all, successfully overcoming the previous universal prejudice against hospitals, to such an extent that those of the government are now thronged with Filipinos seeking treatment.

In doing these things we have had to combat almost unbelievable ignorance and superstition, the remedy for which is to be found, we hope, in the generalization of education which is rapidly taking place. The hundred and seventy thousand children, who formerly took advantage of the meagre educational facilities provided under the previous régime, consisting chiefly of very defective primary instruction, usually given amidst most unsanitary surroundings, and without adequate facilities of any sort, have been replaced by a happy throng numbering no less than five hundred and thirty thousand, who receive from well-trained teachers excellent primary and secondary instruction, both academic and practical. Through the school system we are generalizing the use of the English language which is to-day, after a decade and a half of American rule, spoken far more generally than Spanish was after it had been the official language of the country for three and a half centuries. In this way we are overcoming the very grave obstacle in the way of welding the numerous peoples of the Philippines into one which is presented by their lack of a common medium of communication.

At the same time we are teaching boys and girls the elements of good sanitation and right living. Girls are also being taught to cook, to sew, to embroider and to make lace. Both boys and girls are receiving instruction in gardening, and boys may learn wood working, iron working and other useful trades. Opportunities for higher academic work have been provided in provincial high schools, and at Manila in the Philippine Normal School and the University of the Philippines, while the Manila Schools of Commerce and of Arts and Trades afford ample opportunity for advanced work on industrial and commercial lines, and the Manila School of Household Industries fits women to go out into the provinces and start new centres for the manufacture of laces and embroideries.

We are educating a constantly and rapidly increasing number of highly trained nurses, physicians and surgeons.

The working forces of certain bureaus of the government have been utilized for purposes of special instruction

in surveying, printing and binding, and forestry, and
even the inmates of penal institutions are not forgotten,
but have good schools provided for them.

Quite as important as the development of the minds
of the young is the development of their bodies through
the introduction of athletic games and sports, which
have incidentally promoted intercommunication and
mutual understanding between the several Filipino
peoples.   In many regions baseball is emptying the
cockpits, and thus aiding the cause of good order and
morality.

Educational work has not been limited to the Filipinos,
but has been carried on among the children of the wilder
tribes, many of whom are proving to be apt pupils and
are making extraordinary progress in industrial work.

By educating the masses we are giving to the Filipinos
proper, as distinguished from the *mestizo* politicians,
the first opportunity they have ever had to show what
is in them.

The means of the government are at present insufficient
to educate all of the eight hundred thousand children
who, it is believed, would attend school voluntarily if
given the opportunity.   The insular revenues are derived
chiefly from import duties and internal revenue taxes,
so that there is a very direct relationship between the
amount of government receipts and the volume of business of the country.   Careful attention has long been
given to stimulating the development of the vast natural
resources of the archipelago in order to increase the
prosperity of the people and that of the government,
which are inseparably united.

Owing to the breaking up of the land area of the country
into a very large number of small units, water transportation plays an unusually important part in commercial
development.   More than two-thirds of the very long
coast line has been surveyed, as have the waters adjacent
thereto.

The former scarcity of lighthouses has been remedied. An admirable weather service gives due warning of the approach of dangerous storms, and travel and the transportation of freight by sea have thus been rendered safe.

The previous almost complete lack of good roads has been remedied by the construction of four thousand four hundred miles of well-built, admirably maintained highways in the lowlands, supplemented in the highlands of Luzón and Mindanao and in the lowlands of Mindoro and Palawan, by some thirteen hundred miles of cart roads and horse trails. Hundreds of thousands of small farmers, who previously had no inducement to raise more than their families or their immediate neighbours could consume, because they were unable to sell their surplus products, have thus been brought within reach of the market.

The hundred and twenty-two miles of railway which we found in 1898 have been increased to six hundred eleven.

The government has utilized its coast-guard vessels to build up new trade routes until they became commercially profitable, so that private companies were willing to take them over.

Agriculture, the main source of the country's wealth, was conducted in a most primitive manner, modern methods and modern machinery being practically unknown. Worse yet, it was threatened with complete prostration, owing to the prevalence of surra among the horses and of rinderpest among the horned cattle. At a time when great areas were lying uncultivated because of lack of draft animals, and when the horses and cattle of the archipelago seemed doomed to extinction, a vigorous campaign was inaugurated against animal diseases. It has been carried out in the face of manifold obstacles up to the present day, and is resulting in the re-stocking of the islands through natural reproduction and the safeguarding of the young animals. Strenuous efforts, made through the medium of the public schools and through demonstration stations, are bringing about a slow change in the previously existing antiquated agricultural methods, and the example set by Americans is leading to the gradual introduction of a considerable amount of modern farm machinery.

The placing of the currency of the country on a gold basis has been a powerful factor in promoting material prosperity, and together with the other measures previously enumerated, supplemented by favourable tariff legislation giving the Philippines a market in the United States, has led to an era of extraordinary commercial development.

There has been a very rapid increase in the trade between the Philippines and the United States, the former country purchasing from us, practically dollar for dollar, as much as it sells to us, and furnishing us tropical products of a sort which we should otherwise be obliged to buy from countries with which we have a trade balance on the wrong side of the ledger.

The Philippines have a potential source of great wealth in their fifty-four thousand square miles of forest. We have introduced a conservation system which, if maintained and developed, will permanently preserve the more important forests while at the same time facilitating the establishment of a great lumber industry. The free use of forest products from government lands for other than commercial purposes has been granted to the people.

In the face of quiet but determined opposition from the *cacique* class, material progress has been made in assisting the common people to become owners of agricultural land, while in spite of the restrictions imposed by unwise legislation, several modern agricultural estates have been established. They are not only serving as great demonstration stations, of far more practical value than any agricultural college could be at the present stage of development of the Filipinos, but have materially raised

A Typical Group of Filipinos.

the daily wage of agricultural labourers in the regions where they are situated.

We have established an efficient civil service in which national politics have played no part, and appointments and promotion have depended on merit alone. This rule has been made to apply to Filipinos as well as to Americans, with the result that the former have for the most part been compelled to enter the lower grades because of defective preparation, but with the further consequence that they have been promoted as rapidly as the result of subsequent careful training has fitted them for advancement. The proportion of Filipino employees as compared with Americans has increased from forty-nine per cent in 1903 to seventy-one per cent in 1913.

We have given to the country religious liberty. We have also given it free speech and a free press, both of which have been shamelessly abused. We have created, prematurely in my opinion, a legislature with an elective lower house composed exclusively of Filipinos and having equal powers with the upper house in the matter of initiating and passing legislation.

I reserve for the following chapter a statement of the opportunities which we have given the Filipinos to participate in the executive control of their towns and provinces, and of the results of these experiments.

Never before in the history of the world has a powerful nation assumed toward a weaker one quite such an attitude as we have adopted toward the Filipinos. I make this statement without thought of disparaging the admirable work which Great Britain has done in her colonies, but on the contrary in the conviction that in some particulars we ourselves have gone too fast and too far, and as a result are likely in the end to have forcibly brought home to us the wisdom of making haste somewhat more slowly, and paying more heed to the experience of others, when dealing with new problems.

However, it will do those of us who thought that we

were infallible, if such there be, a world of good to learn that this is not the case; and it will do our Filipino wards good to discover, one of these days, that we can, if necessary, take away as well as give.

Up to the present time our successes certainly overbalance our mistakes, and in my opinion we have just cause for pride in the results of our Philippine stewardship.

CHAPTER XXXVI

Is Philippine Independence now Possible?

This question is one of great importance to the people of the United States, for national honour is involved in finding its true answer.

Both of our great political parties are committed to the policy of granting independence when the Filipinos are ready for it. Are they ready now? If so, the promise should be kept. If not, we should be guilty of an unjust and cowardly act if we withdrew our protection and control.

I have already called attention to the fact that the Filipinos [1] are divided into a number of peoples, sometimes called tribes. The census of 1903 recognizes the following: Visayans, numbering 3,219,030; Tagálogs, 1,460,695; Ilocanos, 803,942; Bicols, 566,365; Pangasináns, 343,686; Pampangans, 280,984 Cagayans, 159,648; Zambalans, 48,823.

The loose use of the word "tribe" in designating these peoples is liable to lead to very grave misapprehension. Their leaders vigorously, and very properly, object to the idea that they have at present anything resembling a tribal organization. The truth is that they are the descendants of originally distinct tribes or peoples which have gradually come to resemble each other more and more, and to have more and more in common.

The very large majority of them have been brought up in the Catholic faith. In physical characteristics,

---

[1] This name is properly applicable to the civilized peoples only.

dress and customs they resemble each other quite closely. They are alike in their dignity of bearing, their sobriety, their genuine hospitality, their kindliness to the old and the feeble, their love of their children and eagerness to obtain for them educational advantages which they themselves have been denied, their fondness for music, their patience in the face of adversity, and the respect which they show for authority so long as their passions are not played upon, or their prejudices aroused, by the unscrupulous. These are admirable characteristics and afford a good foundation on which to build. Such differences as exist between these several peoples are steadily diminishing. This is especially true of the Tagálogs and the numerically comparatively unimportant peoples lying immediately to the north and west of their territory, namely, the Pampangans, Pangasináns and Zambalans. The Tagálogs, Ilocanos, Cagayans, Bicols and Visayans are distinguished by much more marked differences.

In general, the Tagálogs tend to become the dominating Filipino people of the islands, and successfully attempt to assert themselves in their dealings with all the other Christian peoples except the Ilocanos, who are quite capable of holding their own. The Ilocanos have a reputation for orderliness and industry which the Tagálogs lack. The Cagayans are, as a people, notoriously lazy and stupid, although there are of course numerous conspicuous individual exceptions to this rule. The Visayans are comparatively docile and law-abiding. Many of the Bicols are energetic and capable, and they seem to be possessed of a rather keen sense of humour, which their neighbours lack.

Two things tend to keep the several peoples apart. The first is the present lack of any common medium of communication. There are more quite sharply distinct dialects than there are peoples. The Visayans, for instance, speak Cebuano, Ilongo and Cuyuno. The language difficulty is of least importance among the peoples immediately north of Manila where the use of Tagálog is generalized to a considerable extent, but even here it is serious.

Mr. Justice Johnson of the Philippine Supreme Court tells me that when he was serving in Zambales as a judge of first instance the examination of a family of four persons necessitated two interpreters, one for the father, and another for the mother and two step-children, while in the trial of seven men charged with a murder it was necessary to read the complaint in four different dialects.

Taylor cites the following typical instances of practical difficulty growing out of the multiplicity of dialects: —

"In December, 1898, General Macabulos was the commissioner in Tarlac Province. At Camiling the orders prescribing how the elections were to be carried on were read in Spanish and then translated into Ilocano. General Macabulos next delivered in Tagálog a speech informing the assemblage of their duties under the new form of government. This was translated into Ilocano, as the people did not understand Tagálog any more than they did Spanish.[1] When on July 6, 1898, a junta of men in favour of the independence of the Philippines met at Gerona, Tarlac, to elect among themselves the civil officials for the town, the decrees of Aguinaldo, of June 18 and 20, were read in Ilocano, in Tagálog, in Pampanga, and in Pangasinán, all of which languages were spoken in the town."[2]

The head of the town of Antipolo, Morong Province, wrote to the secretary of the interior on October 21, 1898, that his delay in executing orders had been caused by the fact that they were written in Tagálog, which he did not understand. He recommended that Spanish be always used by the central government.[3] Mabini himself at one time proposed that English be made the official language. The constitution of the "Republic," while

[1] P. I. R., 1097. 2.   [2] *Ibid.*, 1157. 8.   [3] *Ibid.*, 1018. 1.

making Tagálog the official language, provided for instruction in English.[1]

There is no literature worth mentioning written in the native dialects, nor do they open a way to the fields of science, the arts, history, or philosophy. Their vocabularies are comparatively poor in words, and they do not afford satisfactory media of communication, especially as words of generalization are almost entirely lacking. This latter fact conclusively demonstrates the stage of mental evolution attained by the peoples which have developed these several languages. Not long since I heard a keen student of Philippine affairs remark that the trouble with the Filipinos was that none of them were more than fourteen years old! There is truth enough in the statement to make it sting.

The use of Spanish never became common, and knowledge of this language was limited to the educated few. After fifteen short years English is far more widely spoken than Spanish ever was. When English comes into comparatively general use, as it will if the present educational policy is adhered to, one fundamental difficulty in the way of welding the Filipinos into "a people" will have been largely done away with.

The second important barrier between the several Filipino peoples is built up of dislikes and prejudices, in part handed down from the days when they were tribally distinct and actively hostile; in part resulting from the well-marked tendency of the Tagálogs and the Ilocanos to impose their will upon the others. The actual differences between a Tagálog and a Visayan are not so great. The important thing, from the American view point, is that

[1] Title X. — Of Public Instruction.

124. . . .

Elementary instruction shall comprise reading, speaking and writing correctly the official language which is Tagálog, and the rudimentary principles of English and of the exact, physical and natural sciences, together with a slight knowledge of the duties of man and citizen. — TAYLOR, 19 MG.

every Tagálog and every Visayan really considers them *very* great.

There would have been no insurrection of any importance in the Visayas and Mindanao if the Tagálogs had kept their hands off. We have seen how they worked their will on the people of the Cagayan valley and the Visayas, and what bitter animosities they provoked. We have also seen how on various occasions the Ilocanos opposed the Tagálogs as such, and even planned to kill them, while the Visayans did kill them on various occasions. However much politicians may declaim about a united Filipino people, certain uncomfortable but indisputable facts reduce such claims to idle vapourings.

At the time when there was great excitement in Manila over the Jones Bill, and many Filipinos believed that independence was coming on July 4, 1913, there took place at the house of General Aguinaldo a very significant gathering of former insurgent generals and colonels. There was then much interest in the question of who would be appointed president of the coming Philippine Republic. It was officially announced that the object of this meeting was to unite those who attended it in an effort to aid in the maintenance of a good condition of public order. I learned from a source which I believe to be thoroughly reliable that one of the conclusions actually reached was that no Visayan should be allowed to become president of the republic, and that one of the real objects of the meeting was to crystallize opposition to the candidacy of Señor Osmeña, the speaker of the assembly. But the undesirability of giving publicity to such factional differences at this time was promptly realized and this attitude on the part of Aguinaldo's supporters was not publicly announced.

Troubles between Ilocanos and Cagayans continue in Cagayan, Isabela and Nueva Vizcaya up to the present day. Several years since, when investigating the cause which lay behind a petition from certain people of the

latter province for an increase in the educational requirement precedent to the exercise of the franchise, I discovered that the whole thing resolved itself into an effort
to disfranchise the Ilocanos, who always voted together
and already controlled elections in several townships.

Without going further into the differences which separate the several civilized peoples, I will say emphatically that the great mass of Filipinos do not constitute
"a people" in the sense in which that word is understood
in the United States. They are not comparable in any
way with the American people or the English people.
They cannot be reached as a whole, and they do not re-
spond as a whole. In this they agree with all other Malays.
Colquhoun has truly said : [1] —

"No Malay nation has ever emerged from the hordes of
that race, which has spread over the islands of the Pacific.
Wherever they are found they have certain marked characteristics and of these the most remarkable is their lack of that
spirit which goes to form a homogeneous people, to weld them
together. The Malay is always a provincial ; more, he rarely
rises outside the interests of his own town or village."

More important than the differences which separate
the Tagálogs, Ilocanos, Cagayans, and Visayans as
such, are those which separate the individuals composing these several groups of the population. Very few of
the present political leaders are of anything approaching
pure Malayan blood. To give details in specific cases
would be to give offence, and to wound the feelings of men
who certainly are not to blame for their origin. Suffice
it to say that with rare exceptions, if one follows their
ancestry back a very little way he finds indubitable evidence of the admixture of Spanish, other European or
Chinese blood. The preëminence of these men is undoubtedly due in large measure to the fact that through

[1] "The Mastery of the Pacific," p. 122, A. R. Colquhoun, Macmillan,
1902.

A Typical Spanish Mestiza.

the wealth and influence of their fathers they had educational advantages, and in many instances enjoyed broadening opportunities for travel, which were beyond the reach of their less fortunate countrymen. To what extent their present demonstrated abilities are due to these facts, and to what extent they are due to white or Mongolian blood, will never be known until the children of the common people, who are now enjoying exceptionally good educational opportunities, arrive at maturity and show what they can do.[1]

Meanwhile there is more or less thinly veiled hostility between the *mestizo* class and the great dark mass of the people. For a time we heard much of *Filipinos de cara y corazon*,[2] and while because of political expediency there is less of this talk now than formerly, the feeling which caused it persists, and will continue to endure. Throughout the Christian provinces the same condition exists everywhere. The *mestizo* element is in control. Until the common people have learned to assert themselves, and have come to take an important part in the commercial and political development of their country, anything but an oligarchical form of independent government is impossible.

There has been complaint from politicians and others of the *mestizo* class that American men are, as a rule, disinclined to increase it by marrying its women and breeding *mestizo* children.

Juan Araneta, a very intelligent Visayan of Negros, put the matter brutally to me by saying that white blood was the only hope for his people, and that if he had his

---

[1] In this connection Bishop Brent has said, "The recognized leaders in the Philippines to-day, so far as racial qualifications are concerned, would have at least equal right to claim citizenship in Spain, China or England. Thus far, it is the men of mixed blood who are the politicians. The degree of capacity in the Filipino will not be revealed until the schoolboys of to-day are in active public life."

[2] Literally, "Filipinos of face and heart." The expression means Filipinos in appearance and in sympathies.

way he would put in jail every American soldier who did not leave at least three children behind him.

Blount pretends to find an obstacle to American control in the fact that American women will not marry Filipinos, and in the further fact that those American men who do marry Filipinas soon find themselves out of touch with their former associates. He says that this is not as it should be.[1] He adds that many Filipinos are sons or grandsons of Spaniards, and therefore have a very warm place in their hearts for the people of that nation.

He neglects to mention the fact that the vast majority of the Spanish *mestizo* class were born out of wedlock.

I believe that the attitude of American women on this subject is eminently proper and that American men, who expect ever again to live in their own country, as a rule make a grave mistake if they marry native women. Even when they are to remain permanently in the islands, such a course is in my opinion usually most undesirable. I have known a limited number of happy mixed marriages of this sort, but in the large majority of cases which have come under my observation they have led to the rapid mental, moral and physical degeneration of the men concerned. While some of the children born of such marriages are very fair, there are occasional reversions to

---

[1] "But there is no doubt that many of the Filipinos after all have a very warm place in their hearts for the Spanish people. How could it be otherwise when so many of the Filipinos are sons and grandsons of Spaniards? Much of like and dislike in life's journey is determined prenatally. On the other hand, the American women in the Philippines maintain an attitude toward the natives quite like that of their British sisters in Hongkong toward the Chinese, and in Calcutta toward the natives there. The social status of an American woman who marries a native — I myself have never heard of but one case — is like that of a Pacific coast girl who marries a Jap. . . . But look at the other side of the picture. When an American man marries a native woman, he thereafter finds himself more in touch with his native 'in-laws' it is true, but correspondingly, and ever increasingly out of touch with his former associations. This is not as it should be. But it is a most unpleasant and inexorable fact of the present situation." — BLOUNT, pp. 554–555.

the ancestral type of the mothers, and the lot of dark-skinned children is not a happy one, as even their own mothers are almost sure to dislike them.

The *mestizo* class is now large enough, and the problems which its existence presents are grave enough, to render undesirable its further growth. Finally, while the light-skinned *mestiza* girl almost always seeks a white husband, the real typical Filipinos, who are brown, are quite content to mate with each other, and do not dislike whites for declining to marry their daughters. The people of this class are friendly toward Americans, if they have actually come in contact with them and learned how much they are indebted to them, and are hostile if their ignorance is so great that they can be led, by unscrupulous politicians, to believe that Americans are responsible for any ills from which they happen to be suffering, such as cholera, which they have often been told is due to our poisoning their wells !

Blount says [1] it is a "verdict of all racial history . . . that wheresoever white men dwell in considerable numbers in the same country with Asiatics or Africans, the white men will rule."

Certainly Spanish and other European *mestizos* dwell in considerable numbers in the Philippines. Are individuals with three-fourths to thirty-one thirty-seconds white blood white men or Asiatics? They certainly would determine what form of government should be established were independence now granted, and it is interesting to determine what they consider to be the requi-

---

[1] "We should either stop the clamour or stop the American capital and energy from going to the Islands. After an American goes out to the Islands, invests his money there, and casts his fortunes there, unless he is a renegade, he sticks to his own people out there. Then the Taft policy steps in and bullyrags him into what he calls 'knuckling to the Filipinos,' every time he shows any contumacious dissent from the Taft decision reversing the verdict of all racial history — which has been up to date, that wheresoever white men dwell in any considerable numbers in the same country with Asiatics or Africans, the white man will rule." — BLOUNT, pp. 438–439.

sites for the establishment of a government by them. One of these men in an address made at the time the congressional party visited the islands, with Mr. Taft, put the case as follows: —

"If the masses of the people are governable, a part must necessarily be denominated the directing class, for as in the march of progress, moral or material, nations do not advance at the same rate, some going forward whilst others fall behind, so it is with the inhabitants of a country, as observation will prove.

"If the Philippine Archipelago has a governable popular mass called upon to obey and a directing class charged with the duty of governing, it is in condition to govern itself. These factors, not counting incidental ones, are the only two by which to determine the political capacity of a country; an entity that knows how to govern, the directing class, and an entity that knows how to obey, the popular masses."

The conditions portrayed might make a government possible, but it would assuredly not be a republic. The advocates of this view are hardly in harmony with the one so eloquently expressed at Rio Janeiro by Mr. Root:—

"No student of our times can fail to see that not America alone but the whole civilized world is swinging away from its old governmental moorings and intrusting the fate of its civilization to the capacity of the popular mass to govern. By this pathway mankind is to travel, whithersoever it leads. Upon the success of this, our great undertaking, the hope of humanity depends."

If what is needed to make a just and stable government possible is "an entity that knows how to obey, the popular masses" and an entity that thinks it "knows how to govern, the directing class," then we might leave the islands at once, if willing to leave the wild tribes to their fate, but we have work to do before the civilization of the Filipinos can safely be intrusted to "the capacity of the popular mass to govern."

Blount has said : —

"Any country that has plenty of good lawyers and plenty of good soldiers, backed by plenty of good farmers, is capable of self-government." [1]

Do the Philippines fulfil even these requirements? Filipino lawyers are ready speakers, but have their peculiarities. When the civil suit which I brought against certain Filipinos for libel was drawing to its close, and the prosecution was limited to the submission of evidence in rebuttal, important new evidence was discovered. To my amazement, my lawyers put the witness who could give it on the stand. They asked him his age, his profession and a few equally irrelevant questions, and then turned him over to the lawyers for the defense, who promptly extracted from him the very testimony it was desired to get on record. Their very first question drew a most unjudicial snort of laughter from the judge, but even this did not stop them.

I was later informed that Filipino lawyers could usually be depended upon to do this very thing, and that their American colleagues habitually took advantage of this fact. The truth is that few of the Filipino lawyers are good, if judged by American standards.

I have elsewhere stated my views as to the excellence of the Filipino soldier, but no military leaders have as yet arisen who were capable of successfully carrying on other than guerilla operation.

The farmers of the islands are as a class anything but good. They are ignorant and superstitious, underfed, and consequently inclined to indolence, and are a century behind the times in their methods.

There are certain undesirable characteristics which are common to a large majority of the people correctly designated as Filipinos. Ignorance and superstition are still to be met at every turn. At the time of the census of

---

[1] Blount, p. 105.

1903 the percentage of illiteracy in the Philippines was estimated to be 79.8. More than half of the persons counted as literate could read and write only some native dialect, and often did even that badly.

More recent, and therefore more interesting, as showing present day conditions, are the statistics obtained in connection with the elections of June 4, 1912. Ability to read and write English or Spanish entitles a male citizen of the Philippines, who is twenty-three or more years of age, to vote.

The total number of registered votes was 248,154 only, of whom slightly less than one-third had the above-mentioned qualifications. In Manila 14 per cent of the voters were illiterate, and in the provinces 70 per cent. This lack of education opened wide the door to fraud and was one of the chief reasons why there were 240 protested elections out of a total of 824, made up as follows: municipal, 709; provincial, 34; for delegate to assembly, 81.

The proportion of literate electors to total population in the territory in question was 1.47 per cent.

One of the easiest kinds of business to start in the Philippines, and one of the most profitable to conduct, is the establishment of a new religion.

We have recently had the "colorum," with headquarters on Mt. San Cristobal, an extinct volcano. People visited this place and paid large sums in order to persuade the god to talk to them. A big megaphone, carefully hidden away, was so trained that the voice of the person using it would carry across a cañon and strike the trail on the other side. If payments were satisfactorily large the god talked to those who had made them in a most impressive manner when they reached this point in their homeward journey.

We have also had the Cabaruan fiasco in Pangasinán, in the course of which a new town with several thousand inhabitants sprang up in a short time. There was a place of worship where the devout were at prayer day and night. There was also a full-fledged holy Trinity made up of local talent. Unfortunately, some of the principal people connected with this movement became involved in carabao stealing and other forms of public disorder, and on a trip to Lingayen I saw the persons who had impersonated God the Son and the Virgin Mary in the provincial jail. We have had "Pope Isio" in Negros, who was in reality the leader of a strong *ladrone* band, and we have had various other popes elsewhere who occupied themselves in similar ways.

Hardly a year passes that miraculous healers do not spring into ephemeral existence in the islands, and the people invariably flock to them in thousands. Conspicuous among this class of imposters was the "Queen of Taytay," whose exploits I have already narrated.

The belief of the common people in *asuáng* and in the black dog which causes cholera has also already been mentioned. A very large percentage of them are firmly convinced of the efficacy of charms, collectively known as *anting-anting*, supposed to make the bodies of the wearers proof against bullets or cutting weapons. Within the past year a bright young man of Parañaque, a town immediately adjacent to Manila, insisted that a friend should strike him with a bolo in order that he might demonstrate the virtues of his *anting-anting*, and received an injury from which he promptly died. Again and again the hapless victims of this particular superstition have gone to certain death, firm in the conviction that they could not be harmed.

The worst of it is that even the native press does not dare to combat such superstitions, if indeed those who control it do not still themselves hold to them.

La Vanguardia, commonly considered to be the leading Filipino paper in the islands, published the following account of the event referred to above : —

"Basilio Aquino, a native of Parañaque, and Timoteo Kariaga, an Iloko residing in Manila, made a bet as to which of them had the better anting-anting, and to settle it Kariaga allowed himself to be struck twice on the right arm and once on the abdomen, but as they say, — Miracle of miracles! Although Aquino used all of his strength and the bolo was extremely sharp, he did not succeed in making the slightest scratch on Kariaga. In view of that, Aquino invited his rival to submit him to the same test. Kariaga was reluctant to do so, for he was sure he would wound Aquino, but the latter insisted so much that there was nothing to do but please him, and at the first cut his right arm was almost severed, and he died from loss of blood two hours later. The wounded man would not report the occurrence to the authorities, but the relatives of the victim were compelled to do so in view of his tragic end."

From the report of this occurrence in *El Ideal*, a paper believed to be controlled by Speaker Osmeña, I quote the following : —

"The trial was made in the presence of a goodly number of bystanders, all of them townsmen, connections and friends of the actors.

"Timoteo Kariaga, that being the name of one of the actors, an Ilocano resident of Manila, was the first to submit to the ordeal. His companion and antagonist, named Basilio Aquino, from Parañaque, bolo in hand, aimed slashes at the former, endeavouring to wound him in the arms and abdomen, without success, the amulet of Kariaga offering apparently admirable resistance in the trial, so that the bolo hardly left a visible mark upon his body."

A very interesting and highly instructive book might be written on Filipino superstitions, but I must here confine myself to a few typical illustrations : —

The following extract from a narrative report of the senior constabulary inspector of the island of Leyte, dated April 3, 1913, is not without interest. It deals with a murder which it describes as follows : —

"Basilio Tarli had given the bolo thrust that killed the deceased, with a small fighting bolo belonging to Pastor Lumantal, who had given Basilio the bolo for this purpose. The deceased

A STRANGE COUPLE.

This photograph shows a feast given by a boy of thirteen years and a girl of twelve on the anniversary of the death of their son. Very early marriages are responsible in part for the poor physical development so common among the Filipinos.

had the reputation of being a sort of witch doctor, and Pastor thought that his wife, Maria Subior, who was pregnant, had a dog or other animal in her womb instead of a child, placed there by the deceased. For this reason Pastor arranged with Basilio Tarli and Cecilio Cuenzona to kill the deceased."

Lieutenant George R. F. Cornish, P. C., stationed at Catubig in Samar, reported on "Pagloon" as follows during August, 1913 : —

"Pagloon, a method of overcoming certain weak traits in children, is practiced by most of the inhabitants of Samar. If, for example, a father who is not in the military service, shoots a man, superstition has it that his child will shortly become sick. The father, to prevent this, uses a method known as 'pagloon,' which, being interpreted, means 'to vaporize,' 'to make clean.' He places the stock of the gun that did the shooting, along with a branch of a cocoanut tree that has been sanctified in incense by the padre of the Catholic church in a fire. The padre furnishes these incense leaves only once a year. The hands are dipped in water and then placed in the smoke. The vaporous healing incense that collects on the hands, from placing them in the fire, is rubbed on the child from head to foot. This operation is repeated three nights in succession and then the child ought to be free from any danger."

Serious trouble was made for men investigating the mineral resources of the island of Cebú by the circulation of a tale to the effect that they needed the blood of children to pour into cracks in the ground.

The following is an extract from a narrative report of the senior constabulary inspector of Pampanga for April, 1913 : —

"April 9. — Between 2 and 3 P.M. in the barrio of San Pedro, Manilan, the two sisters (old women) Maria and Matea Manalili were cut up with a bolo by Hermogenes Castro of the barrio of Santa Catalina of the same town, resulting in the instant death of Matea. Maria, whose right hand was cut off, died on the 21st instant. Castro gave up and on the 10th instant was remanded to the Court of First Instance charged with murder. The two sisters were known in the locality as 'mangcuculan,' or witches, and were charged by Castro with having cast a spell on him, causing a stiff neck, which spell the sisters refused to remove."

A number of comparatively reputable Filipino physicians, in the city of Manila itself, have confessed that they have to pretend to depend, to some extent, on charms and exorcisms, in order to get and keep practice.

In this connection I quote the following decision of the Philippine Supreme Court in the case of the United States *vs.* Mariano Boston, rendered November 23, 1908 (10 Philippine Reports, p. 134).

"The accused in this case was convicted in the Court of First Instance of the Province of Pangasinán of the crime of abortion as defined and penalized in paragraph 3 of article 410 of the Penal Code.

"The guilt of appellant is conclusively established by the evidence of record, the testimony of the witnesses for the prosecution leaving no room for reasonable doubt, despite the fact that there are some inconsistencies and discrepancies in their statements. Counsel for appellant insists that the evidence does not conclusively establish the fact that he intentionally caused the abortion, because there is no evidence in the record disclosing the character and medicinal qualities of the potion which the accused gave to the mother whose child was aborted. The evidence clearly discloses that the child was born three months in advance of the full period of gestation; that the appellant, either believing or pretending to believe that the child in the womb of the woman was a sort of a fish-demon (which he called a *balat*), gave to her a potion composed of herbs, for the purpose of relieving her of this alleged fish-demon; that two hours thereafter she gave premature birth to a child, having been taken with the pains of childbirth almost immediately after drinking the herb potion given her by the appellant; that after the birth of the child the appellant, still believing or pretending to believe that the child was a fish-demon which had taken upon itself human form, with the permission and aid of the husband and the brother of the infant child, destroyed it by fire in order to prevent its doing the mischief which the appellant believed or affected to believe it was capable of doing. These facts constitute, in our opinion, prima facie proof of the intent of the accused in giving the herb potion to the mother of the child, and also of the further fact that the herb potion so

administered to her was the cause of its premature birth.   The
defence wholly failed to rebut this testimony of the prosecution,
and we are of opinion, therefore, that the trial court properly
found the defendant guilty of the crime with which he was
charged beyond a reasonable doubt.

"The sentence imposed is in strict accord with the penalty
provided by the code, and should be and is hereby affirmed,
with the costs of this instance against the appellant.   So
ordered."

It is claimed that the Filipinos are a unit in demanding
their independence.   As a matter of fact, the bulk of the
common people have little idea what the word really
means.   In this connection the following extract from the
report of Colonel H. H. Bandholtz, later director of constabulary, of June 30, 1903, on the bandit Rios, is of interest : —

"Rios represented himself to be an inspired prophet and
found little difficulty in working on the superstitions of the extremely ignorant and credulous inhabitants of barrios distant
from centres of population.   So well did he succeed that he had
organized what he designated as an 'Exterior Municipal
Government' (for revenue only) with an elaborate equipment of
officials.   He promoted himself and his followers in rapid succession, until he finally had with him one captain-general, one
lieutenant-general, twenty-five major-generals and fifty briga-
dier-generals and a host of officers of lower grade.   In appreciation of his own abilities he appointed himself 'Generalissimo'
and 'Viceroy' and stated his intention of having himself
crowned 'King of the Philippines.'   Titles like these not
proving sufficient, he announced himself as 'The Son of God,'
and dispensed 'anting-antings,' which were guaranteed to make
the wearer invulnerable to attack.   Of the *ladrones* killed during
this period, few were discovered who were not wearing one of
these 'anting-antings.'

"The dense ignorance and credulity of the followers of Rios
was clearly shown by the fanatical paraphernalia captured by
Captain Murphy, P. C., on March 8, near Infanta.   Among
these was a box, on the cover of which was painted the word
'Independencia,' and the followers of Rios profoundly believed
that when they had proven themselves worthy the box would
be opened and the mysterious something called independence

for which they had so long been fighting could be secured, and that when attained there would be no more labour, no taxes, no jails, and no Constabulary to disturb their *ladrone* proclivities.

"When this mysterious chest was opened it was found to contain only some old Spanish gazettes and a few hieroglyphics, among which appeared the names and rank of the distinguished officials of the organization."

The affair is typical of an endless series of similar occurrences.

The ordinary Filipino dearly loves mystery, and misses no opportunity to join a secret society. It matters little to him what its supposed object may be, and that end is, as frequently as anything else, the organization of an insurrection. All sorts of fees are collected from the ignorant poor by the leaders of such movements, who are almost invariably of the educated and intelligent classes. At the opportune time they get away with the funds, leaving their ignorant followers to blunder along until caught and lodged in jail. The American government has dealt very gently with such poor dupes, most of whom have been released without any punishment. Within the past few days [1] I have had an interview with an exceptionally intelligent Filipino justice of the peace who sometimes gives me interesting information, in the course of which I asked him what was going on at present. He laughed and told me that the Filipinos in the vicinity of Manila believed that Mr. Harrison, the new governor-general, was coming to give them independence, and that a lot of smart rascals, who pretended to be organizing the army that would be necessary to maintain it, were selling officers' commissions at a peso each to any one who would buy them, and were doing a thriving business.

Until it ceases to be so readily possible to prey on the superstitions, the credulity and the passions of the common people, efforts on the part of the Filipinos to estab-

[1] Written September 15, 1913.

lish and maintain unaided a stable government are not likely to be crowned with very abundant success.

In general it may be said of the Filipino that he is quick to learn, but needs a teacher; is quick to follow, but needs a leader. He is ready to do the things he is taught to do. He accepts discipline, orders, rules. He has a great respect for constituted authority. He lacks initiative and sound judgment.

Let Americans beware of judging the Filipino peoples by the men with from one-half to thirty-one thirty-seconds of white blood, who so often have posed as their representatives.

More important than the interrelations of the several Christian peoples *inter se* are those between the several Christian peoples on the one hand and the non-Christian tribes on the other. This subject has already been discussed at length, so I will limit myself to a brief summary statement.

The Filipinos dislike and despise the non-Christians. They take advantage of their ignorance and helplessness to rob or cheat them of the fruits of their labour, and often hold them as slaves or peons. The non-Christians in turn hate them, and the more warlike wild tribes do not hesitate to take vengeance on them when opportunity offers. The Filipinos as a whole are afraid of the Moros, and with good reason. The Moros frankly assert that if a Filipino government were established, they would resume their long-abandoned conquest of the archipelago, and this they would certainly do. Although the non-Christians are numerically few, as compared with the Christians, they are potentially important because they have the power to make an amount of trouble wholly disproportionate to their numbers. The Filipinos could not rule them successfully, and the probable outcome of any attempt on their part to control them would be the inauguration of a policy of extermination similar to that which Japan is following with certain of the hill men of

Formosa. Because of the inaccessible nature of the country inhabited by many of the Philippine wild tribes, they would be able to hold their own for many years, and there would result a condition similar to that which has prevailed for so long in Achin, while the Moros with their ability to take to the sea and suddenly strike unprotected places would cause endless suffering and loss of life.

Under the Spanish régime the penalty which followed a too liberal use of "free speech" was very likely to be a sudden and involuntary trip to the other world. There was no such thing as a free press. A very strict censorship was constantly exercised over all the newspapers. The things that are now said and written daily without attracting much attention would at that time have cost the liberty or the lives of those who voiced them.

It is hardly to be wondered at that an Oriental people which had never had a free press or liberty of speech should have mistaken liberty, when it finally came, for license, and have gone to extremes which conclusively demonstrated their initial unfitness properly to utilize their new privileges.

Governor-General Smith once told a delegation of leading Filipinos that it was all very well to have freedom of speech and of the press in a country ruled by the United States government, which was strong enough to maintain order in the face of manifold difficulties, but that if the islands ever secured their independence the first official act of those in power should be to do away with the one and the other, for the reason that such a government as they would establish could not exist if either continued.

While the curtailing of freedom of speech or of the press under American civil rule is almost unthinkable, it is nevertheless true that the attitude of many of the politicians who do the talking, and who control the native press, has been poisonous.

A very intelligent student of Philippine affairs has

truly said that nothing more is necessary to demonstrate
the present unreadiness of the country for self-government
than a careful study of the attitude of the native press
toward important public questions.   From the beginning
until now there has been one long and almost uninterrupted
series of lies, innuendoes, sneers and diabolically ingenious
misrepresentations.   Practically every important policy
of the government has been viciously attacked, and the
worst of it is that the people primarily responsible for this
are not honest, or misled.   They know perfectly well what
they are doing and why they are doing it.   They em-
bitter that portion of the common people who are reached
by newspapers at all, and doubtless many of their dupes
really believe that the established government is a rotten
farce, and that its highest officials are steeped in iniquity.

Certainly no people are more skilful than are the Filipino
politicians in pretending to write one thing with the
certainty that another and very different one will be
read between the lines.   In the matter of libel, they are
adepts at skating on thin ice.   Rare indeed is the occurrence of a decent attitude on the part of any native newspaper toward any important public question.[1]

The history of the municipal and provincial governments
is worthy of very careful consideration.

[1] The editor of an American newspaper published at Zamboanga
has accurately described the attitude of the native press as follows : —
   "We have often referred to the great opportunity prevailing for
the native press of the Philippines to aid the material and political
uplift of the inhabitants.   Conditions of race and dialect naturally
conduce to facilitate this work for the native journalist.   With few
exceptions, however, the native press has persistently obstructed every
effort toward general amelioration of the condition of the masses.
Conspicuous efficiency in good government has furnished a target for
its denunciation.   Truth has been garbled, motives maligned, race
hatred kindled, falsehood fabricated and sedition practised, encouraged
and lauded.   The public school system, the intrinsic foundation to
free institutions, instituted under the military régime and constantly
expanded under the civil régime, has been interpreted by the native
press as a pernicious effort to oppress the masses by the enforcement of
a foreign language upon them.   The efforts to stamp out cattle disease

It has been found necessary to exercise close supervision over them in order to correct a constant tendency on the part of those having authority to abuse it.

Practically all the time of three lawyers in the executive bureau is taken up in examining evidence and reports of administrative investigations of charges against municipal officials and justices of the peace, of whom about two hundred are found guilty each year.   Half that number are removed from office.   One of the commonest charges against these officers is "abuse of authority," and one of the most difficult and endless tasks of the American administrative officers is to impress on the elective native official a sense of obligation toward his "inferiors," that is, the plain people who elected him.

He expects obsequiousness and even servility, and if they are lacking, endeavours to get square.[1]

and for the restoration of draft animals have been maligned as being oppressive to personal liberty.   The sanitary measures which have so renovated the very atmosphere of the archipelago have ever been the mark of derision and violent attack.   When cholera and plague have claimed their hundreds daily, efforts at prevention have persistently met with opposition from the native press.   Officials with the most unselfish motives have been persistently insulted, slandered and maligned. The American flag, which is the only emblem giving assurance of safety in the home, peace from abroad, liberty of opportunity, and equality and justice before the law, has been constantly smeared with the opprobrium of a malignant, filthy native press.   Progress of the Philippine people as a whole is retarded."

[1] On March 15, 1913, the Assistant Executive Secretary had occasion to write the following letter to the Governor of Capiz: —

"MY DEAR GOVERNOR ALTAVÁS: I have to acknowledge receipt of your communication of the 28th ultimo, complaining against the Justices of the Peace of Jamindan and Tapaz for failing 'to salute' you when visiting said towns, although your visits were frequently announced in advance, and the Justices of the Peace were in town at the time.

"The theoretical principles of democracy prevailing under this government do not require such courtesies as a matter of law.   It may be that, as your letter intimates, the Justice of the Peace should, as a matter of courtesy, call on you when you are in his town, but failure to do so in no wise constitutes ground for complaint, and were we to take your complaint seriously and cause it to be investigated, we would be indeed in serious danger of receiving a lecture on democracy

A MEMBER OF THE CABARÚAN TRINITY.

This man impersonated Christ at the time a new religious sect established its
headquarters at Cabarúan, Pangasinán. Nevertheless he got into jail for
cattle stealing.

Surely I have given enough illustrations of the ferocious brutality with which Filipino officials treated the common people in the days of the "Republic." Such brutality would again be in evidence were there to be any failure to hold officers strictly accountable.

The following case, called to my attention by a reliable American woman, illustrates the fact that provincial governors are sometimes swayed by other than humanitarian motives : —

"In 1902 when I was living at Capiz, a very pretty little fellow, a child of 7 or 8, often came begging to my house. Finally he ceased to come and I saw nothing of him for several months. Then I met him one morning, stone blind, his eyes in frightful condition. I made inquiry and learned that the people with whom he lived (his parents were dead) not finding him a remunerative investment had decided that he must be made more pitiful looking to bring in good returns as a beggar. So they filled his eyes with lime and held his head in a tub of water. I took the child to the Governor (the late Hugo Vidal) to make complaint. The Governor listened to my story, and then exclaimed, 'You are mistaken. I have known this child for years and he has been like this all the time.' The local sanitary chief agreed with him, and I was forced to give up all hope of having the inhuman wretches that had tortured the child punished."

The attitude of provincial and municipal officials toward very necessary sanitary measures has often been exceedingly unfortunate.

In 1910 the officials of the town of Bautista, Pangasinán, voted to have a *fiesta*, in spite of the fact that the health authorities had informed them that this could not be done safely, owing to the existence of cholera in the

from either the Judge of the Court of First Instance or the Justice of the Peace himself.

"I believe that, under the circumstances, the best course to be taken in the matter would be for you to withdraw the complaint, for even if the Justices concerned admit the charges, no administrative action against them would be possible.

"Very sincerely,
(Signed) "THOMAS CARY WELCH
(Active Executive Secretary)"

neighbouring towns. The town council preferred the merry-making to the protection of the lives of the people, and voted to disregard the warnings of the Bureau of Health, with the result that several of the neighbouring municipalities were infected with cholera, and many lives were needlessly lost. The governor of the province, himself a Filipino, was lax in attention to duty in this instance or the town council would have been suspended before, instead of after, this action on its part.

For a long time municipal policemen were commonly utilized as servants by the town officials, and were nearly useless for actual police work. To put firearms into their hands was little better than to present them outright to the *ladrones*. At present the constabulary exercise a considerable amount of control over municipal police, and there has resulted very material improvement in their appearance, discipline and effectiveness.

Municipal councils in the majority of cases voted all of the town money for salaries, leaving nothing for maintenance of public buildings, roads and public works, with the result that streets in the very centres of towns became impassable even for foot passengers. They were often indescribably filthy, cluttered with all sorts of waste material, and served as a meeting ground for all the horses, cattle, dogs, pigs, hens and goats of the neighbourhood.

In many instances, the first use made of their newly acquired powers by provincial governors and municipal presidents was to persecute in all sorts of petty ways those who had opposed their election, while the latter displayed marked disinclination to accept the will of the majority.

It is not to be expected that the Filipino should understand modern democratic government. Where could he have obtained knowledge of it? Under Spanish rule he saw officials habitually enriching themselves at the expense of the communities they were supposed to govern. He saw a government of privilege where the work of the many benefited the few. How could he have gained experience in modern and enlightened administration for the benefit of the people rather than for the benefit of the administrators? Not only must there be knowledge on the part of officials that this is the proper way to govern, but there must be a demand on the part of the people for such a government, and until the people know and understand that such a government is their right there will be no such demand. There is not yet a sufficient proportion of the Filipino people literate to make approval or disapproval felt.

Incidentally it should be remembered that in the Philippine Islands any provincial or municipal officer may be suspended by the governor-general, or removed for failure properly to perform his duties, for disloyalty, or for other causes. The provincial governors also hold the same power over the municipal presidents. Existing conditions are therefore not comparable with those which would arise without such control. I would as soon say that an automobile could go without a driver because it runs fairly well when there is a driver directing it as that the administration of the municipalities and provinces of the Philippine Islands would go as well as it now does under a system which does not provide for strong central control. It is one thing to administer when you are carefully supervised, and when the power of removal is held directly over you by a superior officer watching your every move, and another to administer equally well when the reins are not firmly held.

Serious consideration must be given to another group of facts in considering the fitness of the Filipinos for independence. It is undeniably true that they have progressed much further in civilization than has any other group of peoples of Malayan origin. It is just as indubitable that their development has not been a natural evolution, but has resulted from steady pressure brought to bear during three and a half centuries by Spain, and during the last decade and a half by the United States.

What would happen were this pressure removed? One may judge, within limits, from what has happened where it has been removed. Take, for instance, Cagayancillo, which is an isolated town on a small island southwest of Panay. Here the Spanish friar was the sole representative of governmental authority in bygone days. Cagayancillo was then a thriving town, with a strong stone fort for defense against the Moros, a beautiful, large church with splendid wood carvings ornamenting its interior, and a fine masonry *convento* of most original architecture, with long rows of giant clam shells embedded in its outer walls. There were a good municipal building and a stone schoolhouse, also excellent for their day. I first visited the place shortly after Palawan was made a province under civil rule. No priest had been there for three years. The town and its inhabitants reeked with filth. The wits of the two or three exceptionally intelligent men of the place were befogged with opium. The church and *convento* were falling into ruin. The fort had already gone to the bad. The *presidencia*[1] was a wreck, and so was the schoolhouse. There were no teachers for the children. The people were rapidly lapsing into barbarism.

In 1910 I visited the town of Malaueg, situated in the province of Cagayan. It was one of the first mission stations in northern Luzón. I found there the walls of an immense church and *convento*. These walls were approximately forty inches thick, and were intact, though roofs and floors had disappeared, in part from decay and in part from the stealing of the boards. Over the door of the church was a thick hardwood beam on which were carved in raised letters Spanish words signifying that the church was rebuilt in 1650. The walls of Manila were built about 1590. When was this church constructed to require rebuilding sixty years later? And what must then have been the size of the town which furnished the necessary hands to erect such a huge structure?

[1] Municipal building.

The Spanish friar in charge had left during the revolution against Spain some time subsequent to 1896, and as a result the town had gone to pieces after so many centuries of life.   Nothing remained but a small collection of grass huts.   The men had reverted to the breechclout, and were again adopting the head-axe.   Many of them had already taken to the mountains.

The Spaniards compelled Filipinos to live in towns, or at least to have houses there.   Under our form of government we allow them to do as they please, with the result that in provinces like Palawan our utmost efforts do not avail to keep them from forsaking settlements and scattering out through inaccessible mountain regions, where they are rapidly gravitating back to the state of barbarism from which they originally emerged.   I might multiply instances of this sort of thing.

In the early days of civil government the commission in many instances combined municipalities which lay immediately adjacent to each other and could readily enough be administered from a common governmental centre.   This action was taken in the interest of economy, and in the belief that the resulting saving in salaries would make possible the employment of more school-teachers, and the construction of better school buildings.

In many, if not most, cases such fusion of municipalities proved a mistake.   The town which happened to become the new seat of government prospered.   There were spent the taxes collected in the other formerly independent centres of population, which, deprived of their *autoridades*,[1] promptly became insanitary, disorderly and unprogressive.

I am firmly convinced that the Filipinos are where they are to-day only because they have been pushed into line, and that if outside pressure were relaxed they would steadily and rapidly deteriorate.

It is not necessary that there should be much retro-

[1] Literally "authorities," by which is meant municipal officials.

gression to cause serious trouble. I have discussed the character and attitude of the present Filipino legislative body. I have shown indubitably what sort of a government the Filipinos themselves established while they had a free hand. I agree absolutely with Blount's contention that they would again establish precisely the same sort of a government if left to their own devices. There would follow, first aggression against the property of foreigners, and then attacks upon their persons, which would not only excuse, but would necessitate, intervention by other governments to protect their citizens. Some of the more intelligent Filipino leaders would set their faces against such conduct as firmly as they did during the rule of the so-called Insurgent government, but now, as then, would be powerless to restrain either the more unprincipled among the intelligent, or the great body of the ignorant rank and file, and nothing more than a fairly plausible excuse would be needed to start the ball of foreign intervention rolling.

Many Americans may, in their present deep ignorance of the value of their most recently acquired possessions, agree with that distinguished representative who announced on the floor of the House of Representatives that the Philippines were "a lemon," but agents and spies of Japan have worked throughout the entire archipelago and she knows better. England and Germany have had their business men in the islands for many years, and they know better also.

The Filipinos are not yet fit to govern themselves, much less to govern the Moros and other non-Christian tribes, even if let alone, and they would not be let alone should we turn their country over to them.

Philippine independence is not a present possibility, nor will it be possible for at least two generations. Indeed, if by the end of a century we have welded into *a people* the descendants of the composite and complex group of human beings who to-day inhabit the islands, we shall have no cause to feel ashamed of our success.

CHAPTER XXXVII

WHAT THEN?

IT has been urged by one class of our citizens that we abandon the islands because they are a source of military weakness, and that we guarantee their independence, which in plain English means that we hold ourselves ready to fight for them! They insist that with our Caucasian origin and our years of hard-earned experience, we are not fit to govern them, but that their Filipino inhabitants, who are the Malayan savages of the sixteenth century, plus what Spain has taught them, plus what they have so recently learned from us, are fit to govern themselves and must be allowed to do so under our protection.

In other words, having brought up a child who is at present rather badly spoiled, we are to say to the family of nations: "Here is a boy who must be allowed to join you. We have found that we are unfit to control him, but we hope that he will be good. You must not spank him unless you want to fight us."

It has been suggested that we get other nations to agree to the neutralization of the islands. Why should they? Are we prepared to offer them any tangible inducements, or do we believe that the millennium has arrived and that they are actuated by purely altruistic motives in such matters?

Blount quotes with approval the following statement of Secretary William Jennings Bryan: —

"There is a wide difference, it is true, between the general intelligence of the educated Filipino and the labourer on the street and in the field, but this is not a barrier to self-government. Intelligence controls in every government, except where

it is suppressed by military force.   Nine-tenths of the Japanese
have no part in the law-making.   In Mexico, the gap between
the educated classes and the peons is fully as great as, if not
greater than, the gap between the extremes of Filipino society.
Those who question the capacity of the Filipinos for self-
government forget that patriotism raises up persons fitted for
the work that needs to be done." [1]

This sounds well, but will it bear analysis? We are
now being furnished a practical demonstration of the
results achieved by people like the Mexicans when they
attempt to conduct a so-called republic. Whether the
gap between the extremes of Mexican society is as great
as that between the extremes of Filipino society depends
on what one includes under the latter term. If one limits
it to the Christianized natives, the statement quoted
is true. If one includes the non-Christians which constitute an eighth of the population, it is not true.

Would the United States care to assume responsibility
for conditions in Mexico without any power to exercise
control over the government of that country? Those
who demand that we guarantee the independence of the
Philippines are advocating a thing precisely similar to
this, except that torture and burying alive do not seem to
be in vogue in Mexico, and would be practised in the
Philippines again, as they have been in the recent past.

Can any one fail to grasp the fact that the following
statements of Bishop Brent embody solid common sense?

"Finally it must be recognized that the Philippine problem
cannot be settled without reference to its international bearing.
Neutralization has been proposed. But can American or any
other diplomacy secure the neutrality of the Powers? Would
it mean anything if promises of neutrality were made? Is it
not so, that though no existing military power, East or West,
would fight America in order to secure possession of the Philippines, there are at least two nations which would seize the first
opportunity for interference if American sovereignty ceased?
Can America afford to protect a government halfway round the
world, which she does not actually and constructively control?

[1] Blount, pp. 296–297.

A TYPICAL OLD-STYLE PROVINCIAL GOVERNMENT BUILDING.

A MODERN PROVINCIAL GOVERNMENT BUILDING.

She has found it difficult enough with one near at hand. It appears to me that it would be a measure of quixotry beyond the most altruistic administration, to stand sponsor for the order of an experimental government of more than doubtful stability ten thousand miles from our coasts. When the Philippines achieve independence they must swallow the bitter with the sweet, and accept the perils as well as the joys of walking alone. There are national risks involved even in a limited protectorate to which I trust America will never expose herself."

We stoutly asserted in 1899 that the Filipinos were not fit to govern their own country, and this was certainly then true. If in the short space of fifteen years, with leaders who have so recently committed almost incredible barbarities still in the saddle, we had rendered them fit, we should have performed the most wonderful political miracle that the world has ever seen. But the age of miracles has long since passed. While the Filipinos have advanced more in the last fifteen years than during any previous century of their history, what they have gained is by no means ingrained in their character, and they yet have far to go. It is our duty and our privilege to guide and help them on their way. We should hold steadily onward disregarding the hostility and the murmurings of selfish politicians, and looking hopefully to the future for substantial results from the broad and generous policy which we have thus far followed.

Many of the politicians want independence under a United States protectorate, by which they mean that their country shall be turned over to them to do with as they please, with a fleet of American warships lying conveniently near to see that they are not interfered with while thus engaged. It would be the height of folly for us to enter into any such arrangement.

We must help the Filipinos to attain for their country commercial prosperity, so that its revenues may be more adequate for the support of government. Before commercial prosperity can exist, the people must learn to employ modern agricultural methods and modern machinery in bringing considerable portions of the present enormous uncultivated areas of fertile land to a state of productivity.

We must set right standards and insist that they be lived up to. The way to stimulate healthful development of the Filipinos is to let the apples hang high and make them climb for them, not to tell them to hold their hats and shake the tree.

This policy of setting right standards has already been very successfully pursued in the education of Filipino doctors, Filipino nurses, Filipino surveyors, Filipino printers and Filipino teachers.

A Filipino should never be appointed to public office merely because he is a Filipino, the clamour of politicians to the contrary notwithstanding. He should be appointed only if, and because, he is fit. Such a policy, unswervingly followed, will do more to promote the real interests of the civilized inhabitants than will all the concessions that could be made in a thousand years.

And what have we ever gained by concessions to Filipino politicians? Can any one point out a single instance in which they have aroused that feeling of gratitude, or even that sense of obligation, which may fully justify the adoption of measures that would otherwise be of doubtful utility? No!

This fact is well illustrated by the attitude of the politicians toward the Jones Bill providing for the establishment of the Philippine republic on July 4, 1913 and independence in 1920.

Hardly were its terms known in Manila when various politicians announced that the Filipinos did not want to wait until 1920, they wanted independence right then!

An editorial in the number of Speaker Osmeña's paper, *El Ideal*, for March 19, 1913, contains the following significant sentence: —

"We accept the test to which the Jones Bill subjects us, because we have full confidence in ourselves. Afterward, we shall do what is most expedient for us." [1]

Gratitude does not enter into the make-up of the average Filipino politician, and we must learn not to expect it. We must do what ought to be done because it ought to be done, and not look for appreciation to a small but very noisy body of men who curse us for standing between them and their prey, as we have stood from the day when Dewey first forbade Aguinaldo to steal cattle until now.

It is just as easy to win the gratitude and the affection of the common people of the lowlands as it has proved to be in the case of the wild men of the hills, but if we are to do this there must be a radical departure from the present policy, and we must deal with them directly.

In this connection it is instructive to study the career of James R. Fugate, Lieutenant-Governor, by appointment, of the sub-province of Siquijor. In spite of wretched health, he has done work of which he and his country have just cause to be proud. No one can fully appreciate it who does not know conditions as they were when he went there and as they are to-day. Siquijor has been converted into a checkerboard by good roads and trails where formerly there did not exist decent means of communication. Dysentery and typhoid fever ravaged the island during each recurring dry season when drinking water was almost unobtainable in many places, and what could be found was really unfit for human use. There are now fine public baths in the towns. Beautiful drinking fountains for men and animals are to be seen, not only in the larger centres of population, but along many of the principal highways.

Municipal officials have been taught their duties and perform them well. A complete telephone system connects the lieutenant-governor's office with all parts of the island. Siquijor was formerly completely isolated from

---

[1] This is a rather open threat to fight.

the outside world, but now has cable communication. Fine schools have been established, and swarm with children. The man who has brought about all this is beloved by the people whom he has helped and protected. They cannot bear the thought of his leaving them. What is the explanation of this phenomenon, when the inhabitants of many parts of the islands seem to remain unmoved by the many advantages which they now enjoy, and murmur against those to whom they are indebted for them? The answer is simple. Mr. Fugate speaks Visayan about as well as he does English, and there have been no intermediaries between him and his people, who consequently understand that they owe to him the benefits which they have received.

Certain evil politicians of Negros Occidental, whom he robbed of their spoils, attacked him with characteristic persistency and ingenuity. A young man of clean life, he was accused of adultery and of seduction of minors. Although he could at any time have had a better position at higher compensation; although he gave much of his inadequate salary to the poor and defenceless; although he carried on public works at a fraction of the cost of similar undertakings in neighbouring provinces, he was charged with profiting by government contracts and with the malversation of funds of the sub-province. All of these attacks failed miserably. His real offence was that he had stayed the hand of the oppressor, and let the people go free.

In many, if not in most, of the Christian provinces we have utilized the services of Filipino politicians who are openly opposed to the policy which we are endeavouring to carry out, and have thus placed between ourselves and the people a screen of shrewd and hostile men who can communicate with them as we cannot, who play upon their ignorance and their prejudices as we would not if we could, who keep them firm in the belief that all their troubles are due to the "*mucho malo gobierno Americano*," [1]

[1] Corrupt Spanish for "very bad American Government."

and that all the advantages which they enjoy have been wrung from the unwilling and unjust Americans by the courage and political ingenuity of the local *politicos*. For this condition of things we have ourselves to thank, and these are the men who would be governors under "self-government."

When the Federal Party was formed, a large number of conservative Filipinos came out into the open and risked their lives to aid in the termination of war and brigandage, and the establishment of peace and tranquillity. At the outset we rewarded many of those who escaped assassination by appointing them to public offices which they seemed fit to fill. In a few instances we even helped the families of those who sacrificed their lives to the cause of law and order. A little later, anxious to show that we were willing to let bygones be bygones, political offices, so far as they were within the gift of the government, were distributed practically without regard to the previous political records of the recipients. In taking this high attitude we assumed that the generous treatment thus accorded our late enemies would be appreciated by them and would win us their confidence and coöperation. We showed our ignorance of the men with whom we were dealing when we allowed ourselves to expect such a result. They interpreted our generosity as an evidence of fear, and each new concession has served only to whet their appetites. For years we gave profitable government advertising to vicious publications which never for a moment ceased to attack us. If there is any one lesson which should have been brought home to us by our experience it is that in the Philippine Islands this sort of thing does not work as yet. In this, as in most other countries, there are just two political parties, to wit, the "ins" and the "outs." Public office is ardently desired by a large percentage of the educated Filipinos who dearly love to exercise authority, and will do without scruple what seems necessary to get it.

We have gone too fast and too far in conferring on the people power to elect their officers. A larger percentage of the public offices should have remained appointive, and should have been filled either with Americans or with Filipinos of recognized ability who were really in favour of the policy which the government was carrying out. Open and active opposition to that policy should have been made ground for prompt removal from office. The men who risked their lives to help us were entitled to recognition and reward, and to the protection which the knowledge that such recognition is being accorded gives in a country like the Philippines. Left out in the cold, they turned against us when they saw our political enemies filling fat offices, and why not? Such a course was safer and more popular, and they thought that we might then be willing to buy their allegiance, judging by our dealings with others!

It has been claimed that the intelligent, highly educated class are a unit for independence. Nothing could be further from the truth, but it would be uncommonly hard at present to prove this fact.

Some time since, I sat beside a very distinguished Filipino at a public banquet. He made a speech in which he expressed the conviction that independence in the near future would be a most desirable thing. When he sat down I said to him, "What would you do if you got it?" His reply was, "Be still! I would take the first steamer for Hongkong!" His attitude is typical of that of a large group of opportunists.

There is a considerable body of intelligent, conservative Filipinos who believe, as do the vast majority of well-informed Americans, that independence at this time would be an unmitigated curse in that it would necessarily be temporary, would result in grave disturbances of public order, would bring foreign intervention and the occupation of the islands by some nation with purposes far less altruistic than ours, and would put the possi-

A REFUGE FROM THE MOROS.

This old fort at Cuyo is typical of many others which were built to afford places of refuge from the murdering, slave-hunting Moros. The building inside it is a church.

bility of real, permanent independence off until a time so remote as to be far beyond the range of our present vision. These men will state their attitude freely in private conversation with those in whom they have confidence, but hardly one of them has the courage to go on record. Why should they? We have seen that in the old days those who opposed the views of Aguinaldo and his associates were given short shrift and that thousands of them were murdered in cold blood, while those who actively opposed the American military and civil governments were without exception freely pardoned when further opposition became impossible, unless guilty of crimes of the gravest character. Nay, more. Under the amnesty proclamation there were turned loose from Bilibid Prison hundreds of murderers, some of whom had taken the lives of scores of human beings. Little attention has been paid at any time to the violation, by Filipinos, of their oaths of allegiance to the United States, and now, when we discover one of the periodic incipient insurrections frequently organized by intelligent natives for the sole purpose of wringing hard-earned pesos from the peasant class, we seldom punish severely even the vicious leaders. It is idle to suppose that these facts are lost upon the conservative Filipinos. They know that if independence does not come no punishment will be meted out to them for remaining neutral, or even for actively advocating it, but that if it does come, and they have opposed it, vengeance swift, sure and dire will smite them. They are afraid, and they have the best of reasons to be afraid, because we have announced no definite policy. Let it be authoritatively stated that American sovereignty will be maintained in these islands for a long period and those who actually believe that there is not a strong element among the Filipinos who favour such a course will get a real surprise.

At present, however, our ears are deafened by the clamour of the noisy politicians, who claim to represent "the Filipino people." In this connection Bishop Brent has pertinently observed : —

"If desire implied ability, the clamor for independence on the part of the Filipinos, which just now is more widespread then at any time in their history, would be the signal for our withdrawal, but only their achievements can determine their ability."

Before we can safely declare the Filipinos ready to try the great experiment of self-government we must bring them to the place where they no longer regard bandit leaders as popular heroes but are able and determined to maintain a state of public order such that life and property will be safe. We must wean them from their present hostility toward legitimate foreign business interests. We must teach them that agriculture comes before art; that a public office is a public trust; that the enormous potential wealth of their forests is worth preserving; that the poor Filipino *must* be encouraged to own and till his own land, not held as a slave or peon. We must go on training physicians, surgeons and sanitarians so that the public health may be adequately protected and individual suffering relieved. We must be sure that our wards have developed the understanding and courage necessary successfully to oppose the great waves of epidemic disease which constantly threaten their country from without. We must train up Filipino engineers, to-day almost completely lacking, in sufficient numbers to make possible the construction of the public works needed in future and the maintenance of those which already exist.

There must be chemists and bacteriologists to do the routine work of the government, to make the investigations necessary to safeguard the lives of the people, and to facilitate the development of the resources of the country. Finally, there must be a sufficiency of just judges, of honourable lawyers, of able administrators, and of legislators unswayed by the childish motives which so often influence those of to-day.

Most important of all, we must bring the Filipino people to the place where they can go on properly teaching their children and their youths.

The day when all this will have been done of necessity lies far in the future, and if, when contemplating this fact, we sometimes grow weary, we should remember that the task, though a mighty and unprecedented one, is well worthy of the best energies of a great nation. It can never be accomplished through partisan politics.

In considering our duty to the Filipinos let us not forget the fate of him "who putteth his hand to the plough and turneth back." The old, old rule applies to nations as well as to individuals.

We are giving the Filipinos a fair chance to develop every latent ability which they possess. In the very nature of the case, their future lies, and must lie, wholly with them. There is no royal road to real independence, much less is there any short cut. Our Filipino wards must tread the same long, weary path that has been trodden by every nation that has heretofore attained to good government.

The case has been admirably stated by that distinguished gentleman who to-day occupies the highest post within the gift of the American people. He has said : —

"There is profound truth in Sir Henry Maine's remark that the men who colonized America and made its governments, to the admiration of the world, could never have thus masterfully taken charge of their own affairs and combined stability with liberty in the process of absolute self-government if they had not sprung of a race habituated to submit to law and authority, if their fathers had not been subjects of kings, if the stock of which they came had not served the long apprenticeship of political childhood during which law was law without choice of their own.

"Self-government is not a mere form of institutions, to be had when desired, if only proper pains be taken. It is a form of character. It follows upon the long discipline which gives a people self-possession, self-mastery, the habit of order and peace and common counsel, and a reverence for law which will not fail when they themselves become the makers of law; the steadiness and self-control of political maturity. And these things cannot be had without long discipline.

"The distinction is of vital concern to us in respect of practical choices of policy which we must make, and make very soon. We have dependencies to deal with and must deal with them in the true spirit of our own institutions. We can give the Filipinos constitutional government, a government which they may count upon to be just, a government based upon some clear and equitable understanding, intended for their good and not for our aggrandizement; but we must ourselves for the present supply that government. It would, it is true, be an unprecedented operation, reversing the process of Runnymede, but America has before this shown the world enlightened processes of politics that were without precedent. It would have been within the choice of John to summon his barons to Runnymede and of his own initiative enter into a constitutional understanding with them; and it is within our choice to do a similar thing, at once wise and generous, in the government of the Philippine Islands. But we cannot give them self-government. Self-government is not a thing that can be 'given' to any people, because it is a form of character and not a form of constitution. No people can be 'given' the self-control of maturity. Only a long apprenticeship of obedience can secure them the precious possession, a thing no more to be bought than given. They cannot be presented with the character of a community, but it may confidently be hoped that they will become a community under the wholesome and salutary influences of just laws and a sympathetic administration; that they will after a while understand and master themselves, if in the meantime they are understood and served in good conscience by those set over them in authority.

"We of all people in the world should know these fundamental things and should act upon them, if only to illustrate the mastery in politics which belongs to us of hereditary right. To ignore them would be not only to fail and fail miserably, but to fail ridiculously and belie ourselves. Having ourselves gained self-government by a definite process which can have no substitute, let us put the peoples dependent upon us in the right way to gain it also." [1]

[1] "Constitutional Government in the United States," by Woodrow Wilson, Ph.D., LL.D., pp. 52–53.

A POSSIBLE OFFICE-HOLDER.

The man with the lance could be elected senator for the Mountain Province were the Jones Bill to be enacted. He has the qualifications therein prescribed as necessary to eligibility for this high office.

These views will be indorsed by every intelligent American who knows the Filipino, and has some adequate conception of the problems presented by the presence, in the same country with him, of the Ifugao, the Igorot, the Manobo, the Bukidnon, and the Moro. They are the views of Professor Wilson, historian and political philosopher, at a time when he was unswayed by party prejudices and untrammelled by party policy. Let us hope that President Wilson, the titular leader of the Democratic party and the dispenser of political patronage, has not entirely abandoned them, and that in embarking so boldly, not to say so rashly, as he has done, on the policy of suddenly giving to the Filipinos a radical increase in the control which they are allowed to have over their own affairs, and of leaving them subsequently to demonstrate their fitness or unfitness to exercise it, he will at least be bound by the actual results of an experiment which, as every one familiar with local conditions in the islands well knows, is fraught with the gravest danger.

After all is said and done, the real Philippine question is not what path they shall take. That has been determined, for all nations alike, by a Divine Providence that is all-seeing, all-wise and inexorable. It is not whether they shall travel the old, old road a little faster, or a little more slowly. That will ultimately be settled, for them and for us, by the unanswerable logic of events, and we need not worry over it. The real question is, shall they make their long and adventurous journey, guided, helped and protected by the strong and kindly hand of the United States of America, or shall they be left to stagger along alone, blind in their own conceit, under the keen and watchful eye of another powerful nation, hungrily awaiting their first misstep?

APPENDIX

Instructions of the President to the First Philippine Commission

> "Department of State,
> "Washington, January 21, 1899.

"My dear Sir: I inclose herewith a copy of the instructions which the President has drawn up for the guidance of yourself and your associates as commissioners to the Philippines.

"I am, with great respect, sincerely yours,

"John Hay."

"Honourable Jacob G. Schurman,
"The Arlington."

> "Executive Mansion,
> "Washington, January 20, 1899.

"The Secretary of State:

"My communication to the Secretary of War, dated December 21, 1898, declares the necessity of extending the actual occupation and administration of the city, harbour, and bay of Manila to the whole of the territory which by the treaty of Paris, signed on December 10, 1898, passed from the sovereignty of Spain to the sovereignty of the United States, and the consequent establishment of military government throughout the entire group of the Philippine Islands. While the treaty has not yet been ratified, it is believed that it will be by the time of the arrival at Manila of the commissioners named below. In order to facilitate the most humane, pacific, and effective extension of authority throughout these islands, and to secure, with the least possible delay, the benefits of a wise and generous protection of life and property to the inhabitants, I have named Jacob G. Schurman, Rear-Admiral George Dewey, Major-General Elwell S. Otis, Charles Denby, and Dean C. Worcester to constitute a commission to aid in the accomplishment of these results.

"In the performance of this duty, the commissioners are enjoined to meet at the earliest possible day in the city of Manila and to announce, by a public proclamation, their presence and the mission intrusted to them, carefully setting

975

forth that, while the military government already proclaimed is to be maintained and continued so long as necessity may require, efforts will be made to alleviate the burden of taxation, to establish industrial and commercial prosperity, and to provide for the safety of persons and of property by such means as may be found conducive to these ends.

"The commissioners will endeavour, without interference with the military authorities of the United States now in control of the Philippines, to ascertain what amelioration in the condition of the inhabitants and what improvements in public order may be practicable, and for this purpose they will study attentively the existing social and political state of the various populations, particularly as regards the forms of local government, the administration of justice, the collection of customs and other taxes, the means of transportation, and the need of public improvements. They will report through the Department of State, according to the forms customary or hereafter prescribed for transmitting and preserving such communications, the results of their observations and reflections, and will recommend such executive action as may from time to time seem to them wise and useful.

"The commissioners are hereby authorized to confer authoritatively with any persons resident in the islands from whom they may believe themselves able to derive information or suggestions valuable for the purposes of their commission, or whom they may choose to employ as agents, as may be necessary for this purpose.

"The temporary government of the islands is intrusted to the military authorities, as already provided for by my instructions to the Secretary of War of December 21, 1898, and will continue until Congress shall determine otherwise. The commission may render valuable services by examining with special care the legislative needs of the various groups of inhabitants, and by reporting, with recommendations, the measures which should be instituted for the maintenance of order, peace, and public welfare, either as temporary steps to be taken immediately for the perfection of present administration, or as suggestions for future legislation.

"In so far as immediate personal changes in the civil administration may seem to be advisable, the commissioners are empowered to recommend suitable persons for appointment to these offices from among the inhabitants of the islands who have previously acknowledged their allegiance to this Government.

"It is my desire that in all their relations with the inhabitants of the islands the commissioners exercise due respect for all the ideals, customs, and institutions of the tribes which compose the population, emphasizing upon all occasions the just and beneficent intentions of the Government of the United States. It is also my wish and expectation that the commissioners may be received in a manner due to the honoured and authorized representatives of the American Republic, duly commissioned on account of their knowledge, skill, and integrity as bearers of the good will, the protection, and the richest blessings of a liberating rather than a conquering nation.

"WILLIAM McKINLEY."

PROCLAMATION OF THE FIRST PHILIPPINE COMMISSION

To the people of the Philippine Islands:

The treaty of peace between the United States and Spain, ratified several weeks ago by the former, having on March 20 been ratified by the latter, the cession to the United States, as stipulated by the treaty, of the sovereignty which Spain possessed and exercised over the Philippine Islands has now, in accordance with the laws of nations, received a complete and indefeasible consummation.

In order that the high responsibilities and obligations with which the United States has thus become definitively charged may be fulfilled in a way calculated to promote the best interests of the inhabitants of the Philippine Islands, his Excellency the President of the United States has appointed the undersigned a civil commission on Philippine affairs, clothing them with all the powers necessary for the exercise of that office.

The commission desire to assure the people of the Philippine Islands of the cordial good will and fraternal feeling which is entertained for them by his Excellency the President of the United States and by the American people. The aim and object of the American Government, apart from the fulfilment of the solemn obligations it has assumed toward the family of nations by the acceptance of sovereignty over the Philippine Islands, is the well being, the prosperity, and the happiness of the Philippine people and their elevation and advancement to a position among the most civilized peoples of the world.

His Excellency the President of the United States believes that this felicity and perfection of the Philippine people is to be brought about by the assurance of peace and order; by the guaranty of civil and religious liberty; by the establishment of justice; by the cultivation of letters, science and the liberal and practical arts; by the enlargement of intercourse with foreign nations; by the expansion of industrial pursuits, trade and commerce; by the multiplication and improvement of the means of internal communication; by the development, with the aid of modern mechanical inventions, of the great natural resources of the archipelago; and, in a word, by the uninterrupted devotion of the people to the pursuit of those useful objects and the realization of those noble ideals which constitute the higher civilization of mankind.

Unfortunately, the pure aims and purposes of the American Government and people have been misinterpreted to some of the inhabitants of certain of the islands. As a consequence, the friendly American forces have, without provocation or cause, been openly attacked.

And why these hostilities? What do the best Filipinos desire? Can it be more than the United States is ready to give? They are patriots and want liberty, it is said. The commission emphatically asserts that the United States is not only willing, but anxious, to establish in the Philippine Islands an enlightened system of government under which the Philippine people may enjoy the largest measure of home rule and the amplest liberty consonant with the supreme ends of government and compatible with those obligations which the United States has assumed toward the civilized nations of the world.

The United States striving earnestly for the welfare and advancement of the inhabitants of the Philippine Islands, there can be no real conflict between American sovereignty and the rights and liberties of the Philippine people. For, just as the United States stands ready to furnish armies, navies and all the infinite resources of a great and powerful nation to maintain and support its rightful supremacy over the Philippine Islands, so it is even more solicitous to spread peace and happiness among the Philippine people; to guarantee them a rightful freedom; to protect them in their just privileges and immunities; to accustom them to free self-government in an ever-increasing measure; and to encourage them in those democratic aspirations, sentiments and ideals which are the promise and potency of a fruitful national development.

It is the expectation of the commission to visit the Philippine peoples in their respective provinces, both for the purpose of cultivating a more intimate mutual acquaintance and also with a view to ascertaining from enlightened native opinion what form or forms of government seem best adapted to the Philippine peoples, most apt to conduce to their highest welfare, and most conformable to their customs, traditions, sentiments and cherished ideals. Both in the establishment and maintenance of government in the Philippine Islands it will be the policy of the United States to consult the views and wishes, and to secure the advice, coöperation and aid, of the Philippine people themselves.

In the meantime the attention of the Philippine people is invited to certain regulative principles by which the United States will be guided in its relations with them. The following are deemed of cardinal importance : —

1. The supremacy of the United States must and will be enforced throughout every part of the archipelago, and those who resist it can accomplish no end other than their own ruin.

2. The most ample liberty of self-government will be granted to the Philippine people which is reconcilable with the maintenance of a wise, just, stable, effective and economical administration of public affairs, and compatible with the sovereign and international rights and obligations of the United States.

3. The civil rights of the Philippine people will be guaranteed and protected to the fullest extent; religious freedom assured, and all persons shall have an equal standing before the law.

4. Honour, justice and friendship forbid the use of the Philippine people or islands as an object or means of exploitation. The purpose of the American Government is the welfare and advancement of the Philippine people.

5. There shall be guaranteed to the Philippine people an honest and effective civil service, in which, to the fullest extent practicable, natives shall be employed.

6. The collection and application of taxes and revenues will be put upon a sound, honest and economical basis. Public funds, raised justly and collected honestly, will be applied only in defraying the regular and proper expenses incurred by and for the establishment and maintenance of the Philippine government, and for such general improvements as public interests may demand. Local funds, collected for local purposes, shall not be diverted to other ends. With such a prudent and honest fiscal administration, it is believed that the needs of the government will in a short time become compatible with a considerable reduction in taxation.

7. A pure, speedy and effective administration of justice will be established, whereby the evils of delay, corruption and exploitation will be effectually eradicated.

8. The construction of roads, railroads and other means of communication and transportation, as well as other public works of manifest advantage to the Philippine people, will be promoted.

9. Domestic and foreign trade and commerce, agriculture and other industrial pursuits, and the general development of the country

in the interest of its inhabitants will be constant objects of solicitude and fostering care.

10. Effective provision will be made for the establishment of elementary schools in which the children of the people shall be educated. Appropriate facilities will also be provided for higher education.

11. Reforms in all departments of the government, in all branches of the public service and in all corporations closely touching the common life of the people must be undertaken without delay and effected, conformably to right and justice, in a way that will satisfy the well-founded demands and the highest sentiments and aspirations of the Philippine people.

Such is the spirit in which the United States comes to the people of the Philippine Islands. His Excellency, the President, has instructed the commission to make it publicly known. And in obeying this behest the commission desire to join with his Excellency, the President, in expressing their own good will toward the Philippine people, and to extend to their leading and representative men a cordial invitation to meet them for personal acquaintance and for the exchange of views and opinions.

MANILA, *April 4, 1899.*

JACOB GOULD SCHURMAN,
President of Commission.

GEORGE DEWEY,
Admiral U. S. N.

ELWELL S. OTIS,
Major-General U. S. Volunteers.

CHARLES DENBY.

DEAN C. WORCESTER.

JOHN R. MACARTHUR,
Secretary of Commission.

INSTRUCTIONS OF THE PRESIDENT TO THE SECOND PHILIPPINE COMMISSION

WAR DEPARTMENT,
Washington, April 7, 1900.

SIR: I transmit to you herewith the instructions of the President for the guidance of yourself and your associates as commissioners to the Philippine Islands.

Very respectfully,

ELIHU ROOT,
Secretary of War.

Hon. WILLIAM H. TAFT,
 President Board of Commissioners
   to the Philippine Islands

     EXECUTIVE MANSION, *April 7, 1900.*
The SECRETARY OF WAR,
  Washington.

 SIR: In the message transmitted to the Congress on the 5th of December, 1899, I said, speaking of the Philippine Islands: "As long as the insurrection continues the military arm must necessarily be supreme. But there is no reason why steps should not be taken from time to time to inaugurate governments essentially popular in their form as fast as territory is held and controlled by our troops. To this end I am considering the advisability of the return of the commission, or such of the members thereof as can be secured, to aid the existing authorities and facilitate this work throughout the islands."

 To give effect to the intention thus expressed I have appointed Hon. William H. Taft, of Ohio; Prof. Dean C. Worcester, of Michigan; Hon. Luke E. Wright, of Tennessee; Hon. Henry C. Ide, of Vermont, and Prof. Bernard Moses, of California, commissioners to the Philippine Islands to continue and perfect the work of organizing and establishing civil government already commenced by the military authorities, subject in all respects to any laws which Congress may hereafter enact.

 The commissioners named will meet and act as a board, and the Hon. William H. Taft is designated as president of the board. It is probable that the transfer of authority from military commanders to civil officers will be gradual and will occupy a considerable period. Its successful accomplishment and the maintenance of peace and order in the meantime will require the most perfect coöperation between the civil and military authorities in the island, and both should be directed during the transition period by the same Executive Department. The commission will therefore report to the secretary of war, and all their action will be subject to your approval and control.

 You will instruct the commission to proceed to the city of Manila, where they will make their principal office, and to communicate with the military governor of the Philippine Islands, whom you will at the same time direct to render to them every assistance within his power in the performance of their duties. Without hampering them by too specific instructions, they should in general be enjoined, after making themselves familiar with the conditions and needs of the country, to devote their attention in the first instance to the establishment of municipal governments, in which the natives of the islands, both in the cities and in the rural communities, shall be afforded the opportunity to manage their own local affairs to the fullest extent of which they are capable, and subject to the least degree of supervision and control which a careful study of their capacities and observation of the workings of native control show to be consistent with the maintenance of law, order and loyalty.

The next subject in order of importance should be the organization of government in the larger administrative divisions corresponding to counties, departments or provinces, in which the common interests of many or several municipalities falling within the same tribal lines, or the same natural geographical limits, may best be subserved by a common administration. Whenever the commission is of the opinion that the condition of affairs in the islands is such that the central administration may safely be transferred from military to civil control, they will report that conclusion to you, with thei recommendations as to the form of central government to be established for the purpose of taking over the control.

Beginning with the 1st day of September, 1900, the authority to exercise, subject to my approval, through the secretary of war, that part of the power of government in the Philippine Islands which is of a legislative nature is to be transferred from the military governor of the islands to this commission, to be thereafter exercised by them in the place and stead of the military governor, under such rules and regulations as you shall prescribe, until the establishment of the civil central government for the islands contemplated in the last foregoing paragraph, or until Congress shall otherwise provide. Exercise of this legislative authority will include the making of rules and orders, having the effect of law, for the raising of revenue by taxes, customs duties and imposts; the appropriation and expenditure of public funds of the islands; the establishment of an educational system throughout the islands; the establishment of a system to secure an efficient civil service; the organization and establishment of courts; the organization and establishment of municipal and departmental governments, and all other matters of a civil nature for which the military governor is now competent to provide by rules or orders of a legislative character.

The commission will also have power during the same period to appoint to office such officers under the judicial, educational and civil-service systems and in the municipal and departmental governments as shall be provided for. Until the complete transfer of control the military governor will remain the chief executive head of the government of the islands, and will exercise the executive authority now possessed by him and not herein expressly assigned to the commission, subject, however, to the rules and orders enacted by the commission in the exercise of the legislative powers conferred upon them. In the meantime the municipal and departmental governments will continue to report to the military governor and be subject to his administrative supervision and control, under your direction, but that supervision and control will be confined within the narrowest limits consistent with the requirement that the powers of government in the municipalities and departments shall be honestly and effectively exercised and that law and order and individual freedom shall be maintained.

All legislative rules and orders, establishments of government, and appointments to office by the commission will take effect immediately, or at such times as they shall designate, subject to your approval and action upon the coming in of the commission's reports, which are to be made from time to time as their action is taken. Wherever civil governments are constituted under the direction of the commission, such military posts, garrisons and forces will be continued for the suppression of insurrection and brigandage, and the maintenance of law and order, as the military commander shall deem requisite, and the military forces shall be at all times subject under his orders to the call of the civil authorities for the maintenance of law and order and the enforcement of their authority.

In the establishment of municipal governments the commission will take as the basis of their work the governments established by the military governor under his order of August 8, 1899, and under the report of the board constituted by the military governor by his order of January 29, 1900, to formulate and report a plan of municipal government, of which his honour Cayetano Arellano, president of the audiencia, was chairman, and they will give to the conclusions of that board the weight and consideration which the high character and distinguished abilities of its members justify.

In the constitution of departmental or provincial governments, they will give especial attention to the existing government of the island of Negros, constituted, with the approval of the people of that island, under the order of the military governor of July 22, 1899, and after verifying, so far as may be practicable, the reports of the successful working of that government, they will be guided by the experience thus acquired, so far as it may be applicable to the condition existing in other portions of the Philippines. They will avail themselves, to the fullest degree practicable, of the conclusions reached by the previous commission to the Philippines.

In the distribution of powers among the governments organized by the commission, the presumption is always to be in favour of the smaller subdivision, so that all the powers which can properly be exercised by the municipal government shall be vested in that government, and all the powers of a more general character which can be exercised by the departmental government shall be vested in that government, and so that in the governmental system, which is the result of the process, the central government of the islands, following the example of the distribution of the powers between the states and the national government of the United States, shall have no direct administration except of matters of purely general concern, and shall have only such supervision and control over local governments as may be necessary to secure and enforce faithful and efficient administration by local officers.

The many different degrees of civilization and varieties of custom and capacity among the people of the different islands preclude very definite instruction as to the part which the people shall take in the selection of their own officers; but these general rules are to be observed: That in all cases the municipal officers, who administer the local affairs of the people, are to be selected by the people, and that wherever officers of more extended jurisdiction are to be selected in any way, natives of the islands are to be preferred, and if they can be found competent and willing to perform the duties, they are to receive the offices in preference to any others.

It will be necessary to fill some offices for the present with Americans which after a time may well be filled by natives of the islands. As soon as practicable a system for ascertaining the merit and fitness of candidates for civil office should be put in force. An indispensable qualification for all offices and positions of trust and authority in the islands must be absolute and unconditional loyalty to the United States, and absolute and unhampered authority and power to remove and punish any officer deviating from that standard must at all times be retained in the hands of the central authority of the islands.

In all the forms of government and administrative provisions in which they are authorized to prescribe, the commission should bear in mind that the government which they are establishing is designed not for our satisfaction, or for the expression of our theoretical views, but for the happiness, peace and prosperity of the people of the Philippine Islands, and the measures adopted should be made to conform to their customs, their habits and even their prejudices, to the fullest extent consistent with the accomplishment of the indispensable requisites of just and effective government.

At the same time the commission should bear in mind, and the people of the islands should be made plainly to understand, that there are certain great principles of government which have been made the basis of our governmental system which we deem essential to the rule of law and the maintenance of individual freedom, and of which they have, unfortunately, been denied the experience possessed by us; that there are also certain practical rules of government which we have found to be essential to the preservation of these great principles of liberty and law, and that these principles and these rules of government must be established and maintained in their islands for the sake of their liberty and happiness, however much they may conflict with the customs or laws of procedure with which they are familiar.

It is evident that the most enlightened thought of the Philippine Islands fully appreciates the importance of these principles and rules, and they will inevitably within a short time command universal assent. Upon every division and branch of the government of the Philippines, therefore, must be imposed these inviolable rules:

That no person shall be deprived of life, liberty or property without due process of law; that private property shall not be taken for public use without just compensation; that in all criminal prosecutions the accused shall enjoy the right to a speedy and public trial, to be informed of the nature and cause of the accusation, to be confronted with the witnesses against him, to have compulsory process for obtaining witnesses in his favour, and to have the assistance of counsel for his defence; that excessive bail shall not be required, nor excessive fines imposed, nor cruel and unusual punishment inflicted; that no person shall be put twice in jeopardy for the same offence, or be compelled in any criminal case to be a witness against himself; that the right to be secure against unreasonable searches and seizures shall not be violated; that neither slavery nor involuntary servitude shall exist except as a punishment for crime; that no bill of attainder, or ex-post-facto law shall be passed; that no law shall be passed abridging the freedom of speech or of the press, or the rights of the people to peaceably assemble and petition the Government for a redress of grievances; that no law shall be made respecting an establishment of religion, or prohibiting the free exercise thereof, and that the free exercise and enjoyment of religious profession and worship without discrimination or preference shall forever be allowed.

It will be the duty of the commission to make a thorough investigation into the titles to the large tracts of land held or claimed by individuals or by religious orders; into the justice of the claims and complaints made against such landholders by the people of the island or any part of the people, and to seek by wise and peaceable measure, a just settlement of the controversies and redress of wrongs which have caused strife and bloodshed in the past. In the performance of this duty the commission is enjoined to see that no injustice is done; to have regard for substantial rights and equity, disregarding technicalities so far as substantial right permits, and to observe the following rules:

That the provision of the Treaty of Paris, pledging the United States to the protection of all rights of property in the islands, and as well the principle of our own Government which prohibits the taking of private property without due process of law, shall not be violated; that the welfare of the people of the islands, which should be a paramount consideration, shall be attained consistently with this rule of property right; that if it becomes necessary for the public interest of the people of the islands to dispose of claims to property which the commission finds to be not lawfully acquired and held disposition shall be made thereof by due legal procedure, in which there shall be full opportunity for fair and impartial hearing and judgment; that if the same public interests require the extinguishment of property rights lawfully acquired and held due compensation shall be made out of the public treasury therefor; that no form of religion and no minister of religion shall be forced upon any community or upon any citizen of the islands; that upon the other hand no minister of religion shall be interfered with or molested in following his calling, and that the separation between state and church shall be real, entire and absolute.

It will be the duty of the commission to promote and extend, and, as they find occasion, to improve, the system of education already inaugurated by the military authorities. In doing this they should regard as of first importance the extension of a system of primary education which shall be free to all, and which shall tend to fit the people for the duties of citizenship and for the ordinary avocations of a civilized community. This instruction should be given in the first instance in every part of the islands in the language of the people. In view of the great number of languages spoken by the different tribes, it is especially important to the prosperity of the islands that a common medium of communication may be established, and it is obviously desirable that this medium should be the English language. Especial attention should be at once given to affording full opportunity to all the people of the islands to acquire the use of the English language.

It may be well that the main changes which should be made in the system of taxation and in the body of the laws under which the people are governed, except such changes as have already been made by the military government, should be relegated to the civil government which is to be established under the auspices of the commission. It will, however, be the duty of the commission to inquire diligently as to whether there are any further changes which ought not be delayed; and if so, they are authorized to make such changes, subject to your approval. In doing so they are to bear in mind that taxes which tend to penalize or repress industry and enterprise are to be avoided; that provisions for taxation should be simple, so that they may be understood by the people; that they should affect the fewest practicable subjects of taxation which will serve for the general distribution of the burden.

The main body of the laws which regulate the rights and obligations of the people should be maintained with as little interference as possible. Changes made should be mainly in procedure, and in the criminal laws to secure speedy and impartial trials, and at the same time effective administration and respect for individual rights.

In dealing with the uncivilized tribes of the islands the commission should adopt the same course followed by Congress in permitting the tribes of our North American Indians to maintain their tribal organization and government, and under which many of those tribes are now living in peace and contentment, surrounded by a civilization to which they are unable or unwilling to conform. Such tribal governments should, however, be subjected to wise and firm regulation; and, without undue or petty interference, constant and active effort should be exercised to prevent barbarous practices and introduce civilized customs.

Upon all officers and employees of the United States, both civil and military, should be impressed a sense of the duty to observe not merely the material but the personal and social rights of the people of the islands, and to treat them with the same courtesy and respect for their personal dignity which the people of the United States are accustomed to require from each other.

The articles of capitulation of the city of Manila on the 13th of August, 1898, concluded with these words:

"This city, its inhabitants, its churches and religious worship, its educational establishments, and its private property of all descriptions, are placed under the special safeguard of the faith and honour of the American army."

I believe that this pledge has been faithfully kept. As high and sacred an obligation rests upon the Government of the United States to give protection for property and life, civil and religious freedom, and wise, firm and unselfish guidance in the paths of peace and prosperity to all the people of the Philippine Islands. I charge this commission to labour for the full performance of this obligation which concerns the honour and conscience of their country, in the firm hope that through their labours all the inhabitants of the Philippine Islands may come to look back with gratitude to the day when God gave victory to American arms at Manila and set their land under the sovereignty and the protection of the people of the United States.

WILLIAM McKINLEY.

THE PAST AND PRESENT ORGANIZATION OF THE COURTS OF THE PHILIPPINE ISLANDS[1]

During the last years of Spanish sovereignty the courts in the Philippine Islands consisted of superior courts, which were the *audiencia territorial de Manila*, the *audiencia de lo criminal de Cebu*, and the *audiencia de lo criminal de Vigan;* the courts of first instance, and justice of the peace courts.

[1] I am indebted to the Honourable Gregorio Araneta, secretary of finance and justice, for a summary statement of the judicial reforms effected since the American occupation, on which this statement is largely based. — D. C. W.

The *audiencia territorial de Manila* exercised jurisdiction in civil matters over the entire Philippine archipelago; in criminal matters it exercised jurisdiction over the central and southern provinces of Luzón and over the islands of Catanduanes, Mindoro, Burias, Masbate and Ticao.

Its legal personnel consisted of a president of the court; two presidents of branches, one of the civil, and the other of the criminal; nine justices (*magistrados*); four associate justices (*magistrados suplentes*); one *fiscal*; one lieutenant-*fiscal*, and three *fiscal* attorneys; five secretaries and four law clerks who were assistant secretaries.

The *audiencia de lo criminal* of Vigan and that of Cebu had only criminal jurisdiction, the former over the northern part of Luzón and the Batanes Islands and the latter over the Visayan Islands and Mindanao. Each of these courts had a president, two justices, two associate justices, one *fiscal*, one lieutenant-*fiscal*, a secretary and one law clerk who was assistant secretary.

There was at least one court of first instance in each province. In some, like Batangas, Ambos Camarines, Samar, Leyte, Cebu and Negros, there were two. In Iloílo there were three and in Manila four. These courts were divided into three classes designated as follows: *de entrada; de ascenso;* and *de termino.*

Subject to the jurisdiction of the *audiencia territorial de Manila,* there were eight *jusgados de termino;* five *jusgados de ascenso,* and fourteen *jusgados de entrada.* Under the criminal jurisdiction of the *audiencia territorial* of Vigan there were three *jusgados de termino,* one *jusgado de ascenso* and sixteen *jusgados de entrada.* Under the *audiencia territorial* of Cebu there were two *jusgados de termino* and thirty *jusgados de ascenso.*

In each court of first instance there was a prosecuting attorney (*promotor fiscal*). In each pueblo there was a justice of the peace subject in his criminal and civil jurisdiction to the judge of first instance of the province. In criminal matters the justice of the peace courts as well as the courts of first instance were subject to the *audiencia territorial* of Manila.

At the present time the courts of justice of the islands consist of a supreme court, courts of first instance and justice of the peace courts.

The supreme court, which is composed of one chief justice and six associate justices, has civil and criminal jurisdiction over all the islands.

In each province there is a court of first instance. Several such courts are usually united to constitute a judicial district, but this does not hold for the court of first instance of the city of Manila, which is presided over by three judges, each in his own court room, nor for the court of first instance of Iloílo, which constitutes a district by itself. The remaining courts are divided between seventeen districts.

The courts of the thirteenth and fourteenth districts have concurrent jurisdiction over all actions arising within the district of Lanao of the Moro province, but the court first acquiring jurisdiction in any cause has exclusive jurisdiction in the same.

There are four judges at large, without territorial jurisdiction of their own, any one of whom may be assigned by the secretary of finance and justice to act in any district. He then has the same jurisdiction as its judge. The services of judges at large are necessary when the judge of any district is absent, or has vacated his position, or when the business of a court requires the aid of an assistant judge.

There further exists the court of land registration, with one judge and five auxiliary judges. It has exclusive jurisdiction over all applications for the registration of title to land or buildings or an interest therein. It also has jurisdiction to confirm the titles of persons who under the Spanish regime acquired imperfect titles to public lands, provided that such persons fulfill the requirements of law for their perfection.

There is now a justice of the peace court in each municipality and by resolution of the Philippine Commission there have been created justice of the peace courts in townships and other centres of population which have not been organized either as townships or municipalities.

In the provinces of Nueva Vizcaya, Mindoro, Palawan, Agusan and in the Mountain province, all of which are organized under the special provincial government act, the provincial governor, the provincial secretary, the provincial treasurer, the provincial supervisor [1] and the deputy clerk of the court of first instance are justices of the peace *ex officio* with jurisdiction throughout their respective provinces.

In the Moro province, which is divided into five districts, called Joló, Zamboanga, Lanao, Cotabato and Davao, there are tribal ward courts which consider and decide minor civil and criminal actions in which the parties in interest, or any of them, are Moros or members of other non-Christian tribes. These tribal ward courts have with regard to these actions the same jurisdiction as is vested by law in justice of the peace courts, but the legislative council of the Moro province may in its discretion vest in such courts jurisdiction in other actions, civil or criminal but not capital, which is at present vested in courts of first instance. In each district the governor and secretary are justices of tribal ward courts and there are as many auxiliary justices as may be needed. The sentences of the tribal ward courts, from which no appeal is taken to the court of first instance, may be modified or remitted by the provincial governor after a review of the case.

In addition to these tribal ward courts there exist justice of the peace courts in each municipality and the governor-general may with the advice and approval of the commission appoint justices of the peace for towns or places in the Moro province which have not been or-

---

[1] The engineer officer of the province.

ganized into municipalities or which, although included within the limits of an organized municipality, are distant from or have no convenient means of access to centres of population. The jurisdiction of the justices of the peace for the municipalities in which such towns or places are situated, and of the justices of the peace appointed for such towns or places, are concurrent over cases arising within the municipality. The several justices of the peace in any district of the Moro province exercise concurrent jurisdiction over cases arising within the district but without the limits of an organized municipality, but the justice of the peace first acquiring jurisdiction over any case has exclusive jurisdiction over it. The justices of the peace in the Moro province have no jurisdiction to try civil and criminal actions in which original jurisdiction is vested in tribal ward courts.

Under the present organization there exists a bureau of justice with the following legal personnel: attorney-general, solicitor-general, assistant attorney-general, and eleven assistant attorneys. There is a provincial *fiscal* in each province with the exception of the Moro province, in which there are an attorney and an assistant attorney. The city of Manila has, besides the city attorney and assistant attorney, a prosecuting attorney with four assistants.

Under the Spanish legislation, justices of the peace had jurisdiction to try civil actions where the value of the thing in litigation did not exceed five hundred pesetas ($50), and actions for unlawful detainer where the action was based on one of the following grounds. The completion of the term stipulated in the contract; the expiration of the time within which notice had to be given for the conclusion of the contract, in accordance with law; the stipulations made or the general custom in each pueblo; and the failure to pay the price stipulated, provided that in neither of these three cases the object of the action was dispossession of a mercantile or manufacturing establishment, or of a rural property the annual rental whereof exceeded two thousand five hundred pesetas ($250). They also had jurisdiction to try *faltas*, which are criminal offences penalized with a fine not exceeding five hundred pesetas ($50) or with *aresto menor*, which is imprisonment not exceeding thirty days, and to conduct the preliminary proceedings in crimes the jurisdiction over which was vested in the courts of first instance. Judges of first instance had original jurisdiction in all civil actions except those in which original jurisdiction was vested in justices of the peace and in actions for crime (*delitos*). The sentences of judges of first instance could be carried in appeal to the *audiencia territorial* of Manila, and in the majority of cases the supreme court of Spain could be petitioned for the cassation of the sentences of the said *audiencia territorial*. The judges of first instance also had appellate jurisdiction in cases of appeal against the decisions rendered by justices of the peace in actions in which the latter had original jurisdiction. All the sentences of the courts of first instance in criminal cases, regardless of whether they were sentences of conviction or of acquittal, had to be submitted for review to the proper *audiencia*, the decision of the former not being final without the approval of the latter. From the decisions of the *audiencia* appeal lay in all cases to the supreme court of Spain.

It naturally followed that legal proceedings were interminable, and one of the worst things which could befall an individual or a corporation in the Spanish days was to become involved in a lawsuit. It is an unpleasant thing to say, but the plain truth is that the character of the judges in not a few instances left much to be desired.

Contrast with the endless complications of the above arrangement the simplicity of that which prevails to-day. Justices of the peace have exclusive original jurisdiction in all civil actions arising in their municipalities which are not exclusively cognizable by the courts of first instance, when the value of the subject-matter or amount of the demand does not exceed $100, exclusive of interest and costs; and where such value or demand exceeds $100, but is less than $300, the justices of the peace have jurisdiction concurrent with the courts of first instance. They also have original jurisdiction in forcible entry and detainer proceedings. They have no jurisdiction to adjudicate questions of title to real estate or any interest therein, or in civil actions in which the subject of litigation is not capable of pecuniary estimation, except in forcible entry and detainer cases, or in those which involve the legality of any tax, impost, or assessment, or in actions involving admiralty or marine jurisdiction, or in matters of probate, the appointment of guardians, trustees, or receivers, or in actions for annulment of marriage. Justices of the peace, except in the city of Manila, have original jurisdiction to try persons charged with misdemeanors, offences and infractions of municipal ordinances, arising within the municipality, in which the penalty provided by law does not exceed six months imprisonment or a fine of $100, or both such imprisonment and fine. In the city of Manila the justice of the peace does not have this jurisdiction; there it is left to a municipal judge, who has jurisdiction to try all the infractions of ordinances and has a more ample jurisdiction to try misdemeanors and crimes against the general laws of the islands. Justices of the peace, except in the city of Manila, also have jurisdiction to conduct preliminary proceedings in all crimes and misdemeanors supposed to have been committed within their municipalities and cognizable by the courts of first instance.

The jurisdiction of courts of first instance is of two kinds, original and appellate. Courts of first instance have original jurisdiction: in all civil actions in which the subject of litigation is not capable of pecuniary estimation; in all civil actions which involve the title to or possession of real property, or any interest therein, or the legality of any tax, impost, or assessment, except actions of forcible entry into or detainer of lands or buildings; in all cases in which the demand, exclusive of the interest or the value of the property in controversy, amounts to $100 or more; in all actions in admiralty or maritime jurisdiction, irrespective of the value of the property in controversy and the amount of the demand; in all matters of probate, both of testate and intestate estates, appointment of guardians, trustees, and receivers, in all actions for annulment of marriage, and in all such special cases and proceedings as are not otherwise provided for; in all criminal cases in which a penalty of more than six months imprisonment or a fine exceeding $100 may be imposed; in all crimes and offences committed on the high seas or beyond the jurisdiction of any country, or within any of the navigable waters of the Philippine Islands, on board a ship or water craft of any kind registered or licensed in the Philippine Islands in accordance with the laws thereof. This jurisdiction may be exercised by the court of first instance in any province into which the ship or water craft upon which the crime or offence was committed may come after the commission thereof, but the court first lawfully taking cognizance thereof has jurisdiction of the same to the exclusion of all other courts in the Philippine Islands. Lastly, courts of first instance have power to issue writs of injunction, mandamus, certiorari, prohibition, quo warranto, and habeas corpus in their respective provinces and districts, in the manner provided in the code of civil procedure. Courts of first instance have appellate jurisdiction over all causes arising in justices' and other inferior courts in their respective provinces.

The supreme court of the Philippine Islands has original jurisdiction to issue writs of mandamus, certiorari, prohibition, habeas corpus, and quo warranto in the cases and in the manner prescribed in the code of civil procedure, and to hear and determine the controversies thus brought before it, and in other cases provided by law.

The supreme court of the United States, according to the Philippine bill, has jurisdiction to review, revise, reverse, modify, or affirm the final judgments and decrees of the supreme court of the Philippine Islands in all actions, cases, causes, and proceedings pending therein in which the constitution or any statute, treaty, title, right or privilege of the United States is involved, or in causes in which the value in controversy exceeds $25,000.

Probably not more than ten Filipinos held judicial or fiscal positions, except that of justice of the peace, under Spanish rule. To-day, three of the seven justices of the supreme court, ten of the twenty judges of districts, two of the four judges at large, and three of the six judges of the court of land registration are Filipinos. In the bureau of justice the attorney-general and seven assistant attorneys are Filipinos. All of the provincial fiscals are Filipinos with the exception of the fiscal of the Moro province and the prosecuting attorney and the city attorney of Manila. All of the justices of the peace except those who serve *ex officio* are Filipinos, and the secretary of finance and justice is a Filipino as well.

Under the Spanish régime justices of the peace did not receive salaries, nor was there any appropriation for the payment of necessary clerical assistance, for office supplies, or for rental of their court rooms. The fees which the law allowed them to charge were their only compensation. These were fifty cents for each civil case tried and twenty-five cents when no trial was held on account of failure to appear on the part of either the plaintiff or defendant or of both.

In criminal cases the fees were seventy-five cents for each case tried, but they could be collected only if the defendant was adjudged to pay the costs and was solvent.

The compensation of justices of the peace was in practice limited to the paltry fees in civil cases, which in many municipalities amounted to almost nothing owing to the small number of such cases tried. Justices of the peace were burdened with orders from the courts of first instance for the service of process, and for this no compensation was given them.

The only appropriations for office, personnel and supplies of the courts of first instance were the following: two Chinese interpreters and sixteen bailiffs, drawing a yearly salary of $48 for the four courts at Manila; interpreters drawing the following ridiculous salaries: $48 per annum in some courts, $36 in others and in still others $24; amanuenses whose salaries in some courts were $48 and in others $36 per annum, while in yet other courts there was no amount appropriated for their salaries. No appropriation was made for clerks, officers, messengers or bailiffs of the courts, for necessary office supplies or for court-houses. The clerks of courts had to pay all subordinate employees. They also had to pay for the building of a court-house out of the money collected as fees from litigants, and in many instances they were compelled to pay for the dwelling place of the judge, who ordinarily lived in the court-house.

The salaries of judicial officers and *fiscals* were also very meager. The prosecuting attorney of a court *de entrada* was paid $750 per annum; the judge of a court of first instance *de entrada*, the prosecuting attorney *de ascenso*, and the secretaries of the *audiencia de lo criminal*, all of whom had the same rank, drew salaries of $937.50 per annum. The judge of first instance *de ascenso*, the prosecuting attorney *de termino* and the secretaries of the *audiencia territorial de Manila* were paid $1125 per annum. The judges of courts of first instance *de termino* and the attorneys of the *audiencia territorial* of Manila and the assistant attorneys of the *audiencias de lo criminal* of Vigan and Cebu drew a salary of $1375 per annum. The assistant *fiscal* of the *audiencia territorial* of Manila and the justices of the

audiencias de lo criminal of Vigan and Cebu, $1750.
The justices of the *audiencia territorial* of Manila and
the presidents and *fiscals* of the *audiencias de lo criminal*
of Vigan and Cebu received $2125 per annum. The
president of the *audiencia territorial* of Manila and the
presidents of the departments of said court and its *fiscal*
received $25 per annum. The president of the *audiencia
territorial* of Manila had an additional allowance of $750,
and the presidents of the departments and *fiscal* of said
court had $250 each for entertainment expenses.

At present, justices of the peace in first, second, third,
and fourth class municipalities receive yearly salaries
of $480, $420, $360 and $300, respectively. The justice
of the peace of Manila receives $1800. The justices of
the peace of Iloilo and Cebu receive $1200 each; those
of the provincial capitals of Albay, Ambos Camarines,
Batangas, Bulacan, Ilocos Sur, Occidental Negros, Pampanga, Pangasinán and Tayabas, $900 each; those of
Cagayan, Capiz, Cavite, Ilocos Norte, Laguna, Rizal,
Samar and Sorsogon, $750 each; those of the remaining
provincial capitals and of any municipalities considered
as capitals of provinces organized under the provincial
government act, $600 each.

Every municipality is required to provide the justice
of the peace with an adequate court room and the necessary office furniture, light, and janitor service. Office
supplies, such as stationery, stamps, printed forms, books,
etc., are furnished by the bureau of justice and paid for
from the appropriation for said bureau.

Clerks and other subordinate employees of the courts
of first instance now have regular salaries prescribed by
law, and the salaries of judges are sufficient to allow them
to live comfortably and with the independence and
decorum which befit their official positions. Judges at
large and some district judges receive $4500 per annum;
other district judges, $5000 per annum; judges in the
city of Manila, $5500. The judge of the court of land

registration receives $5000 and the assistant judges are paid $4000 each with promotion to $4500 after two years of service. The chief justice and associate justices of the supreme court receive $10,000 each.

THE NON-CHRISTIAN POPULATION

The following table gives the present accepted estimate of the non-Christian population of the provinces as now organized, together with the census estimate: —

Province or Sub-province	Census Estimate	Present Accepted Estimate
Abra	14,037	14,037
Agusan	—	85,000
Albay	892	892
Amburayan	—	10,191
Ambos Camarines	5,933	5,933
Apayao	—	20,000
Antique	2,921	2,921
Bataan	1,621	1,621
Batanes	—	000
Batangas	000	000
Benguet	21,828	28,449
Bohol	000	000
Bontoc	—	62,000
Bulacan	415	415
Cagayan	13,414	15,000
Capiz	5,629	5,629
Catanduanes	—	000
Cavite	000	000
Cebu	000	000
Ilocos Norte	2,210	2,210
Ilocos Sur	13,611	13,611
Iloilo	6,383	6,383
Ifugao	—	125,000
Isabela	7,638	7,638
Kalinga	—	76,000
La Laguna	000	(?)
La Union	10,050	000
Lepanto	—	31,194
(Lepanto-Bontoc)	70,283	—
Carried forward	176,865	514,124

Province or Sub-province	Census Estimate	Present Accepted Estimate
Brought forward	176,865	514,124
Leyte	000	000
Marinduque	000	000
Masbate	000	000
Mindoro	7,264	15,000
Misamis	40,210	000
Moro Province	316,664	486,316
Negros Occidental	4,612	4,612
Negros Oriental	16,605	16,605
Nueva Ecija	1,148	862
Nueva Vizcaya	46,515	6,000
Palawan	6,844	20,000
Pampanga	1,098	1,098
Pangasinán	3,386	3,386
Rizal	2,421	2,421
Romblon	000	50
Samar	688	1,390
Siquijor	—	000
Sorsogon	41	41
Surigao	15,814	(?)
Tarlac	1,594	1,594
Tayabas	2,803	2,803
Zambales	3,168	3,168
Total	647,740	1,071,832

Certain of the items in this table require brief explanation. In it the name of each province or sub-province for which the census estimate has been departed from is italicized.

Agusan. This province did not exist when the census was taken. It has since been carved out of the territory which formerly belonged to Surigao and Misamis. The figures given, based largely on actual enumeration, are approximately correct.

Amburayan. This sub-province formed a part of South Ilocos at the time of the census enumeration. It does not appear that any account was taken of its non-Christian population.

Apayao. The territory of this sub-province was a part

of the province of Cagayan at the time of the census enumeration. The estimate is that of its present lieutenant-governor. Lieutenant-Governor Villamor estimated its population at 53,000, but this figure was undoubtedly too high.

Antique. The non-Christian population of this province is probably given too low by the census, but I have allowed the census figures to stand.

Batanes. This province did not exist at the time the census was taken.

Benguet. The present figures are based on an accurate enumeration.

Bontoc. The territory included within this sub-province has been greatly changed since the census was taken. The present figures are based on a recent enumeration.

Cagayan. The present figures were furnished me by Governor Antonio Carag on April 16, 1913. They represent only the supposed Negrito population of the eastern cordillera. There are other non-Christians in the province, but their number is not known.

Ilocos Norte. The census estimate is undoubtedly too low, but is nevertheless adopted, in fault of new and more reliable information.

Ifugao. No such political subdivision existed when the census was taken. This territory then formed a part of Nueva Vizcaya. A recent fairly accurate enumeration has shown the original estimate of the population of Nueva Vizcaya to be grossly in error.

Isabela. This province has lost a part of its non-Christian population to Ifugao and a part to Kalinga. There remain some Kalingas and numerous Negritos east of the Cagayan River, but I have no reasonably accurate estimate of their numbers. The figures given are probably too low.

Kalinga. This sub-province did not exist at the time of the census enumeration. The figures given are quite accurate.

La Union. This province has lost all of its non-Christian population by transfer to Benguet and Amburayan.

Lepanto. The figures now given for Lepanto are accurate.

Lepanto-Bontoc. Carried in the first column, but no entry made in the second because a direct comparison between the territory which was included in this province and the corresponding portions of the existing Mountain Province is not practicable.

Mindoro. No accurate count of the Mangyans of Mindoro has ever been made, but since the census enumeration the island has been crossed in a number of places and the estimate now given is believed to be reasonably conservative.

Misamis. This province has lost its non-Christian population to the sub-province of Bukidnon.

The *Moro Province,* as at present constituted, corresponds to the former districts of Basilan, Cotabato, Dapitan, Davao, Joló, Siasi, Tawi Tawi and Zamboanga, so that a direct comparison between the census estimate and the present estimate is possible. The figures given were recently furnished me by the secretary of the province. They are admittedly inaccurate, but are believed to be approximately correct.

Nueva Ecija. This province has lost its Ilongot population to Nueva Vizcaya.

Nueva Vizcaya. Nueva Vizcaya has lost its Ifugao population to the Mountain Province, but has gained those Ilongots formerly credited to Isabela, Tayabas, Nueva Ecija and Pangasinán, the net result being a heavy loss in non-Christian population.

Palawan. The province of Palawan corresponds closely to the territory included in Paragua Norte and Paragua Sur at the time of the census enumeration so that a direct comparison is possible. There was no real attempt to enumerate the non-Christian inhabitants of this province for the census. Of Moros alone there are some five thousand. There are said to be approximately ten thousand Tagbanuas in the country tributary to the region along the banks of the Iwahig River, which empties into Coral Bay. It is further claimed that there are some five thousand more back of Bonabóna Point. This does not take into account the Tagbanua population on the west coast, nor that of the other Iwahig valley near Puerto Princesa; nor does it include the Tagbanuas inhabiting the islands of Dumaran, Dinapahan, Bulalacao, Peñon de Coron, Culion and Busuanga. I here place the non-Christian population of the province at twenty thousand, but believe this figure rather low.

Romblon. There are some fifty non-Christians in this sub-province, survivors of a much larger number who formerly lived in Tablas and Sibuyan.

Samar. The figures here given are those of a recent estimate by the lieutenant-governor of the hill people of that island. Most of the hill people are rated as Filipinos.

Surigao. Surigao has lost most of its non-Christian population to the sub-province of Butuan, but still has a considerable number of Manobos and Negritos and the figures given are far too low.

INDEX

A

Abacá (Manila hemp), culture of, and statistics of trade in, 891–893.

Abaya, Lino, non-Christian delegate to Aguinaldo's congress, 263.

Abaya, wild Tingian, story of, 549–551.

Abra, conditions in province of, under Insurgent rule, 208–209; estimates of population, 999.

Abra River, trip up the, 344.

Abulúg River, voyage down the, 552–553.

Acevedo, Fernando, 95 ff.

Administration of justice in the Philippines, 400–407, 988–999.

Agius, Monsignor, 445.

Agoncillo, Filipino Insurgent, letters of, 53, 58, 63, 68, 70, 71–72; murder of Spanish recommended to Aguinaldo by, 731.

Agricultural education in Philippine schools, 509–511.

Agricultural lands, action desirable concerning, 842–844.

Agriculture, conditions as to, in Mindoro, 221; general conditions as to, 885 ff.; primitive state of development of, 888, 896–897, 943.

Aguinaldo, Baldomero, attempt of, to open communication with Sultan of Joló, 229; secretary of war and navy in Insurgent president's cabinet, 266; mentioned, 731.

Aguinaldo, Emilio, 17; deceitful statements by, concerning promises of Filipino independence, 19 ff.; insurrection of 1896 against Spain led by, 20; deportation of, 20–21; political activities of, in exile, 21 ff.; meeting between Consul Pratt and, at Singapore, 25–26; statement of, concerning Pratt's promise of recognition of Filipino independence, 26–27; Pratt's work to secure coöperation of, with American fleet, 27–28;

omits all mention of promise of independence at meeting of Hongkong junta, 39; returns to Philippines and meets Admiral Dewey, 46 ff.; reports of conversation with Dewey, 47–52; truth about claim concerning promises of independence, 52 ff.; deceitful proclamations issued by, 56; relations between General Anderson and, 60–62; consideration of extent of coöperation of, with American forces, 76 ff.; assumption of civil authority by, upon capitulation of Spanish, 91; makes plans to get rid of United States troops, 127–134; proclamation of January 5, 1899, equivalent to a declaration of war, 137; plans for attack on Americans, and murder of General Otis, 137–142; character of warfare outlined by, in general orders, 140–142; attack begun by (February 4, 1899), 146–147; conditions in various provinces during rule of, 152–241; action upon receiving news of killing of American soldiers by Insurgents in Cavite, 213; the kind of "republic" that would have been set up by, 242–243; evolution of the government set up by, 244 ff.; conduct of the war by, 270–286; capture of, 287; address issued to Filipino people by, 287–288; guest of Mr. Forbes at Baguio, 470; murder authorized by, as a governmental measure, 730 ff.; meeting of former Insurgent officers at house of, in 1913, 937.

Agusan, province of, divided into Bukidnon and Batuan, 612–613; slave-taking raids into, 711; estimates of population, 999, 1000.

Agusan River, trip up the, 613–617; description of, 615, 800.

Ahern, Major George P., chief of Forestry Bureau, 849.

E

Earnshaw, Señor, denial of existence of slavery in Philippines by, 724.

Eckman, Governor E. A., luncheon given to, by Benguet Igorots, 572.

Edie, Major, efficient medical officer, 413.

Education, under the Spanish, 501–503; system of, established by Americans, 504 ff.

Edwards, General, action in regard to slavery bill, 700, 702.

Elections, under Aguinaldo's scheme of government, 254–256; percentage of illiteracy brought out by Philippine, 523, 944.

Embroidery-making, training of Filipino women in, 507, 509.

Evans, John H., governor of Palawan, 600, 606.

Expositions, exhibition of non-Christian peoples at, 643–645.

F

Far Eastern Association of Tropical Medicine, 443.

Federal Party, the, 341, 967.

Ferguson, Arthur W., 330.

Fiestas held among wild hill men, 564–566.

Filipinos, question of promise of independence to, 18–66; question of coöperation by, with American forces, 67–126; treacherous attitude of, 127–151; conditions in the provinces under Insurgent rule, 152–241; unfitness of common people to govern, 242 ff.; severe treatment of, by Insurgent leaders, 270–275; instances in which severity was used toward, by American soldiers, 281; chief characteristics of, as a people, 340–341; percentage of, employed in the civil service, 359, 366–367; as members of the Philippine constabulary, 380 ff., 399; as judges of courts, 402–407; health conditions among, and educational campaign in sanitary methods begun for, 408–420; training of, for nurses and physicians, 434–435; percentage of tuberculosis among, 444; generally bad physical condition of, 445; establishment of

schools for, 501–505; training of, as teachers, 505–507; change in attitude of, toward manual labour, 508; industrial education of, 508–513; introduction of athletic sports and games, 514–516; drinking habits of, 570; cheating of people of wild tribes by, 570–571, 610–611, 668–670, 951; statement of author's attitude toward, 637–659; lack of sympathy of, for non-Christian tribes, 661–665, 936; question of treatment of wild people by, if given full power, 665, 668–672, 674–675; system of slavery conducted among, 676 ff.; peonage among, 714–729; government by murder and assassination carried on by leaders of, 730–767; granting of legislative power to, deemed to be premature, 772; activities of, in the Philippine Assembly, 773–790; character of Filipinos elected to legislature, 790; doubtful results of turning road and bridge work over to, 882–883; qualities as field labourers, 886; primitive methods of agriculture followed by, 891, 896; lacking as yet in ability to promote commercial prosperity, 917–920; barrier to present complete independence of, found in diversity of peoples and existence of mutual dislikes and prejudices, 933–940; intermarriage of Americans and, 940–941; illiteracy of majority of people, 943–944; superstitions and religious fakes among, 944–949; while quick to learn, lack initiative and sound judgment, 951; irresponsibility of native press, 952–954; other facts militating against fitness of, to govern themselves, 954–960; course to be followed by United States in treatment of, 961–973.

Fish, possibilities for increase of trade in, 904.

Fishing in the Philippines, 806–818.

Flowers of the Philippines, 800–801.

Forbes, W. Cameron, succeeds General Smith as governor-general, 354; excellence of administration of, 354–356; lack of courtesy shown to, in method of requesting resignation, 456; quoted regarding the civil service, 366; assistance given Baguio Country Club by, 465, 467; services of, in developing Baguio, 470–471; credit due, for Benguet Road and Baguio, 487; Quezon's attack on, because of speech on slavery question, 721–723; opening up of game fishing by, 806–807; ocean bonito taken by, 811; plan for coast-guard service evolved by, 868; sensible road policy for which responsible, 882.

Forest products, 847 ff., 852, 858.

Forestry Bureau, reorganization of, 333; work of, 849, 850.

Forests, in Mindoro, 221; legislation for protection and development of Philippine, 347; description, possibilities, and question of conservation and development, 846–860.

Fort, Captain Guy O., 397.

Fortich, Manuel, 618–620, 624, 625, 626, 669, 673.

Franchise, qualifications for securing the, 522–523, 944.

Freedom of speech and the press confused with license, 952.

Freer, Dr. Paul C., superintendent of government laboratories, 414; work as director of Bureau of Government Laboratories, 491–492; death of, 499.

Friar lands question, 376; history of, 834–841.

Friar Lands Act, 836–838.

Friars, torture of, by Aguinaldo's forces, 172–205, 206 ff.; murder of, 731–732.

Fruit production, 903–904.

Fuga Island, shooting on, 820.

Fugate, Lieutenant-Governor James R., work of, in Siquijor, and attacks on, 965–966.

Fullón, Leandro, Insurgent general, murder of enemies authorized by, 736–737.

G

Gallman, Lieutenant Jeff D., valuable work of, in connection with constabulary, 396, 673; work of, among Ifugaos, 577–579; experience of, with people of Lingay, 662–664; liberation of slaves by, in Nueva Vizcaya, 712.

Gambling, among Benguet Igorots, 571; the besetting sin of Filipinos, 715, 777.

Game fish and game fishing in the Philippines, 806–818.

Game shooting, 820–828.

Garchitorena, Señor, 40, 41.

Gilbert, Newton W., secretary of public instruction, 513.

Gilmore, Lieutenant, officer captured and turned loose in Apayao, 556.

Gold, in Mindoro, 221; mines in vicinity of Baguio, 481; in vicinity of Paracale, Luzón, 885.

Gold mining, 885.

Gomez, Manuel, secretary of board of health, 414.

Gonzaga, Gracio, 41; secretary of fomento in Aguinaldo's cabinet, 266; visits first Philippine Commission, 315–316.

Government exchanges, 665.

Government Laboratories, Bureau of, established, 491–492; becomes the Bureau of Science, 494.

Governors, vital importance of work done by American, in the islands, 662–675.

Grant, General Fred D., reminiscence by, 164–165.

Grove, Leo J., barracuda taken by, 808.

Guardia civil, the, 378–380.

Guerilla warfare, authorized by Aguinaldo, 285, 922; horrors of, 285–286.

Guerrero, Leon, 263.

Guzman, torturer of Lieutenant Piera, 190, 204.

Guzman, Governor Pablo, extermination of non-Christians advocated by, 662.

H

Halcon, Mt., marble on, 221.

Hale, Walter F., work of, as lieutenant-governor of Kalinga country, 579–580, 673.

Harbord, Colonel J. G., information given by, regarding constabulary, 387.

Harbours, improvement of, under American régime, 870–872; lighting of, 872–873; charting and survey work in, 873–874.

Hardwood timber in Philippine forests, 847, 849–851.

legislative acts of second Philippine Commission relative to, 334, 335; civil service rules applied to officers in, 363; abuses practised by officers of, 953–957.

Municipal health officers, 439.

Murder, as a part of the Insurgent governmental policy, 730–767.

Museums in Manila, 802.

N

Nanca, Bukidnon village, 622.

Naujan Lake, duck shooting on, 819.

Navigation, Bureau of, 869.

Negritos, 230–231; description of, 532; author's friendly reception by, 553; in Mindoro, 591; pure-blooded, in Palawan, 594; general condition of, 660; reduction of, to slavery, 707–711.

Negros, island of, 230.

Negros Province, area and population of, 218; special interest of first Philippine Commission in, 319; Aguinaldo's policy of assassination and murder in, 738–740.

Newspaper article attacking San Lazaro Hospital, and retraction of, 420–422.

Newspapers, characteristics of Filipino, 420, 446–447, 952–953.

"Non-Christian," discussion of term, 533.

Non-Christian territory, exploration of, 532–558.

Non-Christian tribes, author's visits to, 534–557; number of, 557; government of the, 559–636; corrections of a few of the misstatements made by Blount concerning, 637–659; problems presented by, 660–675; unwillingness of, to accept Christian faith, and hatred of Christian Filipinos, 661–662, 951–952; bad outlook for, with Filipinos in charge of the legislature, 790; census figures, 999–1003.

Normal School, Manila, 502–503, 507, 511, 517, 520–521.

Nozaleda, Archbishop, influence of, on Mr. Schurman, 317.

Nueva Ecija, conditions in, under Insurgent rule, 168–169; estimate of population, 1000, 1002.

Nueva Vizcaya, conditions in, under

Insurgent rule, 170–205; act providing for government of, 559; Blount's view of, and the real facts, 656–658; slavery in, 692–698; estimate of population, 1000, 1002.

Nurses, schools for training, 434, 528–530.

O

Ocampo, Alfonso, quoted concerning Insurgent plan to massacre Spaniards in Cavite, 763.

Ocampo, Pablo, 51.

Office, Governor-General Harrison's view of appointments to, 377; anxiety of Filipinos for, 967.

Offley, Captain R. G., governor of Mindoro, 217, 591, 592, 672.

Ola, Simeon, outlaw chief in Albay, 389.

Opium, the evil of, 789.

Oranges, possibilities for production of, 903.

Osgood, H. D., sanitary engineer, 413.

Ostrand, Judge James A., facts on peonage furnished by, 715–718; removal of, demanded, 728.

Otis, General E. S., a member of first Philippine Commission, 8; dealings of, with Aguinaldo, 115–122; instructions given by Aguinaldo for murder of, 139; men commissioned by Aguinaldo to assassinate, 143; report of supersedure of, by "John Waterly," 284; approval of proclamation of first Philippine Commission shown by, 310 n.; refuses Arguelles' request for temporary suspension of hostilities, 312–313; unfavourable comparison between judgment of, and that of General Lawton, 322–323; laughs at Lawton's proposition looking to prompt conclusion of insurrection and capture of Aguinaldo, 323.

P

Pack, William F., governor of Benguet, 436; credit due, for Teachers' Camp at Baguio, 468; story of the Igorot chief and, 571–572; with

Vigan, conditions at, under Insurgent rule, 207–208; experience in the surf at, 344.

Villa, Simeon, diary of, 54, 279–280, 659; atrocities practised under, in Cagayan valley, 170–205; present powerful position of, 240; secret assassination of Spanish advocated by, 733.

Villamor, Colonel Blas, 538, 549; lack of success as lieutenant-governor of Apayao, 581–582.

Visayan Islands, conditions under Insurgent rule in the, 206 ff., 231–236; Blount's misstatements and actual figures concerning area and population of, 217–219; islands included in the group of, 230.

Visayans, numbers of, and delegates to Insurgent congress, 263; internecine warfare between Tagálogs and, 273 ff.; assassination and murder of, under Insurgent régime, 734–735; number of, 933.

Vocational training in intermediate schools, 523–524.

Volcanoes, 797–798.

Voting qualifications in the Philippines, 522–523, 944.

W

Walters, R. E., governor of Mindoro, 593.

Wantz, scheming engineer, story of, 613–615.

Water cure, the, 177; as practised by American soldiers, 281.

Waterspouts, 796.

Waterways, improvement and development of, 870–874.

Weather Bureau, the Philippine, 886.

Welch, civil service official removed by Democratic administration, 375.

Wilcox, Paymaster W. E., trip made through provinces by, and report of, 153 ff.

Wilcox-Sargent Report, the, 153 ff., 192–196, 206, 211, 236.

Wildman, Rounseville, charges made against, by Judge Blount, 20; Aguinaldo's claim of promise by, of Filipino independence, 45.

Williams, O. F., charges made against, by Judge Blount, 20.

Wilson, John R., efficient official removed by Democratic administration, 376.

Wilson, Woodrow, words of, concerning independence of the Philippines, quoted, 971–972; present policy of, 973.

Women, humane treatment of Filipino, by American soldiers, 278–281.

Wood, General Leonard, enthusiasm of, over Baguio, 473.

Wooden, William M., 609.

Woodworking, education of Filipinos in, 511.

Worcester, Dean C., events leading to first visit to Philippines by, 1–2; spends a year in the Islands (1887–88), 2–3; second visit to Islands (1890–92), 4–6; attitude upon breaking-out of war with Spain, 6–7; interview with President McKinley, 7–8; appointed a member of first Philippine Commission, 8; a member of second Philippine Commission, 9, 325; becomes secretary of the interior in civil government of the Islands, 9, 345; duties and activities of, as secretary, 10–12; long service and final retirement (1913), 12; purposes to correct false impressions concerning Philippine affairs, 12 ff.; adverse criticism of Judge Blount by, 14–15; outline of plan to be followed by, 15–16; arrival in the Islands as member of first Philippine Commission, 304–305; at the taking of Malolos, 306–309; cablegrammed description of battle sent to *Chicago Times-Herald* by, 309–310; activities of, in connection with work of first Philippine Commission, 310–324; in charge of army spies, 321; trip with Professor Moses through Pangasinán, La Union, Benguet, Lepanto, and Ilocos Sur, 341–344; action upon breaking out of Asiatic cholera in Manila, 414–416; forces retraction of newspaper story concerning San Lazaro Hospital, 420–422; work in behalf of training of nurses and physicians, 434–437; takes exploring party to Benguet and Baguio (1900), 451–453; later visits to Baguio, 456–460; services in connection with scientific work in Manila and elsewhere, 488 ff.;

THE following pages contain advertisements of a few of the Macmillan books on kindred subjects.

The United States as a World Power

By ARCHIBALD CARY COOLIDGE

Harvard University

Cloth, $2.00 net

Macmillan Standard Library Edition, 50 cents

In describing the growth of the United States to the position which this country now occupies, Professor Coolidge begins with the people themselves as the controlling force in any political policy, tracing the formation of their ideals, and the conditions under which these ideals have been changed. It has become a matter of common observation that the Spanish War marked a distinct division in the life of the American people, that our horizon has broadened until this country now possesses all the advantages and all the responsibilities that this expanded attitude involves. It is to a consideration of these advantages and responsibilities, and, more particularly, the state of preparedness for them, that Professor Coolidge applies himself in this work.

The material of which the book is constructed was originally gathered for use in the lectures delivered by the author at the Sorbonne as Harvard lectures on the Hyde foundation.

"The extreme lucidity, broad generalizations, and rapid glances at long historical periods are among the chief merits and charms of the book. We know of no volume which sums up so well and in so brief a space the wide interests which have attracted public attention during the last decade, and which, incidentally, are certain, in view of our development, to loom still larger on the national horizon." — *Chicago Inter-Ocean.*

"It is a valuable book, educational and suggestive." — *Pittsburgh Post.*

"The author takes up in detail the relations of the United States with other great Powers, points out the differences which have arisen in the past and which are likely to arise in the future, and discusses the various problems with a sanity and a judicial fairness that cannot be too highly praised. The volume will be an invaluable text-book to every student of contemporary history and a reference manual on all the aspects of the world politics in which the United States has particular interest." — *Public Ledger*, Philadelphia.

"A book of profound meaning, taking up a subject that has grown trite with too much shallow prating, and investing it with new significance." — *San Francisco Chronicle.*

"Remarquable ouvrage, d'information précise, et de haute impartialité." — *La Revue du Mois.*

THE MACMILLAN COMPANY

Publishers   64-66 Fifth Avenue   New York

Cuba   By IRENE A. WRIGHT

Decorated cloth, Illustrated, 12mo, $2.50 net
Travel Series Edition, $1.50 net

" Gives in detail a history of Cuba from its discovery to the present time ; but the work is largely devoted to the new Cuba."
— *Boston Transcript.*

" . . . contains an enormous amount of information."
— *New York Herald.*

Alaska :   *The Great Country*

By ELLA HIGGINSON

Decorated cloth, Illustrated, 12mo, $2.50 net
Travel Series Edition, $1.50 net

" Mrs. Higginson has put the very soul of picturesque Alaska into her pages, and done it with a degree of truth, sympathy, and enthusiasm that will make her book a classic in its domain."
— *Chicago Record-Herald.*

" A spirited and interesting narration." — *Brooklyn Eagle.*

Labrador :   *The Country and the People*

By WILFRED I. GRENFELL, C.M.G., M.R.C.S., M.D., and Others

New Edition. Decorated cloth, Illustrated, 8vo, $2.50 net
Travel Series Edition, $1.50 net

" Not only has Dr. Grenfell drawn a beautiful and comprehensive picture of Labrador, but he has collected all the valuable information about the country and its people that there is, and he has associated with him eight or ten explorers and scientists who have intimate knowlege of the country and have each contributed several chapters." — *Christian Work and Evangelist.*

Dec 17,

Jan 1, 2,

APR 3 _ '73